SAP PRESS e-books

Print or e-book, Kindle or iPad, workplace or airplane: Choose where and how to read your SAP PRESS books! You can now get all our titles as e-books, too:

- By download and online access
- For all popular devices
- And, of course, DRM-free

Convinced? Then go to www.sap-press.com and get your e-book today.

SAP® S/4HANA Finance

SAP PRESS is a joint initiative of SAP and Rheinwerk Publishing. The know-how offered by SAP specialists combined with the expertise of Rheinwerk Publishing offers the reader expert books in the field. SAP PRESS features first-hand information and expert advice, and provides useful skills for professional decision-making.

SAP PRESS offers a variety of books on technical and business-related topics for the SAP user. For further information, please visit our website: www.sap-press.com.

Anup Maheshwari
Implementing SAP S/4HANA Finance
2016, approx. 550 pp., hardcover and e-book
www.sap-press.com/4045

Fisher, Milne, Starmanns
Accelerated Financial Closing with SAP
2013, 296 pages, hardcover and e-book
www.sap-press.com/3227

Malcolm J. Faulkner, William D. Newman
Financial Planning and Analysis with SAP
2014, 440 pages, hardcover and e-book
www.sap-press.com/3507

Manish Patel
Discover SAP ERP Financials (2nd Edition)
2012, 604 pages, paperback and e-book
www.sap-press.com/3133

Jens Krüger

SAP® S/4HANA Finance

An Introduction

Bonn • Boston

Editor Emily Nicholls
Copyeditor Melinda Rankin
Cover Design Graham Geary
Photo Credit Shutterstock.com/173115842/© IM_photo
Layout Design Vera Brauner
Production Nicole Carpenter, Graham Geary
Typesetting SatzPro, Krefeld (Germany)
Printed and bound in the United States of America, on paper from sustainable sources

ISBN 978-1-4932-1385-6

© 2016 by Rheinwerk Publishing, Inc., Boston (MA)
2nd edition 2016

Library of Congress Cataloging-in-Publication Data
Names: Kruger, Jens (Software engineer), author.
Title: SAP S/4HANA finance : an introduction / Jens Krüger.
Other titles: SAP simple finance
Description: Bonn ; Boston : Rheinwerk Publishing, 2016. | New edition of SAP
simple finance : an introduction. 2015. | Includes bibliographical
references and index.
Identifiers: LCCN 2016001715| ISBN 9781493213856 (print : alk. paper) | ISBN
9781493213863 (ebook) | ISBN 9781493213870 (print and ebook : alk. paper)
Subjects: LCSH: Accounting--Computer programs. | Business--Data
processing--Computer programs. | SAP HANA (Electronic resource)
Classification: LCC HF5679 .K78 2016 | DDC 658.150285/53--dc23 LC record available at http://lccn.loc.gov/2016001715

All rights reserved. Neither this publication nor any part of it may be copied or reproduced in any form or by any means or translated into another language, without the prior consent of Rheinwerk Publishing, 2 Heritage Drive, Suite 305, Quincy, MA 02171.

Rheinwerk Publishing makes no warranties or representations with respect to the content hereof and specifically disclaims any implied warranties of merchantability or fitness for any particular purpose. Rheinwerk Publishing assumes no responsibility for any errors that may appear in this publication.

"Rheinwerk Publishing" and the Rheinwerk Publishing logo are registered trademarks of Rheinwerk Verlag GmbH, Bonn, Germany. SAP PRESS is an imprint of Rheinwerk Verlag GmbH and Rheinwerk Publishing, Inc.

All of the screenshots and graphics reproduced in this book are subject to copyright © SAP SE, Dietmar-Hopp-Allee 16, 69190 Walldorf, Germany.

SAP, the SAP logo, ABAP, Ariba, ASAP, Duet, hybris, SAP Adaptive Server Enterprise, SAP Advantage Database Server, SAP Afaria, SAP ArchiveLink, SAP Business ByDesign, SAP Business Explorer (SAP BEx), SAP BusinessObjects, SAP BusinessObjects Web Intelligence, SAP Business One, SAP BusinessObjects Explorer, SAP Business Workflow, SAP Crystal Reports, SAP d-code, SAP Early-Watch, SAP Fiori, SAP Ganges, SAP Global Trade Services (SAP GTS), SAP GoingLive, SAP HANA, SAP Jam, SAP Lumira, SAP MaxAttention, SAP MaxDB, SAP NetWeaver, SAP PartnerEdge, SAPPHIRE NOW, SAP PowerBuilder, SAP PowerDesigner, SAP R/2, SAP R/3, SAP Replication Server, SAP SI, SAP SQL Anywhere, SAP Strategic Enterprise Management (SAP SEM), SAP StreamWork, SuccessFactors, Sybase, TwoGo by SAP, and The Best-Run Businesses Run SAP are registered or unregistered trademarks of SAP SE, Walldorf, Germany.

All other products mentioned in this book are registered or unregistered trademarks of their respective companies.

Contents at a Glance

1 Introduction 27

PART I Exploring the SAP S/4HANA Finance Model
2 In-Memory Technology and SAP HANA 65
3 Removal of Redundancy 81
4 Nondisruptive Innovation 97
5 Unlimited Flexibility Based on Line Items 105
6 Finance in Real Time 117

PART II Using SAP S/4HANA Finance
7 Building Blocks of SAP S/4HANA Finance 135
8 Single Source of Truth: Universal Journal 147
9 Flexible Reporting 169
10 Flexible Analytics with Core Data Services 185
11 SAP S/4HANA Finance Applications 197
12 Revamping the User Experience with SAP Fiori Apps 263

PART III Running SAP S/4HANA Finance
13 Deploying SAP S/4HANA Finance 281
14 Landscape Consolidation with Central Finance 299
15 Adoption Scenarios 313
16 Success Story: SAP SE Runs SAP S/4HANA Finance 323

PART IV Moving Forward with SAP S/4HANA Finance
17 Design Thinking 343
18 Digital Enterprise and the Future of Finance 359

Dear Reader,

Every twenty-first–century business knows that changes are coming—and that the finance department is where digital machinery is breaking new ground.

SAP S/4HANA Finance is a giant leap toward simplified business processes enabled by in-memory technology and streamlined applications—and an integral piece of the SAP S/4HANA suite more broadly. As this innovative solution hits its stride and accelerates today's financials operations, this updated edition is your first good look at what SAP S/4HANA Finance brings to the finance table—and how it then turns the tables on traditional financials operations.

What did you think about *SAP S/4HANA Finance: An Introduction*? Your comments and suggestions are the most useful tools to help us make our books the best they can be. Please feel free to contact me and share any praise or criticism you may have.

Thank you for purchasing a book from SAP PRESS!

Emily Nicholls
Editor, SAP PRESS

Rheinwerk Publishing
Boston, MA

emilyn@rheinwerk-publishing.com
www.sap-press.com

Contents

Foreword 15
Preface 17

1 Introduction 27

    1.1   Market Trends 27
    1.2   Leadership Trends 29
    1.3   Technology Trends 32
    1.4   Introducing SAP S/4HANA Finance 33
        1.4.1   Deployment Modes 37
        1.4.2   Transformative Finance Technologies 40
        1.4.3   Key Areas of Innovation 45

PART I   Exploring the SAP S/4HANA Finance Model

2 In-Memory Technology and SAP HANA 65

    2.1   Keeping Data in Memory 67
        2.1.1   Ensure Durability 68
        2.1.2   New Performance Bottleneck 69
    2.2   Columnar Data Organization 69
    2.3   Data Encoding and Compression 72
        2.3.1   Dictionary Encoding 72
        2.3.2   Data Compression 73
        2.3.3   Operation on Compressed Data 74
    2.4   Parallel Execution 75
        2.4.1   Parallel Execution in Columnar Store 75
        2.4.2   Parallel Aggregation 76
    2.5   Delta Store and Merge 77
        2.5.1   Insert 78
        2.5.2   Delta Store 78
        2.5.3   Delta Merge 79

3 Removal of Redundancy 81

    3.1   Benefits of a Redundancy-Free System 82
    3.2   In-Memory Technology Removes Redundancy 86

Contents

	3.3	Simplifying the Core Data Model	89
	3.4	Immediate Benefits of the New Data Model	92

4　Nondisruptive Innovation　97

	4.1	Compatible Refactoring	98
	4.2	Transitioning to SAP S/4HANA Finance	101

5　Unlimited Flexibility Based on Line Items　105

	5.1	Gaining Unparalleled Insights	105
	5.2	Removing Predefined Aggregates	107
	5.3	Deciding without Information Loss	110
	5.4	Optimizing Operations with Big Data	113
	5.5	Innovating with Line Item Granularity	115

6　Finance in Real Time　117

	6.1	Accepting the Limits of Retroactive Analysis		118
	6.2	Benefitting from Real-Time Finance		120
		6.2.1	Improving Profit	121
		6.2.2	Securing Liquidity	123
		6.2.3	Managing Risk	124
	6.3	Identifying Real-Time Finance Patterns		126
		6.3.1	Data Cases	126
		6.3.2	Method Cases	127
		6.3.3	Process Cases	127
		6.3.4	Ad Hoc Cases	128
	6.4	Becoming a Real-Time Finance Company		128
		6.4.1	Balancing Efficiency and Insights	128
		6.4.2	Examining Industry Requirements	130
		6.4.3	Considering Business Users' Needs	131

PART II　Using SAP S/4HANA Finance

7　Building Blocks of SAP S/4HANA Finance　135

	7.1	Seeing the Big Picture		135
	7.2	Reloading SAP ERP Financials Functionality		138
		7.2.1	Financial Accounting	138

		7.2.2	Management Accounting	140
		7.2.3	SAP Financial Supply Chain Management	142
		7.2.4	SAP Treasury and Risk Management	142
		7.2.5	Cash Management	143
	7.3		New Applications in SAP S/4HANA Finance	143

8 Single Source of Truth: Universal Journal ... 147

	8.1		Mastering Business Challenges without SAP HANA	147
	8.2		New SAP HANA-Based Architecture	151
		8.2.1	Structure of the Universal Journal	152
		8.2.2	Merging G/L Accounts and Cost Elements	154
		8.2.3	Compatibility Views	155
	8.3		Immediate Benefits of the New Model	156
		8.3.1	Depreciation Runs	157
		8.3.2	Multidimensional Profitability Analysis	158
		8.3.3	New Analysis Patterns	160
		8.3.4	Financial Statement Analysis	161
	8.4		Building on Top of the Universal Journal	162
		8.4.1	Fundamental Functional Enhancements	162
		8.4.2	Important Simplification Cases	163
		8.4.3	Prediction Based on Facts	163

9 Flexible Reporting ... 169

	9.1		The Challenge of Flexible Operational Reporting Needs	170
	9.2		Addressing Challenges Using SAP S/4HANA Finance	173
	9.3		Conceptual Advances in Reporting	178
		9.3.1	Merging of Accounts and Cost Elements	178
		9.3.2	Accounts and Other Hierarchies	179
	9.4		Advances for End Users	180

10 Flexible Analytics with Core Data Services ... 185

	10.1		Replacing Complex Analytics with Simplicity	186
	10.2		Paradigms of Core Data Services in SAP S/4HANA	187
	10.3		Building Blocks of Core Data Services in SAP S/4HANA	190
		10.3.1	Domain-Specific Database Languages and Services	192
		10.3.2	Use of Semantic Annotations	192
		10.3.3	Virtual Data Model	193
	10.4		Unified View of Data for Analytics	194

11 SAP S/4HANA Finance Applications 197

11.1 Business Cockpits for Businesspeople 197
    11.1.1 Working with Business Cockpits 199
    11.1.2 Defining a Business Cockpit 201
    11.1.3 Outlook 203
11.2 Financials Operations 205
    11.2.1 Receivables Management 206
    11.2.2 Payables Management 209
    11.2.3 Outlook 211
11.3 Ariba Network Integration 212
    11.3.1 Order Collaboration 213
    11.3.2 Invoice Collaboration 214
    11.3.3 Discount Management 215
    11.3.4 Outlook 216
11.4 Cash Management 216
    11.4.1 Bank Account Management 219
    11.4.2 Cash Operations 220
    11.4.3 Liquidity Management 223
    11.4.4 Simplified Data Model 225
    11.4.5 Outlook 226
11.5 SAP Business Planning and Consolidation for Finance 227
    11.5.1 Business Contexts 228
    11.5.2 Underlying Architecture 229
    11.5.3 Planning Application 232
    11.5.4 Business Planning Process 233
    11.5.5 Outlook 234
11.6 Profitability 236
    11.6.1 SAP Fiori Applications 238
    11.6.2 From Costing-Based to Account-Based Profitability Analysis 238
    11.6.3 Outlook 242
11.7 Financial Closing and Consolidation 242
    11.7.1 Process Management 243
    11.7.2 Avoiding Reconciliation Efforts 244
    11.7.3 Faster Period Close with SAP HANA 245
    11.7.4 New Closing Applications 246
    11.7.5 Outlook 248
11.8 Revenue Accounting 249
    11.8.1 Contract Identification 250
    11.8.2 Performance Obligation Identification 251

		11.8.3	Transaction Price Determination	252
		11.8.4	Transaction Price Allocation	252
		11.8.5	Revenue Recognition	252
		11.8.6	Flexible Adaptability	253
		11.8.7	Outlook	253
	11.9	Real-Time Governance and Compliance		254
		11.9.1	Introduction to Governance, Risk, and Compliance	255
		11.9.2	Changing Trends and Challenges of Staying Compliant	256
		11.9.3	Embedded Real-Time Monitoring of High-Risk Transactions	258
		11.9.4	Outlook	262

12 Revamping the User Experience with SAP Fiori Apps   263

	12.1	SAP Fiori Design Philosophy		264
	12.2	Developing Intuitive Products		265
	12.3	SAP Fiori Design Principles in SAP S/4HANA Finance		266
	12.4	SAP Fiori Application Framework and Finance		271
		12.4.1	Launchpad	271
		12.4.2	Application Types	272
		12.4.3	Application Patterns and Controls	273
	12.5	Extending SAP Fiori		274

PART III Running SAP S/4HANA Finance

13 Deploying SAP S/4HANA Finance   281

	13.1	On-Premise Edition		282
		13.1.1	Architecture Overview	283
		13.1.2	New On-Premise Installations	284
		13.1.3	Landscape Migration for Existing SAP ERP Systems	285
		13.1.4	Handling General Ledger Functionality during Upgrade	286
		13.1.5	Simplification List	287
	13.2	Cloud Editions		288
	13.3	Managed Cloud Options		289
		13.3.1	Service Offerings in the Cloud	290
		13.3.2	Hybrid Scenarios	293
		13.3.3	Subscription Licensing and Options	294
	13.4	Extensibility		296

14 Landscape Consolidation with Central Finance ... 299

14.1 Harmonization and Standardization ... 300
14.2 Principles and Capabilities ... 304
14.3 Evolution to an Operational System ... 309
14.4 Central Finance in the Cloud ... 312

15 Adoption Scenarios ... 313

15.1 Greenfield vs. Brownfield Approach ... 314
    15.1.1 Greenfield Approach ... 314
    15.1.2 Brownfield Approach ... 315
15.2 SAP S/4HANA Finance in SAP Business Suite on SAP HANA ... 316
    15.2.1 Manufacturing Company ... 316
    15.2.2 High-Tech Company ... 318
15.3 Central Finance and Central Reporting ... 319
    15.3.1 Trade Company ... 319

16 Success Story: SAP SE Runs SAP S/4HANA Finance ... 323

16.1 Defining a Finance Vision ... 324
16.2 Moving to SAP S/4HANA Finance ... 326
    16.2.1 System Landscape and Organization ... 327
    16.2.2 Finance Transformation ... 328
    16.2.3 Scope and Structure of the Project ... 329
16.3 Reaping the Benefits ... 334
16.4 Anticipating the Next Steps ... 338
16.5 The Takeaway ... 338

PART IV Moving Forward with SAP S/4HANA Finance

17 Design Thinking ... 343

17.1 Foundation of Design Thinking ... 344
17.2 Impacts on a Business Process Landscape ... 348
17.3 Identify and Define Changes ... 349
    17.3.1 Team Setup ... 350
    17.3.2 Problem Space ... 351
    17.3.3 Solution Space ... 352
    17.3.4 Packaging and Handover ... 353

	17.4	Set Up a Design Thinking Workshop	354
	17.5	Opportunities in the Business Process Landscape	355

18　Digital Enterprise and the Future of Finance ... 359

	18.1	Behind the Term "Digital Enterprise"	360
		18.1.1　Change Has Never Been So Rapid	361
		18.1.2　Automation and Big Data Handling Are Becoming Imperative	362
		18.1.3　Finance Is the Score Keeper of Business Performance	362
	18.2	From Mechanics to Analytics	363
		18.2.1　Eliminating the Drudgery of Accounting	364
		18.2.2　Creating an In-Context Enterprise	366
		18.2.3　Integrating Planning and Analysis with Daily Operations	367
		18.2.4　Enhancing the Use of Information	368
	18.3	Simulation and Predictive Analysis	369
	18.4	Proactive Finance Solution	371
	18.5	Summary	375

Appendices ... 377

A	Changes to the Data Model	379
B	Additional Information	381
C	The Authors	391

Index ... 405

Foreword

Financial processes are at the core of any enterprise. In finance, companies record transactions as they happen and, more importantly, analyze and report the data to fulfill legal requirements as well as internal information needs. In financial operations, companies manage customer invoices and payments to their vendors and ensure a steady cash flow and sufficient liquidity in treasury and cash management. Other important financial topics include profitability analysis, planning, budgeting, risk, and many others. Analyzing large amounts of data to derive valuable insights is the foundation of finance.

In order to handle all of these tasks, companies require the support of enterprise systems. It is for the development of such systems that I co-founded SAP in 1972 with four colleagues, and thus financials has been a core component of SAP's products since the beginning. While SAP's offerings expanded to cover the whole value chain of companies, financials has always remained one of my personal key interests. Therefore, I am happy that with SAP S/4HANA Finance, SAP now provides a next-generation financials solution that makes use of and benefits from another area in which I am personally invested: in-memory database technology and SAP HANA.

In 2009, I presented the vision of integrated in-memory storage for transactional activities (OLTP) and analytical reporting (OLAP). Shortly afterward, SAP launched the in-memory database platform SAP HANA. Since then, the idea of re-integrating OLTP and OLAP in one system has gained a lot of traction. In-memory technology is one of the cornerstones of SAP's Run Simple strategy. SAP HANA enables a significant simplification of enterprise systems, with tremendous benefits for our customers. As technology advisor, I have personally accompanied the development of SAP S/4HANA Finance, the frontrunner of this strategy within the SAP Business Suite and SAP S/4HANA.

This book is not about SAP HANA and its benefits in general, but about how SAP S/4HANA Finance embraces the possibilities of SAP HANA to create additional value for SAP's customers and about the new functionality it provides for them. (If you also want to learn more about the business value of SAP HANA in general, across different domains, and for various use cases, you will find my book on the future of enterprise applications a welcome addition to this resource.)[1] As SAP's new financials solution, SAP S/4HANA Finance evolves and simplifies the traditional SAP ERP Financials. The radical changes underlying SAP S/4HANA Finance have excited many companies but have also led to questions and misunderstandings.

Therefore, let me state some facts clearly, which the book expands upon in more detail: SAP S/4HANA Finance includes all of the functionality—and more—that you are used to from SAP ERP Financials. In addition, it has a much simpler architecture and a simpler data model, opening up entirely new possibilities. All this is provided in a nondisruptive manner for existing SAP customers.

I am glad that you are considering SAP S/4HANA Finance, as I believe it to be the first milestone in an important journey to simplify enterprise systems. This book will help you understand the benefits you gain from SAP S/4HANA Finance. I am confident that after reading it you will understand the fundamental paradigms of SAP S/4HANA Finance and join SAP in simplifying enterprise systems.

Hasso Plattner
Co-Founder of SAP
Chairman of the Supervisory Board of SAP SE
Professor at the Hasso Plattner Institute

---

[1] Hasso Plattner and Bernd Leukert. *The In-Memory Revolution: How SAP HANA Enables Business of the Future.*

Preface

Complexity is the enemy of running your company efficiently. With its Run Simple strategy, SAP sets out to simplify its core offerings to counter complexity. SAP S/4HANA Finance (formerly known as SAP Simple Finance) is the frontrunner product of this strategy and of SAP S/4HANA, which is SAP's next-generation business suite to help its customers run their business processes simply. SAP S/4HANA Finance is a new offering that covers the whole finance value map, based on the well-known and time-tested SAP ERP Financials. SAP S/4HANA Finance has a simpler architecture in all parts of the system but does *not* reduce functionality. Rather, SAP S/4HANA Finance expands the functional scope of SAP's Finance portfolio with a lot of new functionality.

Following SAP's Run Simple strategy, the key mission of SAP S/4HANA Finance is simplification. Increasing complexity—for example, due to proliferating use of devices and unparalleled amounts of information being generated—consumes valuable resources and increases effort for everyone. SAP S/4HANA Finance enables you to overcome needless complexity in your business by removing redundancy, breaking up fragmented silos, and simplifying the financial system of your company. All of this functionality is offered in a nondisruptive manner. The functionality and options of SAP S/4HANA Finance are available in two products: SAP S/4HANA Finance, on-premise edition is an add-on for companies running standard SAP Business Suite on SAP HANA; a similar offering is available to customers who adopt SAP S/4HANA Enterprise Management, which also brings simplification in areas outside finance. With SAP S/4HANA Finance as the backbone of your financial system, you can keep pace with the ever-faster speed of innovations and ever-larger amounts of data. It is optimized for SAP's in-memory database, SAP HANA, and fully leverages SAP HANA's huge potential.

In the view of complexity everywhere, the Run Simple strategy has the goal of letting you focus on your actual business and the needs of your customers. Finance is not an easy topic, and SAP S/4HANA Finance does not claim to make it one. Instead, it promises to be simple from the core of the architecture to the user interface (UI) in order to let you solve financial challenges and embrace business opportunities. SAP S/4HANA Finance makes it simple for your finance departments to focus on their actual responsibilities without any obstructions and with the full scope of functionality.

Because simplification is the key mission behind SAP S/4HANA Finance, this book tells the Run Simple story behind SAP S/4HANA Finance and explains the benefits you can receive from its paradigms and functional features.

Purpose

This book introduces SAP S/4HANA Finance as the next-generation finance solution. What can you expect to learn from this book?

Most importantly, this book describes what SAP S/4HANA Finance offers from a business point of view. If you seek to understand how SAP S/4HANA Finance can help you achieve your financial goals or realize your IT strategy, then you will find the answer in this book. You will also understand the impact of the simplification story behind the product: How does the simplification underlying SAP S/4HANA Finance allow you to benefit and to simplify processes and structures in your company or area of responsibility?

At the same time, we also outline the new flexibility and possibilities that you enable by switching from your current finance arrangement to SAP S/4HANA Finance. We discuss how you can leverage the improvements and new functionality across the whole functional scope of SAP S/4HANA Finance in order to generate business value. You will also learn about the different options you have in areas such as functionality, deployment, or business processes to choose and adapt flexibly to what best fits your needs.

Overall, the focus of this book is on the product side, applying SAP S/4HANA Finance to various use cases. As an introduction to the product, the book is not a how-to guide or a technical manual. In addition, a short legal disclaimer regarding forward-looking statements is in order: At several points in the book, we look to the future. Those sections outline only possibilities and plans for potential future improvements, with no guarantee that they will indeed come to pass at any point in the future. Any decisions you make should be based on official SAP communication material.

This book is meant to give you an impression of how SAP S/4HANA Finance could improve your business. To that end, we give a comprehensive overview of its paradigms and scope. Some of the applications or features mentioned throughout the book require a separate license. You need to check with your SAP contact whether the functionality you require is included in your product bundle when you decide to switch to SAP S/4HANA Finance.

Who Should Read This Book

The target audience of this book is made of financial managers with different global or local responsibilities and other personnel who are responsible for providing and managing their companies' financial IT systems.

Readers with a financial background may be responsible for the accounting processes of their organizations or involved in financial planning, may oversee the processes in financial operations, may be cash managers, or in the case of CFOs will have overall responsibility for their organization's financial processes. This book will give all of these readers plenty of ideas about how SAP S/4HANA Finance can help in their daily business and provide opportunities for further innovation.

Readers that come from a technical background will also find the book useful in order to learn about the options they have to fulfill the needs of their counterparts in business with regard to financial systems. They are interested in providing the financial IT backbone in the most efficient manner and staying at the center of innovation.

We do not assume prior knowledge of SAP systems. In fact, several paths through the book cater to the interest of readers with different backgrounds, as we'll soon discuss. Readers might find it beneficial to have a basic understanding of financial processes and terms, but the book does not require an in-depth technical understanding.

Structure of This Book

This book has four main parts that cover the whole story behind SAP S/4HANA Finance. After describing our objectives and giving an overview of the goals, we begin our in-depth coverage with the underlying paradigms of the SAP S/4HANA Finance model (Part I). We continue by covering new functionality that realizes these goals (Part II), then explain how to run SAP S/4HANA Finance (Part III), and conclude with a look forward to the new opportunities possible with SAP S/4HANA Finance (Part IV). Now, let's preview the structure and chapters of this book in more detail.

Chapter 1 introduces SAP S/4HANA Finance as the next-generation financials solution of SAP and places it in the context of SAP S/4HANA. We describe the financials world as it exists or is developing today. The chapter begins by identifying the new challenges and market expectations that finance departments face and how those trends translate to new requirements for their financials organizations and systems. Meeting these requirements has been the fundamental goal underlying SAP S/4HANA Finance, and subsequent parts of the book elaborate on how SAP S/4HANA Finance delivers solutions to meet these challenges. Chapter 1 briefly outlines the corresponding functionality of SAP S/4HANA Finance on a high level, providing an overview of the finance value map.

Part I, Exploring the SAP S/4HANA Finance Model, looks at the fundamental paradigms that have driven the development of SAP S/4HANA Finance and that are its key differentiators. These include, for example, inherently leveraging the opportunities of in-memory technology, removing redundancy to simplify the system, and facilitating nondisruptive innovation. We explain each paradigm that influenced SAP S/4HANA Finance and outline its impact on the SAP S/4HANA Finance model, also demonstrating the benefits via real-world use cases. Figure 1 illustrates how the topics covered in the chapters in Part I connect to one another in the context of SAP S/4HANA Finance.

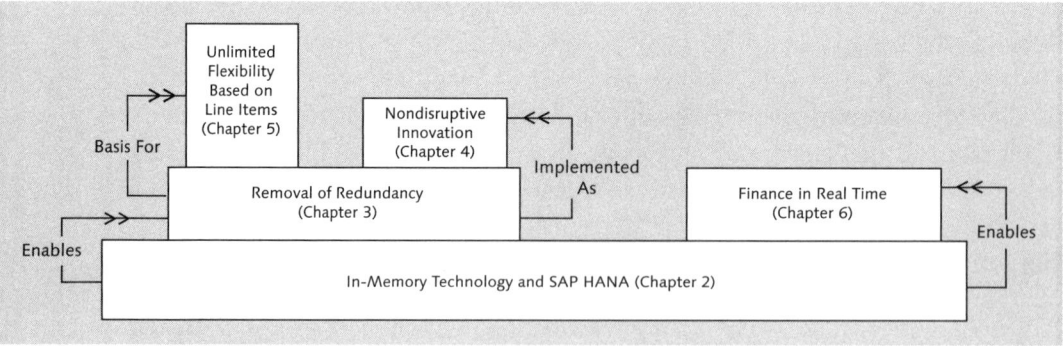

Figure 1 Structure of Part I

Chapter 2 briefly introduces SAP HANA as the in-memory database underlying SAP S/4HANA Finance. It outlines the specific capabilities of in-memory technology that make it especially suitable to meet today's requirements for finance departments.

Chapter 3 covers the benefits of a system without data redundancy and how such a system is feasible thanks to SAP HANA, and it demonstrates how SAP S/4HANA Finance eliminates redundancy on different levels. We highlight the immediate benefits of the removal of redundant data for customers of SAP S/4HANA Finance.

Chapter 4 presents the paradigm of nondisruptive innovation that is key for all improvements in SAP S/4HANA Finance. All changes are offered in a nondisruptive manner so that SAP customers can benefit from their advantages with no need for lengthy implementation or migration projects, safeguarding their existing investments.

Chapter 5 highlights the unlimited flexibility that companies gain with the purely line item–based data model of SAP S/4HANA Finance. It explains the business value in various areas that companies can realize—for example, when freed from rigid hierarchies, in case of organizational changes, or by avoiding aggregate information loss.

Chapter 6 explores the opportunities of real-time finance. The improved performance of SAP HANA and SAP S/4HANA Finance makes it possible to get rid of batch jobs and the issues they entail. Instead, more and more processes can work in real time based on current data. We explain the fundamental shift of real-time finance and how it impacts business processes.

Part II, Using SAP S/4HANA Finance, dives deeper into the specific new functionality provided by SAP S/4HANA Finance, explaining what business value each feature offers. To this end, we map the challenges and requirements mentioned in the introduction to product features. Each individual chapter outlines the impact on business processes by using practical examples, thus outlining the value story of SAP S/4HANA Finance. After presenting the big picture, Part II starts out with the foundation of all accounting and then gradually moves up the stack, as shown in Figure 2. We first consider reporting based on the foundational accounting documents, then cover analytics and applications on top of that, and finally look at the user experience that encompasses both.

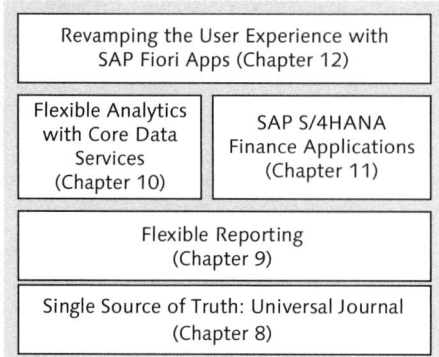

Figure 2 Structure of Part II

Chapter 7 gives an overview of the functional building blocks that make up SAP S/4HANA Finance and outlines the big picture, which is then discussed in detail in the following chapters. Not everything needs to be brand-new, though. We also reiterate applications and features from SAP ERP Financials that are included in SAP S/4HANA Finance. We outline how these components fit into the new world and how they also benefit from the overall simplification of SAP S/4HANA Finance.

Chapter 8 looks in detail at the Universal Journal, which is the single source of truth that brings together the previously separate journals for accounting documents in Financial Accounting (FI) and Management Accounting (CO). After explaining the technical implementation of the Universal Journal, we outline how this next-generation accounting solution in SAP S/4HANA Finance simplifies business processes and enables new capabilities.

Chapter 9 looks at the flexible reporting options offered with SAP S/4HANA Finance. It shows how the change in the way transactional data is stored in the Universal Journal makes it possible to change the paradigms behind legal and management reporting. We highlight how companies receive the flexible reporting options they actually need.

Chapter 10 looks at the flexible analytics capabilities of SAP S/4HANA Finance. Based on Core Data Services, analytics in SAP S/4HANA Finance address the existing pain points of data managers with respect to analytics flexibility, ease of consumption, and extensibility. The chapter begins by looking at the need for a flexible analytics system and goes on to describe how embedded analytics in SAP S/4HANA Finance based on Core Data Services fulfills this need. In addition, we look at some of the architectural building blocks of Core Data Services.

Chapter 11 highlights different applications and areas that particularly provide significant improvements with SAP S/4HANA Finance. These areas cover the whole scope of financials, ranging from cash management to planning to compliance management. We briefly explain the novel functionalities of each application and put them in the context of the overall SAP S/4HANA Finance value story.

Finally, *Chapter 12* presents the revamped user experience that is delivered with SAP S/4HANA Finance. In SAP Fiori, intuitive and beautiful web apps replace existing transactions. Task-based and role-centric apps allow users to follow their processes in an intuitive environment enriched with the capabilities that the web offers.

Part III, **Running SAP S/4HANA Finance**, outlines the different options that companies have to use SAP S/4HANA Finance, such as delivery on-premise or in the cloud. We also outline how new and existing customers of SAP can get to SAP S/4HANA Finance easily and use a success story and adoption scenarios to illustrate how to run SAP S/4HANA Finance and benefit from its capabilities.

Existing customers can seamlessly migrate to SAP S/4HANA Finance. *Chapter 13* covers the wide range of delivery options of SAP S/4HANA Finance: on-premise installation, cloud delivery, or hybrid scenarios. We provide decision support for when to choose what option and how to implement your choice, including when and how to make use of services.

Chapter 14 presents Central Finance, which allows you to use SAP S/4HANA Finance as a centralized system that consolidates complex system landscapes consisting of a large mix of SAP and non-SAP systems. Central Finance offers companies a means to centralize their financial data, harmonize processes, and get better insight into their financial situations. We explain the concepts and benefits of centralization and harmonization, describe the basics of implementing a central reporting scenario, and outline the path from that central reporting option to Central Finance.

Chapter 15 explains how typical implementation projects to adopt SAP S/4HANA Finance look and, in particular, how the nondisruptive paradigm allows SAP customers to switch quickly to SAP S/4HANA Finance. We also outline how organizations can embrace the additional possibilities introduced by SAP S/4HANA Finance.

In order to walk through a success story, *Chapter 16* presents the adoption of SAP S/4HANA Finance at SAP SE. The core financial on-premise system of SAP SE has been replaced with SAP S/4HANA Finance, producing the benefits outlined in the preceding parts of this book.

Part IV, Moving Forward with SAP S/4HANA Finance, discusses how companies can go one step further and rethink their business processes based on the new capabilities that SAP S/4HANA Finance provides. We also provide an outlook into the future of finance.

SAP S/4HANA Finance provides radical new capabilities that allow (but do not require) companies to rethink their processes entirely. *Chapter 17* introduces the Design Thinking approach and contends that it can be used to design business processes from scratch based on the needs of all stakeholders.

Digitalization describes the current trend of rapid movement to a digital economy. *Chapter 18* outlines how SAP S/4HANA Finance helps companies in this process and what options may arise based on this foundation. Thus, Chapter 18 also provides a glimpse into the potential future of SAP S/4HANA Finance.

How to Read This Book

We have now given you an insight into the contents of the book in general and the specific chapters in detail. Because we cover a range of topics, you may find some chapters particularly interesting. The book is organized in a manner that offers you different options to explore the content. For example, during a first read you may want to focus on the business point of view, and later you may want to dive deeper into specific areas.

In general, two main lines of thought—business and technical—are interwoven into certain chapters. Table 1 categorizes each chapter into these two areas. Some fall into both categories. Others mainly take a business perspective, focusing on finance and functionality. Other chapters will be of special interest for readers interested in the technical underpinnings of SAP S/4HANA Finance.

Chapters	Business	Technical
1. Introduction	X	X
Part I: Exploring the SAP S/4HANA Finance Model		
2. In-Memory Technology and SAP HANA	X	X
3. Removal of Redundancy	X	X
4. Nondisruptive Innovation		X
5. Unlimited Flexibility Based on Line Items	X	
6. Finance in Real Time	X	
Part II: Using SAP S/4HANA Finance		
7. Building Blocks of SAP S/4HANA Finance	X	X
8. Single Source of Truth: Universal Journal	X	
9. Flexible Reporting	X	
10. Flexible Analytics with Core Data Services	X	
11. SAP S/4HANA Finance Applications	X	
12. Revamping the User Experience with SAP Fiori Apps	X	
Part III: Running SAP S/4HANA Finance		
13. Deploying SAP S/4HANA Finance		X
14. Landscape Consolidation with Central Finance	X	X
15. Adoption Scenarios	X	X
16. Success Story: SAP SE Runs SAP S/4HANA Finance	X	X
Part IV: Moving Forward with SAP S/4HANA Finance		
17. Design Thinking	X	
18. Digital Enterprise and the Future of Finance	X	

Table 1 Overview of the Chapters and Their Focus

Acknowledgments

I would like to thank all those who have contributed to this book and to SAP S/4HANA Finance in general.

First and foremost, I would like to take the opportunity to thank each of my coauthors: Akhil Agarwal, Alfred Schaller, Arndt Köster, Bastian Distler, Ben Tomsky,

Birgit Starmanns, Christian Klensch, Daniel Lou, David Mahlmann, Ekkehart Seip, Franz Weber, Georg Dopf, Henning Heitkötter, Holger Faber, Janet Salmon, Johannes Wust, Kai Bi, Marc Dietrich, Michael Emerson, Monica Bhat, Oliver J. Kroneisen, Raja Gumienny, Ralf Ille, Reiner Wallmeier, Ric Ratkowski, Sabine Otholt, Stefan M. Fischer, Steffen Vollmert, Susanne Kollender, Tilman Ulshöfer, Torsten Zube, and Winfried Schmitt. All of these authors have been passionate about this book and have invested a lot of time and effort into its creation in addition to their daily work.

I am particularly grateful to the editorial team who successfully managed and completed this large project in a short time frame: Akhil Agarwal, Christin Schmidt, Henning Heitkötter, Peter Cholewinski, and Ralf Sabiwalsky. They outlined this book's content, conferred with all authors, reviewed the text, and organized the overall project.

I also appreciate the support of all colleagues that helped us by answering questions or by reviewing parts of the book. In particular, I'd like to thank Bernhard Fischer, Bettina Zedlitz, Carmen Sucic, Daniel Welzbacher, Dirk Ahlert, Dirk Joachim Henn, Dirk Rohdemann, Fabian Padilla-Crisol, Harald Pflanz, Helge Meyer, Helmut Hofmann, Jan Schaffner, Jens Baumann, Joachim Kenntner, Joachim Mette, Jochen Thierer, Jodi Mazic, Jonathan von Rüden, Julia Schmidt, Kirsten Graß, Lisa Sammer, Manuel Behringer, Marcus Hicke, Marei Dornick, Michael Conrad, Michel Loehden, Michele Boyer, Monika Pfanner, Oliver Sievi, Paul Möller, Philipp Herzig, Qiang Wang, Robert Bieber, Stefan Karl, Stefan Walz, Uwe Mayer, and Verena Patzelt.

I also would like to thank the publisher, SAP PRESS, for gladly embracing the book proposal and publishing it in a short time span. I am especially grateful for the support and work of the book's editor at SAP PRESS, Emily Nicholls. Her input and revision greatly improved the quality of the book at hand.

Of course, a book about SAP S/4HANA Finance could not exist without the product itself. Therefore, I would like to thank all those who contributed to the development of SAP S/4HANA Finance, and, first of all, Hasso Plattner, SAP's founder and the chairman of the supervisory board. He inspired the innovation of SAP S/4HANA Finance and continuously shaped its path. Special thanks go to the developers in the Finance line of business and those in other development units of SAP that made Plattner's vision come true in the product. I also appreciate the feedback and investment of our customers that helped to make SAP S/4HANA Finance most relevant for the needs of enterprises today.

This chapter introduces SAP S/4HANA Finance. We identify trends in the market, in leadership, and in technology that SAP S/4HANA Finance ties together to address today's requirements. The finance value map gives a high-level overview of the corresponding functionality of SAP S/4HANA Finance.

1   Introduction

In today's global economy, finance organizations face unprecedented challenges that have shattered commonly held beliefs and exposed numerous shortcomings in management processes and software applications. Businesses have learned the hard way that if they want to thrive in times of uncertainty, then they need to build functionality that delivers optimal insight and agility. The cost of finance itself remains under scrutiny, and organizations still have to "keep the lights on" for compliance and finance operations. Still, CFOs are stepping up and transforming their organizations to take a more strategic role and help create greater value for the entire business.

Innovations can make possible what was formerly impossible. Imagine eliminating duplication of data, thereby reducing time spent on reconciliation. Or imagine seeing how a large transaction affects a key performance indicator (KPI) on a mobile device the minute that the transaction is made. Now, imagine bringing together your plan and actual data in one place, enabling continuous, event-based forecasting instead of annual or quarterly planning cycles, plus enabling finance to simulate all possible outcomes of business options to make the optimal decision. These scenarios can enable finance executives to provide more value to their entire organization.

1.1   Market Trends

Although the economy is no longer necessarily in a decline, recovery is still slow. We continue to see uncertainty in the economy and volatility in commodity prices and stock valuations. For example, according to Brian Solis' 2013 book *What's the Future of Business?*, over 40% of the companies that topped the Fortune 500 list in 2000 were no longer there in 2010.[1] Adding to that, according to the results of a 2013 SAP-sponsored Bloomberg Businessweek study, most executives expect to contend with low economic growth and expect their own organizations to remain in a low-growth pattern.[2]

As organizations seek growth opportunities, many are expanding globally. Goods and services are increasingly made across the world and not just produced in one country.[3] Such globalization will require a balance between global standardization and localization. Businesses also need an awareness of diverse cultures. Shared service centers are an example of a way to implement consistent processes across an organization. At the same time, companies need to ensure that local regulations are met across finance, operations, and human resources.

Regulation is increasing: More than thirty countries and now some industries have put in place a requirement to file information electronically using eXtensible Business Reporting Language (XBRL). For example, public companies are required to file financial statements for each tax jurisdiction in which they do business and therefore need to meet the different filing requirements of each country and jurisdiction. Companies are offered incentives sometimes for moving to XBRL, even when it is not a legal requirement. For example, according to *XBRL.org*, Dutch banking giant ING announced that on January 1, 2015, it would offer discounts on loan and credit applications for SME customers in the Netherlands who provide XBRL versions of financial statements through the Dutch SBR platform. In addition, industries increasingly require XBLR filings; for example, the Solvency II Directive codifies and harmonizes European insurance regulations, specifically those related to the amount of capital that insurance companies in the European Union (EU) must hold to reduce the risk of insolvency.

Companies continue to focus on risk, including financial risk, so finance departments must determine where to make investments to fund the growth of their organizations. In addition, there is a trend toward analyzing new types of risk that could impact the bottom line, such as analyzing social sentiment, which

---

1 Brian Solis, *What's the Future of Business? Changing the Way Businesses Create Experiences.*
2 Bloomberg Businessweek Research Services, "Finance as Analytical Partner to the Business."
3 OECD Publishing, "Interconnected Economies: Benefiting from Global Value Chains."

could affect brand value. The 2013 Edelman Trust Barometer found that 87% of global consumers believe business should place at least equal emphasis on social interests as business interests, and "purpose" (or organizational identity) has increased as a purchase trigger by 26% since 2008.[4]

Pressure on margins has been another important topic in recent years and will continue to be important in 2016 and onward. Although CFOs look to grow their business, the cost portion of the equation remains important. SAP Performance Benchmarking found a three-times-lower finance cost as a percentage of revenue in the top-quartile-performing organizations versus the bottom-quartile organizations. This is often tied to having the right tools. SAP Performance Benchmarking also discovered a 76% higher operating margin when financial systems provide historical and forward-looking views into financial and operations performance.

Organizations are looking for innovative business models as growth opportunities. Partnerships to create complementary products and services and the creation of digital networks will change the way that companies interact with vendors and customers and will open new channels, especially related to industries focusing on consumers. As an example, Gigaom believes that by 2017 revenues from smart home service automation will amount to at least $11 billion.[5]

Finance is in a unique position to bring together financial and operational information to help guide business as it determines how best to react to these market trends, but there are other important influences—such as leadership.

1.2 Leadership Trends

The primary trend in organizational leadership is a change in the role of the CFO. This shift has been ongoing for some time and will continue to gain traction in 2016 and beyond.

According to a report prepared in 2013 by CFO Research Services in collaboration with SAP, 76% of finance executives who participated in the survey believe that at least half their time should be spent working more closely with their companies'

---

[4] Edelman, "2013 Edelman Trust Barometer."
[5] Adam Lesser, "Projecting the Technology Path to the Smart Home."

operational units in guiding the business, although only 55% feel they actually achieve this goal.[6] In other words, many finance departments still spend much of their time in activities to "keep the lights on" (compliance and finance operations). Although those tasks are necessary, it is the real-time analytic and planning activities that can help finance advise business to provide strategic value.

In a follow-up report prepared by CFO Research Services in 2014, finance executives correlated their ability to become more strategic business partners to their corporations' bottom line.[7] 87% of finance executives said that the finance function will need to improve its capabilities and performance to support profitable growth. Finance executives also saw the need to make financial information more consumable for operational departments, with 58% agreeing that their company's line-of-business managers have difficulty using finance information systems to identify and understand the data to make effective decisions.

Fast forward to a 2015 study by CFO Research Services, in which we see progress in finance being a strategic partner.[8] Now 76% of finance executives reported that finance is central to the use of advanced analytics, and 40% work with other functions to generate business insights. Digitalization also plays a key role. According to this report, 72% of finance executives believe that automating finance processes would raise their importance within their organizations; 71% said automation allows them to meet their goals of being more involved within the business units; and 69% said automation would allow them to have more time available for higher-value work.

Let's look at the categories of activities of the finance function, over which the CFO has domain. Figure 1.1 depicts those activities, the relative time finance managers spend on them today (left), and where they would prefer their focus to be (right). The categories are as follows:

- **Business partnership**
  To provide strategic value, finance must engage with the business to drive value, leveraging instant prediction, analysis, and planning across financial and operational processes. This allows finance to model and analyze the financial

---

6 CFO Research Services, "Shaping the Finance Function of Tomorrow: Finance's Strategic Mandate—and the Innovations That Will Help Them Meet It."
7 CFO Research Services, "The Next Stage in Creating the Value-Added Finance Function: Turning Data into Insight and Business Actions."
8 CFO Research Services, "Thriving in the Digital Economy: The Innovative Finance Function."

implications of business decisions, from evaluating the benefits of a merger or an acquisition compared to building a product, projecting the impact of this decision on forecasts and budgets, and analyzing the profitability drivers across dimensions, including customer, product, geography, and channel.

- **Operational excellence**
  When running finance organizations, finance teams should optimize finance processes for efficient and collaborative relationships with customers, suppliers, banks, and government authorities. Finance can increase operational efficiency by reducing the duplication of finance information, which eliminates delays for updates and the need for multiple reconciliations. With instant insight and self-service access to KPIs, finance can enable real-time decision-making based on real-time data.

- **Compliance and risk**
  Critical to the legal compliance of an organization, finance maintains global regulatory compliance and controls of accounting and tax standards across currencies, languages, and industries. With the ability to run complex processes any time during the period, finance no longer needs to wait until period end to see the financial status of the organization, enabling a soft close at any time, and finance can manage insight into working capital at any time to make the most effective financial investment decisions while mitigating risk.

In order to execute these processes, finance organizations need to undergo their own transformations to provide strategic value to the business, with a focus on instant insight.

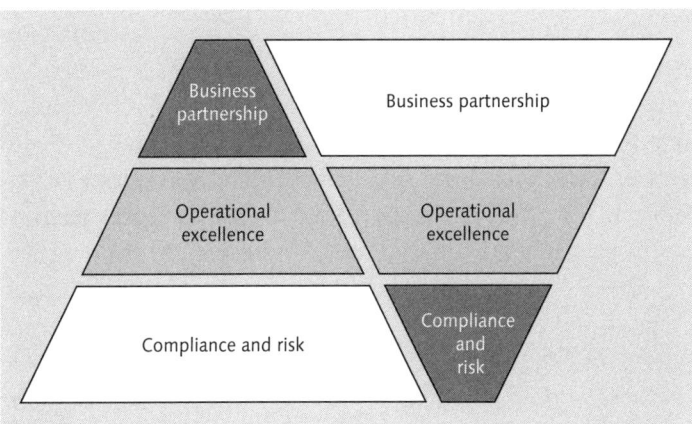

Figure 1.1 As Is (Left) and Desired (Right) CFO Activity Types

1.3 Technology Trends

The three surveys conducted by CFO Research Services in 2013, 2014, and 2015 show a progression in the way that finance executives think about technology. In 2013, organizations strove to understand — and become comfortable with — new available technologies. By 2014, finance executives had made the leap to link the benefits that technology can provide and distinct business results. The survey in 2015 confirmed that finance sees the need to implement these technologies to achieve business value, with 57% of respondents citing that finance needs to take on new responsibilities. In fact, 35% of finance executives expect that IT will be added to their current responsibilities.

Let's look at the major technologies discussed in the surveys:

- **In-memory computing**
  For finance, the focus on *in-memory computing* has increased dramatically. In 2013, only 22% of companies surveyed prioritized deploying in-memory processing capabilities for real-time analysis of data. At that time, the discussion was primarily an IT-based topic with a focus on increasing speed. In 2014, 87% of finance executives agreed that to meet corporate targets for profitable growth managers will need to analyze financial and performance data much more quickly than they can now. This shift indicates that finance organizations have now realized the functional and bottom-line benefits that are available with in-memory computing.

- **Analytics**
  The focus in 2013 was on big data analytics in general, with 78% of finance executives indicating that competitiveness of their organization was a big benefit. By 2014, finance executives began to expect more from their analytics systems, and 83% agreed that better information reporting and data visualization capabilities would help line-of-business managers make better decisions. Associating that improvement with business goals, 91% of finance executives said that to meet targets for profitable growth the finance function will need to become better at providing managers with forward-looking, predictive analytics. In the 2015 survey, 76% of respondents reported that finance is central to the use of advanced analytics; however, 79% still indicate that their companies must invest in advanced analytics capabilities, such as sophisticated tools to predict outcomes, assess risk, model complex business scenarios, and support management decision-making.

- **Mobility**
  In 2013, 77% of finance executives stated that mobile technology can help finance better support business units from on site, and 76% felt that it can empower users with better data retrieval capabilities. By 2014, finance executives had switched the focus to obtaining information using self-services regardless of the technology used to do so, yet 58% believed that line-of-business managers have difficulty using their information systems to identify and understand the data they need to make effective decisions. A customer interview in the 2015 CFO Research Services survey revealed that users will be less forgiving of business systems if they are not as intuitive as the apps available on mobile phones, which highlights a new millennial work style.

- **Cloud**
  Although finance organizations have historically been hesitant to move critical financial information into the cloud, 70% agreed in 2013 that the cloud can help reduce technology costs for the finance function, showing a focus on the bottom line. Others cited cost advantages for data storage and processing, faster implementations, and easier updates. (In the next section, we will discuss the available deployment mode options, including several cloud options.) According to a report from Cisco Systems Inc., 70% of workloads were processed in the cloud in 2015.[9]

It is in this environment, sculpted by these market, leadership, and technology trends, that SAP S/4HANA Finance has emerged.

1.4 Introducing SAP S/4HANA Finance

The right set of finance processes enables people and companies to work together more efficiently and to use fact-based, instant insights to stay ahead of the competition. Holistic finance and operational processes empower executives to maintain regulatory compliance, manage risk, use tools and data to plan and execute strategy, and budget and forecast accurately. These processes also help stakeholders report consistently and quickly on consolidated financial results and manage regulatory disclosures.

---

9 Cisco Systems Inc., "Cisco Global Cloud Index: Forecast and Methodology, 2014–2019 White Paper."

Where does SAP S/4HANA Finance come in, and what makes it work? SAP S/4HANA Finance provides the following advantages:

- More intuitive user experience that provides instant access to any financial insight on any device
- Simpler process execution for real-time financials that are always reconciled
- Streamlined decision making using prediction and simulation, always on the fly
- Simpler solution architecture without aggregates and data redundancies
- Cleaner IT strategy, with on-premise, cloud, or hybrid deployment options
- Accessible pricing structure with pricing bundles, including subscription-based pricing for the cloud
- Simpler business justification of a real-time view of the state of the business across all entities and continuous soft close

As shown in Figure 1.2, the functional scope of SAP S/4HANA Finance is best described through five end-to-end processes that are targeted at the following specific roles in the finance organization, with the CFO presiding over all processes:

- **Financial planning and analysis (VP of finance and controlling)**
  Managing performance is not a one-time event. It is an iterative, ongoing process, driven from the top down and across the entire performance lifecycle: from developing, planning, and executing strategy, through monitoring and analyzing operations, to modeling and optimizing processes for better performance outcomes. The overarching goal is to improve the financial health of the organization on a continuous basis. As business conditions change with increasing speed, organizations must quickly and efficiently adapt budgets, plans, and resources to mitigate risks and take advantage of opportunities as they appear. Predictive analytics helps companies plan better by assessing various possible scenarios and running what-if simulations. Simulations help establish options to maximize profitability in diverse market segments across any dimension of business, including customers, products, geographies, and business units.

- **Accounting and financial close (head of corporate reporting)**
  The ability to close books quickly—with accuracy and in full compliance with global regulatory standards—is a critical management challenge. Failure to close efficiently can adversely impact a company's image. Streamlining the

financial close process not only provides vital decision-making data to stakeholders faster but also frees up their time to pursue activities that add greater value, such as financial and operational analysis. To achieve superior financial close performance, best-run companies standardize the closing cycle into a series of repeatable steps that follow a highly automated schedule. Using communication, collaboration, and automation tools, employees involved in the closing process perform their work smoothly and with fewer errors. The overall result is a faster, less expensive, and more transparent financial close—from the entity close to the corporate close. Plus, disclosures and filings with various regulatory agencies follow with equal efficiency.

- **Treasury and financial risk management (treasurer)**
  In today's unpredictable financial market, risk management for credit, debt, and financial instruments is imperative. Best-run finance organizations optimize cash flow and liquidity management, streamline communications, and integrate treasury functions with multiple banks while maintaining greater control over payment and receipt processes. All of these tasks are accomplished while mitigating financial risks and instituting better financial controls across the enterprise. In addition to managing cash, these finance organizations monitor investments and borrowing activities across multiple geographies and currencies. They strive to secure the best investment rates and lowest possible borrowing costs. Accurate and timely insight into global cash balances and liquidity management processes allows them to finance operations with the best mix of funds while minimizing risks.

- **Finance operations (head of finance operations)**
  Best-run finance departments do not forget to pay attention to the core services they supply to the organization, such as credit checks, collections, invoice management, bank transactions, and travel expense processing. Using shared services to standardize and syndicate business practices, best-run organizations streamline processes across the business to improve transaction speed and accuracy, reduce the number of days for which sales are outstanding (DSO), ease resource demands, and enable fair and accurate handling of payments and receivables. The result is not only superior service but also optimized cost. In addition, enterprise mobility extends core financial processes to mobile devices so that account executives and business managers can access customer account information, payments, travel expenses, and budgets from any device at any time. This enables greater productivity and efficiency, lower cost as a percentage of revenue, and more transactions per full-time employee.

- **Enterprise risk and compliance management (chief compliance officer)**
To protect valuable financial data, best-run finance organizations automate access management. They help ensure that processes are tightly controlled to prevent unauthorized access to sensitive corporate assets while detecting fraud and abuse. These organizations proactively balance risk and opportunity across all finance processes, from transaction management to financial reporting. Continuous monitoring of key risk indicators and compliance effectiveness across heterogeneous systems, business processes, and IT infrastructures helps companies align risks and compliance programs to strategic initiatives, business plans, and process execution. Improved and expanded automated risk and compliance management helps to minimize associated efforts and reduce the cost of doing business in a highly regulated environment. At the same time, organizations can protect revenue streams with greater confidence and optimize financial performance.

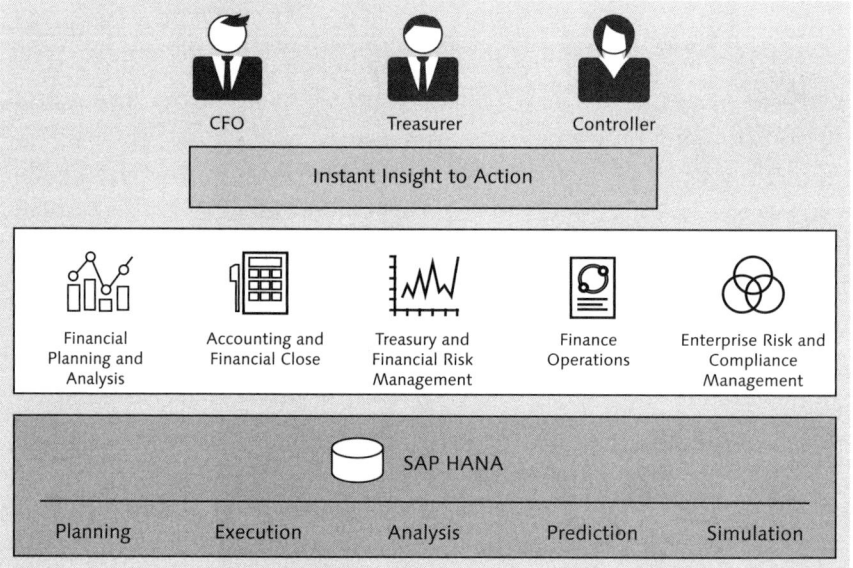

Figure 1.2 SAP S/4HANA Finance across Roles, Processes, and Tasks

The value map for finance (shown in Figure 1.3) identifies the business priorities and strategic solutions, groups them into logical end-to-end processes, and divides these processes further into implementable steps. In the case of finance, the products that support these processes span multiple portfolios of solutions, including SAP ERP Financials; SAP solutions for Enterprise Performance Management (EPM); SAP solutions for Governance, Risk, and Compliance (GRC); and SAP BusinessObjects Business Intelligence (BI).

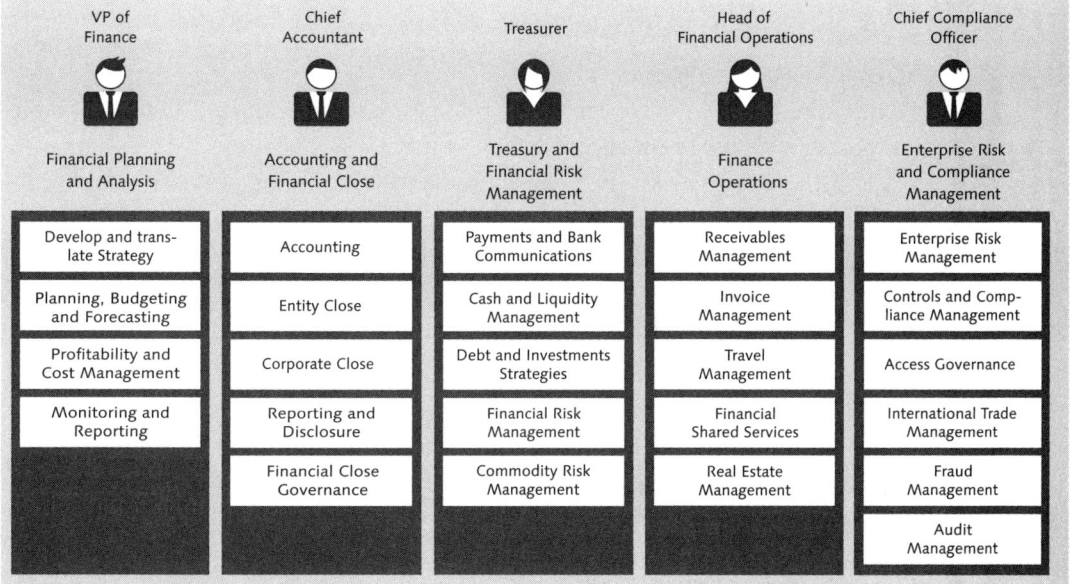

Figure 1.3 Finance Value Map

As the next page in the Finance portfolio of solutions, SAP S/4HANA Finance relies on technological innovations such as SAP HANA and the user experience of SAP Fiori. These innovations benefit finance organizations by enabling them to provide strategic value to the business with instant insight. At the same time, they dramatically simplify the IT landscape with architectural changes to reduce replication and aggregates to benefit the CIO. Embedded within the end-to-end processes are the ability to combine prediction, simulation, and analysis across finance processes in order to identify the best strategic business options and to give financial team members instant and personalized insight for timely and relevant financial decisions.

1.4.1 Deployment Modes

SAP S/4HANA Finance marks the first step of the SAP S/4HANA business suite, which is the next-generation business suite of SAP natively built on the SAP

HANA in-memory platform, fully designed with SAP Fiori user experience. SAP S/4HANA—including SAP S/4HANA Finance—is offered in a variety of consumption models—public cloud (SaaS), managed cloud, and on-premise—for maximum customer choice. Let's look at the deployment options for customers of SAP S/4HANA Finance (summarized in Figure 1.4):

- **On-premise deployment**
  Many installed base customers may prefer to continue to run their SAP implementations on-premise, meaning that software is installed in their own data center in one or more of their sites. The characteristics of an on-premise implementation include having full control over the system and its implementation, including full control over the configuration and the ability to make modifications. The IT organization of the customer also manages security and governance. Each customer maintains the software with any applicable enhancement packs and hot fixes and chooses the timing of implementing any upgrades. From a pricing perspective, customers license the software, which is typically financially managed as a capital expense on the balance sheet that is depreciated over time. Because SAP S/4HANA requires SAP HANA, if a customer prefers to remain on an existing database, then an evaluation is necessary (much of the new development relies on the in-memory capabilities of SAP HANA). There are some options available, such as running only a specific process on SAP HANA—for example, Profitability Analysis (the CO-PA module).

- **Cloud deployment**
  Customers now are able to run their entire enterprise in the cloud with a digital core comprising the most essential scenarios, including finance, accounting, controlling, procurement, sales, manufacturing, plant maintenance, project system, and product lifecycle management. Existing and new customers can adopt the cloud edition of SAP S/4HANA via a simple subscription model. SAP aims to support customers in their journey with predefined migration, system conversion in the cloud, guided configuration, and deployment packages to drive quicker time to value.

  For cloud deployment, there are two options:

  - **Managed cloud deployment**
    Leveraging the SAP HANA Enterprise Cloud, SAP maintains the servers and the software of an organization's implementation as a managed service. The software is installed on servers that are dedicated to a single customer, which

provides the benefit of the customer still being able to configure its business processes; however, modifications are not allowed. The customer still manages the applications and governance rules and has the ability to be on a different release than other customers, again because customers are assigned their own hardware servers. Implementing technical maintenance and upgrades is provided as part of the managed service from SAP. From a pricing perspective, customers still need to license the software capabilities and then purchase the infrastructure and application management on a subscription basis.

- **Public cloud deployment**
 SAP S/4HANA can be deployed in the form of a full SaaS model in which SAP manages both the applications and the infrastructure. Pricing follows a subscription model, which is typically handled as an operating expense by the customer. Configuration is standardized, and modifications are not allowed. All customers are on the same release level. This option enables fast deployment, ensures customers are always up to date on the latest innovations, and provides a lower overall TCO.

- **Hybrid deployment**
 A combination of on-premise and cloud implementations presents an attractive hybrid model. Ideal candidates for these scenarios are point processes that can be easily carved out and do not require close integration with the remaining SAP Business Suite. Examples of such hybrid landscapes include the use of the Ariba Network for invoice management and cloud-based travel and expense. Large organizations that have an on-premise implementation may choose to run specific organizations—for example, remote sales offices, subsidiaries, or recent mergers and acquisitions—in the cloud, with an integration into their on-premise systems for consolidated reporting and disclosures.

For detailed information about deployment modes and migration information, please refer to Chapter 13.

Next, we will take a look at how specific SAP S/4HANA Finance capabilities were built to simplify finance processes for SAP Business Suite customers by leveraging the power of SAP HANA, which can benefit both finance from a process perspective and IT from an architectural perspective.

1 Introduction

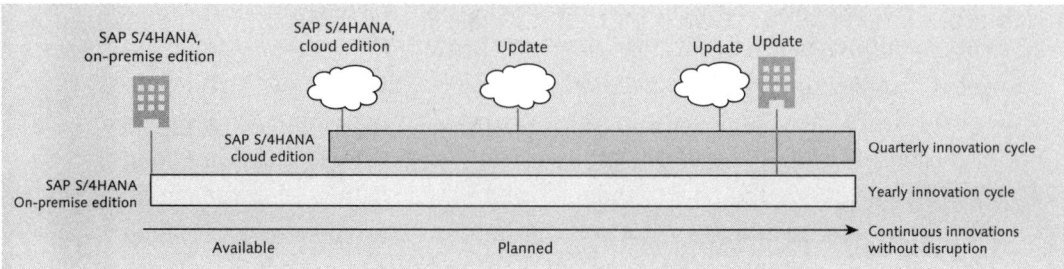

Figure 1.4 Current Deployment Options for SAP S/4HANA Finance

1.4.2 Transformative Finance Technologies

The envisioned paradigm of the future will be the real-time finance organization. These organizations have three major characteristics: alignment, agility, and predictability. *Alignment* means that they need to work from a transparent single source of truth to make sure everyone is working with the same information and no time is lost in reconciling information manually. *Agility* requires real-time finance processes that support instant reactions to changing external conditions. *Predictability* means gaining unmatched insight and foresight in order to preempt potential future changes of conditions before such changes become a reality.

Alignment, agility, and predictability translate to three key finance technologies. Let's look at these technologies now and then apply them to some key areas of finance: accounting, centralized finance, cash management, integrated business planning, business cockpits, and continuous processes.

Single Source of Truth

Alignment is a key prerequisite for any real-time organization. An organization can only act in real time if everyone works from a common set of information provided by a single source of truth.

Such a single source of truth comprises three major elements:

1. The first element is ensuring data consistency across all solutions. This consistency is provided by SAP S/4HANA as the single repository of shared data and shared methods across all finance solutions. All transactional processing (OLTP) and reporting (OLAP) is performed by SAP's finance solutions such as SAP ERP,

SAP Business Planning and Consolidation (BPC), SAP BW, and SAP BusinessObjects BI on the fly from this shared source of information without precalculated aggregates, as shown in Figure 1.5.

2. The second element is providing seamless access to all data, not only financial data, from a single access point. A semantic virtual data model (VDM) on top of SAP HANA provides this capability.

3. Last but not least, in order to ensure data consistency, finance solutions support all personalized analytics within the system of record with a high degree of flexibility and adaptability. This way, there is no need for users to extract and maintain data in local spreadsheets. End users can configure their own data views on the fly any way they want. They can drill down to the line item level and can retain all existing data fields in transaction processing and reporting. They can even flexibly add their own customer-specific dimensions and preserve such additional information in transaction processing and reporting.

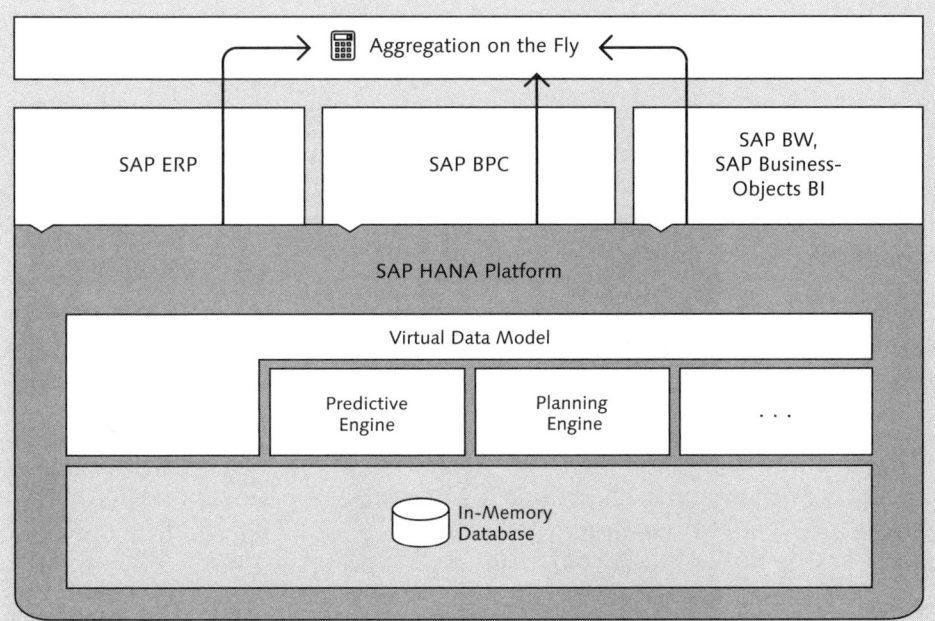

Figure 1.5 Single Source of Truth

This single-source concept enables another important change with regards to report generation. In traditional reporting systems, you preconceive the reporting needs of the business, producing a continuously growing "flood" of static reports. The personalized analytics on a single source of truth allows business users to generate these reports themselves and choose the fields that are relevant to them within these reports, whenever and wherever they need them. This requires finance to focus much more attention on data governance in order to ensure consistent data quality in the central system rather than post-processing data manually in local Microsoft Excel spreadsheets. Once such data quality has been established, freed-up time can be utilized for better strategic advisories. Implementing the financial single source of truth is the decisive means to achieve this data quality.

In classical finance systems, several barriers prevent realization of a single source of truth:

- The same system contains several copies of data stored in different data models.
- Data is stored in decentralized finance systems and copied to a central finance system.
- Data is copied from a finance system of records to a data warehouse.

Why do we have these obstacles? Within a transactional finance system, several data copies are kept for different purposes; for example, in accounting there are different storage areas for external reporting and for managerial reporting. Often, each of these systems and applications has its own data model, optimized for its specific purpose.

Copying data between these models comes with an inherent latency. Systems build separate caches on each copied data set in order to optimize performance. Adjustments to changing business requirements are unwieldy, because all data copies and their predefined caches need to be consistently changed, which is not an easy task when you consider different data modeling within different applications of a finance system. In addition, in day-to-day business these redundant data models result in significant efforts to keep information consistent, so some enterprises establish departments with the single purpose of reconciling data. Further, historical and predictive analytics run on different data sets with a variety of methods—resulting in a multitude of contradicting views of the past, fuzzy snapshots of the present, and ambiguous pictures of the future.

With modern in-memory database technology like SAP HANA, there is now the scalability to provide a single source of truth for a complete enterprise, even with thousands of subsidiaries based on the atomic granularity of each and every transaction of the business: the *line items*. Financial data can be separated into three main categories, reflecting the past, the present, and the future:

- All past economic activities are reflected in accounting, which provides an ex-post view of the enterprise, valuated by accounting principles.
- A single source collects all information about business currently in progress and thus keeps track of all kinds of exposures in the enterprise.
- A third source contains the expectations about the future business: the ex-ante view. Here you record all plans, budgets, and forecasts.

All decisive questions can be answered based on these data categories. The accounting database answers the questions, "What happened?" and "Why did it happen?" in terms of balance sheets, P&L statements, and profitability and market segment reports. The exposure database helps to answer, "What is happening now?" and gives the short- and medium-term predictions. Cash management personnel ask questions such as "When do we have to pay out?" or cost management personnel ask, "What has been spent or committed, but not yet recorded in accounting?" Yearly planning and budgeting cycles bring all three data sources together, usually starting from the ex-post view, combining it with all information about business in progress and external market data to answer the question, "What might happen?" In controlling, you measure current business against these plan figures to answer, "Are we on track?" and thus combine ex-post and ex-ante data. In rolling forecasts, you update the plans based on the most recent information about business in progress.

Real-Time Finance Processes

Real-time finance solutions have three main goals (as shown in Figure 1.6):

- Executing transactional processes in real time (left)
- Providing instant insight on action to the business in order to respond to changed economic conditions without delay (right)
- Putting real-time process oversight and risk-management capabilities in place to make sure that the impact of potential process failures is as limited as possible (bottom)

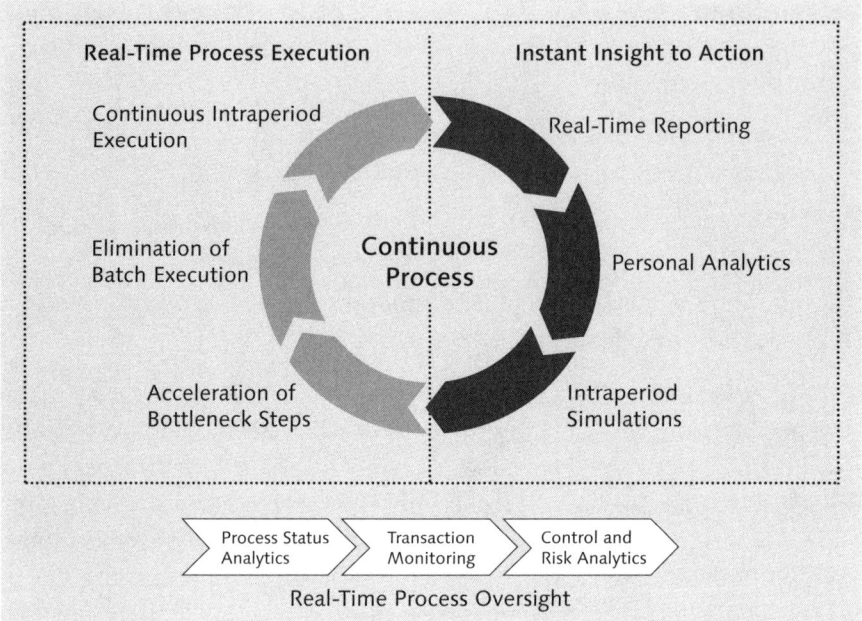

Figure 1.6 Real-Time Process Revolution

The migration to real-time finance processes will constitute no less than a next-process revolution. Today's sequential processes may be replaced by continuous processes in which activities happen simultaneously, driven only by events rather than being driven by an orchestrated sequence of process steps. There will be no more waiting for batch processes, which currently occur only at the period end, in order to obtain current, real-time information.

This is only possible if any process execution—transactional or analytical—happens in real time and if the associated insight to action is made available to decision makers in real time as well. We also believe that novel mechanisms for real-time process oversight will be necessary to ensure compliance and mitigate risks in such novel real-time processes.

As you can see in Figure 1.6, acceleration of process bottleneck steps will be an important element and the starting point of the evolution toward real-time processes. However, many more enhancements will be necessary and in fact are part of SAP's innovation agenda. These include further process automation and new analytical UIs in order to make sure that the processed information reaches the end user in real time, anytime and anywhere.

Insight and Foresight

The ultimate characteristic of being a real-time finance organization is the ability to predict the possibilities of the future better than the competition. This requires unmatched insight and foresight. In practical terms, it means that you need to deeply understand the drivers of your business and develop a quantitative model of your organization based on these drivers. You need to recognize trends and anticipate future risks that may affect these drivers and lead to a better forecast of the near-term future. You need to align around a joint plan and adapt dynamically to changing economic conditions.

In more technical terms, technology innovations will enable finance organizations to be more predictive by providing advanced analytics and novel ways of planning, modeling, simulation, and forecasting.

One particular challenge in this context is the ability for entire organizations to *plan dynamically*. As a consequence of the "new normal," real-world conditions are changing faster and more disruptively than ever before, as seen in the rapidly changing demand in consumer-oriented industries or rapidly changing commodity prices that are relevant for many producing industries. On the other hand, business models of companies are also becoming more complex than ever before, so the impact of changing economic conditions on company plans often will be very complex as well.

Companies therefore need flexible ways to adapt their plans. This means moving away from the traditional, rigid annual planning and budgeting cycle toward an integrated rolling plan for the entire company that finance adapts periodically during the fiscal year. In order to speed up the planning cycle, it is necessary to link the independent plans of the individual business units into the rolling plan for the entire group in real time.

1.4.3 Key Areas of Innovation

Next, we'll discuss six major areas of innovation in SAP S/4HANA Finance that support the real-time finance organization.

Accounting

Accounting and financial close show the financial results of a corporation to external and internal stakeholders. A fast, reliable, accurate, and efficient financial close is a key objective of ambitious corporate finance departments. Business dynamics shrink the available closing windows and require companies to deliver reliable results to the market and to management as soon as possible. Business practices have evolved toward intraperiod "soft closes" that provide relevant top- and bottom-line key figures almost continuously—and definitely not only after period close. We need to take a fresh look at accounting and financial close processes and enabling technologies.

In-memory technology allows SAP to provide an accounting system with an entirely new architecture as part of SAP S/4HANA Finance. Rather than keeping Financial Accounting (FI) and Controlling (CO) documents separate, as in SAP ERP Financials (see Figure 1.7), there is only one single source of truth for financials and management accounting in SAP S/4HANA Finance. As Figure 1.8 shows, all financial data is stored in one repository: the *Universal Journal*, which is used for statutory reporting, profitability analysis, General Ledger (G/L) accounting, accounts payable, receivables management, asset accounting, profit center and cost center accounting, overhead management, and material valuation. The revenue and cost part of the P&L statement includes all relevant detail, such as customers, products, and regions, as well as all dimensions added by the customer. Chapter 8 explains the Universal Journal concept and its benefits in more detail.

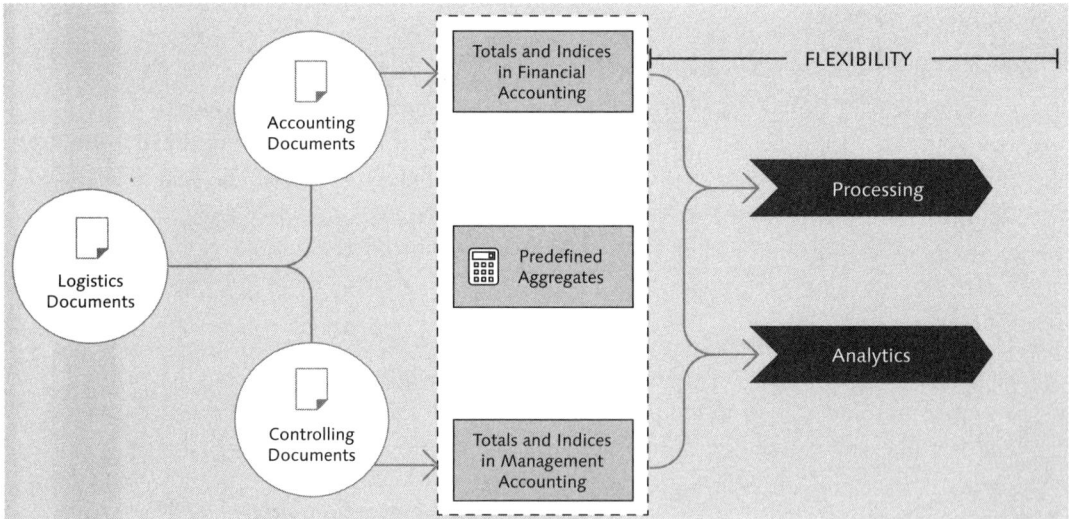

Figure 1.7 Data Flow of Accounting Documents in SAP ERP Financials with Predefined Aggregates

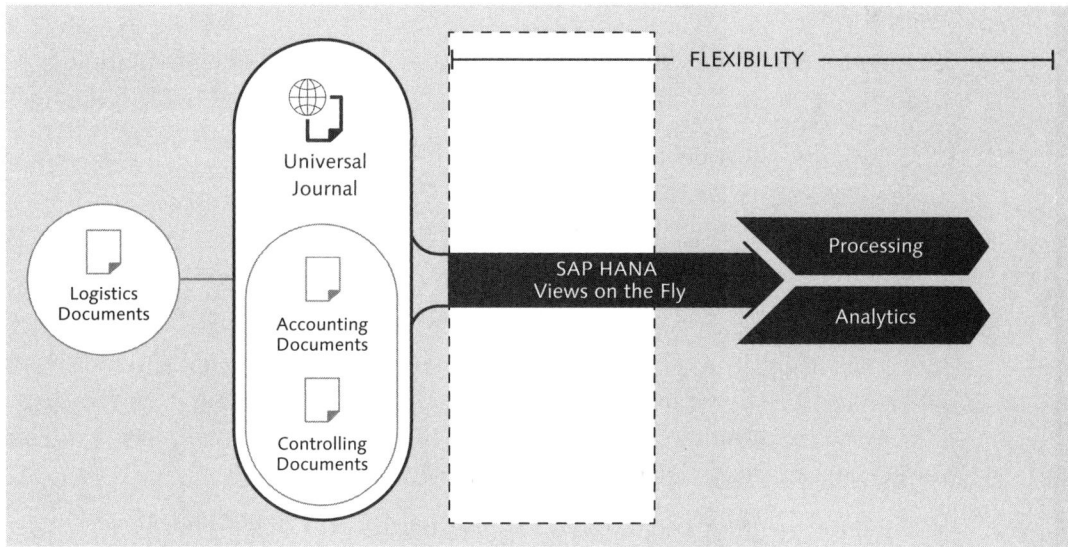

Figure 1.8 Aggregation on the Fly in SAP S/4HANA Finance

Processing and analysis is based on line items, which represent all past economic activities of an enterprise; thus, the highest granularity is available. You can perform any kind of analysis directly on this data set with superior performance; there is no need to preconfigure aggregates for fast data access. This supports on-the-fly analysis in full detail and easier simulation. In the future, consolidations could also be run on the original accounting data. Data replication would become obsolete; some consolidation functionality could even be run on the fly in reporting.

Reporting based on this data is fast and flexible. All SAP BusinessObjects BI solutions can be run on top of accounting data directly within the finance system. This is key to avoiding cumbersome data replication to separate reporting or data warehouse systems.

Accounting in SAP S/4HANA Finance is meant to be easily adaptable. Any number of customer-specific dimensions can be added consistently in accounting. Regulations like the European Solvency Directive or the Basel Accords require companies to extend accounting, sometimes by more than thirty additional dimensions. SAP S/4HANA Finance can cope with this.

Central Finance

Companies today often suffer from heterogeneous landscapes with multiple local finance systems. Root causes for this are as follows:

- Due to limited scalability of traditional ERP systems, the transactional workload has been separated into multiple systems (e.g., regional finance instances rather than a centralized finance instance).
- Systems pile up over the years due to mergers and acquisitions.

A single global instance for finance reporting is a must, because consolidated statutory reporting is legally required, and consolidated managerial reporting is needed to steer the enterprise. Most companies aim to use this required single global system to run the complete range of finance processes and serve as a basis for efficient processes and data quality for decision management.

When implementing a centralized finance solution, the biggest hurdle is to standardize and harmonize global enterprise processes related to master data, configuration, and transactional details for all segments and business areas. We see the following as fundamental approaches toward a centralized finance solution:

- Build the centralized finance system subsidiary by subsidiary, considering all financials processes. This requires standardizing and harmonizing all processes from the beginning.
- Standardize and harmonize one process and deploy SAP S/4HANA Finance in its Central Finance deployment option as a centralized system for this one process.

Most companies prefer the second approach, because it results in fast return on investment. To this end, the best starting point is the Central Finance option of SAP S/4HANA Finance, which is a central system for collecting accounting data (see Chapter 14). This establishes a single source of truth for group reporting, both for statutory and managerial purposes. All accounting records from existing (legacy) backend systems (see bottom of Figure 1.9) are replicated in real time into the single SAP HANA database that is part of the Central Finance system, which runs SAP S/4HANA Finance. Once the infrastructure for onboarding noncentral finance systems to a Central Finance system is available, the finance system of newly acquired subsidiaries can be integrated quickly.

After establishing a central system for financial reporting, the next steps are central planning, central record to report (local and group reporting), central open item management, central bank account management, central payment, central cash operations, and treasury and risk management. Each step adds substantial value for the group, whereas the cumbersome and time-consuming standardization and harmonization endeavor is divided into consumable chunks. Finally, once all finance processes are lifted and shifted this way to a central instance, the noncentral systems become obsolete.

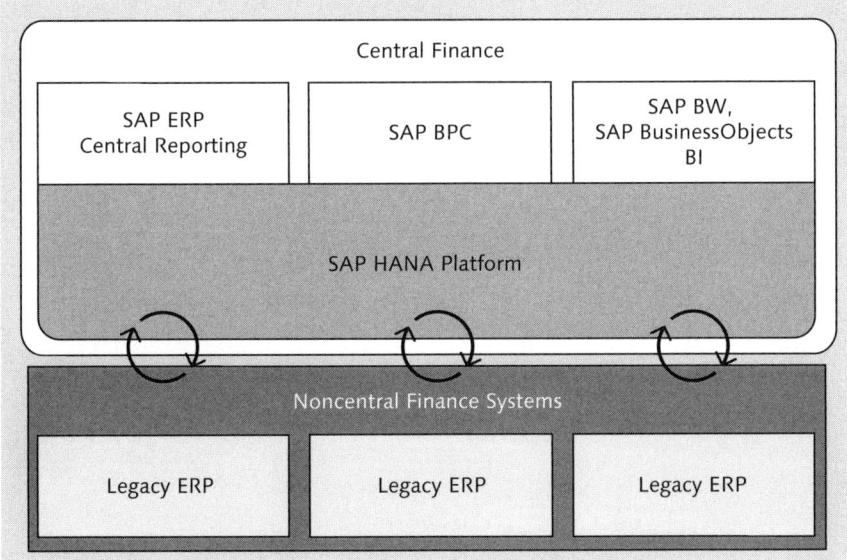

Figure 1.9 Central Finance System Based on SAP HANA Platform

SAP Cash Management Powered by SAP HANA

Profitability and liquidity are essential to sustain and grow the business in a highly competitive, volatile environment that erodes margins and creates substantial liquidity risks. Today, sophisticated cash management practices are used to ensure liquidity and contribute to profitability.

A clear view of historical cash flow, current cash positions, and risks related to financial assets and counterparties along with a reliable estimation of future liquidity are the foundation for effective decisions that mitigate liquidity risks and optimize cash management.

As part of SAP S/4HANA Finance, SAP Cash Management powered by SAP HANA (see Chapter 11, Section 11.4) supports cash managers in their day-to-day business with access to all relevant cash management KPIs on desktops and mobile devices, as shown in Figure 1.10. This includes KPI monitoring, interactive root-cause analysis of deviations, and group-wide forecast of cash and liquidity. It allows cash managers to analyze global bank balances and cash positions based on data from SAP and non-SAP systems. Daily cash operations are easier, because analytics for cash positions is combined with direct actions, like bank transfers. Payments are supported with analytics functions, statistical analysis, and workflow.

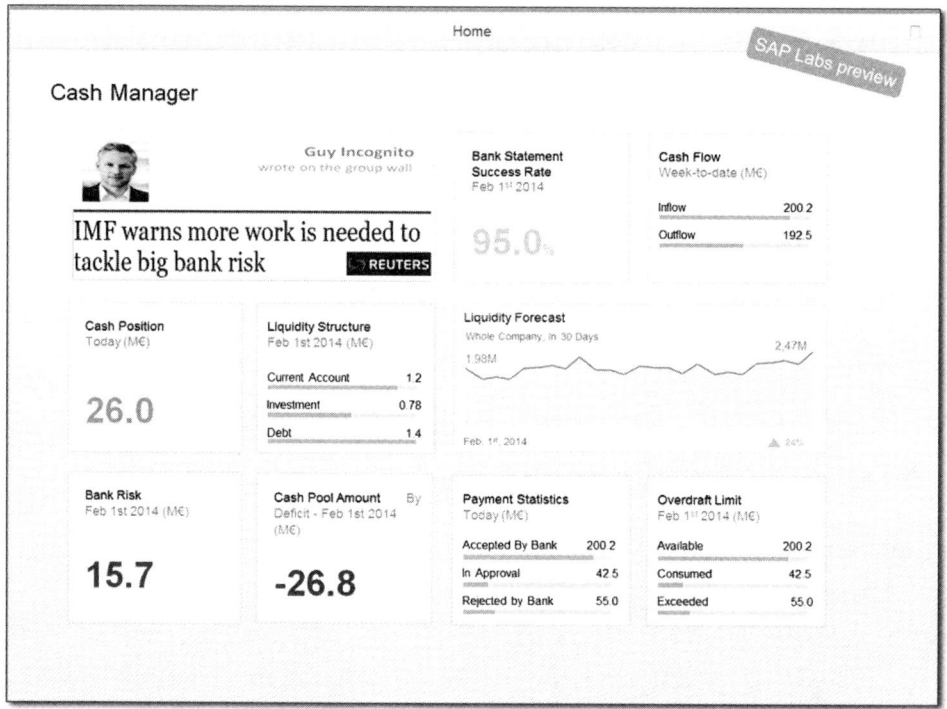

Figure 1.10 Cockpit for Cash Managers

Furthermore, SAP Cash Management includes functions for central bank account management, like overdraft limit analysis, bank risk analysis, and signatory management and workflow, to support the lifecycle management of bank accounts. The net effect is that cash managers can handle their tasks more simply and easily than before in order to achieve compliance and transparency with a systematic approach and reduce potential risk.

The SAP Cash Management application of SAP S/4HANA Finance includes liquidity management with midterm liquidity forecasting, multidimensional cash flow analysis, and rolling liquidity planning and variance analysis. It integrates not only with accounting in SAP S/4HANA Finance but also with the solutions for Treasury and Financial Risk Management, Bank Communication Management, and In-House Cash.

SAP Cash Management is a good example of an application bridging all main data categories of finance: cash position analysis is built on the ex-post view in accounting, cash forecasting combines this with the database for business in progress and thus predicts future cash flow, and liquidity planning even combines this with the long-term planning perspective of the enterprise.

Integrated Business Planning

The first step in the direction of dynamic planning is the real-time integration of different subplans into one integrated business plan. From top to bottom, Figure 1.11 shows how strategic planning directly influences different operational plans and how those feed into other plans, which are based on assumptions made in previous steps. For example, demand planning affects revenue planning, and production planning affects cost planning. Eventually, operational plans feed an organization's overall financial plan in the form of, for example, its profitability plan, balance sheet, and P&L plans.

Strategic planning involves what-if analysis, simulation, and comparison of different scenarios. The strategic targets must be mapped to key figures of operational planning steps in order to ensure the connection between strategic and operational plans. For example, you can break ROI into sales (net sales), production (product costs), and investment planning (investments in new plants) targets.

Developing operational plans and integrating them into one group financial plan is usually a complex process; sometimes the planning operation involves large numbers of staff from different parts of the enterprise. A lot of coordination of standards, procedures, and timelines needs to happen.

1 | Introduction

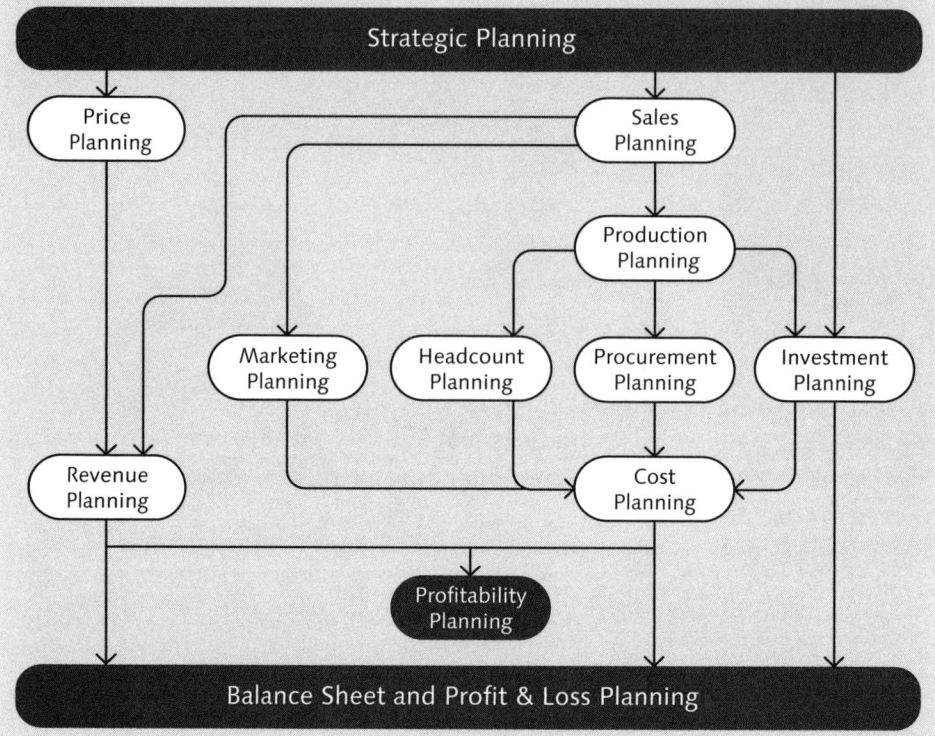

Figure 1.11 Dynamic Planning through Integrated Business Planning

Thus, the need arises for coordination instruments, which structure the planning process and provide complete planning integration at every level. Such instruments help ensure that up-to-date plan data (e.g., in a rolling forecast process) is both reliable and available on time.

A number of functional requirements for a planning solution are available to fully support integrated business planning, as shown in Figure 1.12. These requirements are driven by the need to simultaneously provide the following:

- Strong governance and integration mechanisms for the owner of the central plan
- Far-reaching planning autonomy for the owners of the individual plans
- Seamless integration with SAP ERP in order to accelerate the development of planning models by reusing existing data and data structures

1.4 Introducing SAP S/4HANA Finance

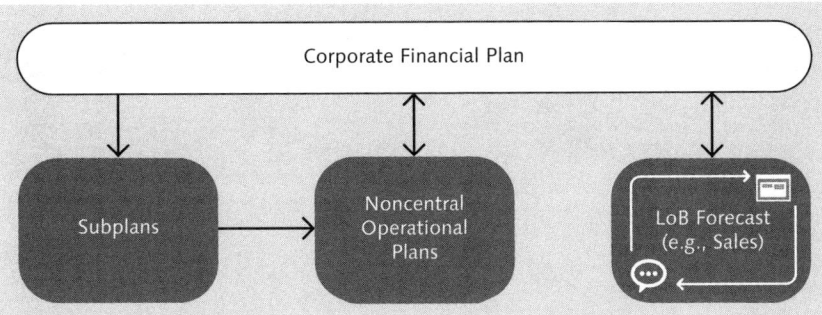

Figure 1.12 System Requirements for Integrated Business Planning

It is a market reality that there is no single planning solution in the market today that supports all of these requirements simultaneously. That's the main reason that many SAP customers still utilize hybrid planning landscapes consisting of SAP BPC, SAP BW Integrated Planning, and planning capabilities in SAP ERP. Although there are integration points among these planning solutions and with SAP ERP, the depth of integration still leaves significant room for improvement. This situation does not improve when employing third-party planning solutions.

SAP Business Planning and Consolidation for Finance in SAP S/4HANA Finance (see Chapter 11, Section 11.5) allows companies to take the ultimate step of unification with SAP ERP by deploying SAP Accounting and SAP BPC on the same SAP HANA platform (see Figure 1.13). In this case, data replication between solutions is no longer necessary, because both applications will share the same data. UIs and workflows are seamlessly integrated, making plans developed in SAP BPC accessible for variance analysis. From the other end, SAP BPC will provide embedded access to master data and actuals that are maintained in SAP Accounting. Both capabilities combined will provide novel end-to-end simulation capabilities.

Furthermore, the operational planning steps share the same planning data set. Thus, the planning steps represent "views" on this single source of truth for planning. Therefore, there is no need to reconcile plans and no latency in the process, because data is not transferred between partial plans. Business users can work collaboratively on the plans; for example, cost planning and revenue planning can happen at the same time, and impact on profitability is visible at any time without "merging plans."

1 Introduction

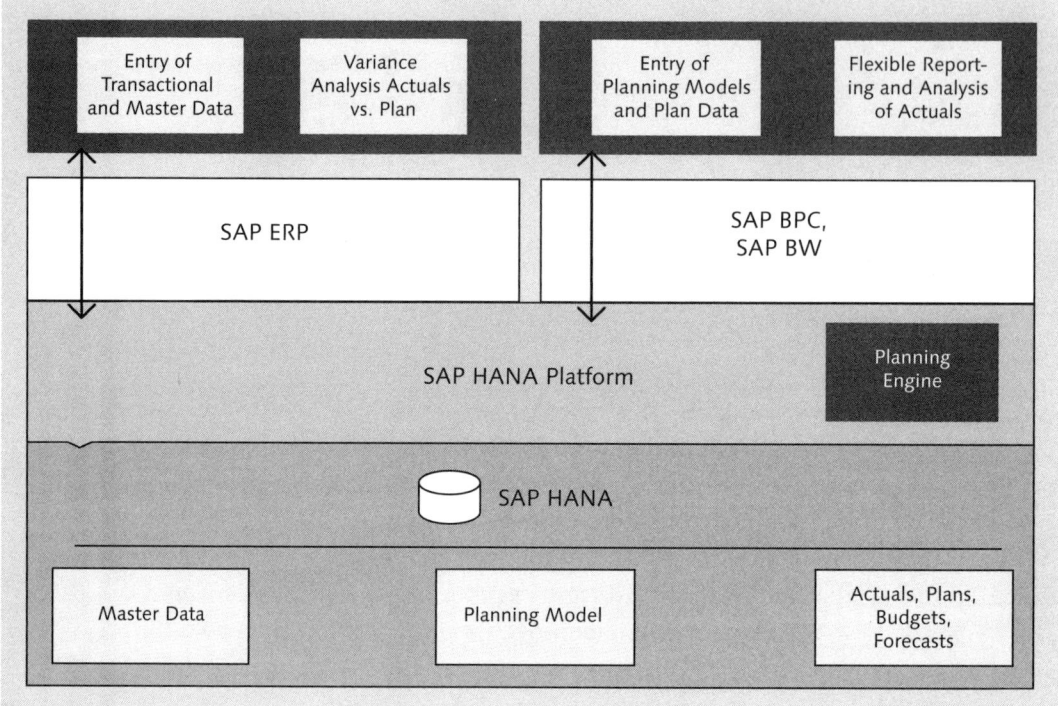

Figure 1.13 Architecture for Next-Generation Financial Planning

Business Cockpits

The business cockpits offered by SAP S/4HANA Finance help to further improve and accelerate the consumption of information by business users. These cockpits aim to provide decision makers in the finance organization with a 360-degree overview of relevant financial data. These cockpits are configurable by end users and provide real-time visualization of the most important KPIs for these roles (see Chapter 11, Section 11.1).

Dashboards and analytics enable actionable insight with real-time access to detailed analysis. Figure 1.14 shows a cockpit that provides the overview for the state of finance. Each of the elements of this cockpit allows for triggering detailed analytical applications, like the net margin analysis shown in Figure 1.15. Other cockpits address the CFO, the financial close manager, the cash manager, and receivables and payables managers.

1.4 Introducing SAP S/4HANA Finance

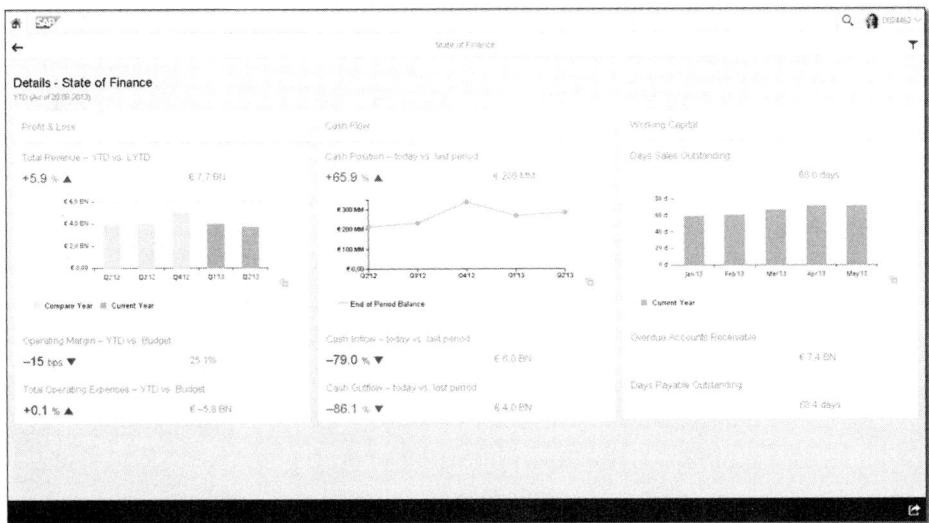

Figure 1.14 State of Finance Cockpit

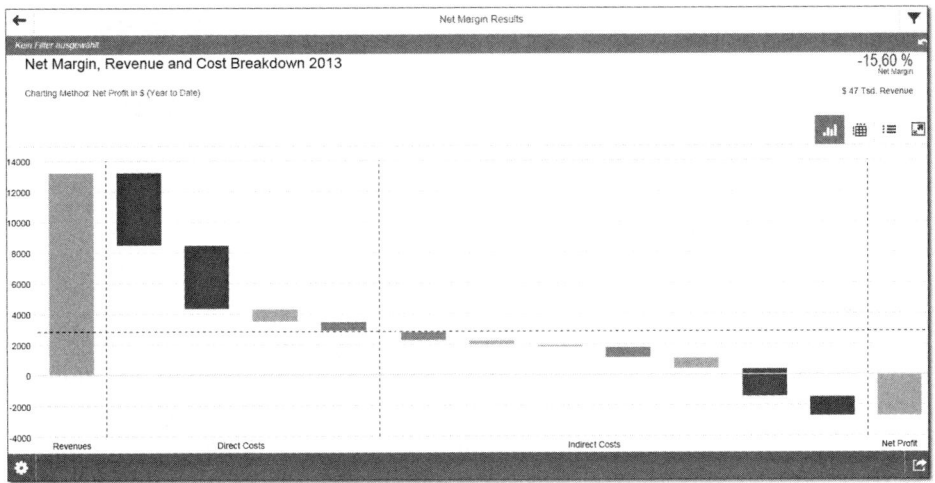

Figure 1.15 Net Margin Analysis Cockpit

SAP Lumira (see Figure 1.16) is another example of how new visualization techniques facilitate end user access to information in the backend system, thereby further contributing to the real-time character of the entire process chain. SAP Lumira is a solution within SAP's Business Intelligence portfolio, which is directly connected to data in SAP HANA.

55

1 | Introduction

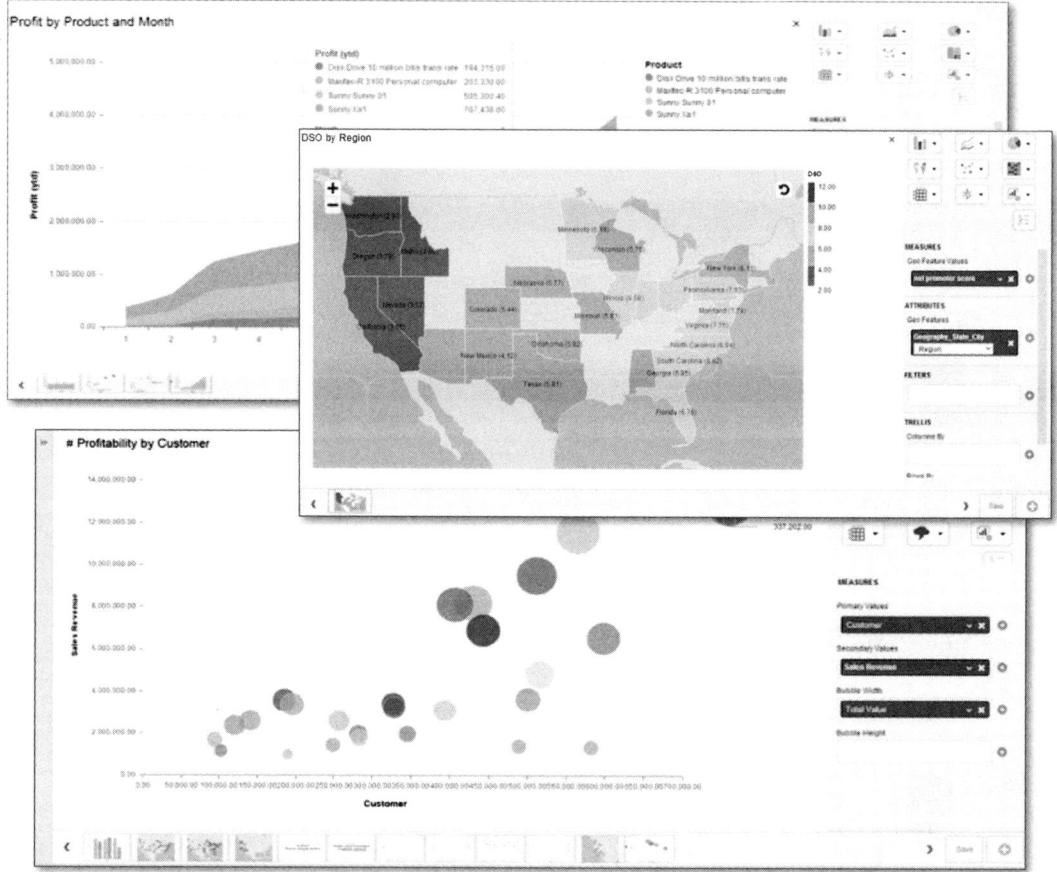

Figure 1.16 SAP Lumira

The solution provides business users in financial departments with the tools to easily visualize any kind of data from any source without the need for IT expertise. It allows users to merge data sets, share models with colleagues, and show results as tables rather than spreadsheets.

SAP Smart Business cockpits are based on a common set of KPIs. They come with a modeler for KPI definition, authorizations, and drilldown definitions. SAP S/4HANA Finance delivers many key figures and cockpits based on this modeler. One example is the SAP Smart Business cockpit for financial close, which is shown in Figure 1.17.

Figure 1.17 SAP Smart Business Cockpit for Financial Close

The SAP Smart Business applications of SAP S/4HANA Finance are device independent, meaning that they are available both in the desktop environment and on mobile devices. Let's look at an example from receivables management that takes advantage of this device independence. The main goal of receivables managers is to keep overdue receivables and days sales outstanding (DSO) low and to minimize credit defaults and bad debt write-offs. With the SAP HANA-based SAP Receivables Manager mobile application, receivables managers can continuously monitor their customers' payment behavior to manage receivables risk and to facilitate efficient cash collection. Configurable alerting and key figures help the receivables manager visualize the customer status in a few seconds (see Figure 1.18).

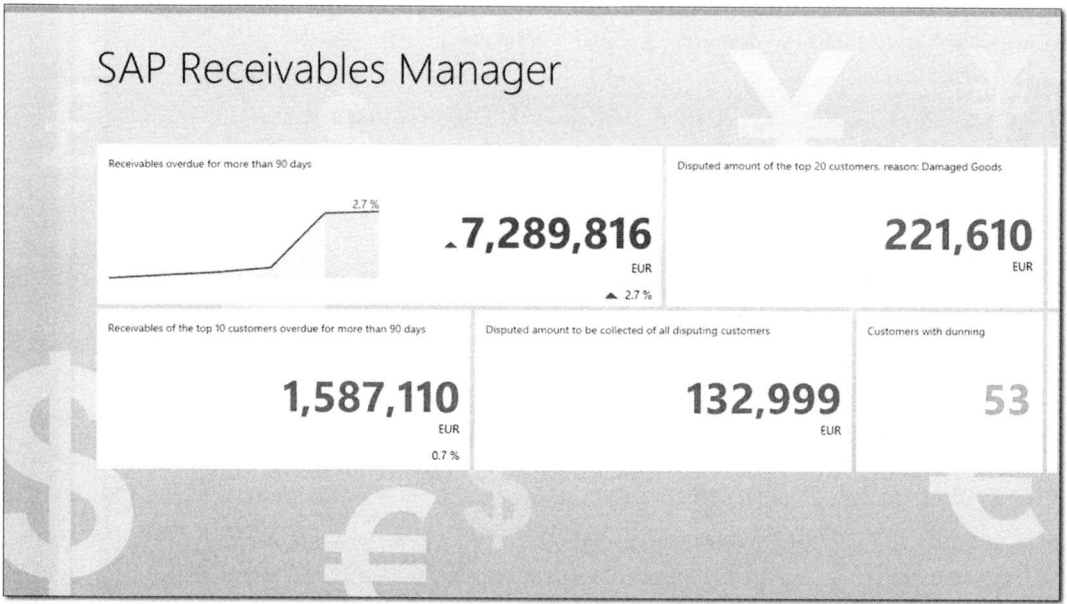

Figure 1.18 SAP Receivables Manager Dashboard on Tablet

A second example is SAP Working Capital Analytics, which provides real-time analysis of drivers for DSO—a main lever for working capital optimization. This analytics application enables interactive creation of flexible data analysis paths with innovative visualizations of the analysis process sequence (see Figure 1.19). SAP Working Capital Analytics helps companies drill down to the business transaction level to analyze all aspects of days sales and payables outstanding. This intuitive and easy-to-use tool allows for interactively building flexible analysis paths. KPI calculations are based on original documents, such as for accounts receivable, and provide new options to explore and drill down, such as analyses by customer down to line items. With classical finance solutions, analyzing data on this level was not possible or at least was complex and time consuming, but with SAP S/4HANA Finance such analysis is both possible and simple.

Introducing SAP S/4HANA Finance | 1.4

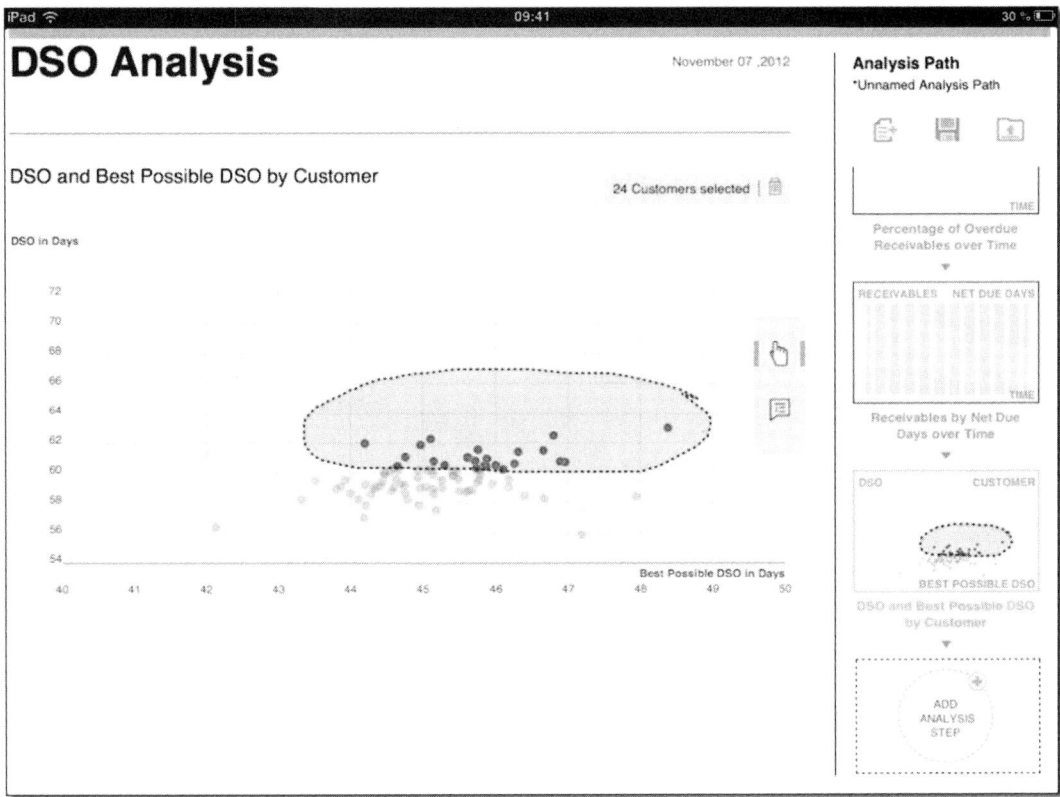

Figure 1.19 Real-Time DSO Analysis

Continuous Processes

As outlined previously, fast period-end closes are a hallmark of an efficient finance organization. They are not only a means of informing shareholders and other external stakeholders of results as fast as possible; companies themselves also benefit from having accurate and up-to-date closing information as early as possible for management purposes. Fast closing requires a perfect choreography of standardized tasks and procedures, whereas "soft closes" during the period benefit from SAP S/4HANA Finance's new architecture.

In SAP S/4HANA Finance, transactional processing generally is accelerated. Because the system records transactional facts only once based on line item tables (remember the single source of truth), the database throughput is doubled. Scenarios that required a high throughput in finance, such as those in insurance, banking, or retail industries, no longer encounter any kind of database-locking issues; these issues are a characteristic of systems using persistent caching means, like aggregates. Due to code pushdown into SAP HANA, some processes can be further accelerated; factors up to thirty are possible, as occurs for work-in-progress calculation for production orders, variance calculation for production orders and cost centers, and results analysis for the percentage of completion method and the revenue method.

In this way, the month-end closing process is significantly accelerated, as shown in Figure 1.20 (see Chapter 11, Section 11.7 for more details).

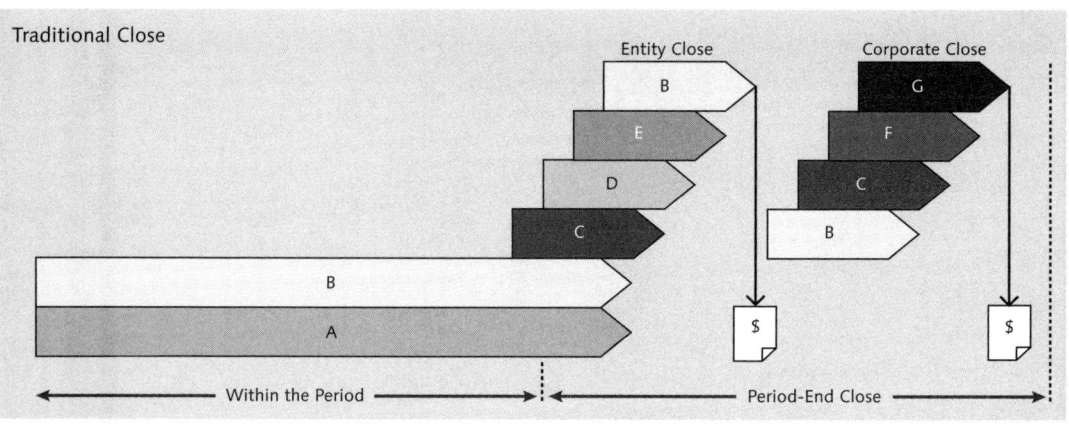

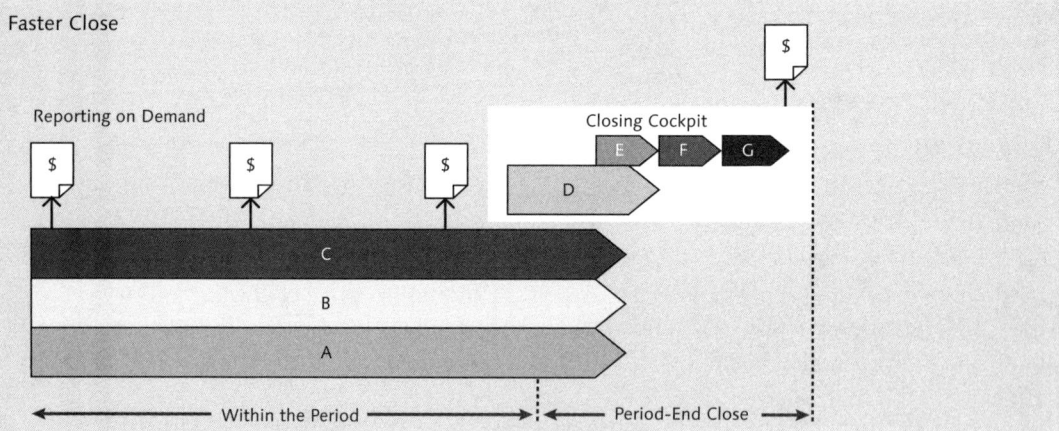

Figure 1.20 Transition to Continuous Processes in Financial Closing

Some steps can even be run on a daily or weekly basis rather than only at period end. Thus, the accounting system provides insight daily or weekly. There are a few key business benefits that can be realized:

- Information for managerial reporting can be provided faster.
- The results of the period-end close can be forecasted more often and with higher accuracy.
- Accounting decisions can be simulated on the fly.
- Each finance organization can better balance its workload throughout the entire period, avoiding today's stressful and error-prone month-end crunch.

A good example for the acceleration is the reconciliation of payables and receivables within the group (intercompany reconciliation). In classical finance systems, this is a batch-dominated process that involves collecting relevant line items from noncentral systems and preanalyzing this data for fast retrieval at a later point in time. The SAP HANA–based process occurs in real time, especially when combined with the Central Finance approach; open items are directly accessed from the single source of truth in accounting, and matching of payables and receivables is calculated on the fly. The UI is easy to navigate, provides good process oversight through dashboards, and includes means for collaboration of the accountants of different subsidiaries.

Let's look at an example of the transition to continuous processes in the area of receivables management—in particular, the collections process—as shown in Figure 1.21.

Today, the collections process has a periodic character and consists of several consecutive process steps, as shown on the left. First, collection-relevant information is extracted from the backend system. After a review of open cases, a collections work list is produced for a dedicated team of collection specialists. These specialists work in the back office and contact their assigned customers in order to resolve open collection cases. The downside of this approach is that a separate team of collection specialists is required. These specialists lack customer proximity and may even work on the basis of outdated information.

It would be much better to involve sales representatives directly in the collections process. However, this is only advisable if they can be equipped with always-up-to-date information about the collection status of their customers. Few situations are more embarrassing for a sales rep than to erroneously complain about an unpaid invoice based on outdated information.

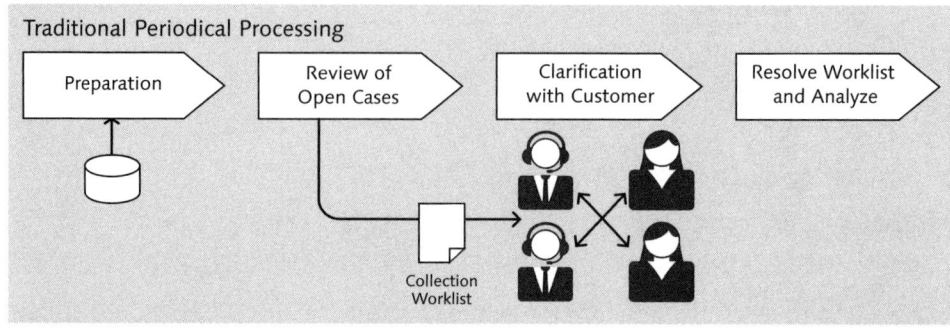

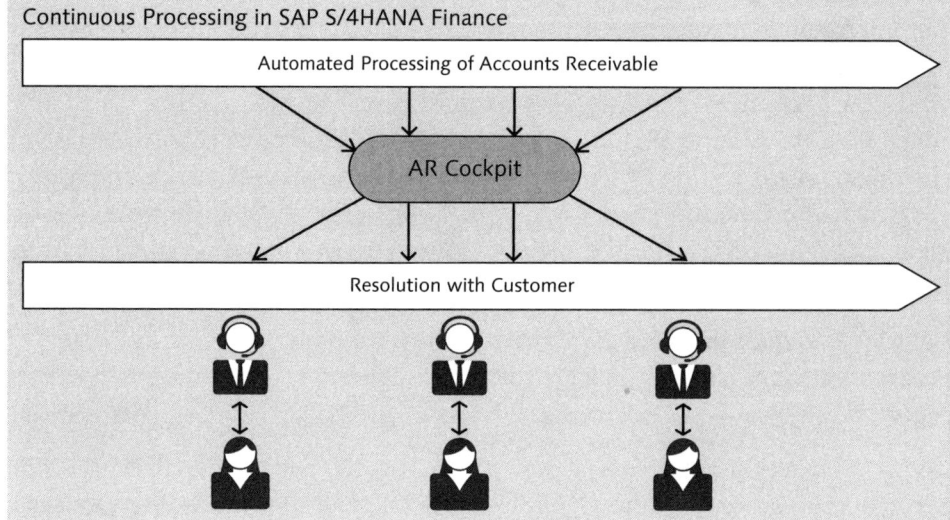

Figure 1.21 Transition to Continuous Process in Receivables Management

With SAP's latest innovations, such direct involvement of sales reps in the collections process becomes a possibility. With real-time information in the hand of sales reps and receivables managers anytime and anywhere, the collection process can be turned into a continuous process without the need for periodic data extraction and quality review steps.

In the next chapters, we will take a more detailed look at the data model for SAP S/4HANA Finance and how it will benefit finance organizations.

PART I
Exploring the SAP S/4HANA Finance Model

SAP HANA is the in-memory database underlying SAP S/4HANA Finance. This chapter outlines the specific capabilities of in-memory technology that make it especially suitable to meet the requirements of today's finance departments.

2   In-Memory Technology and SAP HANA

The purpose of this chapter is to provide an overview of SAP HANA in order to understand the key ideas and concepts behind SAP S/4HANA Finance that will be discussed in subsequent chapters. We will begin with the big picture of SAP HANA. Then, we'll look into some basic concepts of SAP HANA, including its in-memory data storage, dictionary encoding and data compression, parallel execution capabilities, and the concept of using the delta store to optimize write operations. We will summarize the overall vision of SAP HANA as the single unified platform for mixed enterprise workloads—namely, transactional and analytical data processing.

At the core of SAP HANA is a massive parallel database management system (DBMS) that runs fully in main memory. In contrast to traditional DBMSs, which are designed for optimizing performance on hardware with constrained main memory, the SAP HANA database is designed from the ground up around the ideas that memory is available in abundance to keep all business data and that input/output (I/O) access to the hard disk is not a constraint. Whereas traditional database systems put the most effort into optimizing hard disk I/O, SAP HANA focuses on optimizing memory access between the CPU cache and the main memory.

Figure 2.1 illustrates a conceptual overview of SAP HANA, which first and foremost incorporates a full DBMS into a standard SQL interface, transactional isolation and recovery, and high availability. The DBMS is capable of handling row store, column store, and graph store of data. It facilitates massive parallelization of database access threads through a dedicated engine and comes with integrated services, such as search and application extension. It is compatible with standard interfaces, such as SQL, MDX, and others. Here, we will focus on the DBMS aspects of SAP HANA.

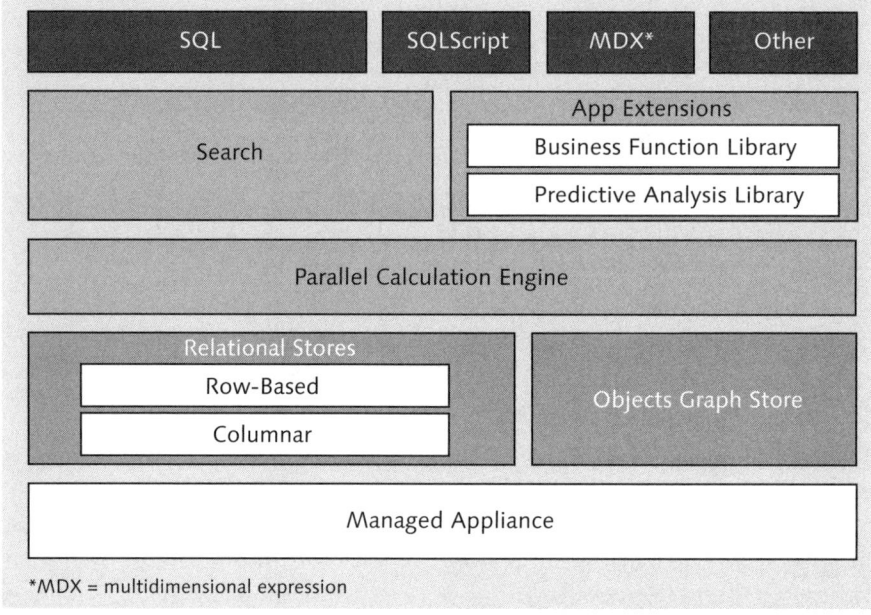

Figure 2.1 Conceptual View of SAP HANA

In order to process massive quantities of data in main memory and provide immediate results for both analysis and transaction, SAP HANA employs the following basic concepts:

- **Keep data in memory (Section 2.1)**
  Although nonvolatile storage is still needed to ensure that write operations are durable, read operations can anticipate that all relevant data resides permanently in main memory and thus can be executed without disk I/O.

- **Optimize in-memory data access (Section 2.2 and Section 2.3)**
  With all data readily available in main memory, data movement between the CPU cache and main memory becomes the new performance bottleneck. SAP HANA resolves this by using columnar store and effective data compression techniques to effectively reduce the overall size of data in memory and achieve high hit ratios in the different caching layers of the CPU.

- **Support massive parallel data processing (Section 2.4)**
  Modern computer systems have a continuously increasing number of processing cores. To natively take advantage of massively parallel multicore processors, SAP HANA manages the SQL processing instructions into an optimized model that allows for parallel execution and scales incredibly well with the number of cores. Optimization includes partitioning the data into sections for which calculations can be executed in parallel.

- **Optimize for writes (Section 2.5)**
  The many advantages of columnar store for fast read performance have their price. Write operations, particularly inserts and updates to a columnar store, are more complicated and less efficient. To overcome this drawback, SAP HANA introduces the concept of the delta store. Incoming updates are accumulated in a write-optimized delta partition, which is merged into the main partition at appropriate times.

The following sections look into each of these basic concepts of SAP HANA in more detail.

2.1　Keeping Data in Memory

Computer architectures have changed over the last few decades. Dramatic drops in price accompany the unprecedented growth of main memory capacity that can be equipped on a single computer. Today, a single enterprise class server can hold terabytes of data in main memory. Main memory is the fastest storage medium that can hold a significant amount of data, making it a viable approach to permanently house the complete business data of an enterprise.

The benefit of keeping data in main memory is most obvious if we look at the storage hierarchy of a computer system. Figure 2.2 shows a conceptual view of storage hierarchy in typical computer systems. In terms of performance, two factors come into play when accessing data from a storage layer. One, performance, is related to the physical speed of the storage medium itself. The other is latency, which is the time delay experienced by the system to load data from a storage medium until it is available in a CPU register. In the end, every operation takes place inside the CPU, and in turn the data has to be in a register of the CPU in order to be processed.

Hard disks are at the bottom of storage hierarchy. Because they are cheap, it is affordable to have a very large amount of storage at this level, but the tradeoff is performance. Not only is the hard disk the slowest medium, but also (because there are typically four layers between the hard disk and CPU register) it has the highest latency.

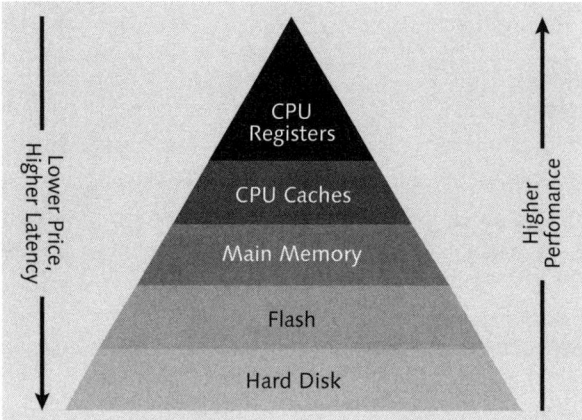

Figure 2.2 Storage Hierarchy

Main memory is the first level of storage next to CPU caches, and it is directly accessible. Compared with accessing data on hard disks, typically data in main memory can be accessed more than 100,000 times faster.

Compared with conventional DBMSs—which employ disks as the primary data store and use main memory as a buffer for data processing—keeping data in memory can improve database performance simply due to the advantage in access time.

2.1.1 Ensure Durability

Keeping data in memory raises a number of questions. First, what happens during a power outage? Main memory is volatile storage. It loses its content when it loses power. In this context, we refer to a set of properties known as *atomicity, consistency, isolation,* and *durability* (ACID) in database technology, which ensures that database transactions are processed reliably and are not susceptible to external disruptions.

In particular, the persistence layer of SAP HANA ensures that changes are durable and that the database can be restored to the most recent committed state after a restart. To achieve this goal in an efficient way, the persistence layer uses a combination of write-ahead logs, shadow paging, and data savepoints. Nonvolatile storage is used for logs and savepoints. Upon restart after a power failure, the database can be restored much like a disk-based database. First the database pages are restored from the most recent savepoints, and then the database logs are rolled forward to redo any changes that were not captured in the savepoints, eventually bringing the database to the same consistent state as before the power failure.

2.1.2 New Performance Bottleneck

With all relevant data in memory, disk access is no longer a limiting factor for performance. With increasing numbers of cores, CPUs are able to process more and more data per time interval. The new performance bottleneck in an in-memory database arises when the CPU waits for data to be loaded from memory into the CPU cache.

The resource "DBMSs on a Modern Processor: Where Does Time Go?" shows that traditional database systems could not address this challenge well.[1] Provided that all data is buffered in main memory in traditional DBMSs, the CPU spends half of the execution time in stalls—that is, waiting for data to be loaded.

In order to achieve desired performance, the key is to work on a minimal set of data and minimize the amount of data that needs to be transferred between the main memory and processor. In the next two sections, we discuss SAP HANA's approach for achieving this goal by organizing data into a columnar layout and into an encoded and compressed format.

2.2 Columnar Data Organization

Conceptually, relational databases represent data in two-dimensional structures called tables. A *table* is a set of data elements organized in terms of vertical columns or attributes (which are identified by their name) and horizontal rows or

---

[1] Anastassia Ailamaki, David J. DeWitt, Mark D. Hill, and David A. Wood, "DBMSs on a Modern Processor: Where Does Time Go?"

records. The main memory, however, is a single-dimensional space, providing memory addresses that start at zero and increase serially to the highest available location. To store the data in memory, the database storage layer has to decide how to map the two-dimensional table structures to the linear memory address space.

There are two basic options: A *row-based layout* stores a table as a sequence of rows in which data elements forming a row are stored in contiguous memory locations. A *column-oriented layout* stores a table as a sequence of columns in which data elements of individual columns are stored together.

Let's look at a simple example, illustrated in Figure 2.3, of a table of persons with four attributes: ID, name, country, and city.

ID	Name	Country	City
1	Paul Smith	Australia	Sydney
2	Lena Jones	USA	Washington
3	Marc Winter	Germany	Berlin

Figure 2.3 Table of Persons with Four Columns

In a row-based layout, all attributes of a tuple (or ordered set of values) are stored consecutively and sequentially in memory, as shown at the top of Figure 2.4. In a columnar layout, the values of individual columns are stored together, as shown at the bottom of Figure 2.4.

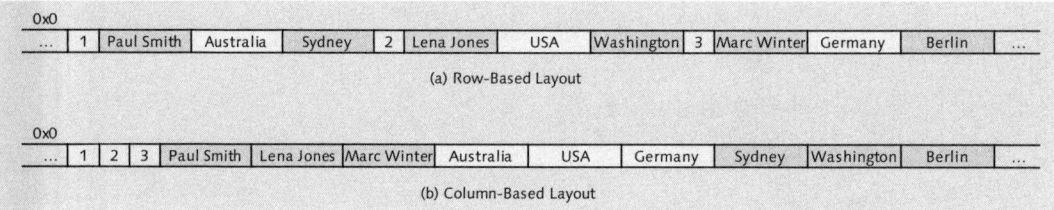

Figure 2.4 Different Storage Layouts

Both storage models have their advantages, which can be traced back to the different memory access patterns required when performing data operations on row-oriented and column-oriented data layouts. These differences are also illustrated in Figure 2.4.

Not surprisingly, the row-based layout is suitable for row operations, as in the following cases:

- The application needs to process only one record at a time (many selects and/or updates of single records).
- The application typically needs to access the complete record.
- The columns contain mainly distinct values, so the data compression rate is low.
- Neither aggregations nor fast searching is required.
- The table has a small number of rows (e.g., configuration tables).

Column-based layout has advantages for column operations, as in the following cases:

- Calculations are typically executed on single or few columns only.
- The table is searched based on values of a few columns.
- The table has a large number of columns.
- The table has a large number of records, and mostly columnar operations are required (aggregate, scan, etc.).
- The majority of the columns contain few distinct values (compared to the number of rows).

SAP HANA supports both row-store and column-store tables. High performance is achieved when column-store tables are used in memory, which shows that workloads on enterprise databases are mostly read oriented and dominated by set processing.[2] In most cases, operations work on many rows but only on a notably smaller subset of all columns. These factors speak in favor of using a columnar layout in an enterprise scenario.

Columnar table layout enables effective projection by accessing only the relevant columns, thus reducing the total number of memory accesses. Operations on single columns, such as searching or aggregations, can be implemented as loops over an array stored in contiguous memory locations. Such an operation has high spatial locality and efficiently utilizes the CPU caches. With row-oriented storage, the same operation would be slower because data of the same column is distributed across memory, causing CPU cache misses and thus stalling the CPU execution.

---

2 Jens Krüger et al., "Fast Updates on Read-optimized Databases Using Multi-core CPUs."

2 In-Memory Technology and SAP HANA

Columnar data storage allows for highly efficient compression. Especially if the column is sorted, there will be ranges of the same values in contiguous memory, so compression methods such as run-length encoding or cluster encoding can be used more effectively. Despite the fact that hardware technology develops very rapidly and the size of available main memory constantly grows, the use of efficient compression techniques plays a key role in in-memory computing in order to do two things: first, to keep as much data in main memory as possible; and second, to minimize the amount of data that has to be read from memory in order to process queries and transfer data between nonvolatile storage mediums and main memory. We will discuss these tasks further in the next section.

2.3 Data Encoding and Compression

Data compression is a set of techniques that decreases the number of bits used for data representation in memory. It reduces the overall memory requirement (and therefore the cost) for keeping business data entirely in main memory. Also, read operations can be performed more efficiently on the compressed data because data movement between the main memory and the CPU is minimized.

2.3.1 Dictionary Encoding

Dictionary encoding is the basis of many data compression techniques. The main effect of dictionary encoding is that longer values, such as text strings, are represented with shorter codes (normally integer values).

Let's walk through translating original values to integer codes using Figure 2.5.

Rec ID	fname		Dictionary for "fname"		Attribute Vector for "fname"	
			Value ID	Value	position	Value
...	...		...	...	...	...
39	John		23	John	39	23
40	Mary		24	Mary	40	24
41	Jane		25	Jane	41	25
42	John		26	Peter	42	23
43	Peter		...	...	43	26
...	...				...	...

Figure 2.5 Dictionary Encoding Example

Dictionary encoding works column-wise. It constructs a dictionary for each column, which translates every distinct value of the column to a distinct integer code. The code can be stored in dictionary explicitly or implicitly (e.g., by the position of the value entry in the dictionary). In our example in Figure 2.5, the dictionary for the column FNAME lists all the distinct values, and the position of each value (e.g., Mary) in the dictionary represents the code for the value. In this case, the number 24 represents Mary. Then, in the actual column store (attribute vector), it replaces all instances of MARY in the column FNAME with the number 24.

Dictionary encoding replaces longer text values with shorter numbers. This can lead to effective reduction in data size in memory when a column contains many identical values (e.g., multiple Johns in the same list, as in Figure 2.5). The more often identical values appear in a column, the greater this benefit of dictionary encoding. In SAP business applications, many columns (e.g., country code, status code, or foreign keys) contain only a few distinct values compared to the number of rows, which allows for a very effective compression of column data using dictionary encoding.

2.3.2 Data Compression

On top of dictionary encoding, SAP HANA applies a number of lightweight compression techniques, such as prefix encoding, run-length encoding, cluster encoding, indirect encoding, and delta encoding. These techniques provide a good tradeoff between higher data compression rates and the additional CPU cycles needed for encoding and decoding.

A more detailed explanation of these techniques can be found in Hasso Plattner's *A Course in In-Memory Data Management*.[3] For now, note that the basic idea of dictionary encoding also is applicable to row-based storage. However, in row-based storage, successive memory locations contain data of different columns. Many compression methods, such as run-length encoding, cannot be applied on a row store. A higher compression factor of up to ten can be achieved in a columnar store as compared to traditional row-oriented database systems.

---

3 Hasso Plattner, *A Course in In-Memory Data Management*.

2.3.3 Operation on Compressed Data

By working with dictionaries to represent text as integers, dictionary encoding not only reduces the memory footprint of data but also increases speed for operations on the encoded data. Users have reported a performance gain of a factor of between one hundred and one thousand when comparing operations on integer-encoded compressed values with operations on uncompressed data.[4] There are several reasons for this result:

- Compressed data can be loaded faster into the CPU cache. Because the new limiting factor is data transport between memory and the CPU cache, performance gain exceeds the additional computing time needed for decompression.

- With dictionary encoding, the columns are stored as arrays of bit-encoded integers. Many predicates—for example, an equality check of join conditions—are evaluated directly on integer codes. This is typically much faster than comparing string values, for example.

- Compression can speed up operations such as scans and aggregations if the operator is aware of the compression. Given a good compression rate, computing the sum of the values in a column will be much faster if the column is run-length encoded, and many additions of the same value can be replaced by a single multiplication.

- Certain operations, such as COUNT or NOT NULL, can be performed directly on the encoded data without having to retrieve the actual values from the dictionary.

- Read operations can further benefit from dictionary encoding if the dictionary itself is sorted. A sorted dictionary can act like an index. The process of retrieving a value from a sorted dictionary can be performed using binary search. Compared to a full scan through the dictionary, this process has a much reduced complexity of $O(log(n))$. Of course, the cost of this enhancement is the need to maintain the sorting order of the dictionary when new values are added.

---

[4] Hasso Plattner, "A Common Database Approach for OLTP and OLAP using an In-Memory Column Database."

2.4 Parallel Execution

Another key aspect of SAP HANA is its ability to achieve optimal parallelism in processing data in memory. This is particularly important in order to take advantage of modern multicore computing systems. It is also key for multinode scale-out implementation and for ensuring scalability in such distributed systems.

SAP HANA is engineered for parallel data processing that scales with the number of cores, even across multiple computing nodes in a distributed setup. Specifically for DBMSs, optimization for multicore platforms accounts for the following key considerations:

- Partitioning the data and executing operations on individual partitions in parallel
- Avoiding sequential processing wherever possible to ensure scalability

Let's look at both considerations ahead.

2.4.1 Parallel Execution in Columnar Store

Column-based storage simplifies parallel execution by using multiple processor cores. In a column store, data is already vertically partitioned, which means that parallelization can be achieved on different levels.

First, operations on different columns easily can be processed in parallel. If multiple columns need to be searched or aggregated, then each of these operations can be assigned to a different processor core.

In addition, operations on one column can be executed in parallel by dividing the column into multiple sections that are processed by different processor cores, as shown in Figure 2.6.

2 | In-Memory Technology and SAP HANA

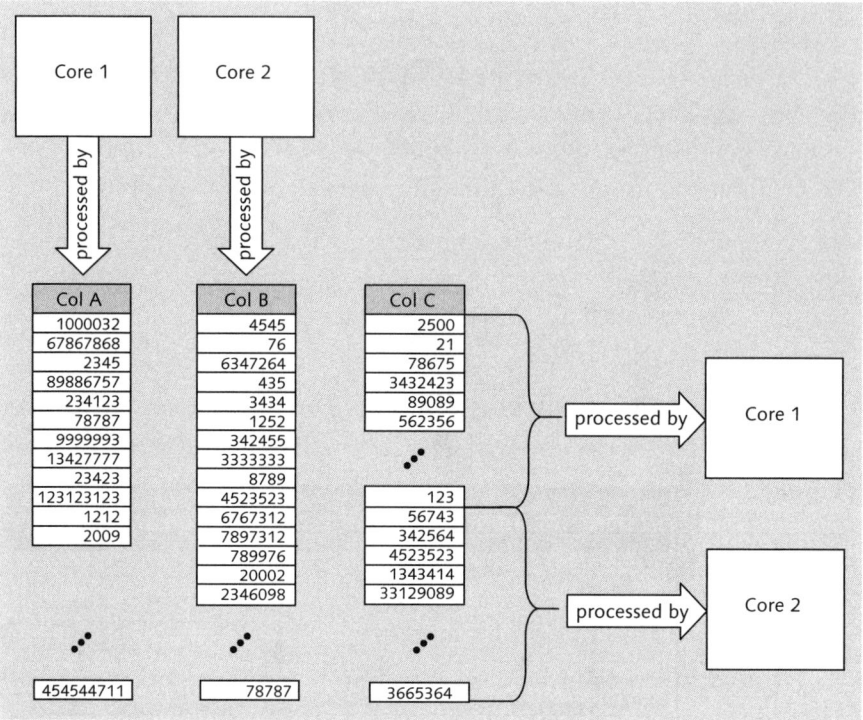

Figure 2.6 Parallel Execution in Column Store

2.4.2 Parallel Aggregation

Aggregation functions such as COUNT, SUM, AVERAGE, MAXIMUM, and MIMINUM are perfect examples for parallel execution. As illustrated in Figure 2.7, SAP HANA performs aggregation operations by spawning a number of threads that act in parallel, each of which operates on a separate segment of data in memory. Each thread executes aggregation functions in a loop-wise fashion as follows:

1. Fetch a small partition of the input data in the shared memory.

2. Calculate the aggregated value on that partition.

3. Repeat steps 1 and 2 until the complete input data is processed.

Each thread has a private buffer in which the local aggregated results are stored. When the aggregation threads are finished, the aggregated values in all private buffers are merged to produce the overall results.

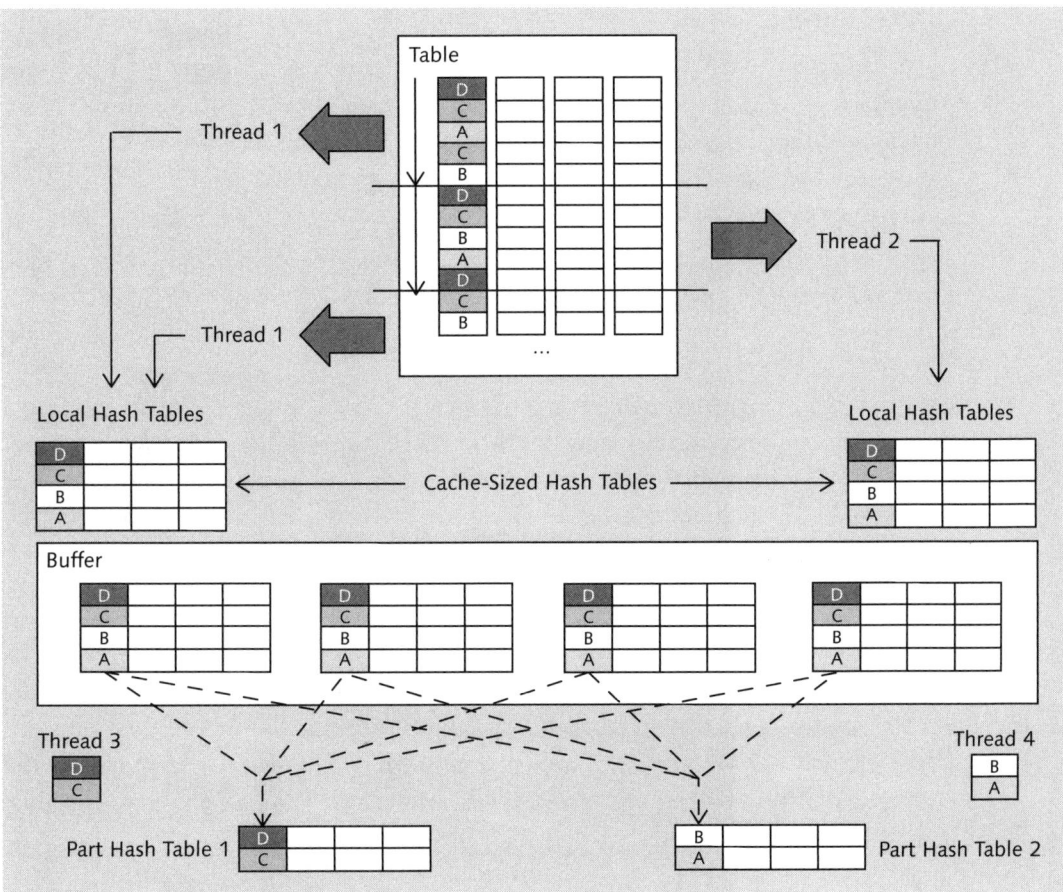

Figure 2.7 Parallel Aggregation Example

2.5 Delta Store and Merge

This brings us to the final key SAP HANA concept: using the delta store to address potential performance issues in a column store during data insert and merge operations. We will look first at the issues faced during an insert operation before moving on to how the delta store and merge help resolve such issues.

2.5.1 Insert

Let's look first at what happens when inserting a new record into a table that is organized in a column-based format. Adding a new record in a column store means adding a new entry to every column of the table. In turn, because every column of the table consists of a dictionary and an attribute vector, adding a new entry to a column comprises the following steps:

1. Look up the dictionary for the new entry, and add a new value if the entry is not found.
2. Add the respective value to the attribute vector of the column.

Processing in particular is more complicated if the dictionary is sorted. Adding a new entry to the dictionary may result in a need to sort the dictionary again. In addition, the attribute vector has to be updated as well in order to reflect the new orders of the dictionary, after which a recalculation of compression may be required. This can have significant impact on insert performance. SAP HANA resolves this problem through the delta store.

2.5.2 Delta Store

As we've just seen, inserting directly into the compressed column can be slow. To resolve this, SAP HANA introduces the concept of the *delta store*, wherein the storage of a column-store table comprises a main store and a delta store, as illustrated in Figure 2.8.

All write operations (insert, update, and delete) happen only in the delta store, which (as its name suggests) is a differential buffer. The main store is not involved during any write operation. Like the main store, the delta store is also column oriented, meaning that every column of the table has a delta store and uses dictionary encoding. To optimize write performance, the dictionary of the delta store is not sorted. When adding a new entry, it is simply appended to the end of the dictionary. In addition, no further compression technique is applied other than dictionary encoding. The delta store exists only in memory and is not included in savepoints. Only logs are written out to nonvolatile storage in order to ensure durability of changes made to the delta store.

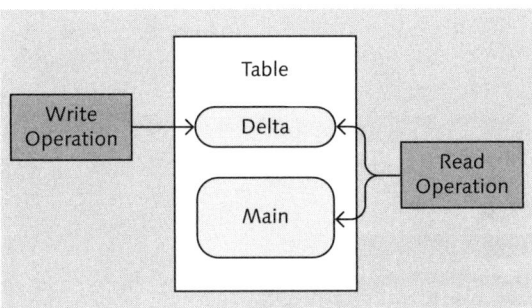

Figure 2.8 Delta Store Concept

The main store is highly compressed and optimized in terms of memory consumption and read performance. Although write operations only affect the delta part, read operations have to be performed on both the main and delta stores, because the overall current state of the table is now the conjunction of the main and delta stores. During query execution, a query is logically translated into a query of the main store and the delta store. The results returned from both parts are then combined to build the overall results.

2.5.3 Delta Merge

The delta store grows as more changes are made to a column table. A large delta store has negative impact on the overall system efficiency and read performance. First, the delta store is not compressed, meaning that it consumes more memory. Second, the dictionary in the delta store is not sorted, which makes it easier to add a new entry but more costly to look up an entry. In order to optimize query execution performance of the system and to ensure optimum compression, the size of the delta store needs to be kept as small as possible. To achieve this, SAP HANA uses an online reorganization process that periodically transfers data from the delta store to the main store. This process is called *delta merge*.

The delta merge process can be costly, because it involves resorting the dictionary and recalculating compression. SAP HANA uses a dual-buffer mechanism to minimize the impact of the delta merge process on the overall availability of the system. Figure 2.9 illustrates the three stages of a merge process:

- **Before the merge operation**
  All write operations go to storage Delta1, and read operations are read from storages Main1 and Delta1.

2 | In-Memory Technology and SAP HANA

- **During the merge operation**
  While the merge operation is running, all changes go into the second delta storage, Delta2. Read operations read from the original main storage, Main1, and from both delta storages, Delta1 and Delta2. Uncommitted changes in Delta1 are copied to Delta2. The content of Main1 and the committed entries in Delta1 are merged into the new main storage, Main2.

- **After the merge operation**
  Main1 and Delta1 storages are deleted after the merge process is finished.

With this *double-buffer* concept, the table only needs to be locked for a short time at the beginning, when open transactions are moved to Delta2, and at the end of the process, when the storages are "switched." As a result, the merge process can be highly parallelized without blocking other read and write operations on the same data.

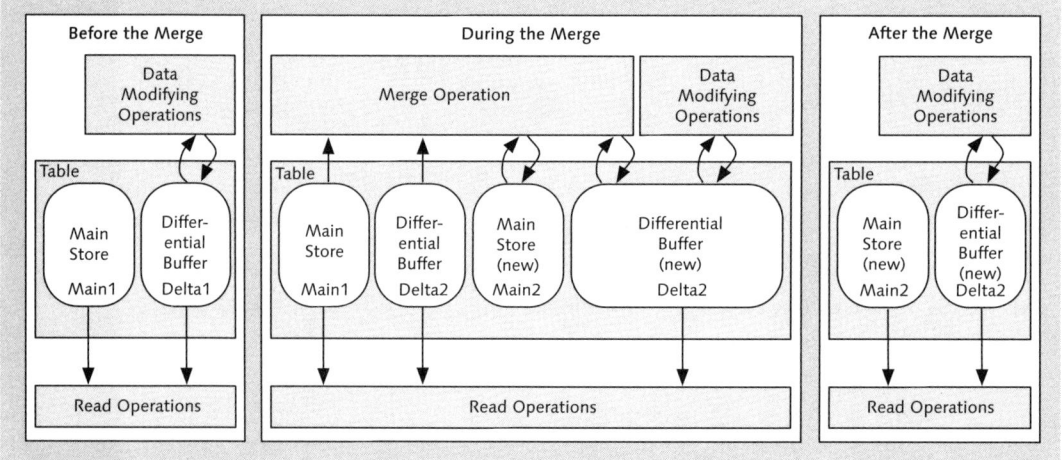

Figure 2.9 Merge Process

SAP HANA introduces a new way of thinking about how to construct business applications, such as financial applications, in an enterprise. The concept of using a columnar in-memory database is now seen as the backbone of enterprise systems, handling both analytical and transactional processing in one system. Techniques such as parallelization, dictionary encoding, data compression, insert only, and the delta store tell a compelling story that lets applications such as SAP S/4HANA Finance become a reality.

This chapter covers the benefits of a system without data redundancy, how such a system is now feasible thanks to SAP HANA, and how SAP S/4HANA Finance eliminates redundancy. We highlight the immediate benefits of the removal of redundant data for customers of SAP S/4HANA Finance.

3   Removal of Redundancy

Redundantly kept data—that is, data derived from other data available elsewhere in the database—is one of the big challenges of software systems.

You may wonder why you would store, for example, the sum of two invoice amounts separately if the same value can easily be derived by calculating it on the fly from the two invoices. In the past, such data redundancy was only introduced to increase performance, because traditional databases could not keep up with user expectations in light of billions of data entries. This came at the costs of significant effort to keep the redundant data consistent, increased database storage, and more complex systems.

Now that SAP HANA improves performance radically, as outlined in the previous chapter, the need for redundancy vanishes. Based on a *single source of truth*, derived data can be calculated on the fly instead of being physically stored in the database. Hence, in the spirit of simplification, getting rid of redundancy is a key paradigm of SAP S/4HANA Finance. We begin our exploration of the paradigms underlying the SAP S/4HANA Finance model by looking at the removal of redundancy in this chapter.

This chapter first introduces the conceptual benefits of a redundancy-free system by contrasting it with the disadvantages of redundant data (Section 3.1). Section 3.2 demonstrates how SAP HANA and in-memory technology enable us to overcome redundancy and avoid its pitfalls. In Section 3.3, we explore how SAP S/4HANA Finance simplifies the core financials data model by nondisruptively replacing materialized redundant data with on-the-fly calculation. Finally,

Section 3.4 highlights the immediate benefits of this simplification for companies switching to SAP S/4HANA Finance.

3.1 Benefits of a Redundancy-Free System

Data redundancy occurs if data is repeated in more than one location—for example, in two separate database tables—or can be computed from other data already kept in the database. In general, all data that you can also derive from other data sources of a system is redundant. Redundant data is distinguished by the fact that you need to maintain its consistency. If you modify the data at one location, then you need to apply corresponding modifications at all the other locations in the database in order to keep the relationship intact and avoid anomalies. Redundant data is high-maintenance data, and it won't take care of itself.

Software engineers spotted the fundamental problems of data redundancy early on. In 1970, Edgar Codd introduced the fundamental relational model that underlies many of today's database systems.[1] In order to reduce redundancy, normalization techniques such as normal forms are an integral part of the relational model.[2]

However, data redundancy remains. We can distinguish four different kinds of redundancy within a database system, depending on the relationship of redundant data to the original data:

- **Materialized view**
  A *materialized view* stores a subset of data from one or several tables as duplicate copies in a second, new, typically smaller table. It materializes the result of a *database view*, which is a stored database query, in order to provide direct access to the result. As such, the materialized view can be compared to an index in the base table. The query may also join several tables.

- **Materialized aggregate**
  If the query of a materialized view aggregates tuples from the base table(s), then we speak of materialized aggregates as a special case. A *materialized aggregate* does not contain one-to-one duplicates, but nevertheless the data is redundant,

---

[1] Edgar Codd, "A Relational Model of Data for Large Shared Data Banks."
[2] Edgar Codd, "Further Normalization of the Data Base Relational Model."

because it can be derived from the original data at any time by applying the same calculation on the fly.

- **Duplicated data due to overlap**
 Data may be duplicated if related information is stored in separate locations. Part of the data attributes overlap, whereas others are present only at one location. The overlap is then a source of redundancy. The different locations are often due to a separation of concerns, whereas the overlap again stems from performance reasons—for example, to avoid joins that are costly in traditional database systems.

- **Materialized result set**
 Long-running programs that arrive at a certain output after several steps of calculation often store the result of their work as a *materialized result set*. Due to the complexity of the program logic, the result is not described as a query but is created by running the program, which then stores its output for fast future reference.

None of these instances of redundancy is necessary from a functional point of view. They have been introduced in the past into enterprise systems to improve query response times in view of slow, disk-based database systems, which made an on-the-fly calculation prohibitively expensive. In-memory technology now breaks down the performance barrier so that SAP S/4HANA Finance can remove all kinds of redundancy. This chapter covers the removal of redundancy with regard to the first two categories: materialized views and materialized aggregates. We'll see these categories come up again later in the book. As described in Chapter 6, eliminating the need for long-running batch jobs makes materialized result sets obsolete in a real-time finance system. The Universal Journal covered in Chapter 8 describes a case in which SAP S/4HANA Finance eliminates duplicated data due to overlap between financial components.

If you look beyond a single database, redundancy also occurs when duplicating the same or derived data in several database systems. In contrast to redundancy within the same database, this cross-system duplication may be wanted in some cases—for example, for data security purposes. In other cases, it is truly redundant—for example, in the case of data warehouses, due to missing analytical capabilities of traditional database systems. As outlined in Chapter 2, this kind of data redundancy on a system level is inherently superfluous because SAP HANA combines OLTP and OLAP capabilities with superior performance.

Coming back to redundancy within a database, what are the benefits of having a redundancy-free system? Why is having a single source of truth in SAP S/4HANA Finance preferable compared to the traditional world of materialized views that serve to improve the performance of read operations?

The fundamental problem with redundant data is the effort necessary to keep it consistent when the original data changes. If you materialize the total amount of all orders of a certain customer, then you need to update that figure every time a new order by that customer comes in. Materializing a figure that needs to be updated frequently—for example, the balance of an often-used account—may even lead to contention, because the balance entry needs to be locked on each debit or credit on the account.

Similarly, a materialized view containing a duplicated subset of accounting data—for example, all open invoices—needs to be reconciled whenever the original data changes. If a customer's payment clears an open invoice, then the payment also has to be removed from the corresponding materialized view.

Regardless of whether this reconciliation needs to be performed manually by each business transaction or is handled automatically by the database system, maintaining consistency leads to additional database operations on top of the actual modifications. Otherwise, your database has more than one "truth"—which means that it is inconsistent. Getting rid of such reconciliation activities is the source of several benefits:

- **Simplicity**
  Overall, the architecture and data model of a redundancy-free system are significantly simpler. There are fewer dependencies and constraints that transactions need to take into account when modifying or analyzing data. As a consequence, transactions are also simpler. The overall simplification also manifests in a few other upcoming benefits.

- **Consistency maintained by design**
  Business transactions that modify data do not need extra work in order to maintain consistency. This makes for simpler programs based on a less complex data model with fewer dependencies. Overall, the architecture of a redundancy-free system is more natural: Transactions record what happens in the database by adding corresponding database records. The system provides everything else as read-only algorithms on top of the data.

▶ **Increased throughput**
Because it is no longer necessary to modify redundant data in parallel, the number of database operations per business transaction diminishes. Only the essential operations to record the transaction occur, and no additional modifying operations are necessary. Fewer database operations and thus shorter duration of each transaction increase the throughput of the whole system so that it can handle more business transactions. Furthermore, materialized aggregates no longer have to be locked for updating, thus removing any contention issues.

▶ **Smaller database footprint**
Redundant data takes up memory and hard disk space that is no longer needed in a redundancy-free system, which shrinks the overall database footprint. A smaller footprint reduces not only the requirements on the main database server but also in turn the disk space needed for backups. A smaller database footprint and higher throughput make a system more cost-efficient. As a consequence, a redundancy-free system has a lower TCO.

▶ **Flexibility in real time**
A redundancy-free system also implies that it is no longer necessary to prebuild aggregates for performance reasons. Fast responses to analytics questions no longer depend on the availability of a materialized answer. Instead of being restricted to questions that can be answered based on what was foreseen when designing the data model of a system, users are given the flexibility to ask any question that can be answered in real time based on the original data. An in-memory redundancy-free system opens up this new level of flexibility with the performance expected from today's fast web applications.

The obvious question that arises from this list of impressive benefits is this: Why haven't all systems always been free of redundancy? Also, why wasn't SAP ERP Financials historically an exception either?

In a traditional disk-based database system, the answer in the past was "performance reasons." Now, in an SAP HANA world, the answer is that there is no excuse left for redundancy, thanks to the speed of in-memory technology. In the past, query response times (especially involving aggregation) were too slow for productive use without materialization. The costs of a redundancy-free system were too high, even compared to the benefits. These days, the superior performance of in-memory database systems means that the fear of slow response times is a thing of the past, as demonstrated in the following section. Figure 3.1 illustrates that, in contrast to the traditional database world, the benefits of a redundancy-free system clearly outweigh the costs, as we'll see applied to the case of SAP S/4HANA Finance in Section 3.3.

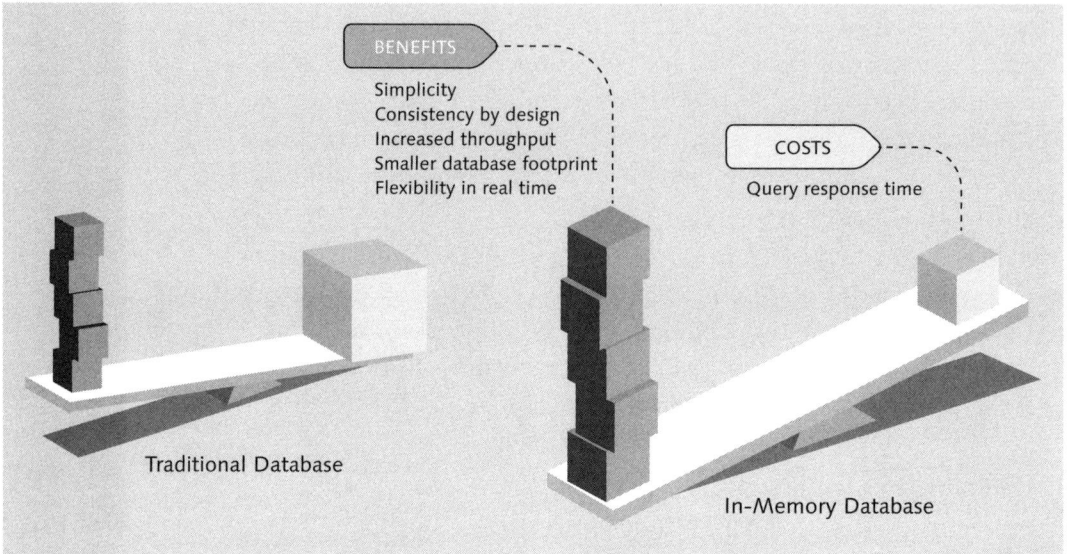

Figure 3.1 Replacing Materialization with On-the-Fly Calculation

3.2 In-Memory Technology Removes Redundancy

For decades, data redundancy has been reluctantly accepted in order to reach sufficient performance. The slow response times of disk-based database systems made a redundancy-free data model impossible. Because latencies and bandwidth of disk access are orders of magnitudes slower than in-memory access, calculating totals on the fly was prohibitively expensive.

Now, a new era is upon us. As outlined in Chapter 2, in-memory technology fundamentally challenges long-standing assumptions. In this section, we demonstrate that SAP HANA indeed enables you to get rid of redundancy without compromising performance.

These days, on-the-fly aggregation is feasible. In order to get rid of redundancy without disrupting businesses processes, on-the-fly calculations replacing materialized aggregates in an in-memory system have to perform at least as fast as users are accustomed to, based on materialization in a disk-based database system. The comparison is thus between *disk-based with materialization* on the one hand and *in-memory with on-the-fly calculation* on the other.

Let's take a closer look. For our demonstration, we'll examine a disk-based system with a typical disk latency of 10 ms (i.e., accessing a random location on disk takes ten milliseconds, or ten million nanoseconds). In comparison, in-memory latency is only 100 ns (0.1 ms). In other words, the database can make one hundred thousand random accesses in the same time as one disk access. The memory bandwidth in case of sequential reads is 4 MB per millisecond per core. For the following example, we consider a simple server that has a single CPU with eight cores. Modern server systems often connect several CPUs, each with 10 cores or even more, further increasing the processing power. For our example, we assume a company with one hundred million accounting document line items in its database and fifty thousand customers.

Total sales in the current month to a particular customer is a typical aggregate value of interest in financial operations. In the disk-based scenario with materialization, a materialized aggregate for this kind of analysis will contain one tuple per customer per month that gives direct access to the answer to such an analysis query. Hence, a user can expect to receive an answer from a disk-based database with materialization after 10 ms, assuming the database system needs a single disk access to retrieve the value and ignoring any further processing for comparability.

In an in-memory system without materialization, the aggregate value is not precomputed as part of every business transaction. As a consequence, calculating the answer to the query takes more steps. Nevertheless, response times are faster, as we'll show. Because the calculation happens transparently for applications accessing the database, the calculation steps will not be noticed by users. To keep the explanations simple, the following sequence of steps assumes a sequential execution of the query. Another advantage of an in-memory system is the in-built parallelization, which further speeds up the execution of more complex queries. The steps are as follows:

1. **Select all accounting document line items for a particular customer.**
   In a column table, the column representing the customer associated with each line item is stored in one continuous block of memory. To identify all items of a particular customer, the database system scans the whole column and keeps track of the positions where the customer number in question appeared.

Thanks to the columnar layout, one such full column scan operates with the full bandwidth of 4 MB per millisecond and core. SAP HANA's built-in compression means that only the compressed integer representations of customer numbers need to be compared. Because there are fifty thousand different numbers, the compressed representation of each customer number only needs two bytes (2^{16} = 65,536 different values). Hence, the customer column for 100 million line items takes up 200 million bytes, or roughly 190 MB. With eight cores, scanning this attribute vector takes 6 ms (190 MB divided by 8 times 4 MB per second).

2. **Apply further selections.**
For each of the items from Step 1, the database next applies further selection conditions, such as the month. For each additional condition, this mandates a lookup in the corresponding attribute vector at every position identified so far. With two thousand line items per customer on average, this leads to two thousand random accesses in a worst-case scenario with entirely noncontiguous positions. Even in that case, this takes only 0.02 ms on a single core (2,000 accesses times 10 ns per access = 20,000 ns).

3. **Add up the sales amount of all line items.**
After all relevant items have been identified in the previous steps, the database retrieves the sales amount for each item and adds it to the result. Again, the database makes one random access per position in the attribute vector for the sales amount and resolves the dictionary-encoded value in one additional access to the dictionary. Even if Step 2 didn't exclude further positions, this requires four thousand accesses and 0.04 ms on a single core.

For the total response time, we can ignore Steps 2 and 3, because they don't contribute significantly to the overall time. In total, on-the-fly calculation of sales to a particular customer in the current month takes approximately 6 ms in an in-memory database system—less than the 10 ms for accessing the materialized aggregate in a disk-based database. Replacing materialization with on-the-fly calculation is thus entirely feasible in this example.

In the case of more complex queries, an in-memory system with on-the-fly calculation may even increase its advantage; for example, a similar query to the one just considered but for all months of the current year instead of only the current month would require up to twelve disk accesses to the materialized values stored per month (unless an additional materialized aggregate is introduced). Although the response time suffers a corresponding increase in the disk-based system up to

120 ms, the on-the-fly calculation only needs to adapt the further selection criteria, keeping the response time of the in-memory system almost the same at roughly 6 ms.

We've already demonstrated the desirability of a redundancy-free system by highlighting the benefits. In addition, these calculations demonstrate its feasibility thanks to the faster in-memory performance. What is possible with fast and stable access times today would have been prohibitively expensive in a traditional disk-based system. Depending on the caching strategy, a disk-based database has to retrieve answers from disk, suffering long latency and slow bandwidth. Compared to that, an in-memory database offers not only faster but also more stable response times, because latency and bandwidth do not vary as they do in a disk-based system that frequently needs to go back to disk to retrieve data.

How does SAP S/4HANA Finance optimize its new possibilities to create a redundancy-free system?

3.3 Simplifying the Core Data Model

As outlined previously, enterprise applications in the past needed to store data redundantly in order to meet performance expectations of their users in view of limited database performance. Applications that remain bound to traditional disk-based databases still experience these limitations. SAP S/4HANA Finance is based on SAP HANA, so it makes use of the dramatically improved performance of an in-memory database. At the same time, its data model is a nondisruptive evolution of the SAP ERP Financials data model, removing any redundancy that has historically been necessary for performance reasons.

Looking at the data model of SAP ERP Financials, several instances of data redundancy quickly become apparent. The fundamental separation of different components (such as Financial Accounting, Controlling, Profitability Analysis, and others) into separate table structures is a case of duplicate data. Chapter 8 describes how the integration of these previously separate components and data models into a Universal Journal enables radically new approaches to finance in addition to the usual benefits of a redundancy-free system.

The data model of each of these components in turn contained data redundancy in terms of materialized views and materialized aggregates. To explain the changes on this foundational level (essentially the first steps toward a redundancy-free system, completed by the Universal Journal), we'll now take a closer look at the data model of Financial Accounting's G/L. The explanations similarly apply to the other components; they, too, have been simplified in the same spirit.

While we take a closer look at Financial Accounting, we'll reference the old tables from Financial Accounting for reasons of comparison; with the Universal Journal (see Chapter 8), you can merge the data structures of hitherto separate components. The fundamental and essential data tuples of every financial accounting system—besides master data—are the accounting documents and their line items. The system records each transaction as an accounting document with at least two line items (one each for debit and credit entry), but potentially more.

Faced with millions or billions of accounting documents (headers, primarily stored in table BKPF) and their line items (table BSEG) and slow disk-based performance, SAP ERP Financials needed materialized views and materialized aggregates in order to provide sufficiently fast access to line items with specific properties or to aggregate values. For this reason, the core data model of Financial Accounting (as illustrated in Figure 3.2) contained, among others, six materialized views (three for open line items separated by accounts receivable, accounts payable, and G/L accounts, and three for cleared line items separated in the same manner) and three materialized aggregates for corresponding totals.

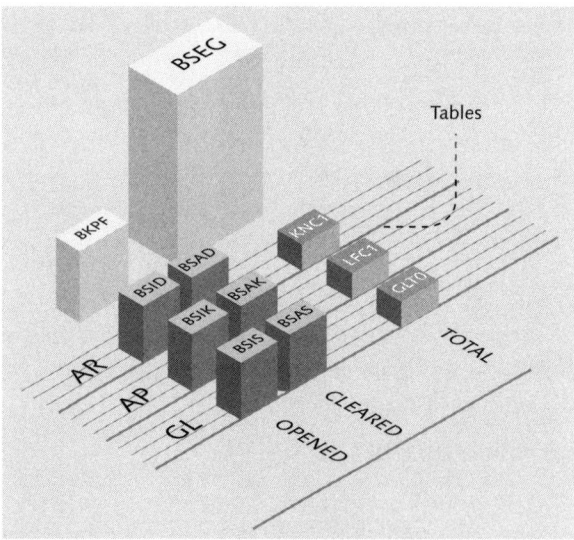

Figure 3.2 Old Data Model of SAP ERP Financials

For example, in an SAP ERP Financials system the materialized view of all open accounts receivable line items (table BSID) contains a copy of each line item (with a subset of attributes) from the original table of accounting document line items that fulfills the following condition: the line item is open (i.e., has not been cleared) and is part of the accounts receivable subledger. Needless to say, when a transaction clears the item, it also has to delete the corresponding tuple from the materialized view of open accounts receivable items and add it to the corresponding materialized view of cleared accounts receivable items.

In contrast, in SAP S/4HANA Finance all of these materializations have been removed in order to take the first step toward eliminating redundancy. The corresponding tables have been replaced with compatibility views. From the accounting documents and line items as the single source of truth, any derived data can be calculated on the fly, most times with higher performance than in a traditional disk-based system. This includes, but of course is not limited to, the views and aggregates that previously existed in materialized versions.

Figure 3.3 illustrates the resulting redundancy-free data model of Financial Accounting (before the Universal Journal) that is functionally equivalent to the previous data model.

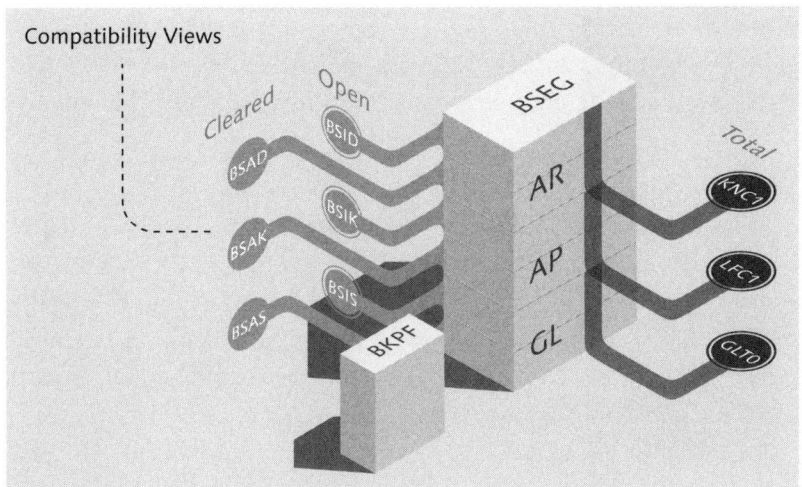

Figure 3.3 New Redundancy-Free Data Model of Financial Accounting

In the spirit of simplification, it consists only of the essential tables for accounting documents and for accounting document line items that record the business transactions. In addition, the compatibility views transparently provide access to the same information that was redundantly stored in materialized views and materialized aggregates before. These redundant tables are in turn obsolete, because SAP HANA calculates the same information on the fly. Appendix A lists the tables that have been replaced with compatibility views.

The compatibility views bear the same name as their historical predecessors to ensure that the changes are nondisruptive and do not require SAP customers to modify their custom programs. Any program—be it part of the SAP standard or a customer modification—that in the past accessed the materialized view of open accounts receivable line items is now seamlessly routed to the corresponding compatibility view. The compatibility view calculates the result for each query on demand—without compromising performance, thanks to SAP HANA (as explained in Section 3.2). In this case, the view selects the open items belonging to the accounts receivable subledger directly from the original table of accounting document line items. Any additional selection conditions—for example, a specific customer—are immediately passed through to the query optimizer and integrated into the query execution plan.

As mentioned at the beginning of this section, the same approach applies to other components as well. For example, materialized aggregates on top of controlling documents are no longer necessary, opening up the ability to combine different accounting components in the Universal Journal. As outlined in Chapter 11, Section 11.4, cash management is another area with similar changes that remove data redundancy.

In summary, the SAP S/4HANA Finance data model is now entirely based on line items, without any prebuilt materialized aggregates or other data redundancy. Not only is the data model simpler, but the program architecture is also simpler: The system "simply" records all business transactions as they happen. Everything else is calculated on the fly by algorithms on top of the data. Without any negative effect on your existing investments in SAP systems, you immediately benefit from switching to SAP S/4HANA Finance. Let's look at how.

3.4 Immediate Benefits of the New Data Model

Removing materialized views and materialized aggregates from the financial accounting data model has an immediate positive impact on the transactional throughput of the system. In the case of SAP S/4HANA Finance, posting an accounting document requires neither inserting redundant duplicates into materialized views nor updating redundant aggregate values. The corresponding effort and database operations to maintain consistency are no longer necessary.

As a consequence, the number of tuples inserted or modified during database operations was indeed cut by half according to experimental measurements. These experimental measurements are based on real-world data of a large SAP customer. Five hundred accounting documents were posted, each with six line items. Instead of twenty-six thousand tuples affected by UPDATE, INSERT, and DELETE operations in a traditional SAP ERP Financials system already running on SAP HANA, SAP S/4HANA Finance only needed to insert eleven thousand database tuples into the tables of the financials component for the entire test—a savings of more than a factor of two.

Of course, fewer tuples translate directly to less end-to-end transaction time spent posting a document. Instead of over 200 ms per document in SAP ERP Financials on SAP HANA, posting in SAP S/4HANA Finance only required 100 ms from end to end, down by a factor of two. As a consequence, the throughput of a system running SAP S/4HANA Finance doubled in this scenario.

The experimental measurements by design did not even include the effect of contention that often appears in systems with data redundancy. Enterprise systems usually handle a lot of transactions in parallel. In the case of materialization, the concurrent aggregate updates in particular can lead to contention, because materialized aggregates have to be locked for updating. In the case of, for example, heavily used G/L accounts, the database system has to handle the otherwise parallel postings sequentially if they access the same G/L account in order to consistently update the totals for this account. This unfortunate situation can no longer occur in SAP S/4HANA Finance, because all transactions simply insert tuples into the database, which does not require locks.

When considering the overall system architecture, the statement that in-memory databases with a column-oriented architecture are not as fast when it comes to modifying operations as they are for reading access no longer holds true. The measurements for SAP S/4HANA Finance show that the speed even of modifying transactions is on par with, or better than, that of SAP ERP Financials running on a traditional database with row-based storage.

The database footprint is another area of improvement. Again focusing on the Financials component, the removal of redundancy in SAP S/4HANA Finance alone has the potential to drastically reduce the database footprint. Memory previously occupied by redundant data, such as materialized views and materialized aggregates, is no longer needed. The database footprint of SAP SE's own internal system for Financials (the main productive SAP system within SAP) has been reduced by a factor of almost three; gaining additional savings is possible by applying concepts such as data aging so that in total a reduction by a factor of fourteen is feasible. Calculations based on SAP customer data show equally impressive numbers—for example, a reduction by a factor of 6.5.

Such a reduction in database footprint immediately translates to hardware savings and a lower TCO. In addition, SAP HANA also enables you to remove your separate data warehouse thanks to integrated OLAP capabilities. By doing so, you gain an additional factor of two across the whole footprint. The numbers shown in both of these cases are for a system already running on SAP HANA as the database. Factoring in additional savings in the database footprint enabled by SAP HANA's storage architecture and compression, the potential savings are even more impressive.

In summary, SAP S/4HANA Finance demonstrates that in-memory technology makes it entirely feasible to remove redundancy from the Financials data model. Redundancy is no longer necessary for reporting or analysis purposes; these tasks can be run in high speed directly based on line items as algorithms, instead of relying on materialized aggregates prebuilt into the data model. As a consequence, users are no longer restricted to only those analytics questions that have been hardwired into the system. Instead, they are free to analyze data flexibly as needed with the performance they expect.

In this chapter, we highlighted the benefits you gain from the redundancy-free data model of SAP S/4HANA Finance. Benefits fall both into the area of TCO reduction (increased throughput and lower database footprint) and entirely new levels of flexibility. Overall, the removal of redundancy in SAP S/4HANA Finance yields a significant simplification of system and processes. We demonstrated the feasibility of these fundamental changes in terms of performance and highlighted some of the key improvements as seen in real-world environments.

We'll see these topics elsewhere in this book. The next chapter outlines the nondisruptive nature of the innovations in SAP S/4HANA Finance, which allows you to switch seamlessly and immediately benefit from the advantages outlined here and throughout the book. Chapter 5 explores the ensuing possibilities in terms of flexibility based on the purely line item–based data model. We focused on the removal of redundancy in the form of materialized views and materialized aggregates in this chapter, and the removal of materialized result sets is explained in Chapter 6 as one of the benefits of a real-time finance system that doesn't require batch jobs. Chapter 8 outlines how further duplicate data stores are unified with the Universal Journal, which is the next big step toward a redundancy-free system that eliminates the need for reconciliation.

This chapter presents the nondisruptive paradigm of SAP S/4HANA Finance, which enables SAP customers to benefit from its advantages without lengthy implementation or migration projects, thus safeguarding their existing investments.

4 Nondisruptive Innovation

Implementing a new system also raises the following key question: "What impact will it have on my existing system, programs, code, and processes?" SAP S/4HANA Finance answers this question in the most favorable way possible: It brings innovation in a truly nondisruptive manner.

We start this chapter by focusing on the existing SAP ERP Financials base and explain the relevant nondisruptive innovation scenarios. Then, we dive into the technical aspects of how such nondisruptive innovation is achievable, both architecturally and from a data access point of view.

As you saw in the last chapter, the new general idea of SAP S/4HANA Finance is to build financial processes and UIs on a redundancy-free architecture. This concept provides benefits such as lower memory footprint, fast data throughput, no reconciliation effort, and high flexibility. The usage of the innovative capabilities of the SAP HANA platform allows us to make all of these benefits a reality. Therefore, any new installation will immediately exploit these advantages and make financial processing new, lean, and efficient at low costs.

However, this is not the whole story. SAP S/4HANA Finance goes even further by providing all of this innovation in a nondisruptive way, meaning that your investments are protected by the compatibility of the solution. SAP S/4HANA Finance safeguards any investment you would have made in SAP ERP Financials through two nondisruptive innovation scenarios:

- **Replacement (Section 4.1)**
  In this scenario, SAP S/4HANA Finance replaces traditional SAP ERP Financials without any process or data disruptions. All external interfaces are kept intact, data is safeguarded, and user experience is not disrupted.

- **Extension (Section 4.2)**

    In this scenario, SAP S/4HANA Finance is implemented side by side with current systems. Data is transferred to the new SAP S/4HANA Finance system by reliable real-time replication mechanisms. You have the flexibility to decide which scenarios to keep running on existing systems and which ones to transfer to SAP S/4HANA Finance.

The following sections will elaborate on these two options. Both are reliable and nondisruptive ways of making use of the benefits that the SAP S/4HANA Finance platform provides for the installed base. SAP S/4HANA Finance is not a "new installation only" offering, nor does it entail immense customer effort due to enforcing tremendous data migration, end user training, or custom code reimplementation.

4.1 Compatible Refactoring

SAP S/4HANA Finance is a nondisruptive replacement of "traditional" SAP ERP Financials. Although it provides a number of new capabilities, including an SAP Fiori user experience, new cash management functionality, SAP HANA-based analytics, and merged Financial Accounting and Management Accounting, it also continues to remain compatible with existing functionality. For example, SAP GUI-based UIs; analytical tools, such as Report Writer and drilldown reporting; and allocation, revaluation, or major parts of period-end closing processes will continue to work as before, though they may have been renovated in some cases.

However, compatibility aspects offered by SAP S/4HANA Finance go further. SAP S/4HANA Finance safeguards customer and partner investments thanks to *compatible refactoring*, in which redundant persistence is eliminated and replaced with views that have the same names (the so-called compatibility views). Thus, any custom-built code accessing the formerly materialized views or aggregates now gets its data from the document level in a seamless manner. SAP HANA does the rest. As a result, existing code is not affected; it keeps running as before.

We saw in Chapter 1, Figure 1.7 and Figure 1.8, that a transition to SAP S/4HANA Finance has no impact on the way data is accessed. This means that a given SELECT statement (such as the following) does not change after SAP S/4HANA Finance has been implemented:

```
SELECT FKONT DMBE2
FROM BSIS
WHERE BUKRS = G_BUKRS
AND GJAHR = G_GJAHR_CURRENT ...
```

The only change is that instead of accessing materialized aggregates, the statement accesses data directly from aggregate views on the fly.

Standard SAP S/4HANA Finance also uses the concept of compatibility views, which form the fundamental principle of enabling seamless running of UIs, reports, and processes as before. During the implementation of SAP S/4HANA Finance, redundant data persistence is eliminated and replaced with these compatibility views (without data persistence) that have identical names to ensure access compatibility. It should also be mentioned that implementation of such a behavior was made possible by the data access capabilities of SAP HANA and their unprecedented response times.

Recall from Chapter 3 that materialized aggregates are now a thing of the past. SAP S/4HANA Finance persists line item–level data. The compatibility views get data directly from this single source of truth. However, in some cases the aggregate tables may have grown such that they are no longer simple. Accordingly, "simple" data dictionary view technology may not be sufficient to tackle the requirements.

This complexity is resolved by compatibility views, which (in technical terms) can be regarded as the uniform technology for accessing SAP HANA through SQL from an ABAP environment. These compatibility views provide necessary interfaces and related capabilities that go far beyond those of traditional data dictionary views and that are needed for our purposes. The implementation of SAP S/4HANA Finance thus acts as one entity toward all consumers: All complexity is hidden, and the compatibility views are accessed in exactly the same way as the former materialized views or aggregates were. Even more complex scenarios, such as balance carryforward, can be handled for full data access compatibility.

This gives us the opportunity to achieve database optimizations at various levels. As illustrated by Figure 4.1, at the transparent ABAP access level itself (the lowest tier), it is possible to perform fast data access and modernize SQL retrieval approaches. At the database near programming level (the middle tier), the compatibility views let us consume the underlying relational data models directly. In addition, specialized database procedures relegated as SAP HANA–specific adoptions (the top tier) help with code pushdown to achieve code/data proximity.

As you have seen, SAP S/4HANA Finance replaces tables made redundant by SAP HANA platform capabilities with compatibility views bearing identical names to safeguard customer and partner investments. A list of replaced database tables is available in Appendix A.

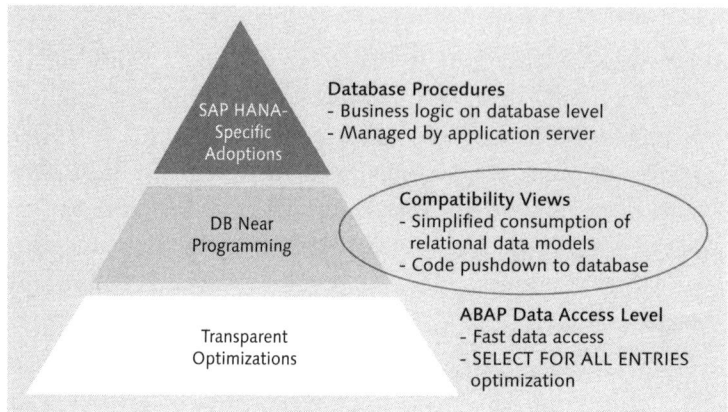

Figure 4.1 Database Optimizations

Figure 4.2 provides a simple illustration of how these tables are accessed through compatibility views.

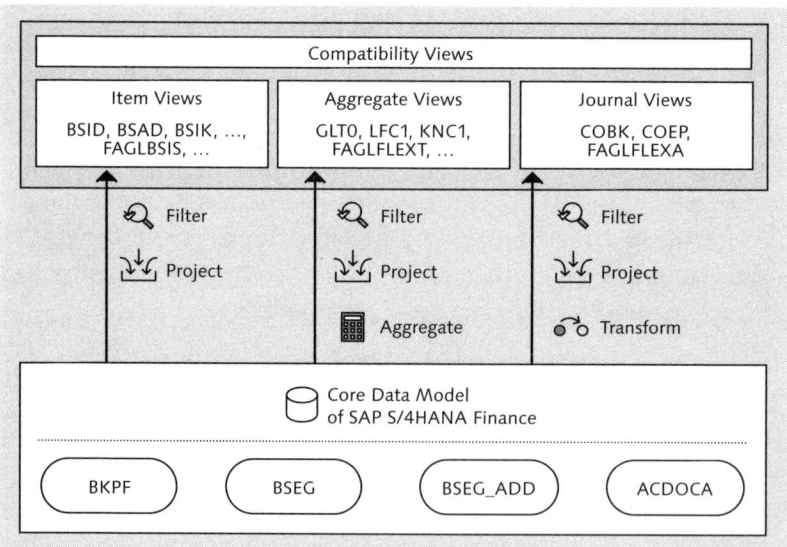

Figure 4.2 Compatibility View Concept in SAP S/4HANA Finance (Accounting)

The various transparent tables at the bottom (table `BKPF`, table `BSEG`, and so on) are read using a combination of relevant filters and aggregation algorithms (in the middle). As before, the compatibility views (at the top) talk to the result set in a seamless manner, thus ensuring that the existing investment is safeguarded.

4.2 Transitioning to SAP S/4HANA Finance

Let's take a brief look at what it means technically to implement SAP S/4HANA Finance from a data access point of view. Note that we'll spend more time looking at deployment models and migrating to SAP S/4HANA Finance from a system landscape point of view in Chapter 13 and Chapter 14.

SAP S/4HANA Finance extensively reduces memory footprint not only by eliminating aggregates but also by merging the line item tables from various application areas into one new persistence, the so-called Universal Journal. During the migration to SAP S/4HANA Finance, tables such as table `COEP` or table `BSID` cease to exist and are replaced with compatibility views that access identical information from the Universal Journal and transform it into the "familiar" structure on the fly, making use of SAP HANA platform capabilities via the compatibility view technology.

Let's take the table `BSID` example. In the SAP S/4HANA Finance data dictionary, table `BSID` is a view that refers to a compatible view implementation. In the migration process, a step is included that switches the data dictionary table definition from "transparent table" to "table with compatibility view implementation," making it possible to implement much more complex logic than simple aggregations. This occurs for the larger number of tables in question.

Overall, migration to SAP S/4HANA Finance is fast and easy. It can be triggered at the end of any period without the need for extensive migration services. The New General Ledger Accounting (New G/L) from SAP is not a prerequisite. You can implement SAP S/4HANA Finance whether you are running Classic G/L or New G/L. In the former case, data is automatically transferred to the new data structures. Other functions, such as existing Profit Center Accounting or Special Ledger, remain in place. Optionally, you may also implement additional optimizations, such as adoption of parallel ledgers or document splitting.

The overall picture of the data migration process is depicted in Figure 4.3. As first steps, we recommend that you acquire the requisite know-how; make a blueprint of the existing configuration; perform prechecks, reconciliations, and period-closing activities; and take a snapshot of the current state before the installation of SAP S/4HANA Finance. In the actual migration of financial data for G/L, accounts payable, accounts receivable, controlling, materials, or assets, line items are moved to the Universal Journal. A final reconciliation and comparison with the premigration snapshot makes the migration complete.

As seen before, all of this is done in a nondisruptive manner.

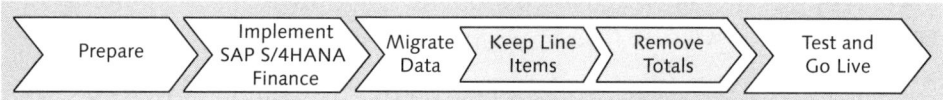

Figure 4.3 Technical Migration Steps for Accounting in SAP S/4HANA Finance

For more details on available migration paths and an overview of deployment options for SAP S/4HANA Finance from a system landscape point of view, refer to Chapter 13.

Presenting SAP HANA–based scenarios that follow a side-by-side approach has been implemented in a number of application offerings:

- **SAP S/4HANA flexible analytics**
  SAP HANA–based analytics on the paradigm of VDMs, which are semantic abstractions of raw data. Consumption on the SAP HANA side is available for all consumers supporting simple SQL—among these, prominently the analytics solutions from SAP. Refer to Chapter 10 for more information on SAP S/4HANA flexible analytics.

- **High-performance applications (HPAs)**
  New applications based on the SAP HANA platform with a new, lean programming model. HPAs are decoupled components that reach new business areas. Examples include SAP Fraud Management and SAP Customer Engagement Intelligence.

- **SAP HANA accelerators**
  Bidirectional, side-by-side integration of SAP HANA for unprecedented application acceleration, primarily for analytical purposes.

With SAP HANA as the underlying platform of SAP S/4HANA Finance, all capabilities provided by SAP HANA accelerators are automatically available in SAP S/4HANA Finance without data replication:

- Profitability Analysis
- New G/L
- Special Ledger
- Profit Center Accounting
- Product Cost Controlling
- Material Ledger

What do these applications for SAP HANA adoption have in common? An SAP HANA server is leveraged for nondisruptive extension of already-installed systems. Because SAP S/4HANA Finance has been based on the SAP HANA platform from the start, the idea of leveraging it in a side-by-side way suggests itself. In this way, centralized finance scenarios are supported. Note that Chapter 14 presents more information on implementation for a Central Finance deployment approach based on SAP S/4HANA Finance and its benefits.

For now, it is important to emphasize that the approach of implementing SAP S/4HANA Finance as a Central Finance instance is a very low-risk (that is, 100% nondisruptive) way to adopt SAP HANA technology. Starting with one new instance of SAP S/4HANA Finance, more and more local systems become superfluous over time because more and more central processes can be transferred efficiently to the central instance. Thus, SAP S/4HANA Finance becomes a perfect lever for complexity reduction and thus lower cost of ownership.

To summarize, there is no denying the fact that implementing SAP S/4HANA Finance is fully nondisruptive. It safeguards your existing investments and brings you to the exciting new world of running finance in a seamless manner.

This chapter highlights the unlimited flexibility that companies gain with the purely line item–based data model of SAP S/4HANA Finance. Companies can realize tremendous business value when freed from rigid hierarchies, disruptive organizational changes, or aggregate information loss.

5   Unlimited Flexibility Based on Line Items

SAP S/4HANA Finance is beneficial to a plethora of business scenarios, but at first it might not be obvious how the removal of aggregates provides significant business value. In this chapter, we begin by looking at how the availability of line item–level information enables deep business insights (Section 5.1). We then move on to examine the removal of predefined aggregates from a business value perspective (Section 5.2) and its benefits for decision making without any information loss (Section 5.3). We also discuss the opportunity in front of us to optimize operations based on big data (Section 5.4) and line item granularity (Section 5.5). Throughout this chapter, you will find example business scenarios to provide direct context and to make the concepts more tangible.

5.1   Gaining Unparalleled Insights

The world and its markets are volatile, and disruptive changes are occurring at an unprecedented rate. Managing these changes with a fragmented landscape, littered with silos of information, puts significant pressure on the responsiveness of businesses. Too often, managers act on information that is no longer relevant to the present situation. On top of this, there are ever-increasing pressures to manage costs, such as IT infrastructure.

Evolution and change is natural and necessary. For an organization to remain relevant, it has to adapt to the constantly changing needs of the market, technological advances, competition, and many other factors. For small companies, it is far easier to adapt quickly, but for larger companies it is difficult to be agile. To understand the complexities of large organizations, information is consolidated or aggregated into something tangible. This allows managers to make meaningful decisions, but vital information is often lost during the aggregation process.

SAP S/4HANA Finance takes a giant leap toward solving this problem, ensuring that essential information is not lost. Lying at the core of business, financials is the foundation for regulatory and internal reporting, providing insight into how well an organization performs at various levels. To transform how businesses fundamentally run and organize themselves, we have to start with the core, which involves looking at all elements and processes of the financial system: how we store and organize the data, the interfaces we use, the way we consume information, and the workflow of the end users.

This business transformation directly impacts a large number of people within an organization, not only providing benefits for accountants and financial managers. It gives a wide range of roles at many levels within an organization unparalleled insights into their domains. These insights can be in the form of better understanding of how to manage a project, can outline which areas of the business are performing well or poorly, or can help a business user choose the best course of action.

Roles and responsibilities evolve regularly. For example, today's CFOs not only have to become more knowledgeable about IT but also must become heavily involved with strategic decision-making. The right combination of financial analysis backed by a financial system that can provide the right insight in real time gives a company a strategic advantage in an increasingly competitive economic landscape.

Performance enables businesses to have real-time analytics and thereby more timely and relevant information to make the right decisions. Analysis no longer has to be constrained by structural definitions, such as geography, organization, or product group. Real-time insight enables companies to be more aligned, agile, and predictive, which are critical capabilities in a volatile environment (see Chapter 6). Because information can be materialized instantly, everyone can have his or her own personalized view into the financials system—yet when they come together there will be no conflicting information, because everyone will work from a single source of data (see Chapter 3).

For example, let's first look at the period-end close, which can be a very arduous task. It takes the effort of many people to align inconsistent transactional and master data. Reconciliation and batch processing can be extremely time consuming, involving many manual steps. Reporting is slow, and it can be difficult to get to the important details.

Because SAP S/4HANA Finance is built upon a single source of truth, in which financial data is aligned with controlling data, the consolidation of FI-CO is rendered obsolete. Now, the reconciliation of line items to aggregated totals, as well as OLTP to OLAP, is also obsolete because aggregates have been eliminated.

The performance of SAP HANA allows for significantly reduced report automation run time, eliminating the need for batch processes, which increases the efficiency of financial activities. Real-time analytics enables direct drilldown into transactions from high-level reports so that we can quickly identify issues to make changes before period close. Visibility into the closing of subsidiaries or other separate financial systems ensures greater alignment.

In total, this frees up a large amount of capacity, enabling people to focus on analysis and interpretation of results rather than data preparation. Along with automated quality checks, this scenario results in much more accurate reporting.

5.2 Removing Predefined Aggregates

The way in which we manage our financial information has evolved organically, in line with business requirements and under the constraints of technology. Let's consider why earlier financials systems were designed around aggregates and why this now needs to change.

In order to adapt, companies need to understand how well they perform in a timely manner. Aggregate dimension granularity can be defined to align to required processes in order to provide this insight in real time. At the simplest level, aggregates are derived from an SQL GROUP BY query, in which facts are associated with a rolled-up dimension—for example, grouping sales figures by geography. The result sets of these operations are stored in separate aggregated tables.

Because the data in these separate tables is precalculated summary data, if implemented in the correct way the tables dramatically improve the performance of querying large sets of data. This is because the required number of rows to be accessed in response to a query is greatly reduced (as described in more detail in Chapter 3). It is then also possible to reuse the aggregated dataset repeatedly without having to recalculate the totals from the underlying data.

However, aggregates are not perfect. Despite the fact that aggregates do have many advantages, they do not form an optimized data model. Aggregates create additional effort at both a technical and business process level in the following ways:

- **Static and complex**
  When change occurs to the underlying structure of predefined aggregates (e.g., due to an organizational change), we have to rebuild them. After these aggregates have been altered, they are no longer comparable. In many different business scenarios, we need to be able to track, analyze, and compare scenarios that are applied to different aggregate structures across a timeline. When we do this, we need to be able to compare oranges to oranges. Making these static aggregates comparable requires a significant effort, normally requiring exports to Microsoft Excel, reconciliation with underlying data silos, and so on.

  Table updates and synchronization create inherent complexity in the system and the dimensional model. Changing the granularity of a particular dimension requires creating new dimensional and fact tables to match the new level of granularity.

- **Information loss**
  Data at the line item level normally has multiple facts or attributes associated with it. This information is effectively lost during the aggregation process. Often, critical information is lost during key processes, such as period-end closing (as described earlier). We will discuss the case of information loss in more detail in the next section.

- **High TCO**
  There are ever-increasing pressures to manage costs such as IT infrastructure. Because aggregation creates additional records, companies require greater amounts of storage space to accommodate the large data footprint. There is also an important cost to maintain these aggregates from a human capacity level.

Acting on the lowest level of data instead of on aggregated data gives businesses the flexibility to free themselves from the direct link between data structures, such as hierarchies, and the underlying data. Because we can aggregate on the fly, information is always up to date and relevant and can be analyzed at any level. Managers can now more easily track trends, managing the changes that occur over time. This leads to more meaningful insights that form the basis of decision-making.

Speed and real-time process oversight will have a profound effect on the way companies operate. End users will enjoy more personalized and context-relevant information in real time from a single source of truth. Colleagues will work concurrently in the system based on the pervasive availability of information. Businesses will be more predictive through dynamic planning and analysis, which includes integrated business planning, system-generated forecasts, and end-to-end simulation capabilities. This all leads to a higher level of corporate agility.

How did we get here? Why couldn't we achieve these outcomes earlier? In short, the answer is that we are no longer under the same technological constraints, with frees us to use a far simpler and more flexible data model.

Speed might not seem like a real business value at first, but when you think of the money saved from processes running multiple factors faster than before on SAP HANA, it is easy to see how speed can make an impact. However, it goes much further than that. Speed is key for enterprise applications because increased performance allows for real-time instead of batch jobs, enables simulation of complex systems, and provides an innovation platform for all business processes. SAP HANA ultimately simplifies all of our processes.

Another example in which the removal of predefined aggregates has an impact is during the process of due diligence ahead of any merger or acquisition. Thanks to the total visibility and flexibility available with SAP S/4HANA Finance, we can now more easily identify issues that need to be resolved or that could be deal breakers. Normally, such identification is a difficult task, especially in a complex organization with multiple subsidiaries.

A key element of any merger is to understand how two organizations, each with its own complexity, can come together in a way that not only works but also provides greater value than the sum of the parts. This process is known as simulation and synergy identification. Typically, a company willing to acquire another will have to pay a heavy premium on top of the current market value, and that goodwill will have to come from somewhere. In the same way that we can identify issues, we can also more easily identify the synergies that drive the strategic reasoning for any merger or acquisition.

Another example of strategic validation is to analyze where revenue comes from. After an acquisition or a merger, it can be very difficult to decipher whether revenue growth comes from an acquisition or whether it was just organic growth within the company. This is only possible by analyzing information at the transactional level and by separating data from the merged data structures.

Working capital is one measure of how well a company operates. If a company's current liabilities exceed its current assets, then it could run into financial issues. Small improvements in DSO for large companies can free up significant amounts of cash flow, which can then be used to drive future investment.

Real-time data availability and increased performance allows for continuous monitoring of the receivables situation anywhere and anytime, including more accurate cash forecasts. As in so many SAP S/4HANA Finance scenarios, we can start from a high-level KPI view and then drill down to an individual line item, identifying root causes of working capital changes and optimizing strategies to improve the company's liquidity, efficiency, and overall financial health. We improve calculation accuracy by eliminating sensitivity to cyclicality, seasonality, and reporting key dates, thus unlocking insight by analyzing millions of transactions.

By removing the offline backend process steps, we can simplify the management of receivables. There is transparency for all users of the information, from the sales executives through to the back office. Sales can trigger actions by directly updating the ERP record, which then becomes instantly visible to the back office.

5.3 Deciding without Information Loss

If information is hidden from decision makers (in this case, in the form of aggregated data), then the situation is like steering a ship partially blindfolded. We may not spot improbable scenarios that could be detrimental to the company or even opportunities for growth. Having total visibility on any issues within a financial system is vital to mitigate any potential risk.

Whenever you choose one silo or dimension to aggregate on, you select it at the expense of losing information from another perspective. Being able to instantly change aggregation or perspective—to test different scenarios for root-cause analysis—results in a more complete and thorough understanding of a company's operations.

In many different business situations, we need to be able to track, analyze, and compare scenarios that are applied to different aggregate structures across varied timelines. This is best achieved when information that is used to perform this analysis is coherent and has relevant business context. In the past, this usually happened in the form of predefined, static aggregates. However, arriving at these static aggregates is time consuming and involves many iterations owing to individual data silos. Critical information is often lost during this process because the real source of truth can become unclear. It is also important that whoever is consuming information at an aggregated level understands the assumptions that went into to creating it: Wrong assumptions lead to wrong decisions.

Information is lost in various ways, some more obvious than others. It is important to understand where and how information can be lost, since it provides the basis for our decision process with regard to how we aggregate data. Some examples of information loss are as follows:

- **Outliers**
  In the presence of outliers, aggregation may mask the real essence of the data. If the aggregation function does not allow insight into the distribution of items with regard to outliers, then decisions or evaluations based on it will be erroneous. For example, a company may have revenue of $1 billion for the first quarter, slightly exceeding the planned target. Everyone is satisfied with the result when looking at the aggregate value. However, without the one large deal that accounts for one-fifth of the revenue, the company would have drastically underachieved its revenue target. Revenue as a simple aggregation by summing sales amount is not resistant to the presence of outliers. Hence, important information is lost in the aggregation process.

- **Data distribution**
  Consider an example in which at the design time of the measure the business equally often conducts deals with small, midsize, and large revenues; that is, sales numbers are uniformly distributed. Therefore, business analysts decide that examining average revenue is appropriate when determining the company's revenue situation at a glance.

  Over time, the distribution changes, and the company now creates more revenue with small and large sales. At the same time, revenue from midsized deals decreases. Total revenue itself remains the same. Hence, the aggregates do not show any problems, whereas the changed distribution implies a noteworthy situation for decision-making. Sustainable midsized deals have been replaced by less profitable small deals and larger deals from a few larger customers.

▶ **Correlation and regression**
On a line item level, different attributes are available for analysis. If the line items are not preserved, then it is no longer possible to identify correlations between different attributes. For example, considering only the average travel costs in a department does not allow you to take other factors into account, such as the travel distance and length of stay. If a cost center manager only knows that trips cost $1,021 on average, then she has no real information to determine whether a cost of $1,000 submitted by an employee is appropriate for a five-day trip over one hundred miles.

However, if the line items were still available, then the cost center manager could perform statistical analyses (e.g., regression) to determine the usual costs for a trip of this kind. Based on that information, she could determine that the average cost for this particular kind of trip is $500 and ask the employee for further explanation.

Perhaps the employee claims that the trip is more expensive due to seasonal factors. However, because the cost center manager still has the line items, she could extend the regression on further attributes and accept or reject the employee's explanations.

Fraudulent behavior such as duplicate invoices, suppliers being paid twice, or invoice interception by fraudsters is an increasing problem in today's corporate systems.[1] If expenses are only reported in an aggregated fashion, then such behavior cannot be detected without maintaining and analyzing line item information. Further, if the association between the aggregate and the corresponding atomic data is lost, then it becomes a cumbersome process to correct the wrong reporting data after fraudulent items have been found.

Organizations and CFOs place risk and control management systems as a vital enabler for ensuring business success in the future. Data is not lost when using SAP S/4HANA Finance, and the platform provides the flexibility to support multiple fraud scenarios, reducing fraud-related financial losses with earlier detection. Costs are kept under control because there is less work for fraud investigation teams to do. There is also no dependency on additional IT resources or specialized analysts. Overall, SAP S/4HANA Finance enables companies to not only more easily identify risk but also secure the key processes of their businesses for the long term.

---

1 Andrew Jesse, "Safeguarding Yourself against Invoice Fraud."

5.4 Optimizing Operations with Big Data

This section will go a little deeper into some of the advantages that have been outlined earlier in this chapter and that are specific to certain areas of an organization.

Business-critical decisions need to be supported on solid reasoning. Far too often, these key decisions are made based on a "gut feeling" rather than on quantifiable information. Many questions should be asked, leading to the need for a system with the flexibility and performance to be able to respond.

If we want to analyze a different business model based on a different structure and a different set of assumptions, then we cannot rely upon our predefined aggregates because there will be vital information lost in these aggregations, as covered in Section 5.3. With SAP S/4HANA Finance, you can easily assess the performance of different parts of the company (e.g., looking at the P&L from different filtered dimensions, such as project, department, segment, profit center, and many others). From here, you can see whether a new business model applied to different scenarios will be better than the current one.

The introduction of the *shared service center model* changed the way many companies operate today. Regional accountants and controllers are responsible for the correctness and completeness of the records, but most business transaction processing is done in so-called centers of expertise. The benefits of moving to this model include pooling expertise, delivering transversal services, improving quality, and reducing cost.

The orchestration of all involved stakeholders is the key to success, so collaboration within the system must become an integral part of the product. Because all reports are based on line items, the information must be also available on this level. This will enable discussions inside the system about processed items, with a history of conversation available to all users and auditors that will ease the closing process. This will also enable a faster decision-making process, because the dialogs are also available to decision makers—for example, in a CFO dashboard with a drilldown from a KPI to the line item that is self-explanatory due to its attached conversation information.

In a highly connected world in which almost everyone is accustomed to communicating via instant messaging, forums, and social media platforms, companies expect the same functionality in their business systems.

Typically, planning rules that will define benchmarks and other company targets are applied to a matrix of aggregates, such as the mix of regions and market categories or product groups. When the organization changes in the middle of a planning cycle, the initial plan becomes very difficult to maintain and therefore becomes diluted. Instead, if you apply the same rules, such as interest rates, expected growth, and so on, directly to line item attributes, then you can later aggregate your line items to whatever hierarchy is now applicable, thereby maintaining a consistent plan.

In another area of the business, understanding how best to organize your sales teams is fundamental to optimizing revenue. SAP S/4HANA Finance puts the right information at the fingertips of the sales force members: The information flows up to them and they can then immediately update the system with new information. This provides greater insight into customer behavior and a better level of service for your customers. Analyzing the cross-selling correlation between products on the fly makes it possible to find the ideal grouping or combinations of products to go to market for a particular customer. As forecasting becomes clearer through more effective simulations, you also can optimize where you should focus your sales resources for potential opportunities.

As companies grow, they traditionally start by organizing their business units around products or product groupings that manage themselves, meaning that they have their own accounting, marketing, IT, and so on.[2] This decentralization creates a suboptimal organization in which each division or business unit is only concerned with its own area, unaware of the impact that its decisions have on the company as a whole. Customers could find themselves contacted by multiple divisions of the same company.

Implementing a customer relationship management system helps to structure customer engagement by managing sales across the product silos. This benefits the company as a whole, improving operations and ensuring that there is no in-house competition or cannibalization of revenue. Typically, data warehousing is used to organize all of this customer information in one place.

This sounds great, but it often occurs that the optimal organization of the sales department does not match the optimal organization of the product department. What does this mean? First, it will be far more difficult to match the revenue on

---

2 Tom Hindle, *Guide to Management Ideas and Gurus* (The Economist).

the sales side to the development cost on the product side. Second, it will be difficult to measure ROI and determine whether resources have been effectively allocated.

Recall that SAP S/4HANA Finance consolidates both financial and controlling information and offers unparalleled flexibility by allowing aggregation on the fly across a much greater array of dimensions. This means that you can now use project style dimensions to match revenue against related costs. Managing multiple hierarchies is now far simpler. The sales organization not only can become more aligned but also can benefit directly from access to whatever information it needs from the ERP system to address customer needs. This situation will benefit customers, who can now receive a far more personalized and targeted offering.

5.5 Innovating with Line Item Granularity

The future lies in taking real-time insight and flexibility to the next level.

SAP HANA and SAP S/4HANA Finance pave the way to unparalleled financial insight. For example, let's consider the case of organizational restructuring. The flexibility of the SAP S/4HANA Finance data model will allow you to create what-if scenarios by designing new potential hierarchies and then applying your current data to these new hierarchies in real time to see what impact they would have on your organization (see Figure 5.1).

SAP has laid the foundation for a fundamental change in the way businesses can gain a deeper insight into their operations. Building on what you can already do and based on what we described earlier in this chapter, there are some key areas that will have a significant impact in the near future. If we add predictive analytics into the mix with integrated machine learning, then we will have real-time simulation that can track trends and the impacts of multiple dimensions in real time. This will ultimately change how businesses approach strategic decision-making.

Overall, SAP S/4HANA Finance provides businesses with a clear strategic advantage. Business leaders will be able to analyze more timely and relevant information to help them make the right decisions. Companies will become more aligned and predictive and run end-to-end simulations, which are all critical capabilities in a volatile environment. Instead of assessing the state of your business based on closed, historical data, you can have a clearer understanding of where you are—not only in the present, but also in the future. In essence, it is now possible to avoid pitfalls that have previously been hidden.

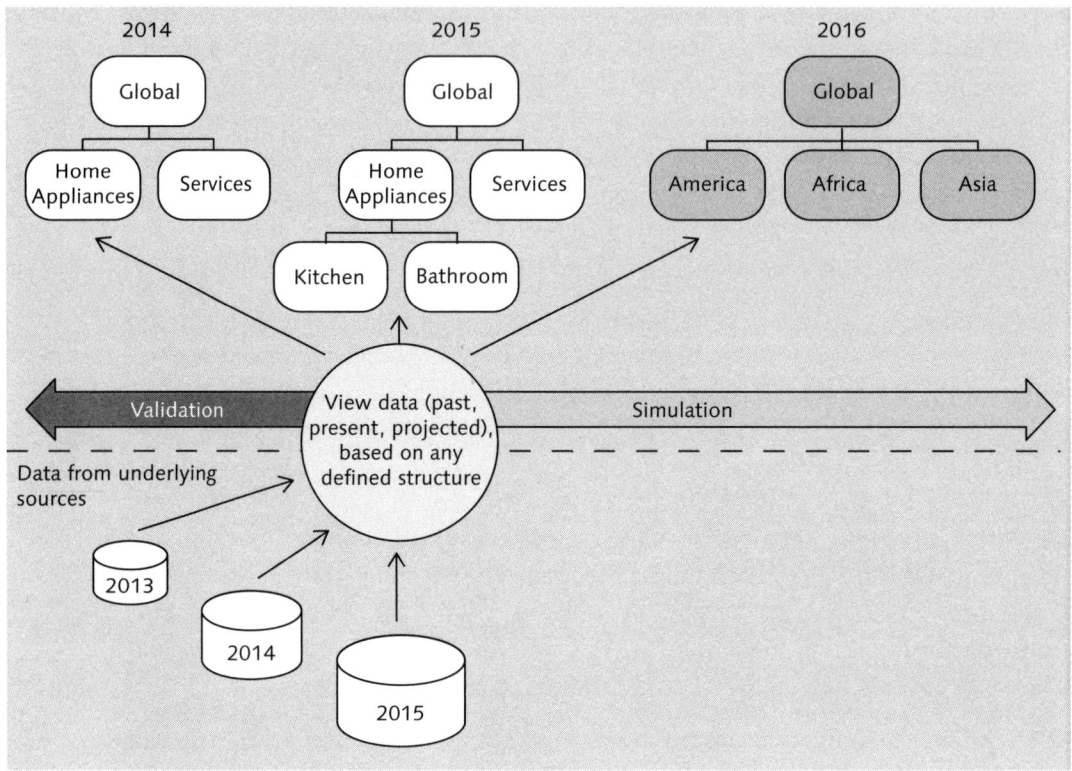

Figure 5.1 Flexibility and Abstraction of Hierarchies from Underlying Data

The improved performance of SAP HANA and SAP S/4HANA Finance makes it possible to get rid of batch jobs and the issues they entail and instead execute finance processes in real time based on current data. Let's examine this fundamental shift and how it impacts business processes.

6 Finance in Real Time

After decades—or, in some cases, centuries—of the same processes (e.g., closing the books on the fourth day of the month), some organizations are at first reluctant to change their finance processes and see no reason to do so. What they do not recognize is that a fundamental shift is in front of us when it comes to real time. New requirements frequently pop up, and new technology is key to at least keep up to date, if not to improve. In other words, even if businesses are happy with their existing processes, the environment around them continues advancing and will leave them behind if they do not adapt.

It is important to understand that although real-time finance is, of course, relevant for your finance department, it also has a significant impact on your entire business. This understanding can guide you up front to make the right business decisions with top-line and bottom-line effects. This idea is not just about another modernized finance system; it's a paradigm shift in how you look at and run your financials. That is where the real value comes from.

Simplified real-time finance starts at design time. Easy line item structures (as described earlier in the book) help avoid permanent changes. Typically, over time, hierarchies in an organization (such as those pertaining to organizational structure, cost or profit centers, products, customers, and regional setup) change, whereas atomic line items within them do not. Furthermore, at the micro level, you must consider not only data, but also methods, processes, and adequate UIs.

Data is the most important factor in finance. If the data foundation is not right, then everything else can easily be wrong. In SAP S/4HANA Finance, there are three main data buckets that may exist in an enterprise:

1. Real-time processes that are reflected in accounting, also known as the *ex-post view*. This is what we just discussed: a single source of truth for accounting.
2. All kinds of exposures for the business in progress.
3. The expectations for future business that act as a basis for planning, budgeting, and forecasting.

Methods (a simple example is currency conversion) play a role in speeding up calculations on one hand while bringing in consistency on the other. Methods create data that we use and post in accounting. Consistency of these methods ensures that a single source of truth is built based on generally accepted calculation principles. That is, results do not change due to different methods of calculation; they only differ because of changed influencing parameters.

Wouldn't it be nice if you could use financial methods in your business before closing a deal and know what would be the impact from a business point of view?

Processes reuse methods, make use of data, and might create new data points. Sometimes, the data created is not an end result but simply an input for further processes. If this chain becomes long, often as a set of batch jobs, then you eventually get the result you are looking for, but only after a long delay.

Wouldn't it be nice if you could cut the batch chain short and get your answers in real time, not only for actuals but also during planning and forecast processes?

In this chapter, we explain how these goals are achieved by a general trend toward simulation and predictive analytics and address the limitations associated with after-the-fact analysis (Section 6.1). We will present examples of business scenarios in which real-time finance really matters and arrive at an understanding of what is possible in addition to what it means to you and your company (Section 6.2). We will also discuss which patterns to look for in your company (Section 6.3) and how to judge your company's capabilities in general, based on a simple classification (Section 6.4). More details and background on these capabilities are available in Part II of the book.

6.1 Accepting the Limits of Retroactive Analysis

When it comes to finance, complexity correlates to business value, as shown in Figure 6.1. It is *good* to know precisely what happened. It is *necessary* to know what is going on now. It would be *great* to know what will happen in the future by making use of simulations and predictions.

Let's look at four key finance questions to see how and where you can benefit from the simplified data model while you carry out decision-relevant real-time simulations—wherever you need them, whenever you need them.

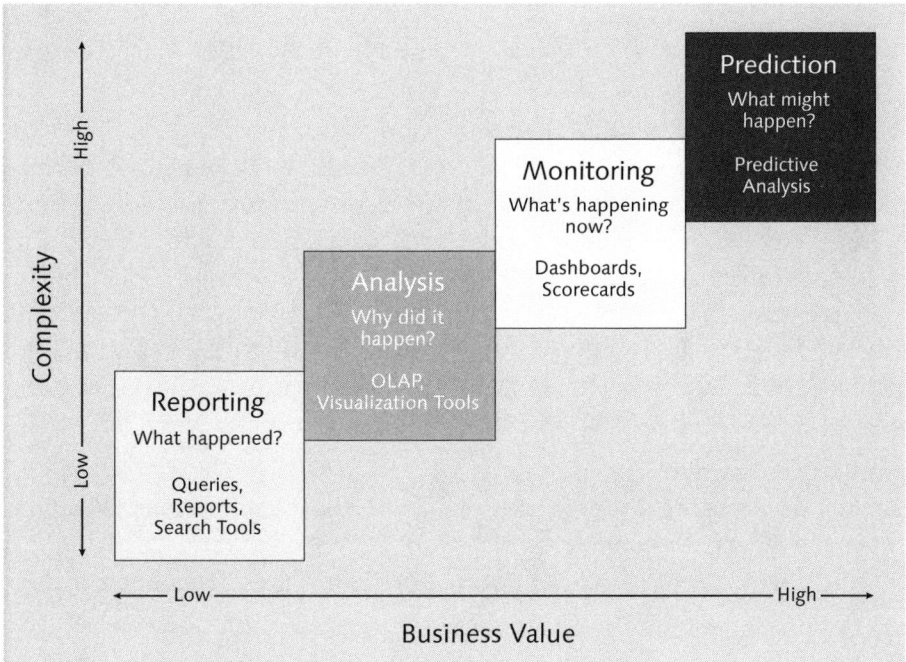

Figure 6.1 Target for Decision Support

- **What happened?**
  This is a typical question answered by your accounting system. Whatever happened in the real world will be recorded in accounting, depending on accounting principles. This is true, for example, for incoming and outgoing invoices.

  Our single source of truth for such information is the Universal Journal (see Chapter 8), with accounting line items that include all dimensions of external and internal accounting, such as company, account, customer, vendor, product, region, and more. Balance sheets, P&L statements, cash flow statements, profitability reports, or market segment reports are typical examples of such ex-post reporting.

- **Why did it happen?**
  Knowing what happened is necessary (and good), but not sufficient. The typical analysis questions concern who did what, where something came from, what purpose it served, and so on. These questions also are answered by our "golden source" for accounting, but here we need additional, more sophisticated tools than just reporting. Interactive tools for slicing, dicing, and drilling down to the accounting line item (and maybe back to the originating transaction) are essential. For recurring questions, a dashboard on top might help.

- **What's happening now?**
  The single source of truth of accounting can no longer help here. We need another source, independent of accounting principles. Of course, it should be possible to drill down to line item level in order to support multiple processes on top. Here, we can store, for example, sales order and purchase order data. Up-to-date information is relevant for all types of processes in the finance department and beyond. Typical candidates are cash management ("When will it hit the cash account?") or cost management ("What has been spent but not yet recorded in accounting?"). Simulations based on actual data ("What's happening now?") allow easy understanding of the short and medium term.

- **What might happen?**
  Here, all data sources come together and provide maximum value. Of course, here again we have a line item–based single source of truth for planning that answers the question "What was planned?" However, as plans often change, the information that tells you about the future was perhaps entered in the system some months ago. That is, your future information is dependent upon data that was correct six months ago.

How can we solve this deadlock? Wouldn't it be nice if you could combine "what happened" with "what is going on" and "what has been planned"? This powerful, fine-grained data source would enable you to answer questions you hadn't thought of yet or that, even if you had thought of them, were taking too long to answer.

6.2 Benefitting from Real-Time Finance

It seems counterintuitive that current expectations for real-time finance lag behind the level of "real-time-ness" that is already a reality in our private lives.

Let's take the example of a family day trip in your car. The dashboard in the car shows the current speed, fuel level, and other critical information *in real time*. The navigation system proposes a new route with a predicted time of arrival based on a new traffic situation *in real time*. When you arrive at your destination, your smartphone provides you with all relevant information about the history of the site, nearby restaurants, and many other things *in real time*.

Why shouldn't you benefit from the same level of "real-time-ness" in your organization? What are the equivalents of speed, fuel level, and other critical information in organizations? Profit might be analogous to speed and financial liquidity to fuel. Other parameters, such as engine temperature, might be represented by financial and operation risk. Because risks are not themselves a problem per se, we need to find the right level of engine temperature, somewhere between too cold and too hot.

As mentioned earlier, integrated information matters much more, because it enables access to greater business insight. The same holds true for enterprise information as well, both on financial and operational levels. Managing this at an enterprise level has, of late, become a significant challenge for CFOs. Their aim is not only to manage information but also to govern it. Typical steps to achieve this end include integrating information from various sources and gaining a deep understanding of which business outcomes are indicated by which information metrics. It is only then that there arises a possibility of time-slicing the information: some of it may be needed ad hoc or daily, some per week, per month, per quarter, per year, and so on, in real time. Only then can it lead to proactive data governance that is accurate and consistent.

In short, knowing *who* needs *which* support *when* and *where* to improve profit, secure liquidity, and manage risk helps to move from financial information provisioning to real business advice—and in the end, business pays the bill!

6.2.1 Improving Profit

In the simplest terms, making more profit means increased revenue and decreased cost, affecting both the top and bottom lines. However, we need to be more specific with our question ("Who needs which support when and where?") in order to keep the top or bottom line of the company healthy.

In practice, all organization activities have an impact on financials. Therefore, the accounting and controlling departments tend to exercise greater control over the various departments and lines of business. However, the real benefit is realized only when the finance functions become enablers to the business, not bottlenecks. This aim can be achieved by providing the individual departments with all the information they need, thus empowering them. That is the power of real-time business.

Next, we'll provide some examples of real-time businesses improving their profitability with real-time data.

Market unit manager Jack checks his business KPIs on his favorite dashboard. He notices that revenue growth is fine, but cost is increasing higher than expected. He wishes to analyze this information in more detail, but unfortunately the predefined KPIs for cost only show direct cost and overhead cost ratio. Clicking on the KPI and drilling down into line item level does not solve the problem completely; it only shows some high amounts on entertainment costs. Jack adjusts his dashboard to show an analysis of this. In a couple of minutes, he has a new KPI showing entertainment costs in relation to revenue by organizational structure. Drilling down into detail now gives him real-time transparency. He knows what action to take.

Sara works as a controller and is in charge of the P&L planning process. She interacts with the various business managers, who perform their financial overhead cost planning on a cost center level, and with the sales managers, who carry out their revenue planning based on the defined market segment structure. Because both sets of users access the same line item–based financial plan, albeit with different dimensions, Sara can see all information in real time. Furthermore, after finishing the first incremental planning she can see the P&L and how it fits into the expected target.

Sally, the product manager of a product line, analyzes the P&L for the period of January to September 2015. She finds the profit figures to be worse than expected. She slices and dices and figures out one specific product that is underperforming. She starts margin analysis for this specific product and finds out that higher transportation cost and customs duty are decreasing the margin. She can now rethink pricing or sourcing for this particular product.

Rini is an accounting manager at an organization. On September 15, she is asked by the management where the company stands as of that point in time. She draws the P&L statement and gets the most recent intramonth figures with exact revenue and cost of goods sold. She checks the contribution margin by market unit structures. Everything is as expected, and she can quickly submit the report to top management.

Next, Rini is asked to take a peek into the future and comment on the expected financial health of the company at the end of the year. She draws the P&L statement and accesses the current financial numbers through September 15. She then uses the system to simulate the report for the rest of the year, making use of planning and exposure data. Her report is 95% accurate. She only needs to make some minor manual adjustments to produce what the management wants.

Production controller Andy wants to revise pricing of his products based on historical data. Instead of running multiple cycles of time-consuming allocations (requiring massive posting in the books), he defines a new pricing method in which actual data is used as an input parameter. The new method is capable of modeling all product cycles and thus gives Andy a lot of flexibility.

6.2.2 Securing Liquidity

In our car analogy, we saw cash liquidity as the fuel to run the company. If your vehicle runs out of fuel before reaching the target, you are in trouble. You do not want to end your journey in this manner. However, there may be several reasons that you ran out of fuel: higher than anticipated consumption, delayed refill, or even an unknown leak in the tank—all of which are avoidable problems.

In finance terms, cash liquidity carries the same relevance, and it is imperative for the cash manager to resolve problems before it is too late. This calls for real-time operations and not just after-the-fact actions.

Some cases can be handled with input from accounts payable and/or receivable systems, but only some. Let's look at a few examples.

Petra works as a cash manager in a multinational enterprise. In light of recent reports of a crisis, the CFO asks her, "How much cash do we have in our bank accounts in country X?"

Fortunately, Petra runs a Central Finance deployment with a single source of truth. With a few clicks, she analyzes the statuses of all the bank accounts, grouped by countries and banks. She reports this information to the CFO, who asks her to move the money to a central account. With one more click, she takes action and makes the transfer.

In general, once or twice a day Petra analyzes the short-term liquidity situation for the upcoming week. One day, she recognizes a liquidity gap of $500,000. She can now choose from among three options: collect more money from customers, pay less money to vendors, or take out a loan from the bank (which is the most expensive option). Collecting money from customers might be time consuming and sensitive, whereas not paying vendor invoices might stop delivery of urgently needed products or services. Thanks to the single source of exposure data, Petra has full transparency on the line item level and can search for receivables and payables in the United States. She finds a suitable candidate and gets all the information she needs. She is now ready to discuss the situation with her colleagues and plan the next course of action.

Petra performs periodic liquidity planning for the medium and long term. Due to line item–based information of actuals, exposure, and planned items, she has easy access to the liquidity situation and can verify the figures by any dimension. To learn from the past, she has the most recent direct cash flow information at hand during the planning process.

Sales manager Steve has had a KPI for working capital since the beginning of the year. In the past, he could reach his revenue targets by demanding higher prices or by adjusting the payment conditions. This typically results in higher interest paid and higher customer credit risk (the customer might become bankrupt). This year, he has his own interest in bringing working capital down. He analyzes what is going on and finds out that there is higher working capital in his product line than expected. Why? Did payment conditions change, or was there a change in customers accepting the goods, or have the number of disputes gone up? He also learns that the given conditions were correct during billing but changed afterward due to a direct change in the open items. He triggers a discussion with his sales team immediately.

6.2.3 Managing Risk

In our car analogy, risk represents the engine temperature. If it's too cold, then you are not taking full advantage of the engine capacity. If it's too hot, then you have to be careful so as to not break the engine.

Figure 6.2 shows a risk-based performance model for an organization with respect to a given risk. On one axis is the probability of failure; on the other is the severity of the consequences (in monetary terms) should there be a failure. Even if the loss is not particularly high in isolation, if it occurs frequently, then you have to fix it. Working on the efficiency and automation of processes increases the probability of default and forces you to embed risk monitoring directly into operational processes. You could look at risk in this way: "It happens today, but cost or liquidity impact will be affected in the future, whether we recognize and understand the root cause or not." Real-time finance can help to optimize profit or liquidity after risk.

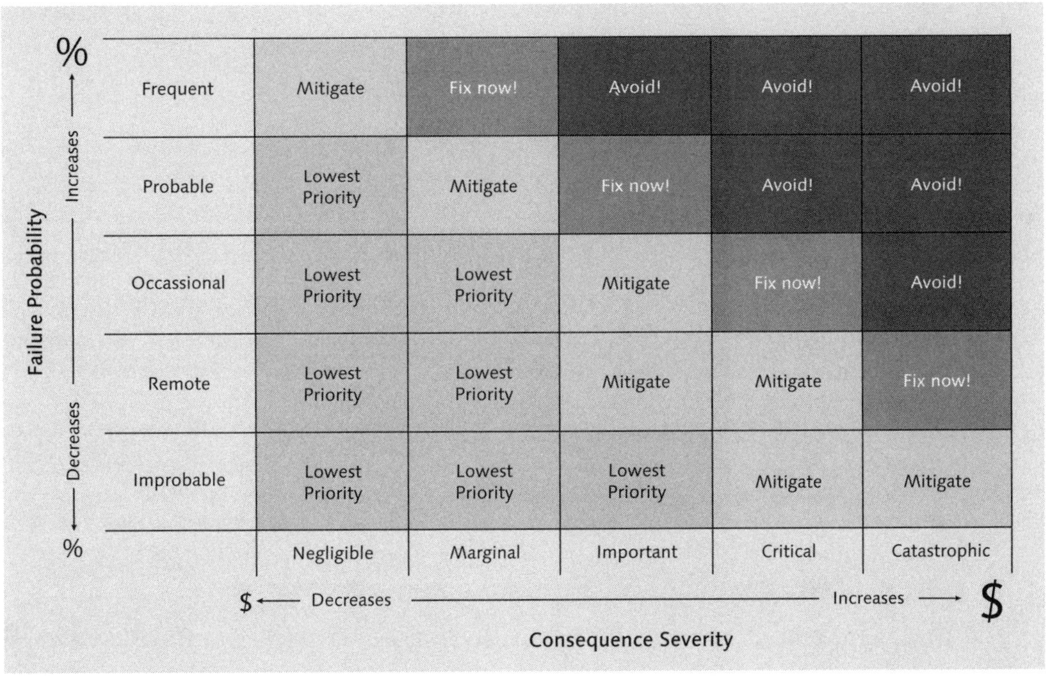

Failure Probability	Negligible	Marginal	Important	Critical	Catastrophic
Frequent	Mitigate	Fix now!	Avoid!	Avoid!	Avoid!
Probable	Lowest Priority	Mitigate	Fix now!	Avoid!	Avoid!
Occassional	Lowest Priority	Lowest Priority	Mitigate	Fix now!	Avoid!
Remote	Lowest Priority	Lowest Priority	Mitigate	Mitigate	Fix now!
Improbable	Lowest Priority	Lowest Priority	Lowest Priority	Mitigate	Mitigate

Consequence Severity

Figure 6.2 Risk-Based Performance Focus Area

Let's look at some areas in which real-time finance can have an impact on managing risk; to do this, we have to clearly differentiate between cases that focus on operational risk (e.g., fraud) and those that focus on financial risk (e.g., foreign exchange risk).

The operational risk manager, Mark, embeds risk- and fraud-based analysis into operational processes. These risk and fraud methods point out critical areas. Mark can see suspicious activities in a timely manner and can act accordingly.

James, working as the treasurer, is the final link in the chain when it comes to financial risk. We saw in other cases that businesses can manage risks on their own to a certain extent. James works in a central office; he does not deal with all the tiny details (even when they are available on a line item level), but he manages multiple risk portfolios. On November 18, he is asked for his opinion on an acquisition scenario (what it would mean from a liquidity and risk point of view). Due to the real-time access he has on central data across relevant portfolios, he receives a precise overview instantaneously. He now has a good view on the group situation today and in the future and is ready to support his CEO on a successful merger and acquisition activity.

6.3 Identifying Real-Time Finance Patterns

We have described several cases in which real-time finance really matters, but they do not present a comprehensive list; they represent only a limited number of cases in only a few scenarios. In practice, there is much more in it for you; in your own company, you will find additional cases.

To help you in this exercise of collecting relevant cases, we have described patterns that we recognized across a wider set. In general, we can group these patterns into the following categories.

6.3.1 Data Cases

Among the most important elements in a successful real-time finance environment is a harmonized data model. SAP S/4HANA Finance achieves this by harmonizing the areas of accounting, exposure, and planning. This means that there is one data model providing information for any application on top of it.

You will benefit most if you have your data harmonized and, if possible, centralized. Without data harmonization, you will limit the number of real-time finance cases. Harmonization is a prerequisite, whereas centralization speeds up information acquisition. There are two potential paths you can take:

1. Harmonize first and centralize second. This sounds good, but it is often not easy with multiple business partners, because they may not experience the same pain points as you and may not be fully committed to your approach.
2. Centralize first and harmonize second. In this approach, you start by centralizing the organization, identify and define problems at the level of the whole organization, and then work toward their resolution over time.

Think about cases in which data solves the problem already, such as the one Sara encountered, as described in Section 6.2.1.

6.3.2 Method Cases

Over the years, the computation power of systems has increased significantly. In the past, we could only compute a single (semi)result and post it to the database. We'd then wait for the next computing cycle to first read the previous (semi)results, then calculate the next step, and finally post to the database again. In SAP HANA, all these complex computations can be executed as a single step, providing two key benefits: Your waiting time is significantly reduced, and the individual computation steps can be reused for actual, planned, and forecast items in applications such as financials or sales (e.g., cost calculation during an available-to-promise, or ATP, process).

6.3.3 Process Cases

In any organization, processes have been standardized and distributed among different departments over time. This comfortable setup is robust and remains stable in cases of any minor changes with respect to content and time. However, when the change needed is significant—for example, pertaining to intra- or interdependencies—then you may hit a roadblock. In such a case, you will need to find an alternative solution.

There may be a need to rethink your processes and ascertain whether they really represent real-world entities or whether the complexity originates from internal steps. Check which methods can do the job in a simpler, quicker, and even more harmonized manner. Don't forget that process simplification will help you simplify your organization.

One simplification mechanism is to get rid of batch-oriented organization models. This forms the essence of real-time finance, in which organization units provide their inputs via automated methods instead of manual processes.

6.3.4 Ad Hoc Cases

In a world in which industries are merging and business models are permanently adjusting to a changing environment, you need the increased agility that real-time finance provides. If your whole organization is more agile, then ad hoc cases are the new normal.

The key to handling ad hoc cases is to question established processes. We figured out that ad hoc cases typically are variants of regular cases, with changes in trigger or timing. In a real-time finance environment, this element no longer makes a difference.

6.4 Becoming a Real-Time Finance Company

IBM published a study based on conversations with 1,900 CFOs across the world.[1] IBM's conclusion was that some finance organizations differentiate themselves from their peers and competitors by stepping into a new role: helping the business make enterprise-wide decisions better, faster, and with more certainty of intended outcomes. They can take complex inputs and arrive at insightful, simple-to-use actions. The IBM study calls these finance organizations "value integrators."

How can your finance organization become a value integrator? Begin by taking a look in the mirror, checking which direction your industry is taking, and asking your business users where they expect additional support from financials. We take a deeper look at this concept in the next section.

6.4.1 Balancing Efficiency and Insights

In general, organizations belong to one of the four financial profiles shown in Figure 6.3, based on scales of efficiency and access to insights.

---

1 IBM, "The New Value Integrator: Insights from the Global Chief Financial Officer Study."

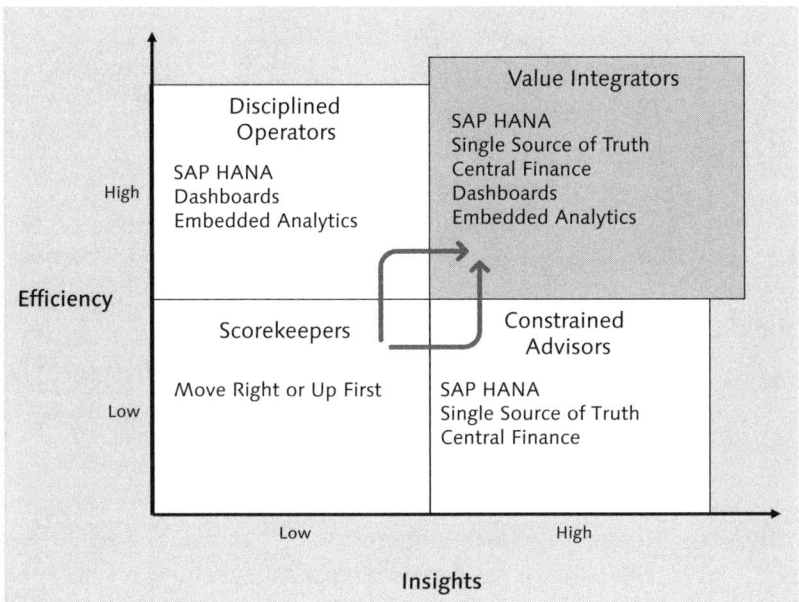

Figure 6.3 Finance Profiles

- **Scorekeepers (low on efficiency, low on insights)**
  Their prime focus is to keep the house in order and run basic finance functions needed for regulatory compliance. They often face challenges with respect to speed and consistency due to an absence of good quality automation and standardization. Hence, they want to start by improving their efficiency or insights.

- **Constrained advisers (low on efficiency, high on insights)**
  These enterprises have developed high analytical capabilities thanks to SAP HANA, a single source of truth, and a Central Finance system, but are restricted by a lack of complete and consistent information. Their processes involve a high degree of manual intervention.

- **Disciplined operators (high on efficiency, low on insights)**
  These organizations run on highly automated financial operations and reporting systems thanks to SAP HANA, with embedded analytics and dashboards running on top. They have at their disposal complete and consistent operational information, but they lack strong cross-functional analytical capabilities, limiting their chances of making informed long-term strategic decisions.

- **Value integrators (high on efficiency, high on insights)**
  These organizations not only have a solid base in but also constantly endeavor to improve their operational efficiency and business insight capabilities. They employ all of the means mentioned previously, such as SAP HANA, dashboards, or Central Finance, to achieve this aim. They are technology adopters and put new technology to good use in order to maintain their competitive advantage.

6.4.2 Examining Industry Requirements

Looking into the different industry clusters, such as production, professional services, retail, insurance, banking, or public services, we see a growing need for improved efficiency and higher insights for the following reasons:

- Traditional industry-separating lines are becoming blurred. On the way to becoming complete solution providers, organizations look to offer additional value-added content, such as professional services and financial services.
- More and more organizations look to get closer to end users, which requires them to make use of mass customization and retail capabilities.
- Structural changes, such as going from the private to the public sector (or vice versa) or the need to go international, leads organizations to face additional reporting requirements, including changes to the way they run their books.
- Business models are changing due to new collaboration strategies. Today, doing everything on your own may not be the best approach. Instead, an organization might (partially) move toward a governance model that includes the following roles:
  - A product specialist who focuses on a subset of the initial offering
  - A service specialist who adapts to the digital economy (from one-off purchases to long-term customer relationships)
  - An orchestrator who owns the customer relationship and makes use of other products and services
  - A layer master who provides high-scale services for others, possibly without owning the customer relations
  - A navigator who is perceived as a trusted advisor and brings business partners together

Whatever may be the case, as an organization you need to get the basics right for your business. Your business managers should feel comfortable that they will make the right decisions. They should be able to answer the following questions, ideally on their own: Do I still make profit? Do I have enough liquidity to run my business? Does the risk fit the profit I make?

Real-time finance helps you to manage these situations in a nondisruptive manner. Remember, as long as your database keeps all relevant information at a line item level it is easy to adjust finance in such a way as to support upcoming changes in business.

6.4.3 Considering Business Users' Needs

In the past, finance was sometimes finance-centric; that is, it focused on using financial data for financial users. Today, finance is about more than just closing the books. Many more users in and outside the finance department need guidelines to proactively manage cost, avoid unhealthy risk, change the business model in the "right" direction, change resource allocation in a profitable way, reduce working capital, watch the right KPIs, and do a good job in (rolling) forecasts and planning.

Ask your colleagues in sales, production, and service functions how you can support them, possibly even on the point of sale (e.g., with an ATP check). There is immense potential in real-time finance, and businesses need to tap into it in order to remain ahead of the competition.

PART II
Using SAP S/4HANA Finance

In this chapter, we take a look at the functional building blocks that make up SAP S/4HANA Finance and outline the big picture.

7 Building Blocks of SAP S/4HANA Finance

Throughout the first part of the book, we explored the simplification approach that gives SAP S/4HANA Finance its name and presented the paradigms that make up the fundamental model underlying SAP S/4HANA Finance. Now, in this second part, we take a closer look at the functionality of SAP S/4HANA Finance that delivers business value built on top of those paradigms. In particular, we explain how the paradigms and simplification lead to benefits in all areas of finance—both "familiar" functionality from SAP ERP Financials and new applications. We explore the most important functional building blocks, such as the Universal Journal, which bring together hitherto separate components, flexible reporting capabilities, exciting applications of different areas, and a new user experience.

Let's take our first close look at SAP S/4HANA Finance, using this chapter as an outline of Part II in general. To this end, Section 7.1 describes the big picture and how it's explained in the subsequent chapters of this book's second part. Section 7.2 explains how SAP S/4HANA Finance is an evolution of SAP ERP Financials and also describes the previously existing functionality. Thanks to overall simplification, SAP S/4HANA Finance essentially "reloads" and improves this existing functionality due to the improved underlying model. Finally, Section 7.3 highlights the individual new applications in SAP S/4HANA Finance, which are later explained in detail in Chapter 11.

7.1 Seeing the Big Picture

The key paradigm of SAP S/4HANA Finance is simplification. Throughout Part I, we showed how technological advances (and most importantly, the advent of in-memory technology for enterprise applications with SAP HANA) opened the road for the fundamental paradigms of SAP S/4HANA Finance: removal of redundancy, nondisruptive innovation, line item–based flexibility, and real-time finance. We also explained the benefits that companies receive from these paradigms woven into the heart of the SAP S/4HANA Finance model—for example, vastly improved performance, simpler system landscape, or entirely new capabilities. The benefits become apparent in all of the functional building blocks of SAP S/4HANA Finance.

Simplification implies a much simpler architecture and handling of the system, allowing you to focus on your finance business and on achieving goals without being impeded by technical considerations. However, simplification most definitely does not mean a reduced functional scope. In contrast, the scope of SAP S/4HANA Finance covers all the important functionality from SAP ERP Financials, as we'll explain shortly. SAP S/4HANA Finance doesn't stop there, however; it brings about an enhanced and even reenvisioned financial system. Now, let's first look at the big picture of the new functionality, as illustrated in Figure 7.1.

The most important functional change is the inclusion of the Universal Journal, which serves as the foundation of all of the following functional enhancements. The Universal Journal, described in Chapter 8, brings together the once-separate data models of different financial components, such as Financial Accounting (FI) or Management Accounting (CO).

In addition to eliminating time-consuming and complex reconciliation activities, the simplification of the data model with the Universal Journal presents entirely new possibilities for companies' external and internal reporting. Closely integrated with the single source of truth, the flexible reporting functionality forms the second layer of the functional basis illustrated in Figure 7.1. Chapter 9 outlines how the Universal Journal allows companies to improve reporting thanks to the increased flexibility and expanded scope of the underlying data model.

On top of this basis of simplified data model and flexible reporting capabilities, we consider first analytical and then transactional applications. SAP S/4HANA Finance allows companies to flexibly analyze their numbers according to their needs. Analytics go beyond legal or management reporting and cover all kinds of business intelligence and performance indicators. SAP S/4HANA Finance provides an easy-to-consume analytics layer on top of the simplified data model, so companies do not have to deal with technicalities but can easily build their analysis based on a rich data model with incorporated business semantics.

Alongside analytics, the Universal Journal also forms the basis for the new and enhanced (often transactional) applications in SAP S/4HANA Finance that work on the data or create it as part of business processes. Recall from Chapter 1 that applications span the entire value map of financials; these new applications form the second half of the third layer shown in Figure 7.1. They all have in common that they follow the simplification paradigms and benefit from the simpler architecture—in particular, the closer integration of financial components, building on top of the basis of the Universal Journal and flexible reporting.

Just providing functionality is not enough if true simplification is the goal. The functionality also has to be offered in a simpler manner with a more intuitive, easier, and delightful user experience. SAP Fiori apps are the means of choice in SAP S/4HANA Finance to achieve exactly that for all of the previously mentioned building blocks: reporting, analytics in general, and financial applications.

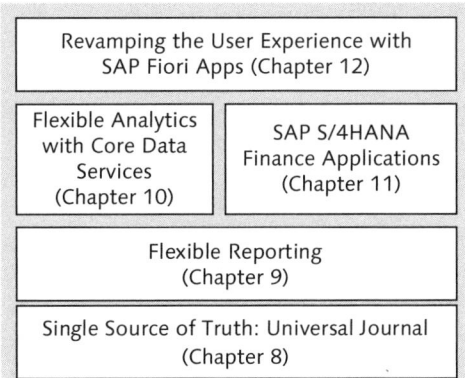

Figure 7.1 Functional Building Blocks of SAP S/4HANA Finance

How do these elements all fit together? In general, the Universal Journal defines how SAP S/4HANA Finance records and stores financial data in a single source of truth, although the impact of this goes far beyond the question of storage alone. Based on the data model, flexible reporting describes how companies can report the recorded financial data in flexible ways, crossing the boundaries of hitherto separate components. Flexible analytics give companies the tools to conduct all of their analysis on top of a simplified consumption model. The new SAP S/4HANA Finance applications make use of the Universal Journal and the simplification paradigms in general to deliver new and enhanced functionality. SAP S/4HANA Finance presents all of this in a more intuitive, more beautiful, and simpler user experience with SAP Fiori apps for both analytical and transactional tasks.

Some of these features and components are brand new, and others are recycled and improved from SAP ERP Financials. Before we dive deeper into what is new along the entire stack, let's take a moment to recall the rich functionality delivered by SAP S/4HANA Finance as an evolution of SAP ERP Financials.

7.2 Reloading SAP ERP Financials Functionality

SAP S/4HANA Finance does not drop all of the time-tested and elaborate SAP ERP Financials functionality you need for your business. Rather, SAP S/4HANA Finance allows you to perform all the relevant tasks you used to perform with the software, but in a smarter, faster, and simpler manner. Existing functionality is reloaded with superior performance thanks to SAP HANA in combination with the improved data model and with new insights thanks to the underlying fundamental paradigms (explained in Part I). In addition, much of the existing functionality is now offered with a new UI. SAP Fiori apps offer an intuitive, personalized, and simple user experience for financial tasks (see Chapter 12).

What is this reloaded content? Does it really extend across the finance value map? Let's take a closer look at the individual building blocks.

7.2.1 Financial Accounting

Financial Accounting (FI) records all expense, revenue, and asset-related business transactions of a company, such as customer invoice, vendor invoice, or payment documents in (sub)ledgers as financial documents. Legal reports, such as balance sheets or P&L statements, are generated, and companies then report these to the government, investors, and other interested parties. For these purposes, FI comprises the areas of G/L, Accounts Receivable, Accounts Payable, and Asset Accounting.

New General Ledger Accounting

The central task of G/L accounting is to provide a comprehensive picture of external accounting and accounts. Recording all business transactions (primary postings as well as settlements from internal accounting) in a software system that is fully integrated with all the other operational areas of a company ensures that the accounting data is always complete and accurate.

Beyond fulfilling legal requirements, New G/L Accounting also fulfills requirements for modern accounting. In Chapter 8, we'll focus more on the closer integration with management accounting (controlling) on the level of the data model that leads to a closer functional integration. New G/L Accounting allows you to perform parallel accounting by managing several parallel ledgers for different accounting principles.

New G/L Accounting also serves the purposes of internal management reporting in parallel with legal reporting. For example, it integrates the Profit Center Accounting functions. As outlined in Chapter 8, SAP S/4HANA Finance takes this integration to the next level with the Universal Journal. Based on this integration, you can generate financial statements for any dimension (such as profit centers).

New G/L Accounting supports the segment reports required by the International Financial Reporting Standards (IFRS) and US Generally Accepted Accounting Principles (GAAP).

Accounts Receivable

The Accounts Receivable subsidiary ledger records and updates customer-related business transactions—such as invoices, credit memos, or down payments—on a detailed level and maintains the G/L in parallel on an aggregated level. Open invoices, credit memos, and so on are collected in accounts receivable until they are processed in the payment process.

The postings made in the Accounts Receivable module are also automatically recorded in the G/L, where the accounts related to receivables are updated. The respective account for posting is obtained based on the master data of the customer and type of the transaction. In the master data, each customer is assigned to a G/L account in which the respective customer invoices, credit memos, and so on are recorded.

Accounts Payable

The Accounts Payable subledger records and updates all vendor-related business transactions (e.g., invoices, credit memos, payments, and down payments), similar to how accounts receivable handles customer transactions. Accounts Payable is closely integrated with the Purchasing component in SAP ERP Operations. Invoices can be either created directly within accounts payable or transferred via the accounting interface from the Invoice Verification component of SAP ERP Operations. Similar to Accounts Receivable, the postings made in the Accounts Payable module are also automatically recorded in the G/L, where the accounts related to payables are updated. In the case of accounts payable, the respective account for posting is obtained based on the master data of the vendor.

New Asset Accounting

Asset Accounting allows management of assets from the creation or purchase of a new asset to its retirement. During this lifecycle, an asset can be depreciated; that is, its value can be reduced over a period of time.

As a "reload" of this SAP ERP Financials content, SAP S/4HANA Finance provides New Asset Accounting, which is integrated with New G/L Accounting. You can handle parallel valuation of your assets using either the accounts approach or the ledger approach known from G/L—meaning that you either create alternative accounts to handle parallel valuation or use multiple ledgers. Both cases offer you flexible options to deal with parallel accounting principles or other valuation differences at low cost. New Asset Accounting posts values of leading and parallel valuation in real time for all accounting principles. You can track the postings of all valuations without having to take into account the postings of the leading valuation, as was partly the case in classic Asset Accounting. With the Universal Journal, asset accounting in SAP S/4HANA Finance is more closely integrated into accounting, so less reconciliation is necessary and more fine-grained exploration across components is possible (see Chapter 8).

7.2.2 Management Accounting

Based on the same data model as Financial Accounting, Management Accounting (also known as Controlling, or CO) is used for internal accounting within a company to prepare operating data, such as product costing, cost of goods sold, overhead, and actual costing of inventory. This operative data is used for the business analysis of the company and to support management decisions. It provides the basis for contrasting the cost of sales with the revenue earned and for explaining the value added by production and investment activities within the organization. In addition to documenting actual costs, the main task of Management Accounting is planning. You can determine variances by comparing actual data with planned data.

Management Accounting consists of various components:

- Cost Element Accounting classifies the cost and revenue objects into various object types and value types. SAP S/4HANA Finance elevates cost elements as a special kind of G/L account, thus enabling additional reporting possibilities (see Chapter 8, Section 8.2.2).

- Overhead Cost Controlling manages the costs due to overhead processes in a company and consists of the following subcomponents:

    - Cost Center Accounting enables managing the overhead costs according to the management units where the costs were incurred.

    - Internal Order Accounting manages the costs occurring due to internal activities. You use internal orders to collect and control according to the internal activity that incurred the costs. You can assign and monitor budgets for these internal activities to ensure that they are not exceeded.

    - Overhead Cost Planning enables planning for the costs that could be incurred in the next periods.

    All of these subcomponents greatly benefit from faster allocation processes and improved in-period insights.

- Product Cost Controlling calculates the costs that occur during manufacture of a product or provision of a service. It enables you to calculate the minimum price at which a product can be profitably marketed. The integrated Universal Journal makes it easier to look at the various stages of a product's lifecycle and calculate costs over the whole lifetime.

- Profitability Analysis analyzes the profit or loss of an organization. The system allocates the corresponding costs to the revenues for each market segment. It provides a basis for decision making—for example, for price determination, customer selection, conditioning, and distribution channel selection. Account-based Profitability Analysis has undergone significant improvements, which we outline in detail in Chapter 11, Section 11.6.

7.2.3 SAP Financial Supply Chain Management

SAP Financial Supply Chain Management optimizes the financial and information flows, such as payment- and invoice-related processes within a company and between business partners, and thereby supports daily financial operations. It is integrated with Financial Accounting, especially Accounts Receivable and Accounts Payable, to exchange financial information. SAP Financial Supply Chain Management contains various components, including the following:

- Collections Management provides users a work list of receivables to be collected. Companies use Collection Management to collect outstanding receivables according to a prioritized list and thus optimize their cash flow.
- Dispute Management allows for managing and tracking disputes with customers over receivables. Dispute Management stores the information about a dispute in a so-called *dispute case* in order to collect all relevant information at a central place and resolve disputes more quickly.

Chapter 11, Section 11.2 has more details on how SAP S/4HANA Finance supports companies in their financial operations with new applications. Closely related are the components of SAP Treasury and Risk Management as well as SAP Cash Management, outlined in the following sections.

7.2.4 SAP Treasury and Risk Management

SAP Treasury and Risk Management helps companies recognize, assess, and manage the risks they face in different areas, such as interest or currency rates. It is based on a series of solutions such as the following that primarily analyze and optimize business processes in the financial area of a company based on a single source of truth:

- The Market Risk Analyzer analyzes market risks in financial positions. Changes in market prices represent important influencing factors for company success. Changes to market prices can influence the value, transaction value, or timing of payment flows. Risks can be analyzed according to risk factors such as exchange rates, interest rates, stock price risk, index price risk, or volatility.
- The Credit Risk Analyzer controls the risk of losing money due to customer defaults when goods or services are sold on credit. By computing total amounts and specifying limits, counterparty risk—that is, the risk of loss of value of a receivable due to the degradation of credit standing of the business partner—

is monitored and reduced. Integrated with SAP Financial Supply Chain Management, companies can assess a customer's credit rating before selling on credit, limit credit given to customers based on their rating, and monitor their exposure to credit risks.

- The Portfolio Analyzer groups tools for the calculation of yield and performance figures as well as for the comparison of those key values with benchmarks. It is designed to measure the success of investments from different custom-defined perspectives independently from the transactional entities and by using a variety of methods.

7.2.5 Cash Management

SAP S/4HANA Finance embraces SAP Cash Management powered by SAP HANA, which enables the group treasury or the cash department to manage cash and liquidity centrally. Its major features include Bank Account Management and Cash Management. Bank Account Management enables cash and bank accountants to centralize the management of bank accounts.

In SAP Cash Management, liquidity planning allows cash managers in subsidiary organizations to plan the cash flows in their organizations with the help of the embedded actual and forecasted cash data. Cash managers and CFOs in higher-level organizations and headquarters can then get a consolidated forecast of the future liquidity situation and also set targets for the planning in their subsidiaries.

SAP Cash Management provides several reports so that cash managers can monitor and forecast bank account balances and cash flows in their company. Thanks to close integration and the line item–based data model, they can look into financial transaction details and identify what has contributed to the cash movements in an organizational unit during a certain period of time.

Chapter 11, Section 11.4 further explores the benefits and new functionality of SAP S/4HANA Finance in the area of cash management.

7.3 New Applications in SAP S/4HANA Finance

SAP S/4HANA Finance has been built to help meet today's business needs in finance departments. In addition to the important capabilities of SAP ERP Financials, it contains advanced capabilities and innovations to achieve the following goals—and more! We'll use the following overview of new features as a roadmap for the remaining chapters in Part II:

- Provides a single source of truth between transactions and analytics to streamline and eliminate cycle times and reconciliations of data (see Chapter 8)
- Offers new reporting and analytics capabilities for finance users with self-service access to all information, allowing instant insight to action (see Chapter 9 and Chapter 10)
- Connects business networks in real time to establish an integrated business ecosystem and help drive optimal collaboration with customers, suppliers, banks, and government authorities
- Combines innovative rapid planning and forecasting with predictive analysis to explore new business models and immediately assess potential effects on the bottom line
- Provides new on-the-fly capabilities for moving finance processing, such as month-end closing activities, from batch to real time
- Extends global regulatory compliance capabilities across currencies, languages, and industries with continuous risk assessment along all enterprise processes

In Chapter 11, we'll explore these last four themes and more as we take a closer look at applications across the scope of SAP S/4HANA Finance:

- As a follow-up to Chapter 10 on the flexible analytics data provisioning, in Chapter 11 we'll begin by considering business cockpits for analysis purposes (see Chapter 11, Section 11.1). SAP S/4HANA Finance provides an easy-to-use cockpit solution that enables business users to configure KPIs and cockpits according to their needs, based on the easy-to-consume analytical model.
- Chapter 11 continues by looking at Financials Operations (see Chapter 11, Section 11.2), which constitutes the interface of a finance system for customers and vendors and takes a crucial role in the daily operations of companies. As such, a close integration to business networks is critical in this context. SAP S/4HANA Finance in particular provides integration capabilities with the network of SAP Ariba (see Chapter 11, Section 11.3). The financial operations of a company have a direct impact on its cash flow. Managing cash flow, liquidity, and bank accounts is supported with SAP Cash Management powered by SAP HANA, a part of SAP S/4HANA Finance that is covered in Chapter 11, Section 11.4.

- When we are expanding our focus from day-to-day business into the future, planning solutions become an essential topic. The key improvement of SAP S/4HANA Finance with regard to financial planning is an integrated solution (see Chapter 11, Section 11.5) that builds on the simplification paradigms and, in particular, the Universal Journal to offer a more streamlined planning experience.

- Profitability Analysis now operates on top of complete financial data and, in addition to better performance, offers new capabilities for analyzing the profitability of different entities, such as products or organizations (see Chapter 11, Section 11.6). At the end of each fiscal period, companies need to perform an accurate and fast financial closing and consolidation process in order to fulfill their legal reporting requirements. At the same time, they also desire a more up-to-date view on their financial figures within a period. By moving toward a real-time close, SAP S/4HANA Finance supports companies in both of these goals, as outlined in Chapter 11, Section 11.7.

- A specific topic of relevance for closing and other financial activities is revenue recognition. SAP S/4HANA Finance delivers with SAP Revenue Accounting and Reporting (see Chapter 11, Section 11.8), a solution that implements the latest legal regulations and offers unprecedented insight into the state of revenue recognition. All of these financial activities in a system are highly sensible and require strict governance to avoid fraud and manage risks. SAP solutions for Governance, Risk, and Compliance (GRC; see Chapter 11, Section 11.9) provide such functionality with smart means to consistently monitor and update detection strategies.

In summary, once we apply innovative SAP ERP Financials features and assemble some new, powerful applications, we can see the big picture in Chapter 11 to get a deeper insight into the entire application landscape of SAP S/4HANA Finance. Chapter 12 describes the new user experience of SAP Fiori that spans all of these features. The upcoming chapters explain the basis of such functionality (as described in the previous lists), starting with the Universal Journal as the single source of truth on the level of the data model.

SAP S/4HANA Finance is a major step forward in changing how enterprise software is deployed and used across the financial operations of a company. It combines the ease of cloud-based deployment (or the full control of an on-premise installation), a full set of standard financial functions, and net new functionality that enables a company to conduct a soft financial close and model different financial scenarios. The result is not only better day-to-day financial management but also an improved financial planning and execution function that can help companies stay abreast of rapidly changing market conditions.

Let's begin our inspection of SAP S/4HANA Finance's working parts by looking in detail at the Universal Journal, which is the single source of truth that brings together the hitherto separate journals for accounting documents in Financial Accounting and Management Accounting.

8   Single Source of Truth: Universal Journal

The Universal Journal is the single source of truth and the holistic basis for next-generation accounting in SAP S/4HANA Finance. It changes the game with respect to reconciliation-free transparency, seamless navigation, and superior insight into financial data. The new Universal Journal is a harmonized and redundancy-free data store of actual data serving the General Ledger (G/L), Management Accounting/Controlling (CO), Asset Accounting (AA), and Material Ledger (ML) components.

After explaining the technical implementation of the Universal Journal, we outline how this next-generation accounting solution in SAP S/4HANA Finance simplifies business processes and enables new capabilities. We begin by describing the approach of the past and the challenges resulting from this approach (Section 8.1). Section 8.2 covers the new SAP HANA-based architecture; it provides some technical details about how the Universal Journal addresses the aforementioned challenges and explain the easy way for companies to adopt the new solution. In Section 8.3, we describe and explain important benefits for companies that are an immediate consequence of the new structure. The chapter concludes in Section 8.4 with an outlook on further great ideas and innovation potential that companies can now leverage with the new architecture.

8.1   Mastering Business Challenges without SAP HANA

In many software solutions used today, Financial Accounting and Management Accounting are two separate components; sometimes, they are separate systems that are only loosely coupled from an architectural perspective—if at all.

This design was due to the historical belief that Financial Accounting and Management Accounting are independent areas in terms of content. The decoupled approach came along with posting data into the two components with different details, different structures, and different key figure systems. Moreover, it allowed for local corrections and manipulations of the data. As a consequence, reporting figures differ at first view, although the two areas provide financial information based on the same underlying business processes.

Today's CEOs and CFOs, however, demand a holistic financial and management accounting picture that fits together and leaves no questions open. To tackle this fundamental reconciliation challenge, companies miss out on a lot of reporting and analysis capacities, because they first have to perform time-consuming reconciliation and understand the differences. This leaves less time available to focus on the content and prepare high-quality decision support for the executive level. This is particularly critical during high-pressure situations in period-end closing activities.

This new era of big data provides larger and, in terms of content, richer data sets—but the urgency to make decisions faster every day is still increasing. Hence, avoiding the reconciliation challenge has become even more important. There is simply no time left for tedious reconciliation activities. However, this is not only an "internal" challenge. The walls between financial reporting and management reporting are under heavy fire by financial regulations as well. International Financial Reporting Standards (IFRS) 8 clearly states that operating segments, which are regularly reviewed by management via internal reports, have to be published as part of the official financial statement. This increases the pressure to create a single source of truth.

Looking at SAP financials functionality in particular, SAP ERP Financials historically also followed the decoupled approach. However, already the evolutionary development of the system and the subsequent introduction of new components, such as Profit Center Accounting, Joint Venture Accounting, or Public Sector Funds Management, have shown that FI and CO have more in common than previously thought, because the new components added the same driving dimensions (fields such as profit center, venture, fund, and the respective partner fields) simultaneously in both components.

In the past, developments such as the "reconciliation ledger" or the New G/L realtime integration tackled the reconciliation challenge between FI and CO and brought the components closer together. However, even these developments never performed the last logical step of combining FI and CO into a single physical table. At the time, there were technical arguments and good reasons not to do so—for example, the breadth of the data structures or the sheer volume of data in a combined table that would slow down specific reports. These arguments no longer hold true, thanks to the superior compression capabilities of SAP HANA.

Another big technical challenge is a thing of the past as well. Recall from Chapter 3 that totals tables were needed in order to cover the performance requirements with respect to analytics and mass processes at period end. Due to the limitation of sixteen key fields in transactional tables—and because the fulfillment of new requirements often meant creating new fields and dimensions—new tables had to be created (often accompanied by precisely fitting line item structures) for every bigger new requirement. Around these tables, new components (such as Profit Center Accounting, Joint Venture Accounting, the Functional Area Ledger, and some of the Public Sector modules) have been built in order to cover the business requirements. Moreover, SAP offered the Special Ledger module (FI-SL), a tool that allowed customers to create new totals records and process logic on their own.

The powerful Profitability Analysis (CO-PA) module is also a separate component in SAP ERP Financials. Although it was originally designed as a freely configurable module to analyze profit margins down to the product level, companies often want to reconcile the data of CO-PA with the P&L statement. This is particularly challenging in the widely used costing-based variant in which, architecturally, the G/L account is explicitly not part of CO-PA's structure. Because each component covered a specific part of the holistic accounting context, they all kept to a high degree of redundant data and therefore had to be reconciled as well.

In general, reconciliation comes in the following two types:

- **Reconciliation within a single component**
  An example of this type is the reconciliation of persisted totals records with the underlying line item records. Because the totals are a straightforward projection of the line items, this task is inconvenient, but usually not difficult to fulfill for the end user. SAP provided reports such as Report SAPF190 in order to automate this task in the past. Now, with SAP HANA and the elimination of materialized aggregates (see Chapter 3), this challenge has vanished.

- **Reconciliation across components**
  This tends to be the much harder task, because individual components do not necessarily have an identical structure. You first have to figure out what dimensions or key figures can be compared and reconciled at all. A good example is the reconciliation between the P&L and the costing-based CO-PA.

In this chapter, we focus on the reconciliation challenge across components.

The redesign of the G/L in ERP2004 (New G/L) brought a first wave of harmonization to the accounting landscape. Because New G/L bundled the advantages of different modules (e.g., customer field extensibility, parallel views, and document splitting from Special Purpose Ledgers or rich content from Profit Center Accounting) into a new module, this led to overall simplification. SAP customers could work with fewer components, which meant less reconciliation effort. However, the aim of New G/L was never to replace classical subledgers, like AA, ML, CO, or CO-PA, so the reconciliation challenge among all these components remained, as shown in Figure 8.1.

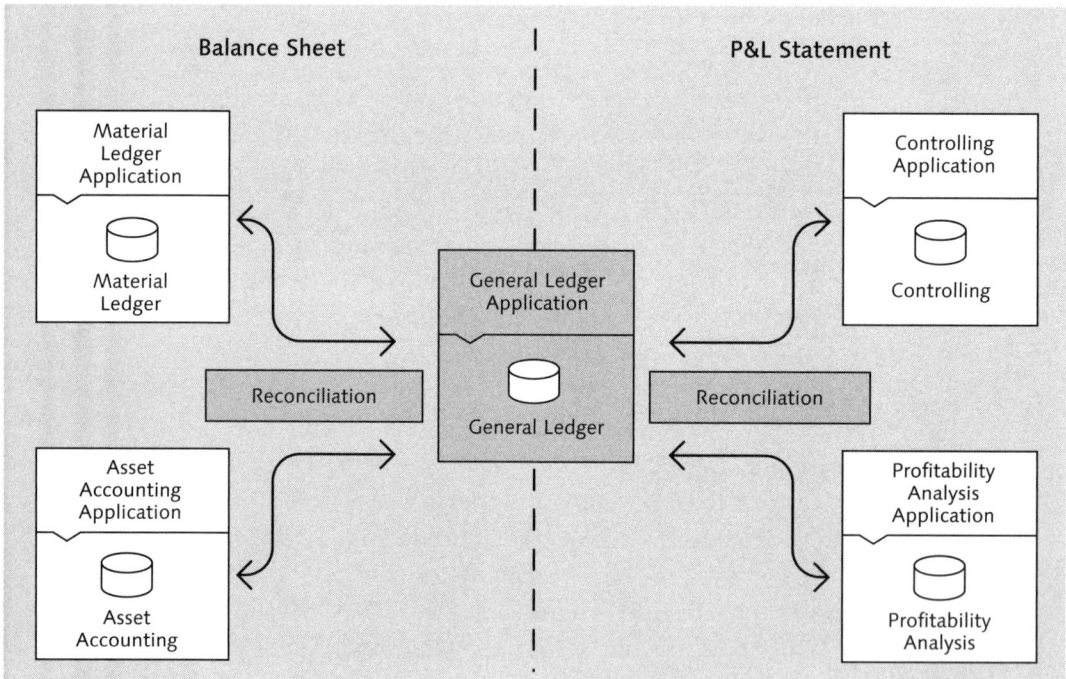

Figure 8.1 Main Accounting Tables after New G/L Harmonization

For the sake of simplicity, we'll refer to New G/L as just G/L from now on. Take a look back at Figure 8.1; the integrated system needs at least the reconciliation of the G/L, AA, and ML components on the balance sheet side and G/L, CO, and CO-PA on the P&L side.

Important and widely used components, like the ones included in Figure 8.1, tend to develop some kind of independence from other components over time. A decoupled architecture seems to make that independence easy, but it ignores the reconciliation challenge. In practice, this leads to code, configurations, and concepts that work perfectly only for the specific component and do not fully reflect the other components with their specific needs. As a consequence, the underlying tables, data structures, or capabilities are not as consistent as they could be.

To illustrate this point, let's consider a few examples from today's system. In the G/L, you can have up to three parallel currencies, but only two in CO. In G/L, parallel ledgers are available to reflect scenarios with multiple accounting standards; CO uses concepts like delta version, and AA has depreciation areas. G/L has accounts, but CO has cost elements. Extensibility with customer fields works quite well with some components, but not in all of them.

These little "disharmonies" belong to the second reconciliation type. Usually, there is quite a bit of manual effort required to be sure that everything is as expected. For instance, when comparing costs in the P&L with costs in a CO report you have to figure out how the ledger in G/L and the (delta) version in CO fit together or how the G/L account can be mapped to the cost element.

What kind of architecture can address the reconciliation challenge and pave the way for important new functions and real-time business insight? Let's find out.

8.2 New SAP HANA-Based Architecture

SAP HANA has some stunning features. One of them is the capability to aggregate hundreds of millions of line items of one table within seconds. Wouldn't being able to write all detail that is needed by all components (G/L, CO, AA, ML, and CO-PA) into one single table constitute the ideal architecture?

With Figure 8.1 in mind, the approach we take is straightforward: combine the data structures of the different components into a single combined line item table: the Universal Journal. This is our single source of truth that replaces the previously separate physical tables, as shown in Figure 8.2. Similar to the removal of redundant materialized views and materialized aggregates, SAP S/4HANA Finance provides compatibility views that give transparent access to the obsolete individual tables, thus offering a nondisruptive path to the innovative Universal Journal.

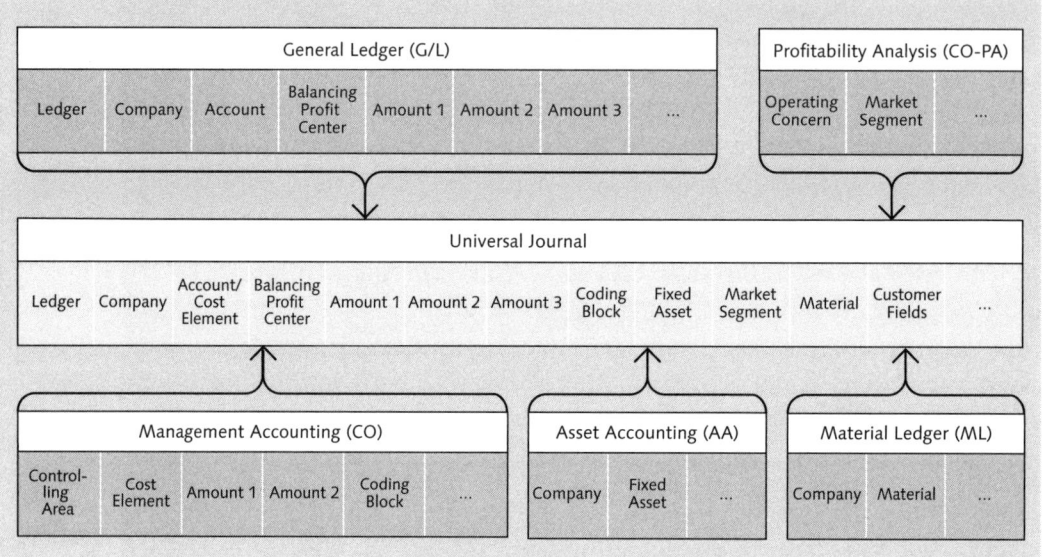

Figure 8.2 Universal Journal: Combination of Different Sources

8.2.1 Structure of the Universal Journal

By definition, the Universal Journal has all fields (columns) required by the business processes and the individual components. Whereas the technical handling of a table with so many fields would have created significant difficulties in the past, now we can dare such a feat thanks to SAP HANA's superior compression technologies and columnar layout.

We have talked a lot about G/L (FI), CO, AA, and ML. The new architecture merges all components into a holistic accounting, keeping the respective good qualities and bringing them together in a system with additional novel capabilities. When talking about G/L, CO, AA, and ML in this context, we refer to the rich functionality provided by these now-integrated components, which the Universal

Journal protects and expands. It takes the best attributes of each component and combines them into the new structure, as the following examples highlight:

- From G/L, the Universal Journal takes the ledger entity in order to handle multiple accounting principles in parallel. This multi-GAAP capability is now used in many SAP customer installations with increasing tendency. It also takes the capability to run three currencies in parallel from G/L. This is more than the two currencies that are currently handled in CO. The inheritance of G/L is the ability to produce balance sheets by any dimension via document splitting. *Document splitting* guarantees balanced documents for entities other than the complete company, thus allowing, for instance, a full balance sheet per segment. This is integrated in the Universal Journal as well.

- From CO-PA, the Universal Journal brings the customer-definable market segment information into the new structure. We fill the market segment fields by leveraging the rich field derivation capabilities of CO-PA. Because the journal entry is based on the account, the Universal Journal leverages the account-based CO-PA capabilities via this approach and enhances them with dedicated developments. The costing-based CO-PA is untouched and can run in parallel.

- From CO, the Universal Journal takes the complete set of controlling entities (e.g., cost center, project, and internal order) that is the coding block. It also takes the cost element that will merge with the G/L account. We provide some details about mapping cost elements and G/L accounts shortly.

- From AA, the Universal Journal takes the asset number, asset transaction type, depreciation area, and further relevant attributes.

- From ML, the Universal Journal takes the material number, inventory quantity, movement category, and other data.

SAP customers can, of course, enhance the new comprehensive table according to their needs. The Universal Journal integrates the coding block extension (structure `CI_COBL`), allowing the input of customer fields on many UIs. The CO-PA extension technology is also used in order to bring customer-defined market segment information into the new structure.

The very existence of the Universal Journal allows you to harvest the first important improvements immediately. Earlier, we mentioned the increasing demand of companies for a holistic handling of multiple accounting standards (e.g., IFRS and US GAAP) throughout the whole system. Working with parallel ledgers supports this requirement in G/L. Now, you can start to enhance the well-known and still-working functionality in CO in this way this as well. As shown in Figure 8.3, the reposting of primary costs is one of the transactions (Transaction KB11N) offered with the ability to post to ledgers (or ledger groups) individually.

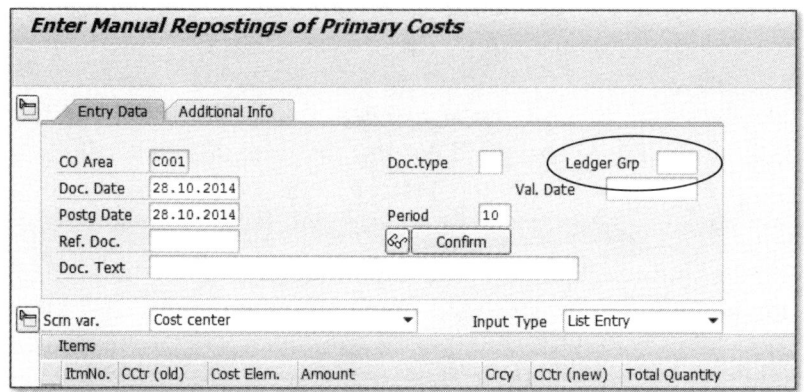

Figure 8.3 Ledger-Specific Reposting of Primary Costs: Ledger Group

The vision for the future is to have the ledger entity available in the complete CO functionality. This is the wish of many companies and would, for example, allow for having multiple prices in activity allocations or for distributing costs with different rules in separate ledgers.

8.2.2 Merging G/L Accounts and Cost Elements

Before the Universal Journal, we had G/L accounts in G/L and (secondary) cost elements in CO mapped to those G/L accounts. Because the user always had to trace the mapping rules backwards, this architecture hindered navigation from FI to CO.

In the SAP HANA architecture, you use only one field in the Universal Journal entry to store both G/L account and cost element. The trick is that you simply declare a cost element to be a special kind of G/L account. You maintain the "new account" via one single UI, as shown in Figure 8.4. The screenshot shows the creation of a new G/L account of the SECONDARY COSTS type. You can now post documents that include line items with secondary cost elements directly to FI.

From an account perspective, navigation between FI and CO is now seamless.

8.2 New SAP HANA-Based Architecture

New Account	
* G/L Account:	600400
* Description:	Internal Settlement
* Chart of Accounts:	YKON
* G/L Account Type:	Secondary Costs

Figure 8.4 Harmonization of G/L Account and Cost Element at the Example Secondary Costs

8.2.3 Compatibility Views

Recall from earlier in the chapter that there are many programs in the system working with the data structures of a specific component—for example, with the table of controlling document line items, table COEP. Read accesses to this table are common in these programs. How can you now change the underlying database table without having to rewrite the whole code?

The answer is technically elegant and refreshingly simple: Use compatibility views, similar to the removal of materialized aggregates (see Chapter 3).

As outlined in Figure 8.5, read operations in the ABAP code are redirected toward a view (V_COEP) via a specific setting in the data dictionary definition of table COEP.

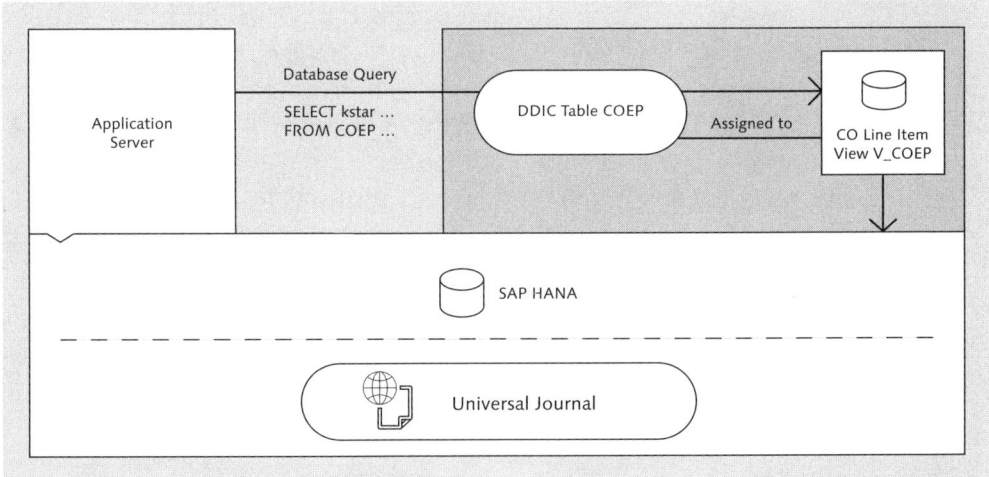

Figure 8.5 Compatibility View for Table COEP

155

This view then no longer reads the physical table COEP but the new Universal Journal; it now maps the data back to the structure of table COEP. From the perspective of the program code, there has not been any change. It still uses statements like SELECT FROM kstar, kostl, … COEP. The redirection is performed in the database interface, invisible for the source code. Using this technology safeguards not only the rich standard processes delivered by SAP but also customer-specific reports. Table A.3 of Appendix A lists the tables that have been part of the Universal Journal refactoring.

Now that we've described the new SAP HANA-based architecture of the Universal Journal in SAP S/4HANA Finance, let's turn our attention to the first benefits resulting from this architecture.

8.3 Immediate Benefits of the New Model

We've talked a lot about the pain of reconciliation. With the new architecture, this challenge in accounting has simply vanished. Let's look at the mileage you can get out of finances when you avoid reconciliation among the following:

- Between data structures within a component in order to compare line items and persisted totals, because SAP S/4HANA Finance eliminates the materialized aggregates.

- Between FI and CO (or a reconciliation ledger) or real-time integration within G/L, because with the new architecture you merge CO and FI so that real-time integration is guaranteed by design. Users can natively drill down to the same line items from the key figures and reports of both components. Secondary cost elements are simply G/L accounts that can be assigned to financial statement versions as well. This is a big simplification in the day-to-day work of companies, because navigating from a source G/L report to a target CO report will show the same account number. The user no longer has to trace the mapping rules backwards in each navigation step.

- Between CO-PA and G/L, because account-based CO-PA is implemented by enriching Universal Journal entries with market segment attributes. As a consequence, profitability reports nicely fit the P&L statement, because both refer to the same line items.

- Between fixed Asset Accounting and G/L, because both components rely on the same line items.
- Between ML and G/L, because ML reports and G/L reports can be traced back to the same line items.
- Between OLTP and OLAP, because SAP HANA provides multidimensional access to line items with unprecedented speed, and therefore it is no longer necessary to replicate data to an OLAP system in most use cases. Even for the rare cases in which a company needs financial data in an OLAP system, the Universal Journal offers a dramatic simplification: Today, data needs to be extracted from different independent data sources, at least one data source for each component. Thereafter, OLAP data has to be reconciled with the OLTP data source by source. In the new architecture, you need only one single data source for all accounting components. Hence, reconciliation between OLTP and OLAP is needed for this single data source only. This is an immense benefit in terms of effort and cost.

Instead of writing highly redundant information in separate tables, SAP S/4HANA Finance now writes data into one single store. Line items are written once, reducing the memory footprint and increasing the throughput of the system. In the end, companies thus also have a lower TCO thanks to the Universal Journal.

8.3.1 Depreciation Runs

We explained earlier that separate components with individual persistency tend to focus on their own needs. Let's now consider an example from AA prior to the new journal entry. When posting asset depreciation as part of the closing process, the AA module writes all the value adjustments on the detailed asset level into its specific persistent data structures. G/L and CO are only informed on a summarized (totals) level, without detailed asset number information.

Focusing on totals like this has several disadvantages:

- In G/L, it is not easy to break a fixed asset account down to the individual assets that are assigned to the account, simply because the information was not sent to G/L.
- The cost center manager analyzing depreciation costs on his cost center cannot quickly determine the fixed assets causing the costs. He cannot easily check if the costs have been assigned correctly to his cost center.

Because the Universal Journal based on SAP HANA provides a unified storage, AA, G/L, and CO all rely on the same integrated data structure. The depreciation process now writes the fully detailed information into this single structure all at once so that it is transparent to all components. All needed fields are available by definition and are filled accordingly.

Figure 8.6 shows some exemplary line items that such a depreciation run may have posted. On the separate depreciation cost items, the fixed asset number is now filled as an attribute, offering more detailed insights for cost center managers. The depreciation process provides all the data to fulfill the requirements of G/L and CO.

G/L Account	Fixed Asset	Cost Center	Profit Center	Credit	Debit
Accumulated Depreciation (Vehicles)	A-100		Car Fleet	$750	
Accumulated Depreciation (Vehicles)	A-200		Car Fleet	$850	
Accumulated Depreciation (Vehicles)	A-300		Car Fleet	$400	
Depreciation Costs (Tangibles)	A-100	4711	Car Fleet		$750
Depreciation Costs (Tangibles)	A-200	4711	Car Fleet		$850
Depreciation Costs (Tangibles)	A-300	4711	Car Fleet		$400

Figure 8.6 Depreciation Provides New Insights for Cost Center Manager

8.3.2 Multidimensional Profitability Analysis

With respect to multidimensional profitability analysis, there are totally new options.

Without the Universal Journal, profitability analysis learns about the impact of certain business processes very late—usually at period end via the settlement to CO-PA during closing runs. This happens when costs or revenues are first posted to a CO object (cost center, project, etc.) without assigning a market segment. For example, think of posting salary to the respective cost centers or invoicing work done within a consulting project, thereby posting revenue to the respective customer project. The disadvantages of this architecture are clear: Companies see meaningful profitability information in the reporting only very late—after the settlement runs have taken place. Furthermore, the respective CO-PA reports show the information on summarized settlement cost elements and not with the original G/L account—which leads to further reconciliation efforts. Furthermore, the company has to ensure that the settlement run is indeed scheduled to be executed periodically.

The Universal Journal follows a different, integrated approach based on the following observation: Why not write market segment attributes such as the corresponding sales order or customer directly and automatically into the document while data is posted to a CO object? In these examples, this would mean assigning salary postings directly to the respective market segment or assigning the revenue for a consulting project both to the project itself and also to the respective market segment. Figure 8.7 shows how market segment attributes could be derived from the project.

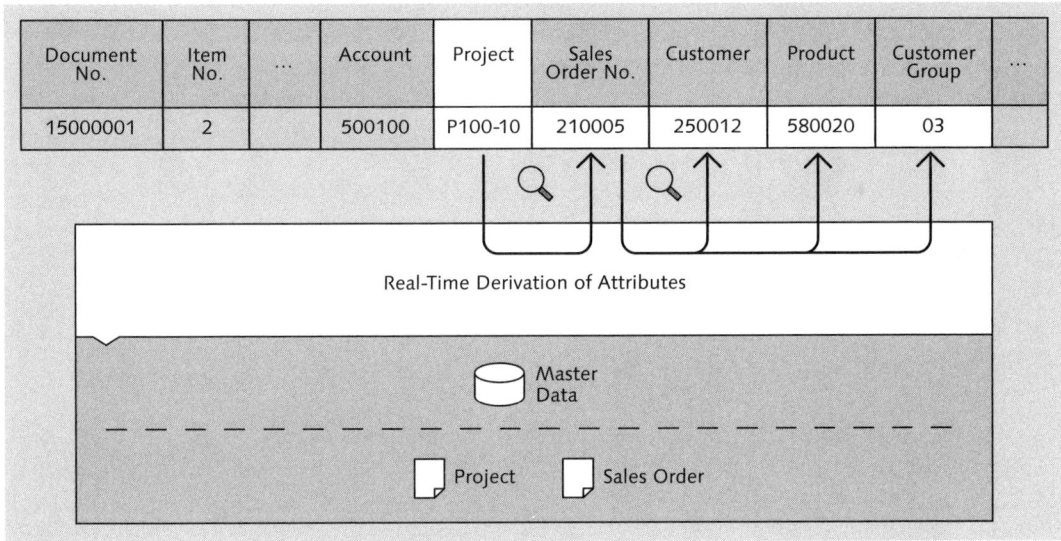

Figure 8.7 Real-Time Provisioning of Profitability Attributes

In general, you derive profitability characteristics at the point in time of primary postings for each P&L line item. You can thereby follow a simple approach: Take all information that is available and known at that point in time. Of course, this also encompasses the use of customer-specific derivation rules and the corresponding posting of the respective profitability characteristics. In the example shown in Figure 8.7, the project P100-10 can be analyzed according to division and territory, for example.

8.3.3 New Analysis Patterns

There are also new and flexible options for analyzing costs. In classical CO, costs were analyzed specifically per cost object type. Companies had to run reports for cost object types such as cost centers, projects, or internal orders separately. With the Universal Journal, companies can now easily analyze costs for all cost object types together. This is shown on the left in Figure 8.8 with the example of air travel costs.

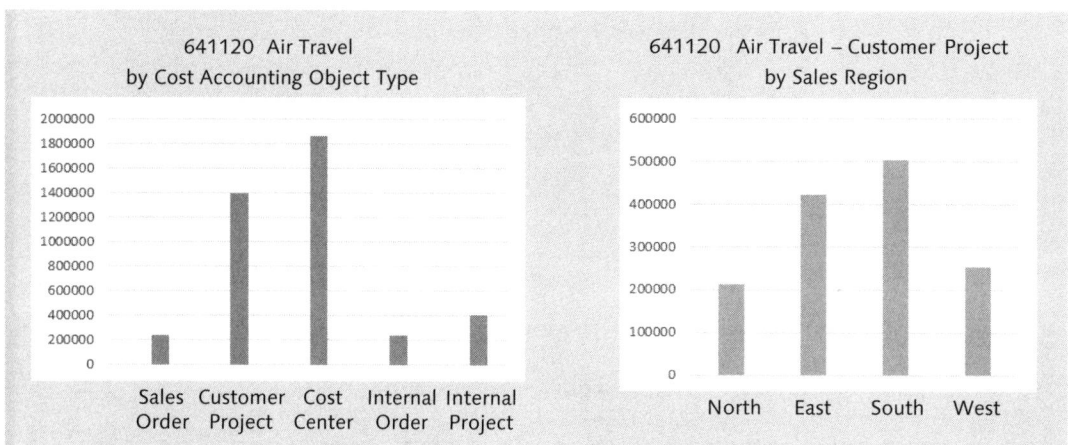

Figure 8.8 Examples for New Flexible Options in Cost Analysis

Account 641120 can be broken down to contributions of cost types such as sales order, customer project, or cost center. The further specific analysis of one dedicated cost type is also possible; on the right of Figure 8.8, you can see the analysis of air travel costs on customer projects according to sales regions (market segments). This kind of analysis can now be performed in real time without waiting for the closing process. (We'll take a closer look at reporting in the next chapter!)

8.3.4 Financial Statement Analysis

The Universal Journal also opens up totally new options and possibilities for analyzing the balance sheet. Users can drill down from each balance sheet position to natural objects such as fixed assets or materials, which wasn't possible before the Universal Journal.

However, the pinnacle is the flexible analysis of the P&L statement in real time. Using SAP HANA, the P&L statement can now be broken down according to any dimension available in the Universal Journal (see Chapter 9 for more details on available dimensions).

Figure 8.9 illustrates a deep dive on market segments that displays customer and product dimensions for each line of the P&L statement. Remember that SAP customers can define these dimensions themselves; they should be derived as early as possible in the business processes. This fundamental capability is already game changing, because it allows real-time analysis at any point in time. The cherry on top is the perfect fit of the P&L statement to any profitability report without a need for any reconciliation.

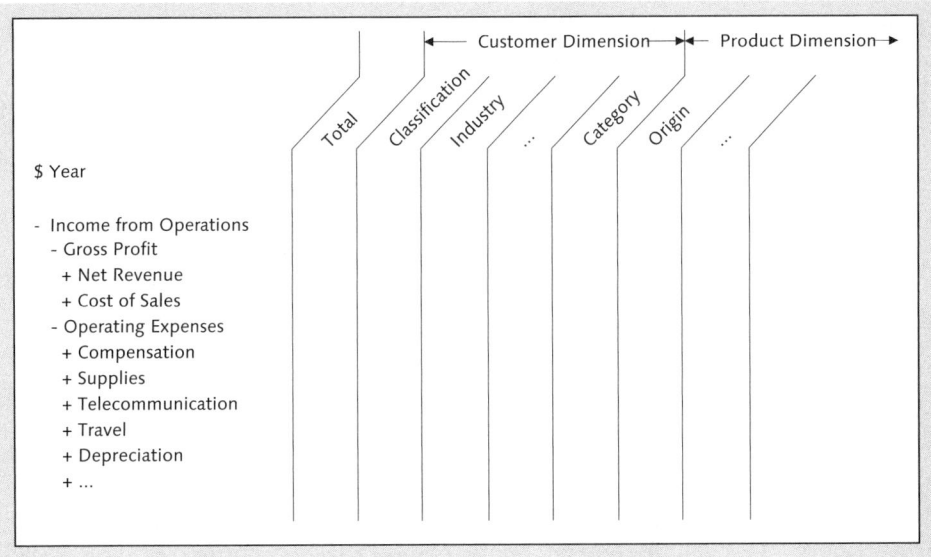

Figure 8.9 P&L Statement with Embedded Market Segment Analysis

As another significant benefit, the new structure includes built-in extensibility capabilities. In the era of totals records, extending structures with customer-specific fields was cumbersome and very limited, especially with regard to using the customer fields in reports or processes. Technically, extending the data structure for totals was very difficult to master, because it meant extending the key. Now, only one line item table has to be extended. The Universal Journal makes it much easier for companies to perform this process consistently for all accounting components.

So far, we have demonstrated that the Universal Journal immediately delivers highly relevant and reconciled information for managers and decision makers much earlier and in much better quality than ever before, both in the P&L/profitability and the balance sheet types of reporting. The Universal Journal also lays the foundation for additional improvements in the future, as we'll now explain.

8.4 Building on Top of the Universal Journal

In this section, we describe "ideas from the lab" based on the Universal Journal. Although the Universal Journal itself is already groundbreaking, the innovation potential on top is huge as well. Remember that we can't make any promises that these possibilities will come to fruition, but we can get an idea of what would make for increasingly powerful financials capabilities.

8.4.1 Fundamental Functional Enhancements

We showed in Section 8.1 that currency handling has been slightly different in the respective components. The G/L, for instance, currently supports three parallel currencies, whereas CO can handle only two. From the structural perspective of the data model, the Universal Journal harmonizes the currency handling in the different components. However, companies expect more flexibility in currency handling. The road is now paved toward a third currency in CO and, if needed, a fourth currency in all components.

The Universal Journal implements the ledger approach as known from the G/L in order to handle the widespread wish of companies to simultaneously post different valuations (e.g., US GAAP next to IFRS, local, or statutory valuation). However, it is not sufficient to have the ledger criterion as a column in the database;

it also needs to be integrated into the business processes. SAP S/4HANA Finance already takes the first fundamental step by implementing the ledger in CO transactions such as Transaction KB11N. By taking this further in the future, all processes can take advantage of the ledger concept. Imagine a system in which, for example, all essential closing processes could handle different valuation scenarios posting into different ledgers. This would give companies a lot of additional flexibility and eliminate costly auxiliary calculation in Microsoft Excel. Therefore, achieving full and seamless parallel valuation capability in all components has to be the target.

8.4.2 Important Simplification Cases

Bringing FI and CO closer together makes more simplification possible.

For example, today the different components have their own individual allocation solutions. This challenges companies to figure out which allocation to run for which purpose and in which sequence. Moreover, there are functional differences: The allocation in G/L is not able to run cross-company, but the allocation in CO is. G/L allocation can run on customer-added fields, but the CO allocation can't. G/L allocation supports parallel ledgers, but CO only does so indirectly and not completely (using delta versions). The goal is to have one single allocation solution that serves both the needs of CO and G/L and unifies the advantages of the currently different solutions into one single solution. The Universal Journal is the foundation for this development.

Statistical key figures are another example, because they are defined with individual and different transactions in G/L and CO. Again, based on the Universal Journal, we can harmonize and simplify the definition of these key figures.

8.4.3 Prediction Based on Facts

Let's close by describing a big vision: the prediction of a P&L statement not only based on extrapolation or other mathematical algorithms but based on facts—facts that are *already available in the system* and could be used as the basis for predictions. The Universal Journal gets us closer to this vision, because its integration of components lays the foundation for such predictions across financial processes.

Today, financial accounting and management accounting systems mirror the past of a company. The main reason for this is the fundamental historical purpose of financial systems: to produce a legal balance sheet and a legal P&L. As a consequence, accounting today becomes aware of a business transaction usually only at the point in time when legal regulations enforce its recording.

In a sales process today, for example, accounting receives process data for the first time only when the invoice is entered, but not before, such as during the negotiations or contract completion. The invoice posting and, in turn, notification of accounting happen quite late in the course of the business process, but insight for the financial business is not available until even much later. A system usually requires the period-end closing activity of revenue recognition in order to show the correct revenues and expenses in the P&L. Revenue recognition is required by law, because certain conditions (such as delivery of a good or service) have to be fulfilled before a company can recognize the respective revenue. Moreover, additional steps, such as settlement, are required to derive the correct market segment or business area for presentation in an analytical report.

Today's managers need and could have much more: true real-time insight not only into the past but also into the future. Many workarounds are available to fulfill the CFO's wish for an outlook of the upcoming quarter. For example, many companies currently analyze the sales pipeline and the incoming orders in order to get a forecast of revenue at period end. This manual prediction of revenue has to consider revenue recognition as well, because an order entry in, for example, September does not automatically lead to revenue in September. Projects in professional services usually generate revenues according to the percentage of completion method. Long-lasting contracts leading to a constant stream of revenues are becoming more important as well—for example, in subscription-based cloud services. The manual collection of revenues may work for a limited number of objects and for simple cases that are not impacted by revenue recognition, but for real mass data in larger companies users do not see this as a viable option, because collecting the information by hand would require too much effort and lead to inaccurate results. If the business also requires complex revenue recognition processes by law, then companies find themselves in a situation just like the one witnessed by a particular company, the manager of which said, "We are steering blind during the posting period."

Let's look at an example to illustrate the principal idea of prediction based on facts. Companies know the lifecycle of a sales order in their processes very well.

A typical process proceeds along the steps of order entry, order fulfilment—for instance, reflected via time confirmation on the customer project behind the sales order—invoice, and revenue recognition until payment. What if you could use this common knowledge to anticipate the effect of a sales order on the financial books and immediately get the insight that you need—long before the actual entries hit the books?

The technical idea would be simple: once the sales order is entered into the system, you would anticipate and already "post" the whole process chain, including virtual *prediction journal entries*. Figure 8.10 shows a simplified example of such a visionary process chain with anticipated invoice, anticipated revenue recognition, and anticipated payment.

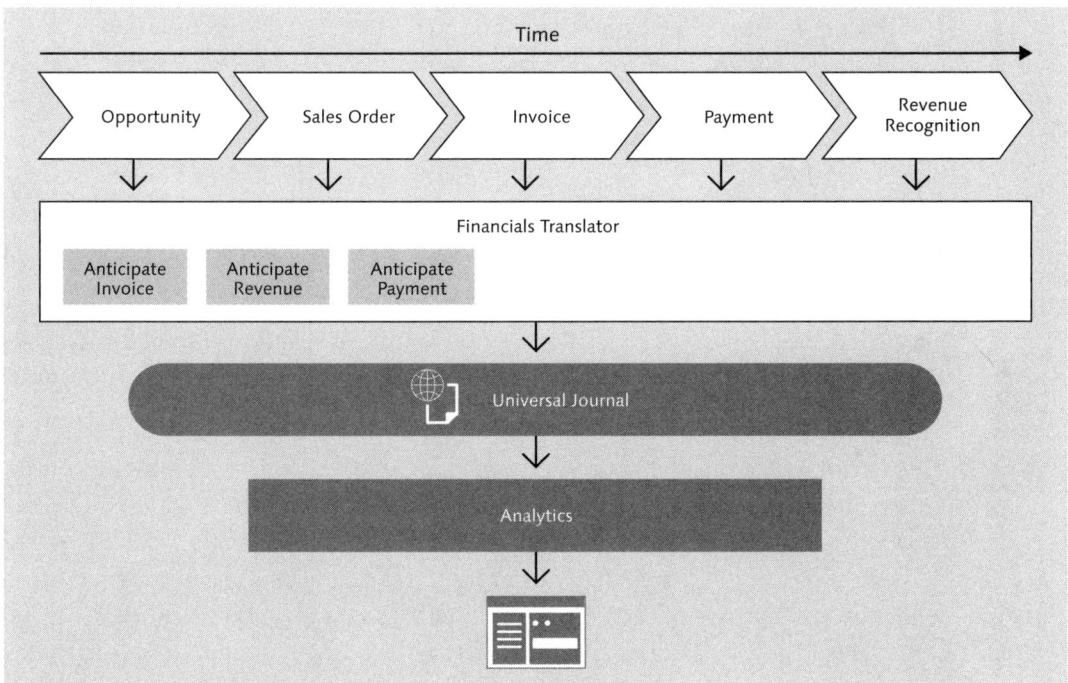

Figure 8.10 Creation of Prediction Journal Entries Based on Real Data

As the machinery to prepare actual journal entries, the Financials Translator would be extended in order to produce prediction journal entries for invoice, revenue recognition, and payment. In structure, the predicted journal entries would be compatible with the Universal Journal entries, but marked as "predicted" to differentiate them from actual postings. Because accounting analytics as a whole is based on the Universal Journal, this approach would have an immense advantage. The predicted information would be immediately available for use in all accounting reports as well—in other words, not only in the P&L, but also in profit center reporting, profitability reporting, and all others. Of course, the prediction journal entries would follow basic rules of actual journal entries (such as zero balance of the line items) and use the same methodologies for deriving important characteristics (such as profit center) automatically and seamlessly, without any user effort.

To have meaningful reporting, you would have to post the anticipated journal entries (the prediction journal entries) with the correct chronological sequence and timing. By analyzing historical data, SAP HANA can tell you the typical time lag between order entry, invoicing, revenue recognition, and payment. To have the best possible insight in your P&L statement, the prediction journal entries would follow along with the progress of the process chain. In this example, the posting of the customer invoice would refresh the prediction data created by the order, triggering the current revenue recognition rules and an adjustment to the anticipated payment. The actual payment would finally supersede the anticipated payment.

Because companies want to anticipate the future, prediction journal entries created for past periods could be aged quite soon, keeping the memory footprint under control.

This example described a simplified process chain that starts with a sales order. Other objects, such as sales contracts or sales opportunities, would be treated similarly. Process reality is often more complex—for example, due to partial deliveries or complex revenue recognition mechanisms. The existing posting logic that creates the "real" actual journal entries already handles all these deviations from the straightforward case for actual postings. By applying exactly this logic for the prediction, it would be possible to handle complex cases as well.

As a consequence of this idea, the P&L statement could be evolved to visualize the past, the present, and future of the whole company.

In the visionary example illustrated in Figure 8.11, management has a clear view on already-fixed revenues of the analyzed period (the REVENUES column). The revenue based on incoming orders and orders at hand is pretty certain, but revenue contributions resulting from opportunities and quotations (the PIPELINE and QUOTED columns) are less reliable. For analysis purposes, a drilldown to the individual opportunity would be possible thanks to the Universal Journal. Moreover, the columns of the P&L statement are now available for any market segment, showing their contribution to the company's overall performance. In this example, the ORDERS AT HAND column could be explored for detailed information along the Customer Group, ABC Classification, and Industry dimensions.

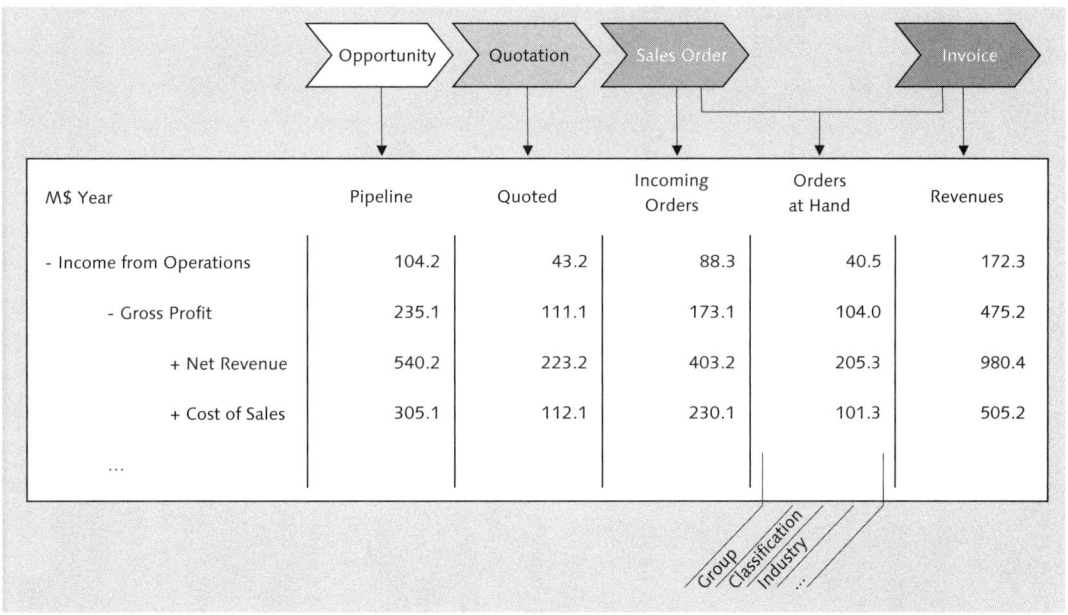

Figure 8.11 P&L Statement as Focal Point for the Company Performance in Past, Present, and Future

Financial statement notes are another interesting use case for prediction journal entries. In these notes, companies have to present a future-oriented assessment of the company's financial condition that is true and fair. We believe that a future-oriented P&L statement would allow companies to produce notes more accurately and with less effort. Even if the future deviated from the statements made in the notes, companies could easily argue on a fact basis. This is highly relevant for ensuring compliance.

In this section, we described a fundamental new type of application that would expand accounting from a purely backward-looking system into an application that looks forward as well. The Universal Journal as the new architectural foundation delivers the needed structuring of the data and reconciliation-free insight, and SAP HANA delivers the needed speed. As we've already seen, the Universal Journal already provides companies with tremendous effort savings and entirely new insights, providing decision support at its best without artificial boundaries. In the future, its importance will grow even more.

In the next chapters, we describe in more detail the new capabilities and options in reporting and analytics based on the Universal Journal that SAP S/4HANA Finance offers today.

This chapter shows how the change in the way transactional data is stored in the Universal Journal with SAP S/4HANA Finance makes it possible to change the paradigms behind legal and management reporting. We highlight how companies receive the flexible reporting they need.

9   Flexible Reporting

The Universal Journal provides the raw data for operational reporting, but SAP S/4HANA Finance offers new capabilities for reporting on top of the Universal Journal. To introduce these new capabilities, we will start the chapter with the reports that every project delivers as part of the first implementation: the financial statements, basic asset and inventory reporting, and basic management reporting. (Understanding how to get to these reports will also show how SAP S/4HANA Finance offers innovation without disruption!) With SAP S/4HANA Finance, you still have financial statements, basic asset reports, and so on as before, thanks to the compatibility views that select data according to the fields in the old aggregate tables—but you also have the option of getting far greater insight from what is essentially the same raw data: the fields that were available in the line items but not in the aggregates.

To understand this switch, consider the P&L statement. We are all used to seeing an account structure grouped by company code, perhaps with the option to drill down by segment, profit center, or functional area. Now, imagine that instead of only seeing such a broad P&L statement, you could focus on each of the account groups in turn and understand the business transactions behind the values shown on those accounts.

You might start by selecting a group of salary accounts and pulling in the cost centers for the employees for whom these salaries were paid or by looking at a group of material accounts and pulling in the projects and orders for which these materials were procured. This would show you which parts of your organization were responsible for certain spend categories. Imagine being able to select a group of revenue accounts and viewing the regions, products, and customers behind these postings. This would show you which parts of your organization were responsible for generating revenues.

Although we have had this information in the past, companies had to look for it across components. For example, to understand the details behind revenues, you had to choose a report in Profitability Analysis; to understand costs, a report in Cost Center Accounting; and so on. Now, one report can take you from the aggregated P&L statement showing the financial health of the company as a whole to a deep dive that shows which regions are spending heavily and which are earning high revenues. If you pull in the planned costs for these items, then you will start to understand where you are meeting your targets and where you have a challenge.

Of course, there's more to it than integration. The salary costs, for example, don't generally remain salary costs but are charged in the form of allocations, building up sender–receiver relationships in which the cost centers are credited and, for example, the orders or projects debited while costs flow through the organization. Thanks to the design change whereby secondary cost elements are treated as part of the chart of the accounts (see Chapter 8), the new reports include these postings, so you'll be able to track how overhead costs are gradually converted to cost of goods sold or assets under construction. In the past, organizations remained in the dark until period close, when order and project settlement moved overhead costs to the appropriate part of the balance sheet.

We'll now look at the current challenges in operational reporting and how SAP S/4HANA Finance provides a host of new options. We'll look at changes to our understanding of accounts, how to group accounts, cost centers, and profit centers, and what this all means from an end user perspective.

9.1 The Challenge of Flexible Operational Reporting Needs

Everybody who has used SAP ERP Financials has worked with a financial statement report like the one shown in Figure 9.1. It shows the accounts structured by the groups in the financial statement structure.

Such a report is the heart and soul of financial reporting and won't disappear. Compatibility views on the old totals tables (see Chapter 3 and Chapter 4) will ensure that no matter what version of this report your organization is currently using, you will still see the same data in these reports as before. The challenge with a report like this is that it shows highly aggregated data, giving you a good overview but not much insight into what business events drive the various postings.

Financial Statement Item/Account	Tot.rpt.pr	tot.cmp.pr	Abs. diff.
ASSETS	10.839.394,95	9.569.821,16	1.269.573,79
Fixed assets	2.836.625,00	1.587.625,00	1.249.000,00
Current assets	8.002.769,95	7.982.196,16	20.573,79
LIABILITIES	10.839.394,95-	9.569.821,16-	1.269.573,79-
Capital and reserves	2.399.326,87-	2.498.638,40-	99.311,53
Provisions	100.000,00-	100.000,00-	0,00
Payables	8.340.068,08-	6.971.182,76-	1.368.885,32-
Profit and loss statement	1.323.381,01	1.115.250,00	208.131,01
Sales revenues	9.166,50-	0,00	9.166,50-
Other operating income	416,03-	0,00	416,03-
Raw materials and consumables	6.170,14	0,00	6.170,14
Depreciation	0,00	152.531,00	152.531,00-
Other operating charges	1.326.793,40	962.719,00	364.074,40
Financial statement usage	130.578,01-	51.017,00	181.595,01-
Balance-sheet loss carried	1.174.332,60	875.695,60	298.637,00
Profit from profit and loss	1.304.910,61-	824.678,60-	480.232,01-
Accounts not assigned	2.254.237,48-	1.873.317,00-	380.920,48-
Supplement	1.192.803,00-	1.166.267,00-	26.536,00-

Figure 9.1 Financial Statements Report from SAP ERP Financials

In this context, we have to think about potential drilldown options. If you were using the G/L, then it was already possible to take this same report and drill down by segment, profit center, functional area, and so on without navigating to a different report. Of course, you could have extended the G/L to include further dimensions in this table, but due to the technical limitations outlined in Chapter 8 most organizations would not have added more than a handful of custom fields. If you only used cost centers, then it made sense to activate the cost center scenario for the G/L.

In previous releases, this required building your own reports to look at the costs by cost center. More often than not, organizations wouldn't go down that track at all, because they also use orders, work breakdown structure (WBS) elements, business processes, and so on to collect costs, and these weren't available as G/L scenarios. Instead, they would report in the Controlling module, thereby moving into a different world in terms of the types of reports offered and the granularity of the information available. Figure 9.2 shows a classic cost center report displaying the following costs:

- Costs that were posted directly to the cost center (salaries, buildings, insurance, etc.)
- Costs that this cost center received from other cost centers (cafeteria, telephones, etc.)
- Costs that it charged to other cost centers in the form of an allocation for corporate service costs

This is typical of the object-focused reporting we typically know in Controlling, in which the assumption is that one manager is responsible for all costs on his cost center.

Cost centers: actual/plan/variance				
Cost Center/Group: 1000 — Corporate Services				
Person responsible: Pfaehler				
Reporting period: 1 to 1 2013				
Cost elements	Act.costs	Plan costs	Abs. var.	Var. (%)
430000 Salaries	63.430,11	13.785,10	49.645,01	360,14
431900 Holiday premium				
435000 Annual Bonus				
440000 Legal social expens	3.813,29	3.932,85	119,56-	3,04-
440100 Soc. secur., salary	9.259,06		9.259,06	
449000 Other pers. costs	51,55	53,17	1,62-	3,05-
451000 Building maintenanc	2.137,60	2.141,03	3,43-	0,16-
466000 Insurance expenses	622,78	642,31	19,53-	3,04-
470000 Occupancy costs	2.515,80	2.569,24	53,44-	2,08-
471000 Machinery rental	2.075,94	2.141,03	65,09-	3,04-
473000 Postage	1.794,36	1.926,93	132,57-	6,88-
476000 Office supplies	1.594,99	1.712,83	117,84-	6,88-
476100 Data proc. material	488,36	513,85	25,49-	4,96-
476500 Misc. admin. costs	863,26	856,41	6,85	0,80
476900 Miscellaneous costs	513,03	513,85	0,82-	0,16-
481000 Cost-acctg deprec.	38.016,00	45.860,96	7.844,96-	17,11-
483000 Imputed interest	5.385,00	90.434,75	85.049,75-	94,05-
618000 DAA IT Development		619,47	619,47-	100,00-
633000 IAA Canteen	397,71	397,71		
634000 IAA Telephone Units	18,87	9,43	9,44	100,11
635000 IAA Telephones	142,30	142,30		
636000 IAA Vehicle Admin.	62,54	31,27	31,27	100,00
637000 IAA Human Resources	1.172,35	1.172,35		
* Debit	109.260,94	175.503,23	66.242,29-	37,74-
632000 IAA Corporate Serv.	175.596,72-	175.596,72-		
* Credit	175.596,72-	175.596,72-		
** Over/underabsorption	66.335,78-	93,49-	66.242,29-	70.854,95

Figure 9.2 Cost Center Report in SAP ERP Financials

The working assumption behind this kind of report is that when the cost center manager notices an anomaly—for example, that actual costs that are hugely different from planned costs—then he will select the offending line and navigate to the relevant line items to understand what exactly has been going wrong. Essentially, what he does here is leave the report and navigate to another one via a report–report interface. We have all been conditioned to do this, because the totals records only contain a handful of fields (the cost center, the cost element, the period, etc.).

The challenge with such reports is that in order to see the materials that were ordered, the employee submitting travel expenses, or indeed most of the detail that tells a manager what really happened, the manager has to navigate away from the overview report and down into the line items without fine-grained control of the filter criteria due to the coarse-grained overview report. This leads to the risk that he will be overwhelmed by the sheer number of detailed line items, not all of them relevant to his cause.

More to the point, a report like this forces a manager to think in period blocks. If he is looking at orders or projects that often exist over multiple periods, then he has to be careful about the time frame he selects, because orders and projects rarely fit neatly into the year viewed in P&L statements, and it is easy to start comparing apples with pears if you have orders and projects that run over several years.

The financial statements and the cost center report thus outlined represent business as usual. Let's turn our attention to how operational reporting changes with SAP S/4HANA Finance and solves the challenges and information needs mentioned so far, thanks to the new possibilities from SAP HANA and the Universal Journal.

9.2 Addressing Challenges Using SAP S/4HANA Finance

Let's now look at a P&L statement in SAP S/4HANA Finance to understand what we mean by drill down.

Figure 9.3 shows a P&L statement broken down by accounts—essentially a more modern UI used for the example we looked at in Figure 9.1. The difference lies in the NAVIGATION PANEL button in the top-left corner of the screen and its associated panel, which takes us into a new world in which drilling down no longer means navigating through a set of prebuilt aggregates or to the other report that contains the data that the manager is really interested in. Instead, we have the option to access many of the fields in the Universal Journal entries. We can start to understand, line by line, what transactions are driving business forward.

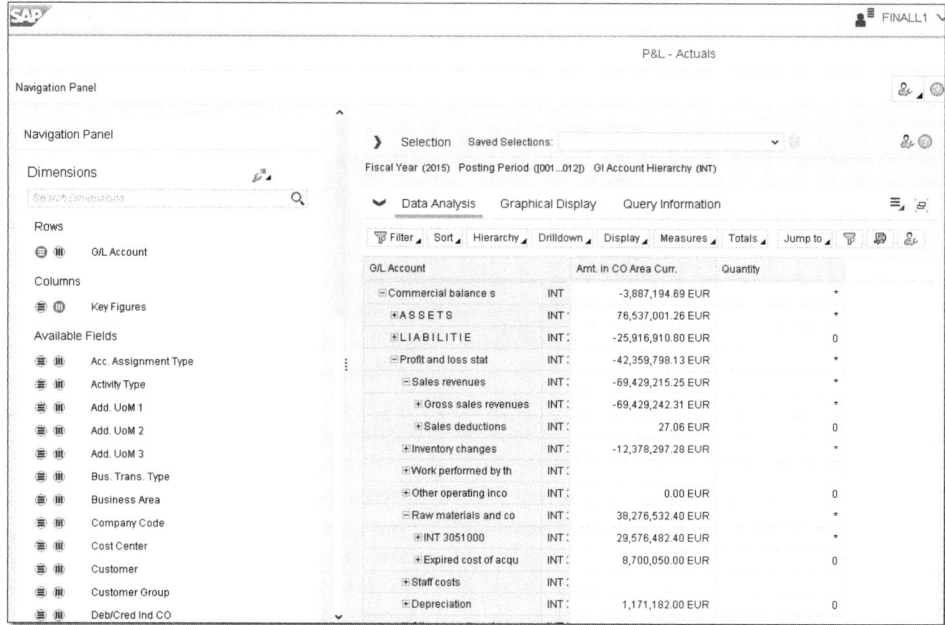

Figure 9.3 Income Statement in SAP S/4HANA Finance

To illustrate what we mean by this change, let's drill down to look at the revenues by material group. Instead of navigating to a different report, scroll down to the field labeled MATERIAL GROUP under AVAILABLE FIELDS and select the icon showing three parallel lines to the left of the MATERIAL GROUP field. This changes the number of lines shown in the report, giving a line for each of the material groups for which revenues have been recorded as shown in Figure 9.4. You'll notice that the column MATERIAL GROUP is empty for the account groups ASSETS and LIABILITIES. This is because the material group is an income statement dimension and is captured for the sales and cost of goods sold lines using the characteristic derivation functions in Profitability Analysis.

Now, remove the drilldown by material group and instead select a new dimension to show which cost centers are assigned to the RAW MATERIALS, STAFF COSTS, and DEPRECIATION accounts. Figure 9.5 shows the cost centers assigned to these accounts. You'll notice that there are some raw material costs that could not be

9.2 Addressing Challenges Using SAP S/4HANA Finance

assigned to cost centers. To see the account assignments for these costs here, you'll have to pull in a different field, such as WBS element or an order.

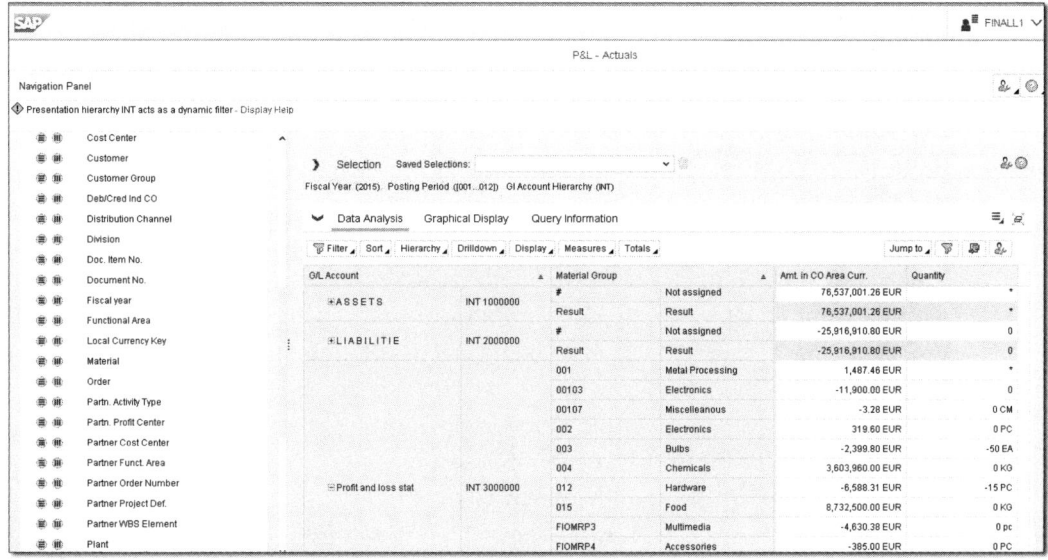

Figure 9.4 Income Statement with Drilldown by Material Group

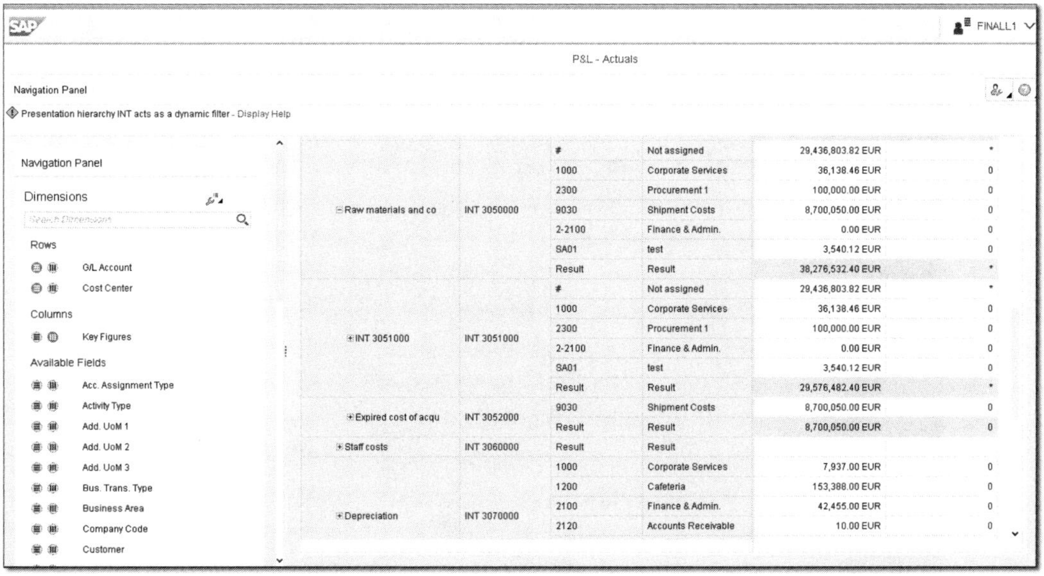

Figure 9.5 Drilldown of Income Statement by Cost Center

These are just a couple of examples of drilldowns. Figure 9.6 shows more of the drilldown options for the P&L statement. The G/L already offered some drilldown options (company code, functional area, business area, segment, profit center, and—with specific configuration—cost center), but drilling down always meant navigating through the dimensions of the materialized aggregates. Now, we are aggregating on the fly using the data in the Universal Journal. In the past, to see reporting dimensions that represent account assignments—cost centers, orders, projects, and WBS elements—you would have to navigate to separate reports, like the one in Figure 9.2 or the equivalent reports for orders and projects. Matching totals on the cost centers and in the G/L was usually relatively straightforward, but orders and WBS elements were tricky, because they often have a different periodicity than the income statement (very short orders in the food industry, longer orders in the automotive industry, and so on). Remember that SAP S/4HANA Finance still has dedicated order and project reports, but it now provides them directly as part of the P&L statement as well. Typically, costs captured on cost centers and orders do not remain there but are charged from cost centers to orders and from orders to profitability segments using allocations, settlements, and so on. This type of sender–receiver relationship is represented by partner relationships. Therefore, you'll notice the reporting dimensions partner activity type, partner cost center, and partner profit center at the bottom of the list so that you can trace the value flow of your costs from cost center to order (with an offsetting posting to the partner cost center) and from order to profitability segment (with an offsetting posting to the partner order).

Figure 9.6 also includes reporting dimensions, such as customer, customer group, distribution channel, division, material, and material group, which allow you to view costs and revenues by dimensions where you would previously have had to choose a CO-PA report. Although CO-PA has long been able to deliver reports by region, product, customer, or whatever dimensions organizations have chosen to create, there has typically been a shift from an account-based model in cost center accounting and order and project accounting to a key figure–based model in Profitability Analysis, in which all accounts are assigned to key figures (value fields) in cost-based Profitability Analysis. We'll return to the mechanics of this shift in Chapter 11, Section 11.6. For now, know that this switch in taxonomy makes it even more difficult to reconcile revenues and costs in the G/L with revenues and costs in Profitability Analysis. In SAP S/4HANA Finance, cost-based CO-PA continues to exist for specific requirements, but otherwise the new paradigm is to use account-based CO-PA to ensure that the figures in the income statement can be broken down by whichever dimensions you have chosen to activate in your operating concern (typically product, customer, region, sales office, and so on).

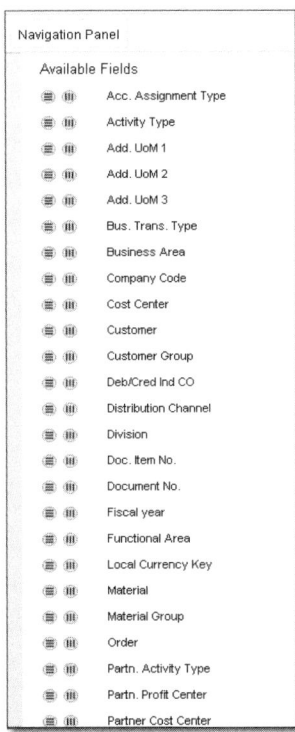

Figure 9.6 Income Statement with Drilldown Options

Finally, you'll notice partner objects bringing up the rear in Figure 9.6. These are available for reporting whenever you look at a sender–receiver relationship in which one cost object charges costs to another. This represents quite a radical change. In the early days of SAP ERP, such costs were stored in the reconciliation ledger and transferred to the G/L at period close. With the G/L, real-time integration created journal entries for these postings on a reconciliation account, but only with SAP S/4HANA Finance can you immediately see such postings as allocations for marketing costs, allocations for sales costs, and so on. There is no need to wait for period close to report on such transactions.

The P&L statement is just one example of how operational reporting is changing in SAP S/4HANA Finance. We'll now look at some of the other shifts that change the approach to reporting in SAP S/4HANA Finance.

9.3 Conceptual Advances in Reporting

As you start to bring together financial data that has long been kept apart, it's also important to consider the organizational structure of this data. Thanks to the Universal Journal, SAP S/4HANA Finance can overcome conceptual limitations of the past. The handling of entities relevant for organizing reporting has been enhanced to make the conceptual setup of reporting easier. We will look at the most important entities—namely, accounts and hierarchies—ahead.

Students starting out in Controlling learn that P&L accounts are primary cost elements and that whenever they need to document a cost flow they are working with secondary cost elements. SAP S/4HANA Finance removes this distinction that many consider unnatural, treating cost elements and accounts as one and the same. Working with hierarchies of accounts, cost centers, and other entities is now simpler because of this unification.

9.3.1 Merging of Accounts and Cost Elements

If you refer back to Figure 9.3, Figure 9.4, Figure 9.5, and Figure 9.6, you'll see that only the term account is used. The cost elements that structured the screen in Figure 9.2 are gone. As explained in Chapter 8, the chart of account maintenance has been extended behind the scenes to cover balance sheet accounts and three types of P&L account:

- P&L accounts with no reference to Controlling
- P&L accounts for postings to cost centers, orders, projects, CO-PA dimensions, and so on (formerly primary cost elements)
- P&L accounts to document cost flows from senders to receivers (formerly secondary cost elements)

This small change makes reporting much simpler: You don't need to set up a workflow to create a primary cost element whenever you create an account, and all cost flows in Controlling will automatically be included in the G/L, provided that you include the new accounts in your financial statement versions. This effectively supersedes the notion of real-time integration from the G/L and ensures that the value added represented by each time recording and order confirmation is immediately captured in the financial accounts.

9.3.2 Accounts and Other Hierarchies

You'll also notice that the reports in Figure 9.3 and Figure 9.6 use an account hierarchy. Organizations have always used financial statement versions, cost element groups, and so on to group related accounts for reporting purposes. The difference here is that we are using one structure to cover balance sheet accounts, P&L accounts, and what we formerly called cost elements. We now exclusively use the financial statement versions to structure accounts for reporting purposes. In previous iterations, the only structure available to achieve this same end was the account hierarchy in Profit Center Accounting, and organizations had to keep this structure in sync with their financial statement versions and cost element groups as accounts changed. In contrast, cost element groups remain in SAP S/4HANA Finance for your legacy reports and to control account selection for allocations and settlement, but the financial statement version becomes the account group of choice for reporting.

As you think of other hierarchies, such as cost center hierarchies and profit center hierarchies, remember that one of the challenges that organizations have struggled with in the past was having organizational structures in a constant state of flux. SAP S/4HANA Finance introduces new, simpler UIs to maintain these hierarchies, as shown in Figure 9.7. This makes it easier to search for existing hierarchies, copy and extend hierarchies, and create new ones.

One of the key functional enhancements offered with the new UI is the ability to copy an existing cost center or profit center group as an inactive hierarchy and then prepare for changes that you know are coming within your organization. When you are ready to release the changes, the system copies the inactive hierarchy into the table for the active hierarchy and makes the old hierarchy inactive. This can vastly reduce the number of hierarchy nodes that are available for selection in your applications, limiting availability to those that are active.

We've looked at the way the changes in the Universal Journal enable a new type of reporting that will primarily impact financials practitioners tasked with laying the foundation for reporting by setting up the organizing entities. Now let's look at what changes arise for the end user.

9 | Flexible Reporting

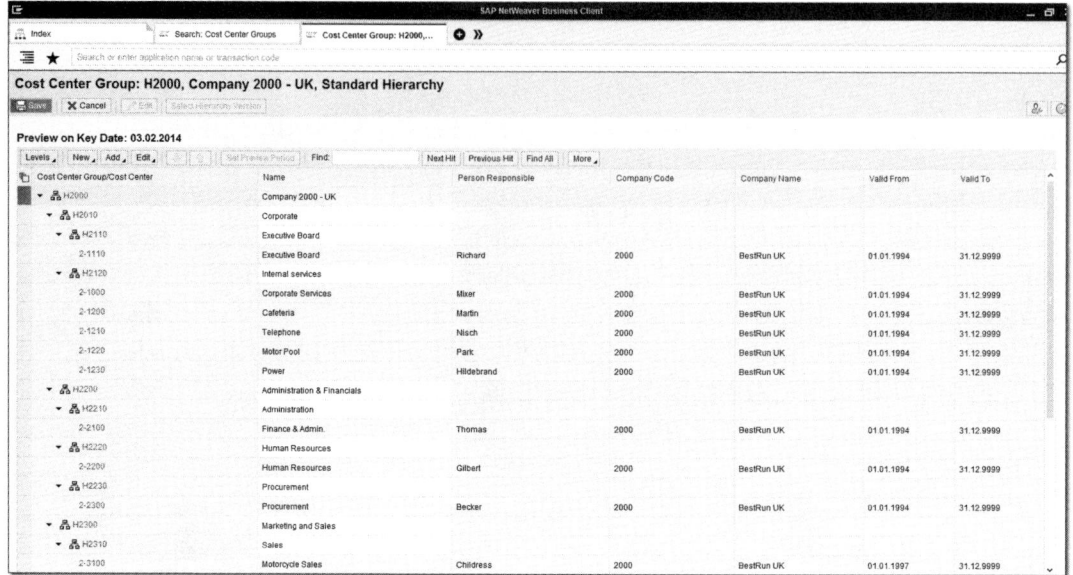

Figure 9.7 Cost Center Hierarchies in SAP S/4HANA Finance

9.4 Advances for End Users

As we will explain in Chapter 12, SAP Fiori is the umbrella term for the new UI of SAP S/4HANA Finance (and other SAP products).

Figure 9.8 shows My Spend, one of the first SAP Fiori applications. My Spend gives managers on the move access to their spending on a tablet or mobile device as well as on the more traditional desktop. Here, you can see the manager's spending grouped by cost center group, with the relative size of each box determined by the total spend for each cost center. To see the details, users click on the box to show the actual costs, the committed costs (for open purchase orders), and the budget. From there, users can access the details for each account group and finally navigate from there to the line items.

Alternatively, you can view the way different account groups are trending. At the beginning of the year, when little has been spent, you can switch to BUDGET to see the relative budget per cost center. Thanks to these features, the My Spend app gives managers with busy schedules full control over their spending at any time and enables them to react early.

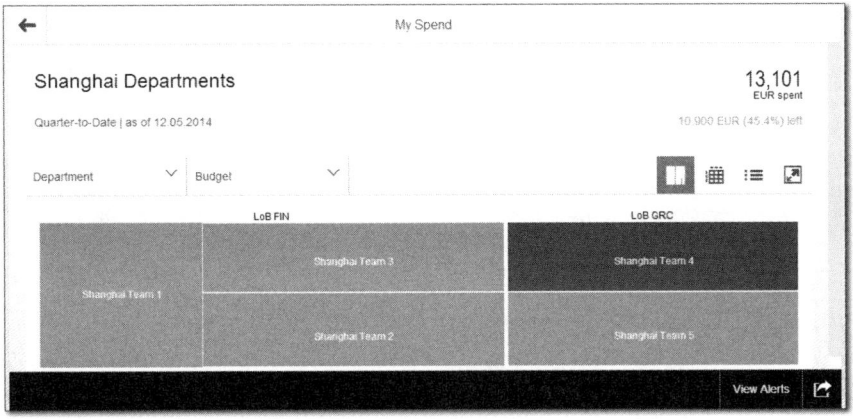

Figure 9.8 Operational Reporting for Managers on the Move: My Spend

Another paradigm shift in SAP S/4HANA Finance has been to redefine selection screens. Figure 9.9 shows the SAP Fiori version of the customer line items report. Notice the selection boxes across the top of the screen and the FILTER button next to the RESET button, which allow you to add more selection fields as required. The simple act of including the selection screen in the main screen of the report makes working with such a report much easier, because you no longer have to back out of the report to change the selection criteria.

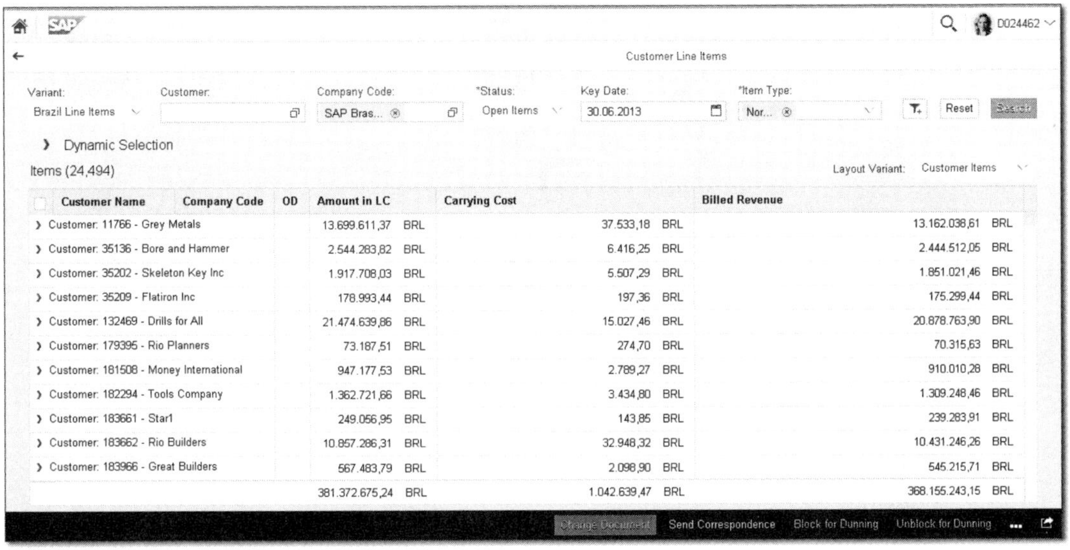

Figure 9.9 SAP Fiori App: Customer Line Items

As an example of how end users struggle today, consider Linda, the head of a kindergarten. The salaries for Linda's staff are assigned to cost centers, the state support for offering childcare in various age categories is assigned to projects, and she has a handful of orders for "other costs." She is an occasional user of SAP ERP and has neither the time nor the inclination to become an expert user. Because the costs for all of those objects are now available in one table, it is easy for Linda to build a simpler version of the report shown in Figure 9.3 that only contains drilldowns relevant to her role as the head of the kindergarten.

Now consider the audit requirements typical in the utilities industry. Utilities have huge volumes of fixed assets, with huge capital expenditures for assets under construction and vast spending on maintenance of these assets. Due to their reporting requirements, utility companies first need to pull together the orders and WBS elements that represent their capital investments on a group of assets. Then, they build lookup tables to link these items with the maintenance orders used to capture the costs of servicing these assets. With SAP S/4HANA Finance, the assets and the associated expenses simply come together, because there is no longer a distinction between modules in reporting.

Because orders and projects rarely fit neatly into reporting periods, any sort of lifecycle reporting becomes a challenge. It is even more of a challenge when the various orders have no relationship to one another. In the automotive industry, it is common to analyze the costs of producing cars alongside the costs of servicing the same vehicles. Production costs are managed on production orders and the service costs on service orders. Production orders and service orders have always had a similar data structure, but there was no link between the two, even though what companies *really* wanted to know was whether there was a correlation between the cost of servicing the car and of delivering the car initially. The production order completed on delivery of the car, and the service order completed on the return of the car to the customer. Such orders need to be tagged as belonging to the same production model or the same customer to make clear that the same car model is being produced and serviced, and then it becomes possible to look at the profitability of that car over its lifecycle, perhaps also including the initial development costs (also on orders or projects) in the equation in order to get an overview of the complete lifecycle.

In this chapter, we highlighted the flexible reporting capabilities that SAP S/4HANA Finance offers on top of the Universal Journal. You have seen how separate data structures and working with aggregates limited the scope of reporting in the past and how you can now easily start from the P&L statement and drill down according to many dimensions. You have examined one SAP Fiori application, and we'll return to this topic in Chapter 12.

We will now look at the mechanics behind the analytical applications in terms of the Core Data Services model that translates the raw data in the Universal Journal entries into information that can be consumed easily by a manager or business analyst.

In this chapter, we take a look at the Core Data Services–based embedded analytics capabilities of SAP S/4HANA Finance and how they address data managers' existing pain points with respect to analytics flexibility, ease of consumption, and extensibility.

10 Flexible Analytics with Core Data Services

In Chapter 2, we saw that SAP S/4HANA Finance follows the key paradigm of uniting both transactional and analytical data in a single SAP HANA database, effectively making data latency a thing of the past. This enables you to consolidate and combine data from disparate systems into a centralized database.

These fundamental shifts in enterprise data availability and governance create a unique opportunity. It is possible now to perform business analytics that meet the requirements shown in the right-hand column of Table 10.1.

Old Analytics Model	New Analytics Model
Use old data	Use real-time data
Access data in multiple places	Access single source of truth across systems
Use generic UI	Use role-specific UI
Perform transactions and analytics individually	Perform transactions and analytics simultaneously

Table 10.1 Transformation into Real-Time Analytics

In order to gain a competitive advantage in today's world, it is imperative that you have access to business insights into your data in real time. Having access to the full potential of your data enables you to make smarter decisions, react quicker to changes in the market, and accelerate or simply trigger new business models for the future. As we noted in the preceding chapters, the new, simpler data model of SAP S/4HANA Finance enables companies to record all relevant data in an integrated manner. This lays a good foundation for an analytics system that taps into the business benefits that can be derived from this opportunity.

In this chapter, we discuss such an analytical system that turns this opportunity into reality: the *virtual data model* (VDM), based on Core Data Services (CDS), which is a preconfigured, extensible data model. We start by describing the typical system landscape of an enterprise and the challenges it presents (Section 10.1) before moving on to CDS (Section 10.2) and its building blocks (Section 10.3). We conclude the chapter with a summarized look at the unified view on data that SAP S/4HANA Finance provides based on CDS as compared with other analytical tools (Section 10.4).

10.1 Replacing Complex Analytics with Simplicity

"Complex" is how most data managers would describe their analytics landscapes. Figure 10.1 depicts one such landscape, comprising a multitude of data sources spread across separate OLTP and OLAP systems. As a result of this complexity, each cross-application analytical information request by a business user accesses predefined aggregate formulations that stand in for the various underlying systems. Such a setup that uses predefined aggregates can be compared to a stovepipe, because you only receive a one-eyed view of the data.

This limitation results in the following issues:

- **Mountains of data in the system, not freely accessible**
  You only see what is offered to you through the prebuilt analytical data models. Any change to these data models is cumbersome.

- **Need to slice and dice data for every analysis**
  You do not receive ready-to-use natural data drilldowns with the prebuilt data models. For in-depth analysis, you must perform analytical operations such as slicing and dicing on the heavy result set.

- **Not-always-consistent analysis**
  A change in the system data landscape is not automatically reflected in the analytics data models, giving you incomplete information in certain cases. Also, the data model may not access all data sources in certain scenarios and may operate on older data.

Prebuilt aggregate models do provide role-based information, but in a complex manner. This makes the analytics exercise inflexible and time-consuming. What is needed instead is a flexible, extensible, easy-to-use analytics data model that turns around how systems look at data: from challenge to opportunity. The VDM based on CDS fits the bill.

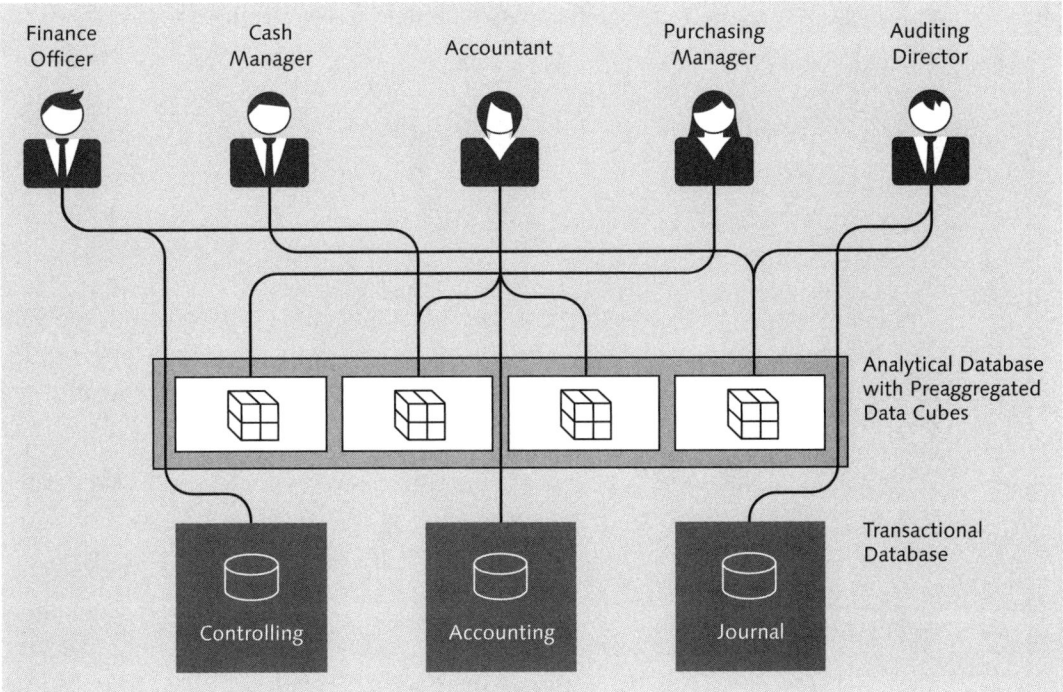

Figure 10.1 Typical Analytical IT Landscape of an Enterprise

10.2 Paradigms of Core Data Services in SAP S/4HANA

CDS is an out-of-the-box family of database languages that enables application developers to access SAP S/4HANA Finance data in a standardized manner.

CDS allows an application developer to enhance SAP S/4HANA Finance data for semantically rich data models, consumable directly in analytic applications. Specific analytic models can be developed based on CDS models delivered with SAP S/4HANA Finance for the most important analytic questions in finance areas such as financial operations or P&L statements. This leads to the following advantages:

- Improved productivity for analytics model development
- Higher consumability of data
- Better performance of analytical models
- Increased interoperability of analytics models across applications

CDS observes the following fundamental paradigms:

- Domain specificity, which is similar to conceptual thinking
- Declarativeness
- Extensibility
- Reflexiveness

These advantages enable you to connect your business processes with relevant data in a contextual manner. You now have the power to see the relevant information at the place where it needs to be used for your analytics purpose, not merely at its original source.

With CDS, you have the opportunity to define your own analytical data models based on the CDS models already available in SAP S/4HANA Finance and use them in combination with your transactional data via a common interface.

Thanks to the preconfigured semantic data model on top of the financial components, CDS let you tap into the potential of data that changes with high velocity. By using CDS, you get better business insights presented in an easy-to-consume, business-relevant manner.

This is a huge step forward toward ease of consumption for business users, because they no longer need to work with technical data structures and work out business semantics by themselves; instead, business users have a VDM with truly business-like semantics for their use.

Let's revisit the complex analytics landscape we saw in the last section and redefine it with CDS as the analytics platform, as shown in Figure 10.2. You now have an abstraction layer to shield business users from the technical complexity of underlying data sources. The result is an enterprise-wide view of your data through VDMs specific to business user roles. These data models carry meaningful business semantics, making it easy for users to understand and use the results with unprecedented performance. The entire data model is highly user-friendly and ready to be consumed or extended. Owing to the single source of truth concept, issues related to data duplication and inconsistencies are avoided.

Another advantage of combining analytics with transactions is that users now have a unified view of information backed by relevant context without having to go back and forth between various applications at different points in time. This setup provides a holistic vision across the entire business process, enabling users to interact with the system in real time.

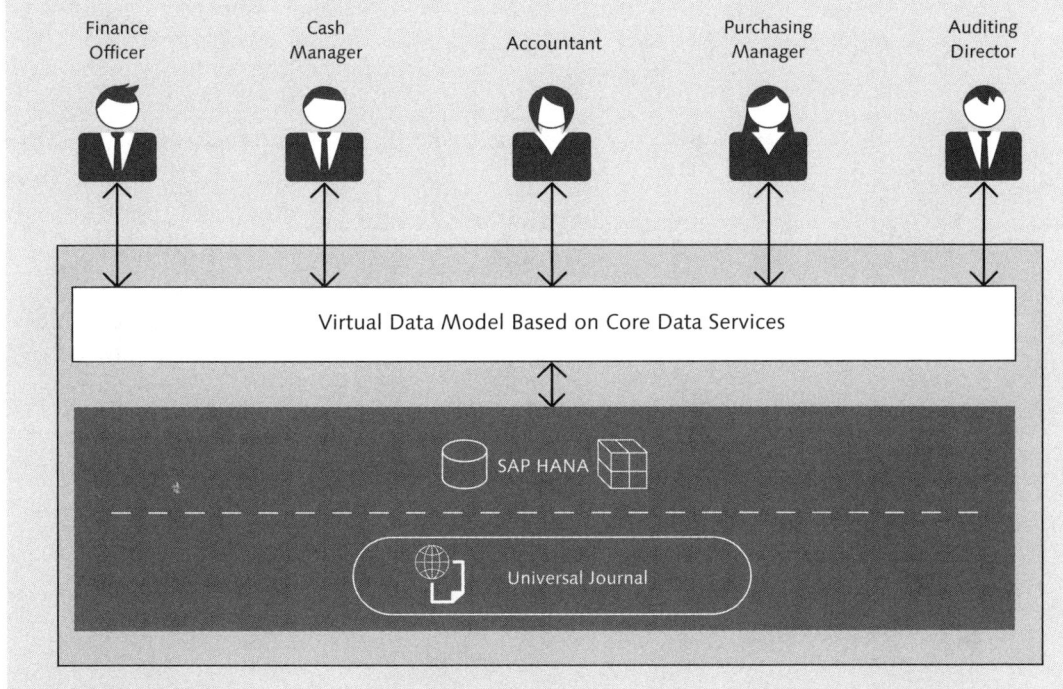

Figure 10.2 Simplified Analytical IT Landscape with CDS in SAP S/4HANA

Let's look at a real-world business example. Rachel is the purchasing manager at a global toy manufacturing company, vToyz. Fifteen days before the end of the current financial quarter, she knows that she has all the information she needs for the upcoming global quarterly financial review meeting, hosted by the CFO. One of the key pieces of information she is supposed to present is a reconciled view of the vendor invoices received without goods received, as well as the goods received without invoices received (GR/IR) for the quarter. Unlike in the past, when she had to fetch individual data points from vendor invoices and goods receipts and manually match them, she now uses the SAP Invoice and Goods Received Reconciliation data model from the VDM. For Rachel, managing and settling invoices was never so easy.

This VDM on top of the technical accounting data model helps her in the following ways:

- Presents a single-source of truth
- Shows a list of all open invoice items with an option to view them grouped by vendor, account, period, or value
- Matches currently unmatched open items from invoices to goods received
- Provides a mechanism to track progress of items with notes and status information
- Gives a deep dive into the historical purchasing data
- Lists contact details of respective business partners

As a result, Rachel not only can provide clear, consistent status reports to the stakeholders within the company, but also can derive the following business benefits:

- Fast and accurate invoice clearing
- Prevention of payment of incorrect invoices
- Availability of purchasing history for verifications

In the next section, we'll take a deeper look at what constitutes the CDS and VDM in SAP S/4HANA and what makes them easily consumable to technical and business users alike.

10.3 Building Blocks of Core Data Services in SAP S/4HANA

In this section, we will focus on the VDM in SAP S/4HANA based on CDS. CDS is a common set of domain-specific languages (DSLs) and services to define and consume VDMs in a contextual and semantic manner. CDS is available in two flavors with similar capabilities that differ mostly with regard to the underlying platform: SAP HANA CDS and ABAP-managed CDS. SAP HANA CDS is specific to SAP HANA, whereas ABAP-managed CDS views are handled by SAP NetWeaver and thus integrate with the data dictionary. Therefore, SAP S/4HANA employs ABAP-managed CDS. CDS comprises a family of such DSLs and services making up a coherent and common core data model.

The following are the two main languages of CDS:

- **Data definition language (DDL)**
  Using DDLs, you define semantically rich data models, which can be enhanced further using annotations. We will discuss the concept of annotations in this section.

- **Query language (QL)**
  QLs let you read data from the earlier defined data models in a coherent, efficient and convenient manner. You are also free to define further logical views on top of existing data models, thus adding even higher semantic abstraction.

The placement of these components in the overall data and application landscape is depicted in Figure 10.3.

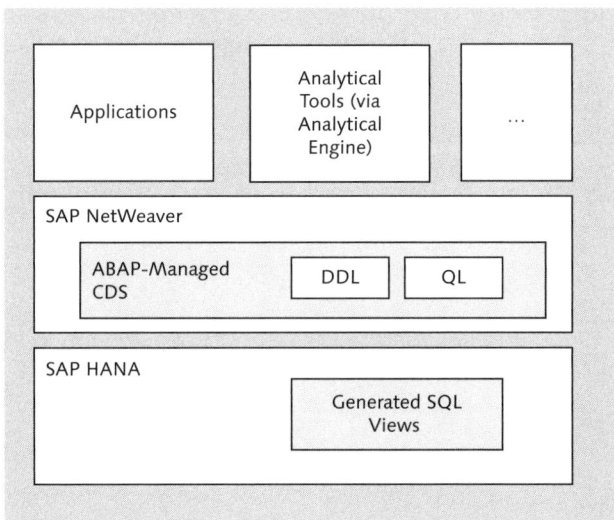

Figure 10.3 Positioning of CDS as Part of SAP S/4HANA

ABAP CDS is managed by SAP NetWeaver. Views defined in the DDL of ABAP CDS define data types and data models as part of the data dictionary. Those elements are consumed by applications in SAP S/4HANA, such as SAP Fiori apps. They are also accessible through an analytical engine for generic analytical tools.

On the database level, ABAP CDS supports any database—SAP HANA in the context of SAP S/4HANA. CDS views generate base views in plain SQL that represent the interface between database and upper layers and lead to a code pushdown to the database.

Let's take a deeper look at the DSLs, annotations, and overall VDMs.

10.3.1 Domain-Specific Database Languages and Services

Perhaps you're wondering why we even need DSLs. Can't everything be handled with plain SQL?

The answer is yes, every data fetch can be achieved with plain SQL. However, doing so can often become complex, far too technical, and miles away from business semantics. In most cases, the result is imperative SQL with loops within loop(s).

This is where DSLs come to the rescue. They help pull data modeling, retrieval, and subsequent processing closer to the conceptual thinking of domain experts such as finance managers by using the concepts of entities with structured types, semantic types, associations, annotations, and expressions.

In simple terms, the following steps apply:

1. Define business-like entities.
2. Define associations between these entities with possible parameters or aggregates.
3. Define further views on top of these associations if needed.
4. Perform calculations on these artifacts.
5. Query the now-defined model.

10.3.2 Use of Semantic Annotations

Annotations are typed records of metadata. Each annotation corresponds to a structure type and may have its own cardinality definition and other constraints. Once created, you assign these annotations to data model artifacts, such as an entity.

The use of annotations has the power to massively enrich data models by way of semantic references in real-world-like terms.

10.3.3 Virtual Data Model

The overall collection of entities enriched with associations and annotations forms the VDM. A VDM represents a harmonized and simplified data model with high business orientation. VDMs are easy to understand, directly consumable in transactional or analytical applications internally or externally, and are reusable and extensible by SAP, customers, and independent software vendors.

The data model views thus created are best designed as a layered set, with the following levels:

- **Interface views**
  These are prepackaged and ready to be consumed by applications or consumption views on top. They represent a stable, logically complete view of technical data structures that makes relevant business semantics visible.

- **Consumption views**
  These are built on top of interface views for a specific end-user application. They are domain-specific and use standardized notations.

These views are co-related via associations, which on the one hand eliminate the need for long lists of fields, and optimize the system performance significantly on the other.

Standardization of field names, through a global field catalog, makes consumption far easier.

The real power of SAP S/4HANA's CDS-based VDM comes from the fact that you can easily consume it to meet your specific requirements without disrupting the SAP-delivered content. All standard views follow consistent development guidelines, making it easy for you to comprehend and process them. Standardized naming of fields and views makes it easy to pick the right ones. For consumption, you can use standard technologies such as OData, openSQL, or standard SAP Fiori UIs. SAP S/4HANA's VDM is also easily extensible: On the level of individual views, you can add additional fields using CDS syntax. Furthermore, you can create and expose your own analytical views by building on top of the delivered CDS views.

10.4 Unified View of Data for Analytics

The CDS-based VDM in SAP S/4HANA presents a comprehensive and business-ready data model that offers the following benefits compared to other operational intelligence solutions:

- **Open**
  Access to SAP S/4HANA CDS is based on open standards and interfaces. You only need basic data modeling skills to be able to access data from the underlying data models and build on top of it. This provides the flexibility to create analytic applications specific to your requirements without being restricted to premodeled content.

- **Uniform**
  All data models of SAP S/4HANA follow a common approach. This makes it easy for you to comprehend all data models, including those that spread across more than one application.

- **Intuitive**
  Use of business-like semantics abstracts from the complexity and cross-references that exist within the underlying application-level data. As a result, you understand the data model more intuitively.

- **Fast**
  CDS pushes business semantics down to the database. Thus, it leverages the performance of SAP HANA, enabling you to analyze large volumes of data quickly.

- **Real time**
  Because all reporting happens on primary data (which is consistent by definition, thanks to the paradigm of a redundancy-free system), there is no need to wait until data has been loaded into a data warehouse. This saves any cycle time from recording to reporting. There is no additional data reconciliation effort.

Thanks to these benefits, companies can use SAP S/4HANA Finance and the CDS-based VDM for finance to build up their analysis suite. Ultimately, this allows companies to have a more detailed and flexible view of their business. In turn, they react more quickly and make better decisions, because they can analyze all data on the fly and, if required, even in a self-service approach.

SAP plans for the VDM to serve as the foundation for future analytics applications development. The goal is to provide a standardized and stable starting point and framework for companies and partners that use SAP S/4HANA Finance and to build analytical applications on top of it.

This chapter highlights applications and areas that provide significant improvements within SAP S/4HANA Finance. These areas cover the whole scope of financials, ranging from cash management to planning to compliance management. We briefly explain the value of each application.

11   SAP S/4HANA Finance Applications

So far in this book, we've covered the core functionalities of SAP S/4HANA Finance based on the simplification paradigms outlined in Part I. The Universal Journal and the flexible reporting capabilities it offers form the basis for a wide range of applications across the whole finance value map.

In this chapter, we look one by one at the most important new functionality that SAP S/4HANA Finance applications provide to make areas such as financial operations, cash management, business planning, or financial closing simpler. All of these areas benefit from the overall simplification and the groundbreaking Universal Journal; moreover, these improvements give companies using SAP S/4HANA Finance entirely new possibilities. Thus, these applications accompany the flexible analytical capabilities of SAP S/4HANA Finance.

Let's start by looking at business cockpits, which are a natural extension of analytics because they offer a comprehensive view of key figures.

11.1   Business Cockpits for Businesspeople

Get an overview of your business situation, gain insight into it, and start action on it: This is the use case of a business cockpit. Like the cockpit in an airplane for the pilot, a business cockpit gives businesspeople an overview of their companies' or departments' situation in one view, allows the further analysis of the situation, and then enables them to take action to avoid impediments and improve the situation. Managers starting their work in the morning by looking at the state of their areas or preparing for a quarterly board meeting are typical real-life situations in which cockpits are needed.

Typically, today's businesspeople have static reports prepared by controllers or assistants in a time-consuming process. The reports refer to a point in time in the past and have a fixed structure. An ad hoc request for a drilldown requires a further iteration through this process. A restructuring of the reporting often requires IT involvement. This is not a working mode suitable for the modern, volatile business world of an agile enterprise.

What businesspeople need instead is real-time analysis with up-to-date information and predictions for the future. A cockpit must support fast insight with adequate visuals. The business world requires ad hoc drilldown capabilities along unforeseen analytical paths. This requirement goes beyond numbers; correlations among different areas also have to be shown so that the root causes of problems and the impact of decisions are made transparent. Adaptation to new business situations must be possible within minutes or hours by businesspeople without time-consuming IT involvement. A business cockpit is expected to facilitate this kind of insight to action.

SAP S/4HANA Finance provides built-in analytics such as adaptable cockpits along with cockpits for various roles based on SAP Smart Business. With its fresh and simple UI design based on SAP Fiori, SAP Smart Business is easy to use on desktop and mobile. SAP Smart Business cockpits put the business department into the driver's seat when it comes to creating the cockpit the department needs. Business defines the relevant KPIs and business semantics within a tool environment that is easy for end users to work with. Thanks to the simplified data model of SAP S/4HANA Finance and the virtual data model of SAP S/4HANA based on Core Data Services (see Chapter 10), this process is simpler than ever before without requiring huge data federation and integration projects upfront. The Universal Journal guarantees consistency and flexible drilldowns across FI and CO. With SAP HANA as the database, the cockpit displays all KPIs at high speed and based on real-time data. The cockpit also offers suitable collaboration functionality for discussing the company's situation (displayed in the cockpit) and for taking further actions. Simulation and prediction for decision making are on the roadmap to be added to the solution.

Let's look in more detail at what SAP Smart Business cockpits provide to address typical use cases. The next section looks at a typical scenario supported by a cockpit.

After that, we outline how SAP S/4HANA Finance makes it easy for businesspeople to define and adapt their cockpits. We'll conclude with an outlook on upcoming improvements.

11.1.1 Working with Business Cockpits

Let's walk through an example of the typical use of a business cockpit to get insight into an organization's data.

One morning in October 2015, Mary, the CFO of Candies United, sees the screen shown in Figure 11.1 on her tablet.

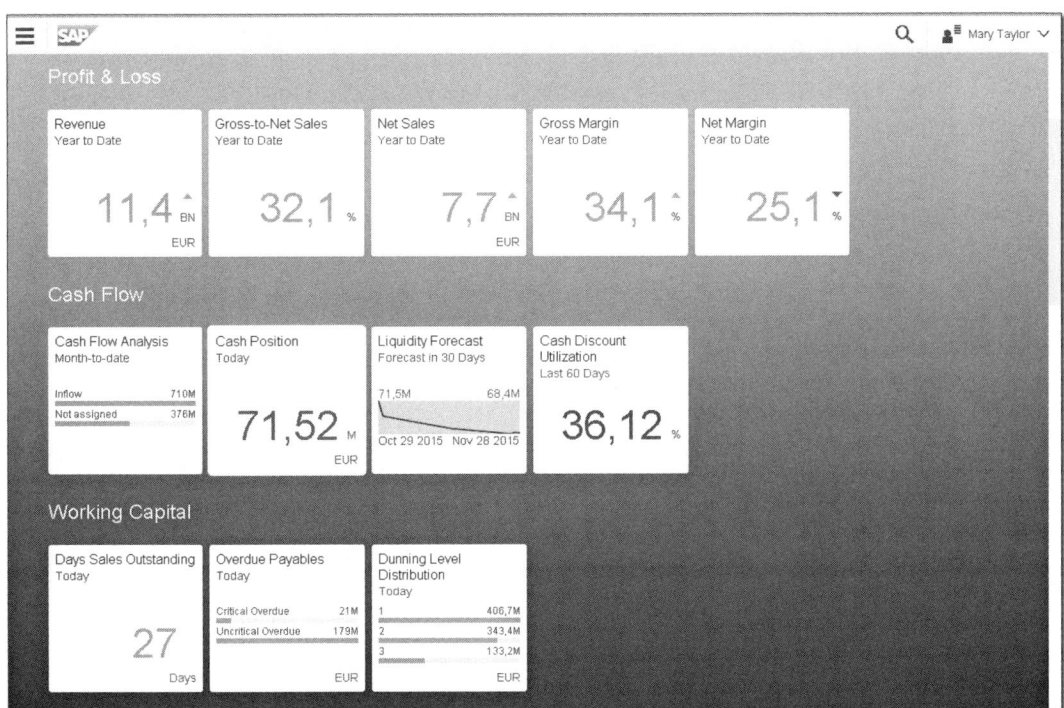

Figure 11.1 SAP Fiori Launchpad with SAP Smart Business KPI Tiles for CFO

With one glance at her screen, Mary sees the most important information about the financial situation of Candies United, presented in an easy-to-consume manner. Beyond delivering pure information, the cockpit directs Mary's attention to points of interests, such as deviations, and to issues that require attention, such as

199

the red net margin of cash discount utilization. After skimming over the rest, which seems to match her expectations, Mary decides to focus on the net margin for now and clicks on the NET MARGIN tile to open a time series analysis, as shown in the top right of Figure 11.2.

Based on this overview, Mary analyzes further by looking at particular aspects through filtering or drilldown. Filtering allows Mary to focus all actions on a certain business area, such as a product group or a certain customer. Drilldowns (e.g., for time, product, customer, geography, or organization) allow her to examine details in order to find the root cause and single events impacting the business.

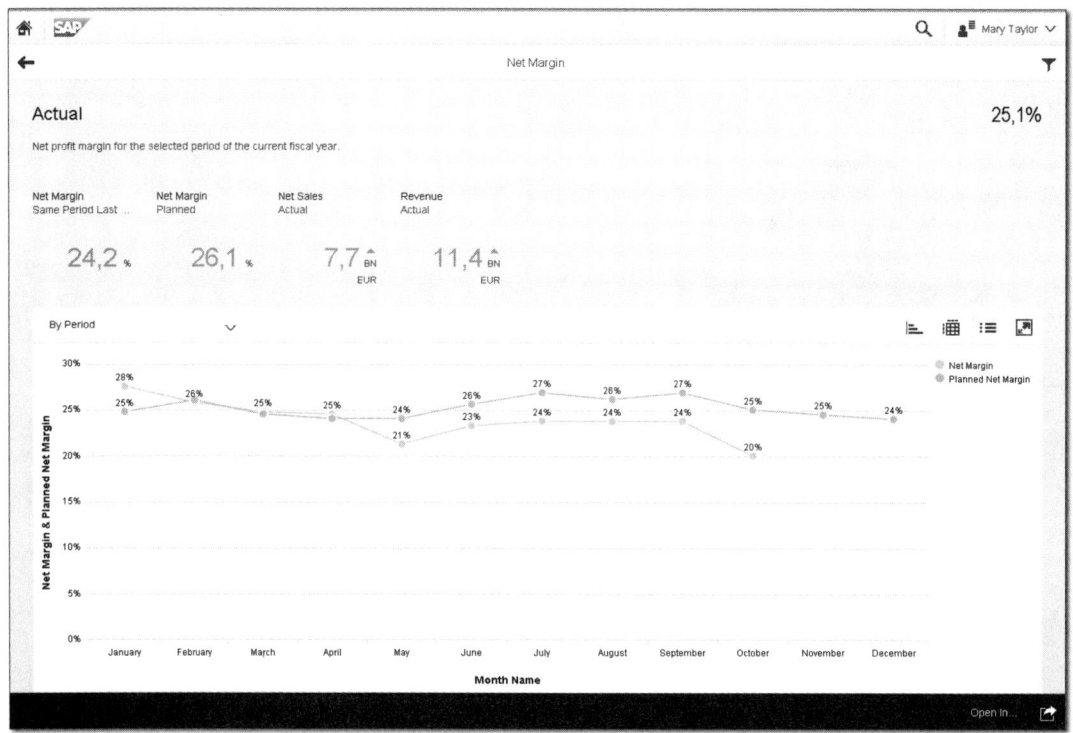

Figure 11.2 Drilldown into Margin over Months with Plan to Actual Comparison

From the screen shown in Figure 11.2, Mary sees that the margin has been trailing since the middle of this year and that there was an especially steep decrease in October. She could now navigate to other analytical applications to further drill into the root cause of this margin decrease—for example, by using My Spend (see

Chapter 9, Section 9.4). In this case, she identifies the spending on travel as the root cause. She can take immediate action and inform the responsible persons via the built-in collaboration features.

11.1.2 Defining a Business Cockpit

Let's take a step back from Mary's specific scenario and look at finance business cockpits in general. At a first glance, it may appear that designing a cockpit means designing an analytical tool for a single user. However, a business cockpit needs to be based on the business model of a company—that is, the common mental model of the people driving the company. This model defines the goals of the organization though KPIs, the valuation of these KPIs, the drivers influencing them, and other factors (actual, plan, forecast, etc.). With this information in mind, a business cockpit serves as the common navigation system for managing a company. It supports both the work of individuals and the collaborative reasoning over the situation of a company, the insights, and the necessary actions. Therefore, SAP Smart Business organizes this business model in a central repository. The business model can then be presented by using a stringent information design throughout the entire company.

The meaning of a KPI in the context of a business model represents its semantics. Think back to Mary's net margin KPI. The basic number for that KPI is the net profit—but that number can be displayed in many ways. Margin is the percentage in relation to the net revenue. The relevant trend may be the comparison to the previous period or the period year. Relevant drill-down capabilities are by product category and product and by customer group and customer. These features and relationships are described in the semantics of a KPI. Hence, the semantics comprises the relation to overall business terms, relevant currencies or units of measure, thresholds, benchmarks, trends, variants, relevant granularities of measures and time, and drilldown as well as filtering dimensions.

To become the tool of choice for executives and managers, a cockpit has to be simple and effective to use. In this context, less is more. Business is volatile, so the cockpit must be easy to adapt. Employees from the business side must be able to personalize dashboards for their needs without developer support; the basic composition and adaptation of the dashboard must be in their hands. Business experts must be able to compose dashboards on their own, because they are the ones who know the business and its information needs. The task of IT is to provision all necessary data in a form in which business can consume it.

SAP S/4HANA Finance's cockpit solution is based on SAP Smart Business. SAP Smart Business allows business users to maintain a common repository of KPIs and their visualizations. Figure 11.3 shows an example of the definition of the net margin KPI and its different *evaluations*. Evaluations represent different variants, trends, and thresholds for a KPI as part of its business semantics. On the left side of the figure, you can see other P&L-relevant KPIs, such as open disputes or net sales. The lower part of the right side displays several evaluations of the net margin KPI, such as the comparison of the KPI with the same period last year or with the plan for that KPI. These are the definitions that we refer to as business semantics. The KPI is linked to database views that SAP provides as part of the virtual data model of SAP S/4HANA (see Chapter 10) or by which the IT department of a customer extends the predelivered VDM.

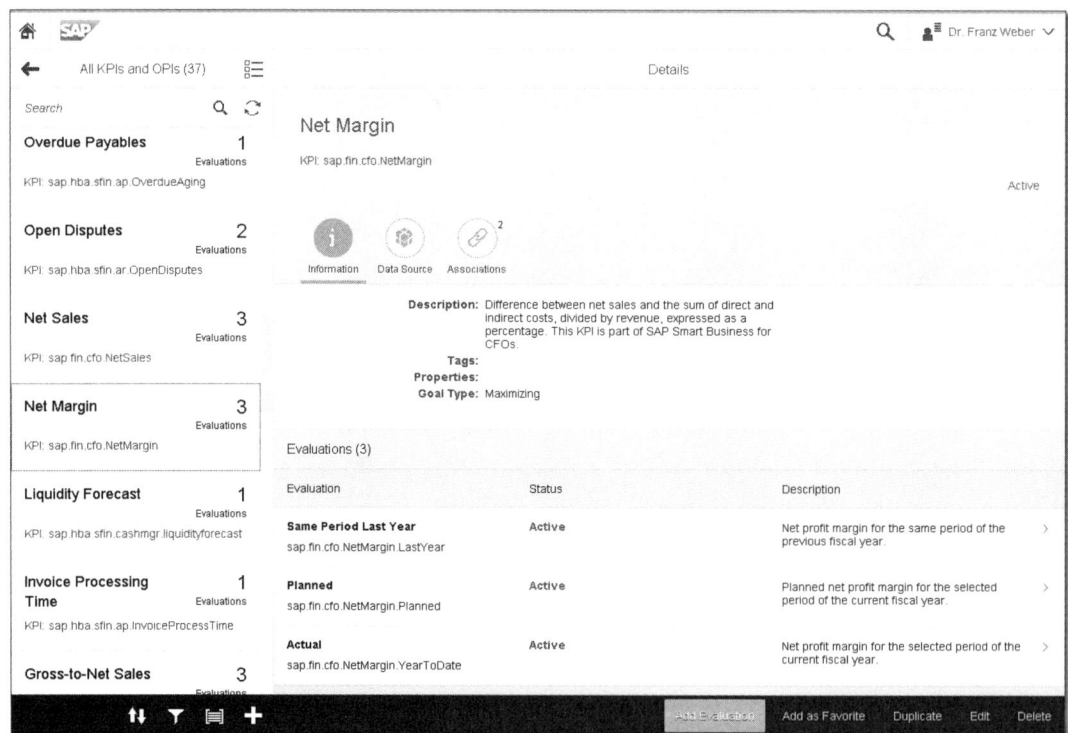

Figure 11.3 SAP Smart Business Expert Tool to Define KPIs

On top of this, businesspeople can now choose the appropriate visualization of KPIs and their evaluations for display on a dashboard. Typical visualization patterns, such as single KPIs, bar charts, or benchmark comparisons, are supported. In Figure 11.4, the net margin KPI is connected to a generic drilldown visualization tile that offers drilldown capabilities out of the box based on the underlying data model. Return to Figure 11.1 to see the resulting launchpad with this tile.

Figure 11.4 Choosing KPI Visualizations with SAP Smart Business

11.1.3 Outlook

To provide even greater insights, embedded analytics will become a standard feature of SAP S/4HANA Finance. Overview pages could become the next-generation dashboard in which content and tools are optimized specifically for a particular role. Visualization of the relationships between KPIs provides greater insights for business users on which to make decisions or take actions. Users can visually see potential impact by simulating an action before actually executing a transaction. These are domain-specific applications.

There is an intuitive and consistent information design across these applications that users quickly will become familiar with. For example, you could look at your accounting line items side by side with analytical views that represent your current line item groupings, providing in-context analytics where you can navigate or drill down further by clicking on the graphic and the line item tables update, or vice versa by altering the line item filters or groupings. This functionality enables a far more natural interaction paradigm for "slice and dice" analysis.

In addition to the analytical elements (as discussed in Chapter 10), other important functionality needs to be part of cockpit solutions. Typically, users of financial information are not alone in their work and need to collaborate in different ways. When one user finds a particular insight in the system, he or she should be able to comment on that finding by annotating directly on the ERP data. Such annotations provide greater context for others who use the system. For example, if there was a spike in a chart somewhere, an analyst could tag that trend with text that explains the movement. The ability to share information using integrated communication tools is key to enabling teams to share insights and drive value for the company. It provides a "context handover" from one user to another. In line with sharing information, snapshot functionality allows users to easily create reports that can be organized in a gallery.

However, embedded analytics are dedicated to the domain that they are built for. Many users want to have the flexibility to pull in data from different data sources and to design their own analytical views. SAP S/4HANA Finance was a frontrunner in the simplification of the ERP data model. Now other ERP modules are following suit, meaning that we now have the flexibility to align supply chain, HR, and finance data across a huge array of dimensions.

The ultimate cockpit is one that consumes all enterprise data, can combine it with external unstructured data such as interest rates and commodity prices, and is built on a platform that enables fully flexible simulations on top of both planning data and external variables. In Q4 of 2015, SAP released SAP Digital Boardroom, which is built on the SAP Cloud for Analytics platform. This application provides top-level executives with the flexibility to build stories in hours. *Stories* are made up of components that include different metrics, ratios, graphs, KPI driver trees, and so on. Because these components or KPI views are built from transactional line items, they can be viewed from any perspective on live data. This means that there is no need for anyone to work outside of the system, and the result is an aligned and agile decision-making unit.

11.2 Financials Operations

Handling receivables and payables as efficiently as possible and optimizing the cash flow is at the core of Financials Operations, the next category of SAP S/4HANA Finance applications on our list.

Financials Operations covers all kinds of payment processes and collection activities to bring in money as quickly as possible. Accordingly, the business value of a state-of-the-art Financials Operations system comes both from the effectiveness of the measures it can provide for collecting outstanding receivables (to increase cash flow) and from the efficiency and degree of automation to run those volume activities with high reliability and minimum labor investment for headcount-intensive tasks (to reduce costs).

In SAP S/4HANA Finance, companies benefit from high-efficiency gains both for the processing of accounts payable (AP) and accounts receivable (AR) due to real-time information and faster line item reporting. The runtime of key activities has been reduced from as much as one hour down to mere seconds.

Another common denominator of both areas is that both payables and receivables managers usually monitor activities on a daily basis, typically with a handful of key indicators. With SAP S/4HANA Finance, managers can see all real-time KPIs relevant for steering their businesses at a glance. Here, the advantages of overcoming the traditional divide between transactional and analytical processing become particularly apparent:

- KPIs are directly derived in real time from line items and without the need for additional, redundant, analytical data sets.
- Users can drill down from the aggregated values to the single line item level, including full availability of all information, such as document attachments, correspondence, or dispute cases.

Let's look more closely into the capabilities of Receivables Management before we present the Payables Management side. In both areas, we'll look at applications for both managers and accountants.

11.2.1 Receivables Management

In Receivables Management, the main goals are as follows:

- Keep overdue receivables low.
- Keep DSO close to the agreed payment terms (sometimes referred to as *net DSO*).
- Minimize write-offs for bad debts without sacrificing possible business opportunities.
- Guarantee high operational efficiency for all internal processes—for example, the processing of incoming payments or closing activities.

SAP S/4HANA Finance supports receivables managers and accountants in fulfilling these goals via improved performance and new, streamlined applications.

Accounts Receivable Manager

SAP S/4HANA Finance provides rich, real-time analytical capabilities that support the receivables manager in reaching his goals. The main idea is to push relevant information to the user instead of relying on the user pulling information from the system.

Using the SAP Smart Business cockpit of SAP S/4HANA Finance (see Section 11.1) and corresponding KPIs from AR, the manager can see at a glance if the ratio of total overdue receivables in his area of responsibility is above a certain threshold, what his DSO is, or if the cash collection process is running smoothly. Because all data is shown in real time, unnecessary inquiries due to stale data—for example, concerning a customer that is on top of the overdue receivables list—no longer happen. A payment from this customer posted in the system just seconds ago would make the customer disappear from the overdue receivables list.

Furthermore, executing analytics directly on the operational system allows the receivables manager to drill down to the lowest level of detail (e.g., a single customer or a single invoice) whenever needed.

Accounts Receivable Accountant

SAP S/4HANA Finance allows for establishing common business practices across various organizational units and countries in order to standardize and streamline the AR-related processes. For example, the Process Collections Worklist app in

SAP S/4HANA Finance (shown in Figure 11.5) supports a rule-based cash collection process based on predefined strategies. These strategies model the best business practices for selecting customers to contact that proved to be successful in the past for collecting outstanding amounts most efficiently. The system assigns individual worklists of customers with outstanding receivables to the accountants. Based on the collection worklists, the accountants prepare their collection calls with the customers.

The goal here is to not leave the decision to call a specific customer to the accountant, because this might lead to mixed results. For example, experienced accounts call the "right" customers, whereas accountants with less experience might call the "wrong" customers, because they either fail to analyze which customers are the right ones or they prefer to have a more enjoyable conversation and thus only call the "easy" ones. With SAP S/4HANA Finance, accountants do not need to spend time analyzing which customers to call; instead, they can focus entirely on customer interaction. Based on the best practices and strategies that proved to be effective for the company, the system ensures an efficient selection of the most promising customers to call.

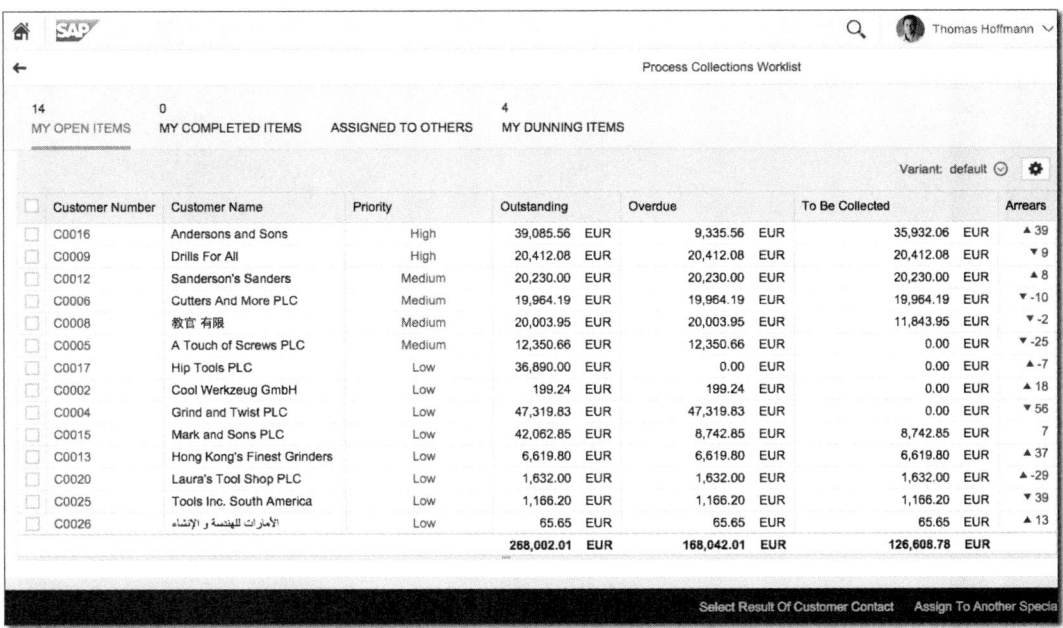

Figure 11.5 Process Collections Worklist

11 SAP S/4HANA Finance Applications

The Process Receivables app in SAP S/4HANA Finance (see Figure 11.6) allows a user to document this customer interaction directly in the system (e.g., whether the customer agrees to pay an outstanding invoice by a certain date, whether the customer was reached at all, whether he asks for a later call back, and so on). Subsequently, the system automatically monitors agreements and deadlines stipulated with the customer. Customers who subsequently break their promises to pay are reinserted into the accountant's worklist with the highest priority.

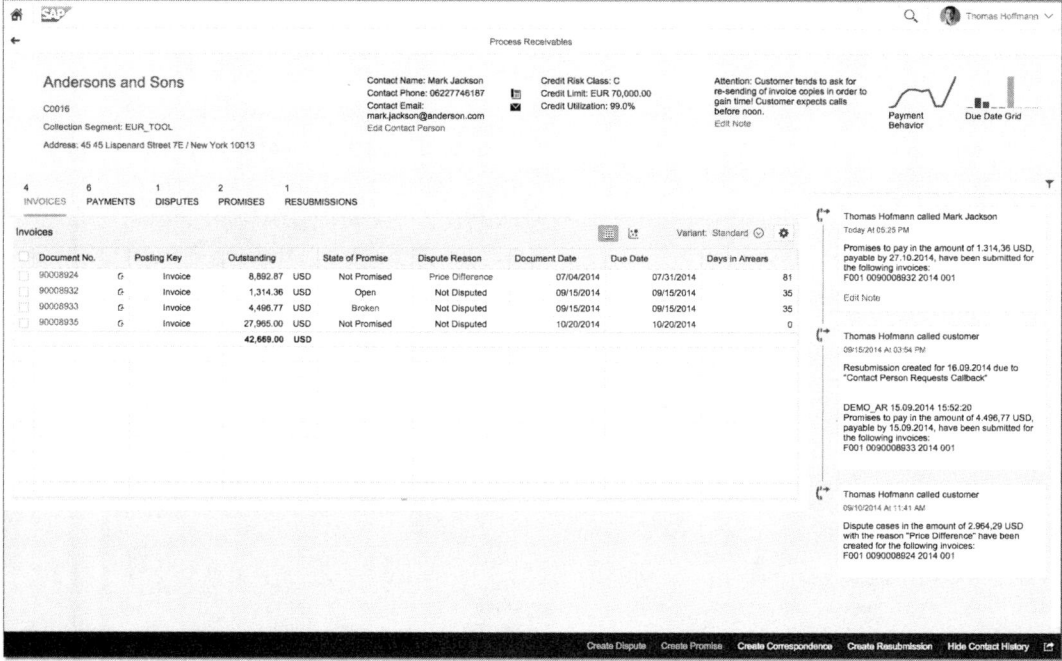

Figure 11.6 Process Receivables

In addition to streamlining the collections process, the documentation of the customer interaction also allows the receivables manager to monitor the whole process in real time. He can immediately react to deviations and identify possible improvements either with regard to his team setup or collection strategy fine-tuning.

The mechanism of work lists that are generated based on collection strategies allows the receivables manager to optimize his cash collection process and consequently reduce his overdue receivables, DSO, and even bad debt write-offs.

Collection strategies can be a combination of several weighted factors, such as the amount of overdue receivables surpassing a certain threshold per customer, a customer still failing to pay one week after receiving a dunning notice, the credit exposures of a customer exceeding 80% of his credit limit, and so on. Another collection strategy could be to call customers with large invoices one week before the due date in order to verify that the invoice is correct and to proactively prevent eventual disputes.

11.2.2 Payables Management

The main goals of Payables Management are as follows:

- Achieve highly efficient processing of supplier invoices by maximizing automation and reducing the cost per invoice.
- Systematically use cash discounts by paying at the right point in time.
- Ensure timely payments for key suppliers or high-priority items.
- Enforce compliance with company strategy.

As with Receivables Management, Payables Management in SAP S/4HANA Finance supports AP managers and accountants.

Accounts Payable Manager

Again, the focus is on pushing real-time information to the user. The following KPIs particularly support the manager in optimizing cash discount utilization and optimally scheduling payments:

- Available cash discounts in a recent period or exceptional invoices with cash discount before the next payment date
- Cash discount utilization by different business dimensions, such as company, country, payment term, vendor group, and cause for cash discount loss
- Simulations of available future cash discount

For example, the Cash Discount Utilization app in SAP S/4HANA Finance (shown in Figure 11.7) supports managers in monitoring cash discount utilization across the organization. They can identify unnecessary losses in cash discounts and avoid such losses in the future. AP managers can analyze insufficient utilization

11 | SAP S/4HANA Finance Applications

by different business dimensions and quickly trigger actions from within the app (e.g., via email or via SAP's collaboration solution, SAP Jam).

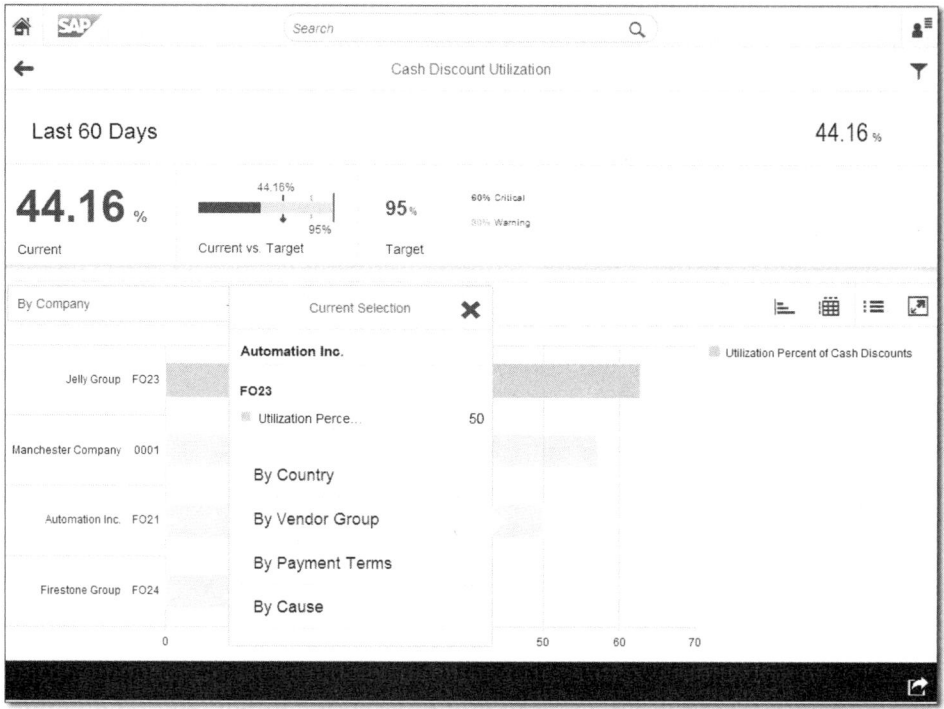

Figure 11.7 Cash Discount Utilization

Accounts Payable Accountant

SAP S/4HANA Finance transforms processes in AP from batch-oriented, periodically scheduled tasks to people-driven business with faster and more accessible user experiences for the AP accountant. The accountants themselves should drive and make decisions based on information from the system instead of being driven by batch jobs. As a first step, SAP S/4HANA Finance provides intuitive and simpler state-of-the-art UIs to improve, for example, user efficiency for creating and processing payment proposals.

SAP S/4HANA Finance enables partners to bring their established and proven solutions in the AP arena to the same high level of user experience (e.g., in the area of vendor invoice management and approval workflow).

11.2.3 Outlook

Automation remains a central goal for accounts payable and for accounts receivable accounting. In other words, in a perfect world, only exceptions should require manual attention from accountants.

With the networked economy closely connecting buyers and suppliers, this target now comes into reach (see Section 11.3). On the accounts receivable side, networking buyers, suppliers, and payment providers will dramatically reduce manual reconciliation efforts by conveying precise remittance information via the network. Accounts payable processes, on the other hand, can be directly determined by subsequent sourcing and procurement steps—thus avoiding expensive "repair" steps in accounts payable. The effort spent in accounts payable and receivable can then shift from highly automatable processes to tasks that generate more value or to innovative instruments, such as factoring (selling receivables) or reverse factoring (prefinancing suppliers).

Another aspect to consider is a closer integration of AP with Cash Management. Beyond simplification and performance improvement, future development in accounts payable will leverage the simulation capabilities of SAP S/4HANA Finance and SAP HANA, as demonstrated by the following use case in payment processing. Today, reducing the amount of outgoing cash can only be achieved by manual, time-consuming, unstructured editing of the payment proposal.

In the future, simulated and predictive payments will enable the user to interactively set various criteria and rules for the selection of open invoices to pay. Based on these parameters, the payment proposal and total outgoing cash amount are dynamically recalculated within seconds. The user can optimize the payment parameters until the total of outgoing payments meets the requirements of the cash manager, who monitors the overall liquidity of the company.

In this section, we showed how SAP S/4HANA Finance changes the game for both receivables and payables management:

- The high degree of automation makes manual user interaction obsolete wherever possible.
- UIs are optimized for professional users but allow new users to become familiar with them easily.

For your receivables department, SAP S/4HANA Finance in particular leverages built-in business knowhow, allowing you to establish state-of-the-art business practices. Real-time capabilities allow you to focus on the relevant customers, exceptions, and tasks.

Your payables department benefits from smarter business decisions, simpler AP processes, and faster user interaction with a much better user experience. For the future, SAP plans to provide simulated and predictive payment functionality, which will allow you to simulate short-term outgoing payments, optimize the payment process efficiently, and benefit from a joined view of payables and cash positions. This will help payables clerks to make the right financial decisions and will reduce payment risks. With these measures, you will be able to further optimize your cash flow.

11.3 Ariba Network Integration

Integration and business networks are key topics of collaboration across companies, and they go a long way toward simplifying interorganizational procurement and sales processes. For example, the network can instantly notify buyers the moment a purchase order is confirmed or a shipment has been sent by a supplier. When receiving the shipment, the buyer can enter quantities accepted or rejected and request replacement or credit for damaged goods via that same network.

SAP Ariba runs the world's largest business network, Ariba Network. As shown in Figure 11.8, Ariba Network extends accounts payable and receivable processes in SAP S/4HANA Finance systems at the buyer and supplier sides. Making use of this collaborative e-procurement and e-payment platform streamlines processes, reduces processing costs, and provides a single point of integration.

For on-premise scenarios, the Ariba Network Integration add-on provides technical integration (also deployable on many older SAP ERP releases). Because the network has become an integral part of SAP's cloud setup, SAP S/4HANA Finance consumed as a cloud service includes this integration by default.

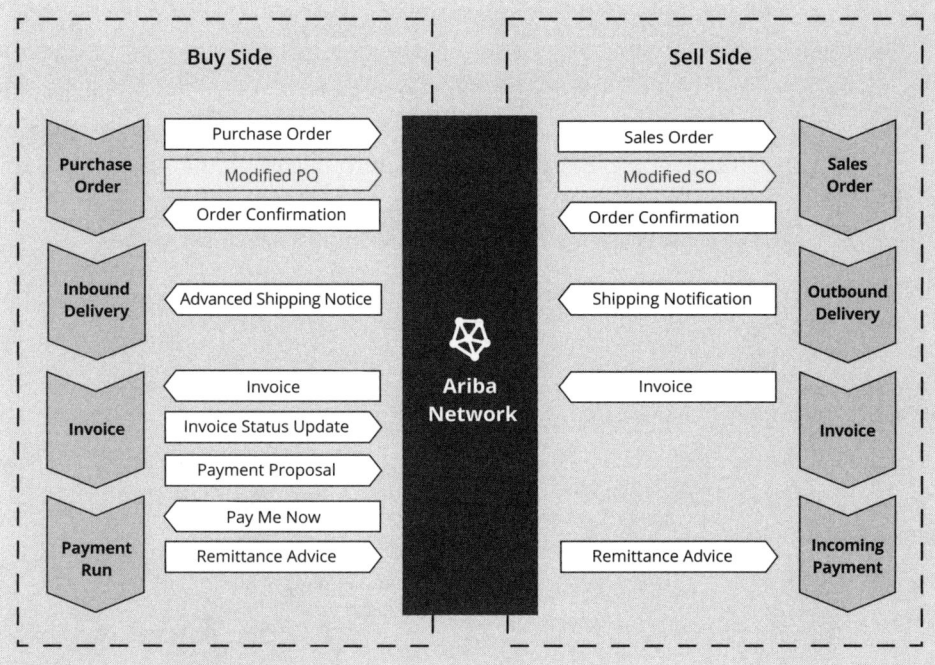

Figure 11.8 Integration between Buy Side and Sell Side via Ariba Network

This section highlights some of the most important benefits when integrating SAP S/4HANA Finance with Ariba Network, which provides end-to-end connectivity for order-to-invoice and invoice-to-pay processes, helping buyers and suppliers to collaborate better, improve compliance, and go paperless across these processes. In addition to other offerings, Ariba Network supports order collaboration, invoice collaboration, and discount management. Let's get an overview of the value within each of these areas.

11.3.1 Order Collaboration

The intuitive buyer and supplier dashboards for order management in Ariba Network provide three benefits (see Figure 11.8):

- Centralized and streamlined communication with customers, using a consolidated view for order collaboration. This consolidated view provides a complete picture of the buyer–supplier relationship. Both sides have a consolidated view of the current state of orders, which reduces effort spent checking the status and transmits information in a timelier manner.

- Suppliers can automate their order management end to end and collaborate with their customers. Orders and subsequent communication on change orders, confirmations, cancellations, or advanced shipping notices are sent through the network and automatically show up at the other side.
- Ariba Network also offers rules-based order routing for fast, accurate order information delivery via various electronic interfaces, such as email or electronic data interchange (EDI).

11.3.2 Invoice Collaboration

When they are connected via Ariba Network, trading partners can more easily view and manage invoices and payments while controlling cash flow and risk, thus strengthening the financial supply chain.

The SAP Ariba invoice capturing solution transforms paper-based processes to 100% digital, automated, and paperless processes. This solution is preconfigured with best practices content for invoice review and for approval and exception management. In this way, the solution dramatically improves productivity by providing real-time transparency of all aspects of invoicing. Seamlessly transmitted via Ariba Network, invoices are automatically matched and validated to cut cycle time from an industry average of twenty-three days to five days or less.

The Smart Invoicing feature goes beyond basic connectivity by automatically detecting errors and exceptions at the line item level. This helps invoices not only reach accounts payable faster but also move faster through the entire process. SAP Ariba's automated approval routing ensures that the right people are immediately notified and working to get the problem solved.

PO-Flip technology gives suppliers the ability to create an invoice directly from a purchase order with just one click, leveraging the system's automatic validation against business rules. Errors are detected before an invoice ever reaches a buyer, thus ensuring smooth and efficient processing and faster payments.

The Carbon Copy (CC) Invoices app provides a central dashboard for suppliers, showing all invoices for a buyer. Suppliers see both invoices they created on Ariba Network themselves and invoices that the buyer created on their behalf in his SAP S/4HANA Finance system. For example, if a buyer receives an invoice by mail or fax, then the original invoice was created in the SAP S/4HANA Finance system and transferred to Ariba Network, from where suppliers can use the invoice in subsequent processes.

Optimization and prediction of cash flow is supported by the following means:

- Secure electronic funds transfer and fast reconciliation via AribaPay
- Support for all typical payment methods, such as check, credit card, wire transfer, and others

Ariba Network can accelerate payments and increase productivity thanks to the following features:

- Multiple e-invoicing options, including PO-Flip, invoices without purchase orders, and system-to-system invoicing via cXML, EDI, and CSV upload
- Easy-to-use dashboards and notifications for insight into invoice and payment status
- Support for multiple languages and 172 currencies, plus compliance with local VAT laws

11.3.3 Discount Management

As shown in Figure 11.8, buyers can submit payment proposals in line with their payment strategies to their suppliers on Ariba Network. This enables buyers to offer early payment with corresponding discounts and thus take advantage of favorable payment conditions.

For suppliers, on the other hand, the system provides an integrated cash optimizer that instantly determines the most preferable of these payment proposals with regards to the supplier's working capital requirements.

Using Ariba Network's PayMeNow feature, suppliers can then respond to the payment proposal and indicate the desired early payment date and discount, which leads to an automatic update of the corresponding accounting documents.

Furthermore, buyers can keep their suppliers informed by means of payment advices about the payments they will receive. Whenever a payment is made, the SAP S/4HANA Finance system sends a remittance advice to Ariba Network (see Figure 11.8).

11.3.4 Outlook

Deploying business applications in the cloud further lowers the threshold to a networked economy drastically, because the network becomes an integral part of the business-to-business (B2B) or business-to-customer (B2C) relationship. Hence, a future solution for cloud-based procurement may have the potential to provide an even more proactive and more intelligent interaction between business partners, beyond enforcing best practices for business rules and checks.

In the cloud, complementary processes do not exist in isolation from each other any longer. This means that the pay part of the invoice-to-pay process can seamlessly feed the cash part of SAP S/4HANA Finance's order-to-cash process—going even beyond today's invoice collaboration.

Although these are exciting future possibilities, the current integration of SAP S/4HANA Finance and Ariba Network already provides huge additional value in terms of automation and thus increased process efficiency and cost reduction. The potential of process automation cannot be overstated; as the Aberdeen Group identified in a 2013 survey, best-in-class companies who regularly employ AP automation have less than half the industry average of the cost per invoice.[1]

11.4 Cash Management

These days, many enterprises' operations are driven by cash flows. Among the top concerns of CFOs or treasurers are transparency on cash deposits, forecasting of cash flows, and their company's liquidity structure—on top of the risks coming from fluctuating currency exchange rates and interest rates and the credit worthiness of counterparties in business transactions.

Cash management constantly faces contradicting requirements:

- **Manual operation vs. automation**
  Some companies pursue automation as much as possible, whereas other companies only trust the results from manual actions. Moreover, automated liquidity forecasts from cash management systems do not produce estimations that

---

[1] Ankita Tyagi, "From the Shadows to the Forefront: AP Automation and the Strategic Vision."

are thorough and precise enough. (This is an industry-wide fundamental problem, due to the complexity in the system landscape and varying quality from different information sources.) As a consequence, some manual steps to collect, scrutinize, and adjust forecasted amounts cannot be avoided. The big challenge is to balance gaining efficiency by automation with ensuring that analyses and forecasts are reliable and trustworthy.

- **Decentralization vs. centralization**
  Cash needs to be centralized in order to be leveraged most efficiently. The same goal applies to cash-related information, which unfortunately is decentralized along the purchase order, sales order, invoice, and payment processes and is also distributed over different systems. Consequently, the biggest challenge for any cash management system lies with this scattered cash-related information, and the management of cash, bank accounts, payments, and liquidity needs to be highly centralized. It's remarkable how much it costs for enterprises to come up with a thorough view of their bank accounts, cash positions, or liquidity statuses.

- **Separation vs. integration**
  Typically, an enterprise's cash and treasury department operates separately from its accounting department, and each department has different concerns and focuses. SAP's classic cash management product had tight dependencies to the Accounting module, introducing overlaps between the accounting department and the cash department. On the other hand, to have better liquidity forecast or cash flow analysis, cash management requires a tight integration with the Treasury, MM, SD, AR, AP, and even HCM modules in the SAP ERP system. Balancing the separation and integration among these modules with Cash Management is always a subtle matter.

As part of SAP S/4HANA Finance, SAP Cash Management powered by SAP HANA is SAP's next-generation cash management product, designed to cope with these business and technical challenges. (Note that SAP Cash Management powered by SAP HANA has a separate price tag; you need a separate license in order to use this function.) It handles these challenges by providing three sets of benefits:

- True technical innovations in accordance with the paradigms of SAP S/4HANA Finance: real-time analytics without information redundancy, insight-to-action, and merging of transactional and planning systems

- New functions and features, such as Bank Account Management, which forms the cornerstone for cash managers to manage bank accounts of the whole enterprise group centrally
- A brand-new UI with SAP Fiori technology to simplify the daily tasks of cash managers

The SAP Fiori launchpad for cash managers, shown in Figure 11.9, provides a first impression of the new user experience available with SAP Cash Management powered by SAP HANA. Thanks to the calculation power of SAP HANA, the launchpad can show multiple KPIs for cash managers, including bank statement import status, cash positions, bank risk, deficit cash pool, liquidity forecast, and payment statistics. From this high-level overview, you can either drill down into details or trigger actions directly.

Figure 11.9 SAP Fiori Launchpad for SAP Cash Management Powered by SAP HANA

Let's dig into the major function modules for end users and the architectural concepts behind them. The description of functionality follows the typical workflow in Cash Management, starting from the prerequisite bank accounts and then following the daily work of cash managers with regard to cash operations and liquidity management.

11.4.1 Bank Account Management

Bank accounts are one of the core assets of a cash department. Bank accounts need to be owned and controlled centrally to improve efficiency and to ensure compliance. Many companies struggle to have a thorough view of all bank accounts opened by their subsidiaries.

SAP Cash Management powered by SAP HANA introduces Bank Account Management as a brand-new function module with the following key features:

- It provides bank accounts as master data with simpler handling by the cash department and many additional attributes compared to the classical house bank account. These additional attributes reflect the daily business of cash departments and the truth on the bank side.
- It allows cash managers to group banks and bank accounts into a hierarchy for more flexible reporting and easy access by different users.
- In order to manage bank accounts centrally, it allows group cash managers to establish their own centralized governance processes for opening, closing, or changing bank accounts.

As shown in Figure 11.10, Bank Account Management shows the overall bank structure of a company and the bank accounts opened in those banks.

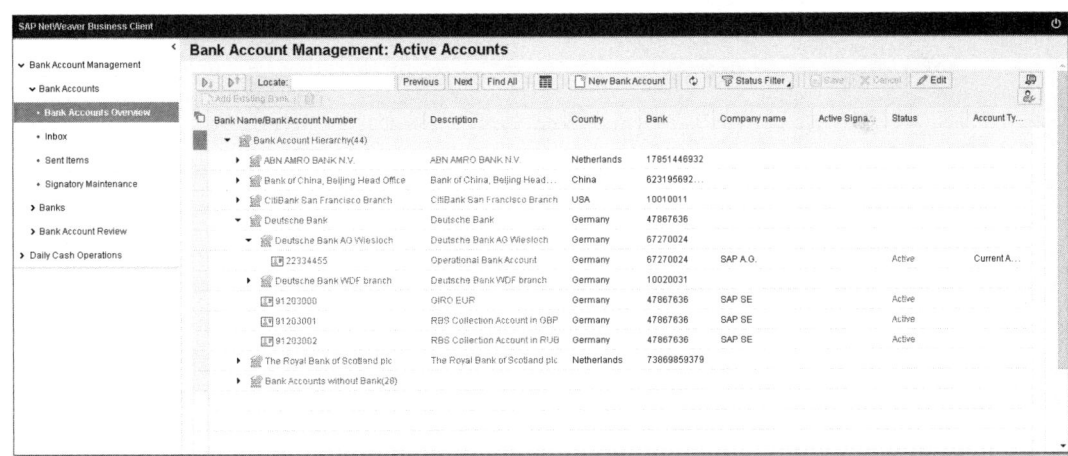

Figure 11.10 Bank Account Overview in Bank Account Management

11.4.2 Cash Operations

Typically, the most important tasks each morning for a cash manager are to review the cash position in order to understand the cash distribution and to check whether bank accounts have sufficient funding for today's payments obligations or whether there is a surplus to be invested.

Cash managers will find it an easy task to accomplish these morning exercises with SAP Cash Management powered by SAP HANA. First, two important KPIs are shown directly in the SAP Fiori launchpad: bank statement import status (BANK STATEMENT MONITOR) and CASH POSITION, as shown in Figure 11.9. The bank statement import status shows clearly how well the bank statements have been imported into the system as scheduled so that cash managers can have a clear understanding of how trustworthy and up to date the cash position is. If the bank statement hasn't been imported 100% successfully, then the cash manager can drill down to the bank account details to identify the external contact person on the bank side in order to contact that individual, or the cash manager can go to the Bank Statement Monitor to retrieve the details of the imported bank statement. The complete process doesn't require any value input; the end user only needs to click through the screens and act accordingly.

Once the bank statement import status is confirmed, the cash manager looks at CASH POSITION for an intuitive view of where the cash is distributed among countries, company codes, or banks, as shown in Figure 11.11. She can drill down to the cash position details to identify which bank accounts have deficits and the expected inflow or outflow during the day.

If there is any questionable cash flow, she can drill down to the Payment Details app (see Figure 11.12) in order to understand each payment and its status. Here, she can answer the following questions:

- Has the payment reached the bank?
- Did the bank acknowledge the transaction with a success message?
- Have the intraday statement and the bank statement been imported?
- Have the payment and bank confirmation been reconciled?

If necessary, she can even drill down to all the payment details, including the accounting document.

Cash Management | 11.4

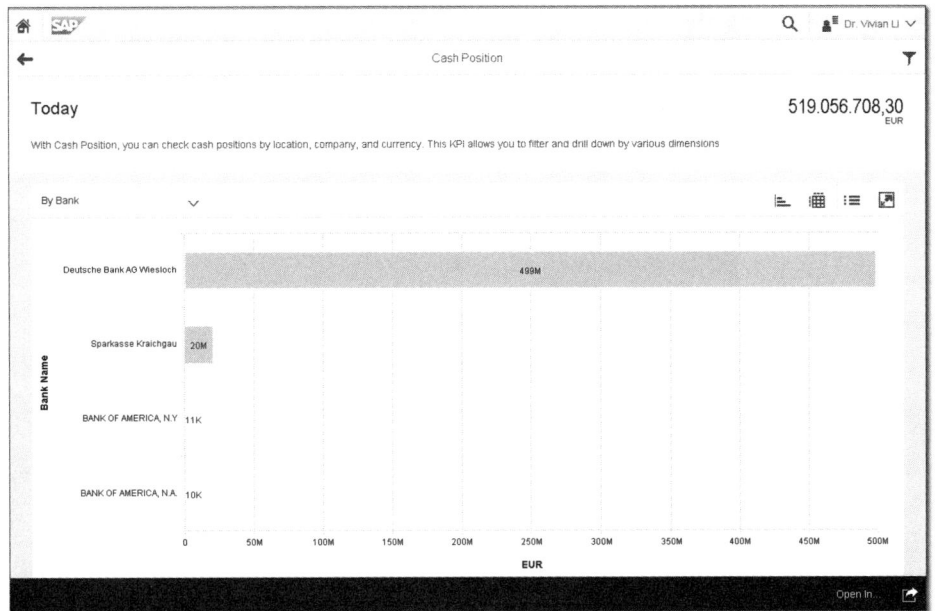

Figure 11.11 Cash Position by Banks

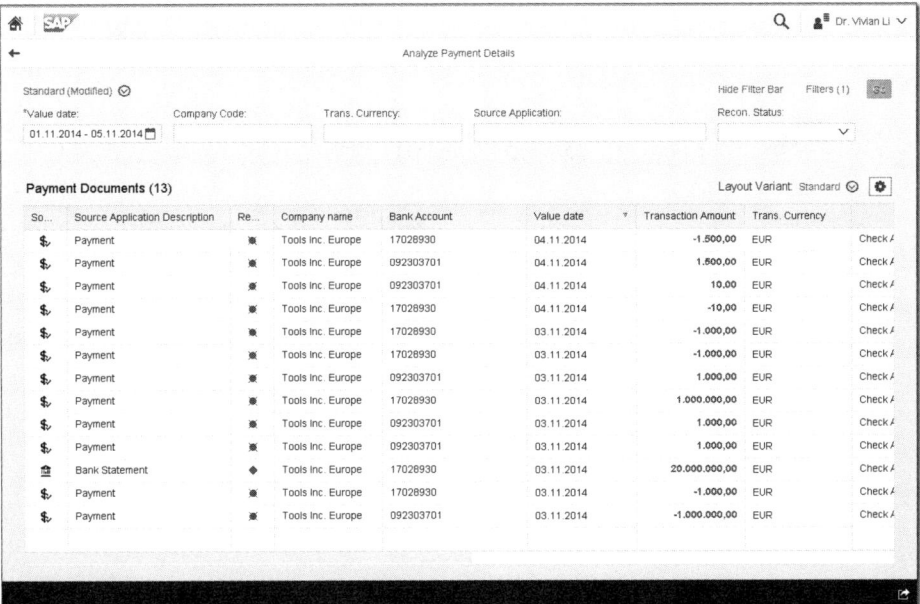

Figure 11.12 Payment Details

Once the cash manager is sure that the bank account position is okay, she might decide to make a bank transfer (see Figure 11.13)—for example, if there is a deficit that needs to be covered or a surplus that would be of better use in a different bank account. She can trigger the bank transfer directly from the Cash Position app.

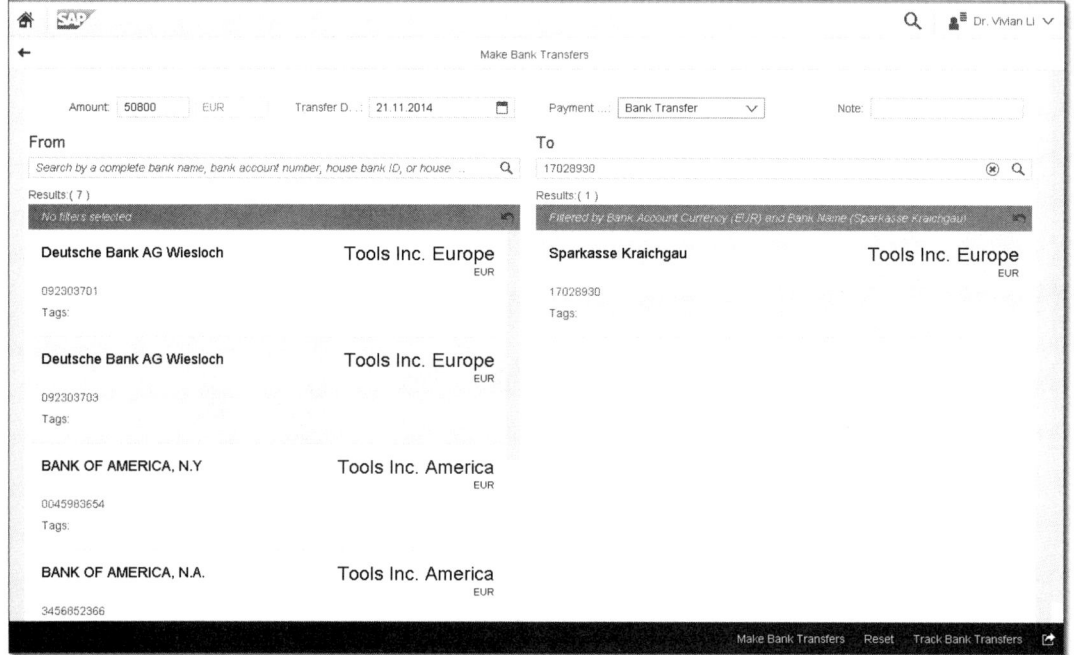

Figure 11.13 Bank Transfer

The bank transfers, together with other large payments, will go to the company's head of cash operations for approval before being sent out. The head of cash operations directly sees the number of payments pending his approval on the APPROVE BANK PAYMENT tile in his launchpad, as shown in Figure 11.9. From there, he opens the list of payments needing approval and decides to approve or reject them, as shown in Figure 11.14. Only with his approval will the payment instruction be sent to the bank automatically.

All of these steps run as web apps on both desktop and mobile devices. When the cash manager starts her work in the morning, she sees a high-level overview and a detailed insight into payments that is easy and intuitive to use. She can then take actions directly over the course of the day. Ultimately, she is able to send out all the instructions to banks before the cutoff time in the early afternoon.

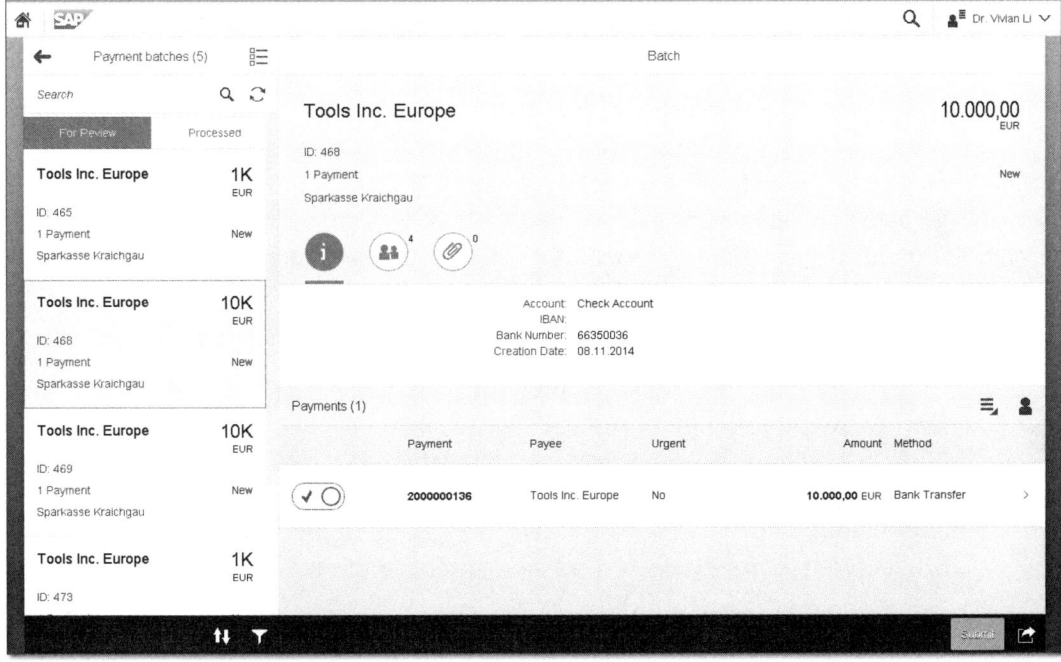

Figure 11.14 Approve Bank Payment

11.4.3 Liquidity Management

Having finished their morning tasks, in the afternoon cash managers will typically look at a longer time horizon to understand whether the enterprise group has sufficient liquidity in the next months and whether the cash flow might introduce outstanding risk (e.g., foreign currency exposure) before deciding on the strategy for the next months.

To do this, cash managers need to collect information from subsidiaries and departments. They not only acquire high-level aggregated figures but also drill down into line items to trace the root cause of exceptional cash flows. What makes the activity even more difficult is that quite often the information is distributed in different systems.

SAP Cash Management powered by SAP HANA provides extensive liquidity management functionality to help cash managers to cope with these challenges. The app respects the fact that the rolling liquidity forecast still needs people's input, judgment, review, and approval—but the application successfully streamlines and supports these manual processes.

First, the rolling forecast/plan process is enabled by the embedded SAP Business Planning and Consolidation for Finance functions (see Section 11.5). Group cash managers can trigger a planning process that will be distributed to all the involved people via fine-grained workflow management capabilities that lead the responsible subsidiary cash managers directly to the respective applications.

When the subsidiary's cash manager enters planning data, the system automatically suggests amounts for different liquidity items based on the data collected from the system. The suggested amounts can come from the automated liquidity forecast, actual cash flows that happened in the same month last year, or last planning cycle's planned amounts, as shown in Figure 11.15. Cash managers can take those suggested amounts, increase or decrease them with a specified factor, and copy them into the planned columns of this planning cycle. The end user can also drill down into the details behind a suggested amount.

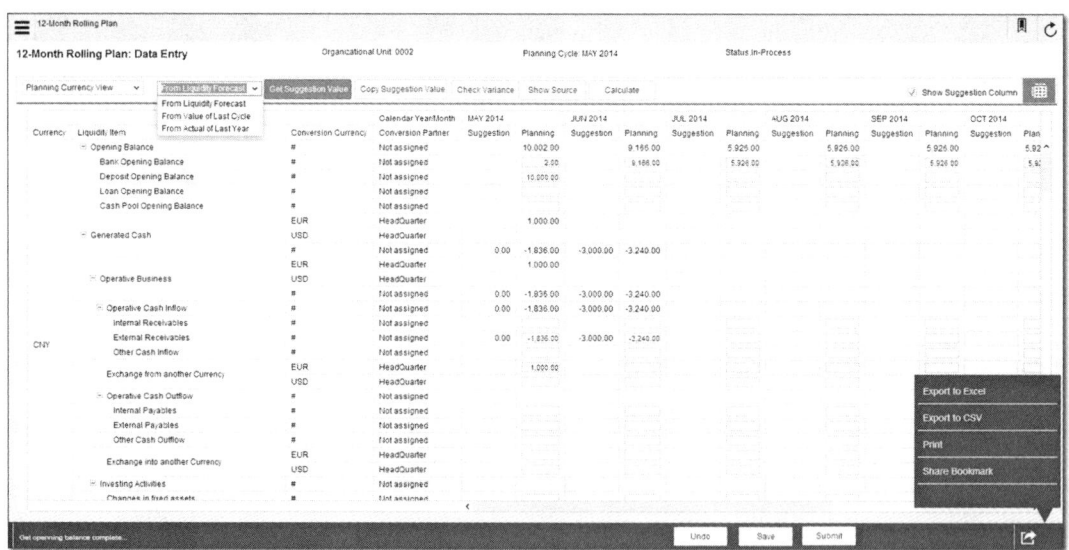

Figure 11.15 Liquidity Planning Data Entry Screen

The subsidiaries' cash managers submit their results to group cash managers. SAP Cash Management powered by SAP HANA will automatically aggregate the collected liquidity plans from subsidiaries for the group cash managers. Because this process also integrates the opening balance of the cash position as well as other financial assets and liabilities into the planning data entry sheet, the group cash manager may perform further investment or funding planning based on the complete picture. The aggregated results clearly show the liquidity structure forecast, which will be the guidance for next month's treasury operations.

As time progresses, the group cash manager can conduct a variance analysis via the Analyze Liquidity Plan app (see Figure 11.16) to check how far the forecast is from the actual and whether each subsidiary is operating according to the agreed-upon guidance.

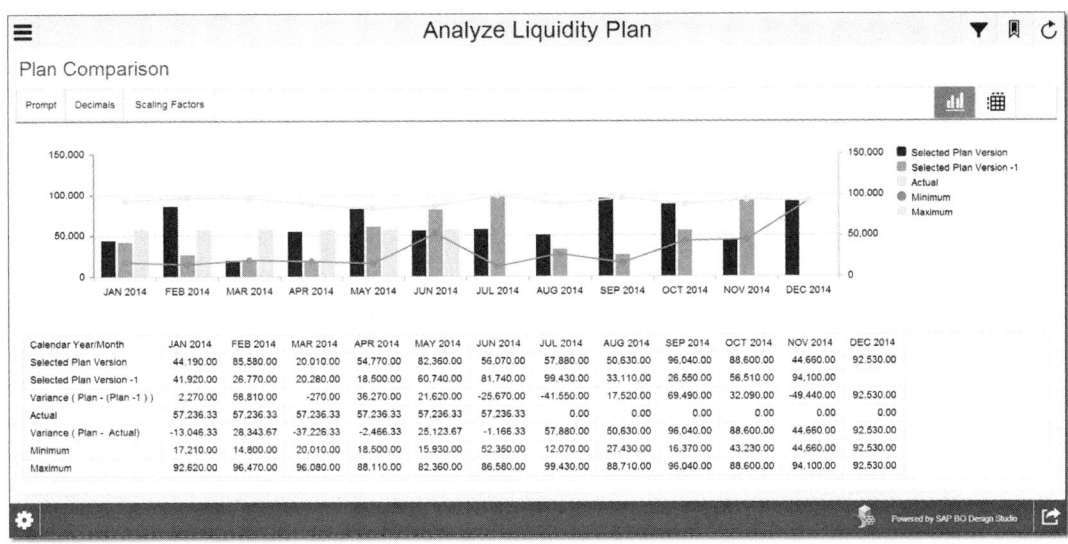

Figure 11.16 Analyze Liquidity Plan

11.4.4 Simplified Data Model

These innovative features are based on several fundamental backend simplifications that apply the paradigms of SAP S/4HANA Finance to Cash Management.

First, Bank Account Management removes the one-to-one binding between General Ledger (G/L) accounts and bank accounts. Companies only need to predefine a static set of G/L accounts to be used by all hundreds or thousands of bank accounts. When a new bank account is opened, there is no need to create one or several G/L accounts specifically for this bank account. This in turn simplifies the work of both the cash department and the accounting department, much reducing their potential conflicts.

Second, SAP Cash Management powered by SAP HANA introduces the Exposure Hub, a central component for data provisioning. The Exposure Hub collects all the operational information from the local system and from remote systems and stores this information in a consistent format, with the following advantages:

- It ensures that planned, forecast, and actual data have the same granularity. This is a prerequisite for variance analysis of planned, forecast, and actual data.
- In line with the removal of redundancy in SAP S/4HANA Finance (see Chapter 3), it stores only the line items and calculates aggregates for reporting on the fly. End users can always drill down to line items.

Last but not least, the embedded planning and OLAP framework of SAP S/4HANA Finance (see Section 11.5) allows companies to run liquidity planning directly on top of the transactional cash management system, making separate planning and reporting systems and extraction processes obsolete.

SAP S/4HANA Finance supports cash managers in all phases of their daily business and allows for a more efficient management of cash positions. In this way, it supports companies in navigating the challenges outlined at the beginning of this chapter.

11.4.5 Outlook

The improvements outlined so far represent the first phase of a renewal of cash management in SAP S/4HANA Finance toward centralization of bank accounts, payments, and liquidity status. More functionality and a continuously improved user experience will continue to evolve. The simplified architecture forms the basis for these improvements.

Central management of bank accounts over their lifecycles remains a focus topic. More SAP Fiori apps will become available to allow cash managers to handle their daily activities with regard to bank accounts via a simpler and more intuitive user experience. Also, other areas of cash management, such as risk assessment and corresponding proposals for action, can be automated and accelerated further.

The forecasting and simulation capabilities in cash management will improve thanks to the comprehensive data foundation. Similarly, cash planning benefits form an integrated planning solution.

11.5 SAP Business Planning and Consolidation for Finance

After discovering the enormous potential that columnar databases like SAP HANA have for purely analytical applications, the next bold move is into the area of financial planning. Here, you typically find a combination of analytical steps (e.g., displaying actual data for the previous year) and transactional process steps (recording plan data). As a consequence, empowering a new financial planning solution by using SAP HANA technology can be considered mandatory!

Let's look at the business requirements, architectural changes, process innovations, and resulting benefits that have been implemented in SAP BPC for Finance. We first look at how planning in SAP S/4HANA Finance can be summarized in the following four layers of improvements:

1. New plan data record design:
   - Combines all planning dimensions from Financials and Controlling (like G/L and CO-PA)
   - Eliminates redundant information (like cost element and G/L account)
2. State-of-the-art architecture:
   - Based purely on line items
   - Lacks aggregates
   - Optimized for SAP HANA
3. Intuitive frontend:
   - Microsoft Excel data sheets for power users and casual users
   - New functions (e.g., comments and provisional master data)
4. True business benefits:
   - Seamless plan versus actual reporting capabilities, from a group-level income statement to detailed customer/product profitability information
   - Built-in reconciliation, which reduces time to close
   - Simulation capabilities that allow better business decisions

11.5.1 Business Contexts

Planning, be it on the strategic or operational level, is one of the major processes for managing a company and individual organizations. Planning captures the expectations, defines the goals to achieve, and outlines the course of action. The process of planning business activities in a company is not limited to financial planning and in fact can involve many different stakeholders. Therefore, planning can be a time-consuming process that requires detailed preparation in order to ensure consistent execution and alignment among the planners and thus avoid waiting time and redundant planning.

The top management agrees on the strategic goals of the company. These goals are broken down to tactical and, eventually, operational goals and to the different areas of responsibility within the company, such as sales or production. The operational planning process itself typically starts in the sales department. The outcome (portfolio and quantity of products sold) then has to be translated into the impact that it has on other areas of the company.

For example, a significant increase or decrease of planned units sold for a given product will influence the following areas, among others:

- Raw materials and semifinished products needed for the product's production (Materials Management)
- Number and skills of workforce involved (Human Capital Management)
- Storage space needed (Asset Management)
- Sourcing and distribution infrastructure (Accounts Payable and Accounts Receivable)
- Cash flow (Finance)

SAP's new planning application, SAP BPC for Finance, addresses these dependencies by integrating financial planning processes that in previous releases could not be run in an integrated way because the disparate architecture of the system and data model did not allow it.

The breakdown of strategic goals to actionable operative measures can have a financial impact that needs to be analyzed and planned. Table 11.1 highlights the possible financial impact.

Source	Description	Corresponding Planning Activity in SAP BPC for Finance
Machine runtime increased	The service cost center must deliver the machine maintenance service more frequently.	Cost center planning activity output
Storage capacity increased	The company enlarges the warehousing capacity with its own resources.	Project planning
Strategic cost reduction	Overall transportation costs will be reduced by changing the transportation service provider.	P&L planning
Internet sales market penetration	By introducing an Internet sales platform, the company diversifies its distribution channels.	Market segment planning
Collections management	DSO will be reduced by implementing a new payment terms concept.	Balance sheet planning for receivables

Table 11.1 Examples of Operative Measures and Corresponding Impacts on Planning

11.5.2 Underlying Architecture

Within the SAP BPC for Finance solution, all of these SAP applications store their plan data in a single table (a BPC cube). Such an integrated data model inherently makes it possible to take the dependencies into account. Let's first look at the table structure for plan data before expanding the view to the system landscape architecture.

Plan Data Table Structure

Similar to actual data, planning in the past also faced the issue of separate data stores per component, such as G/L or CO. Similar to the Universal Journal for actual data, the SAP BPC for Finance solution now stores all financial plan data in the same data structure. This single source of truth is shown in Figure 11.17.

The simplified architecture entails a wide range of benefits for companies in their planning activities, as shown in Table 11.2.

11 SAP S/4HANA Finance Applications

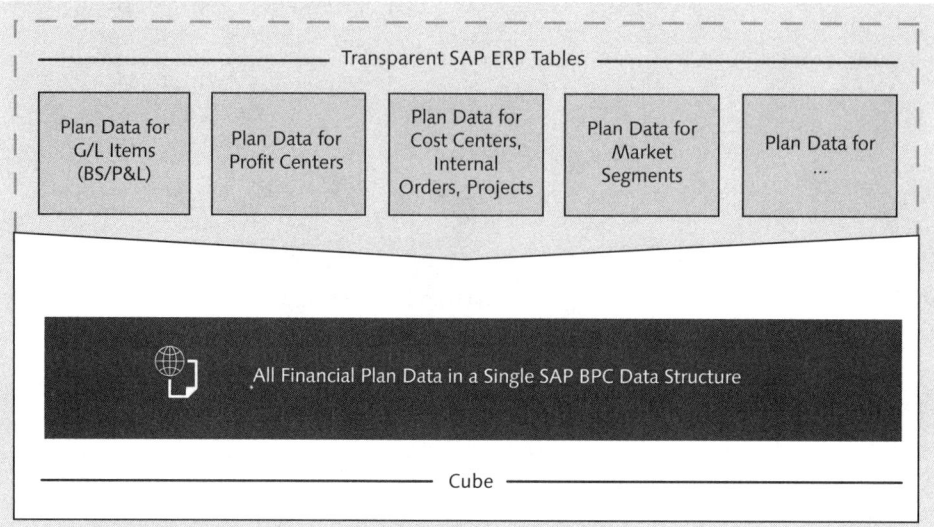

Figure 11.17 Single Source of Truth for Financial Plan Data

Challenge	Solution	Business Benefit
Long planning cycles due to data replication between tables	All data stored in a single table	Reduced planning cycles
Planning silos with separate data stores	All plan data have the same structure and validation rules	Data integrity increases
Long-running batch jobs for replicating data	All data stored in a single table	Data replication not necessary
Simulation impossible due to performance limitations	Availability of SAP HANA–enabled Planning Application Kit	Simulations and prediction algorithms can be implemented quickly
Different reports show data based on different tables	A single SAP HANA–based SAP BW report reading a single table	Reports show consistent and comparable data
Plan data from Management Accounting (CO) redundant with G/L (FI) plan data	Redesigned table brings together CO and FI	Drill down from high-level G/L plan data to detailed market segment plan data

Table 11.2 Business Benefits of Simplified Planning Architecture

System Landscape

Even with companies that work across global markets, regulations that become more complex, and reporting requirements that change frequently, users expect to record plan data in a few keystrokes and to retrieve information in the blink of an eye. In the past, planning required a landscape with several different systems with specific duties.

SAP's response to these changing requirements is straightforward: with SAP BPC for Finance, it is now possible to run a full-fledged planning system (SAP BPC 10.1 for SAP NetWeaver) within the same instance of SAP S/4HANA Finance. This architecture (optimized for a low TCO), also known as the *unified SAP BPC planning model*, is shown in Figure 11.18.

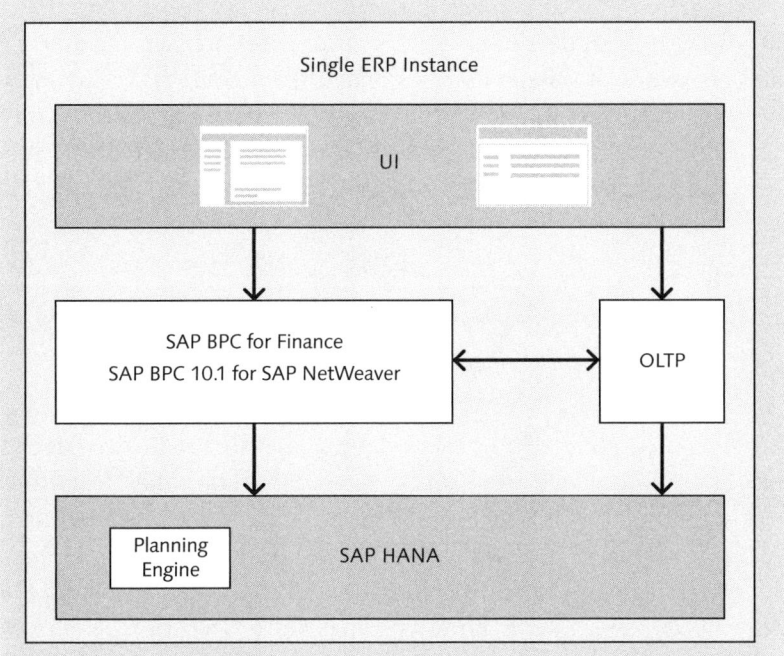

Figure 11.18 Simplified System Landscape for SAP BPC for Finance

Compared to the challenges of a distributed landscape, the simplified system landscape offers companies significant advantages, as listed in Table 11.3.

Challenge	Solution	Business Benefit
Separate systems for SAP ERP and planning	Now possible to run a full installation within an existing SAP ERP system	Reduced TCO
Data replication between systems	All data resides in same instance	Replication no longer necessary
Latency between systems	Data access via virtual providers	True real-time reporting for transactional plan data and master data

Table 11.3 Business Benefits of Simplified System Landscape

11.5.3 Planning Application

The drastic changes in the plan data table architecture with a single table and the simplified system landscape are the enablers for further innovations in the planning application itself. SAP BPC for Finance brings together financial and controlling information for actual and plan data. This enables seamless drilldown reporting based on integrated and fully reconciled data instead of separate reports.

Because plan data changes frequently, controllers often want to add notes to plan data in order to indicate, for example, why a certain figure has changed. Based on the simplified data model, SAP BPC for Finance now offers this functionality.[2]

Another property of the planning process itself is the fact that it is sometimes necessary to plan financial data for items that are not yet available in the current year. A typical example is the need to plan revenue data for a product for which no official master data record exists in the SAP system yet. In previous releases, this requirement forced customers to leave the core SAP ERP instance (here, plan data is validated against existing master data) and to set up their planning applications in a dedicated system. This is no longer necessary. The functionality to record plan data on provisional master data is now available.[3]

In order to accelerate the planning process, controllers frequently copy past years' actual data into the plan data for the upcoming year. These basic functions

---

[2] Günter Graf, "Enhancing an Input-Ready Query with a Comments Column in Integrated Business Planning for SAP Simple Finance."
[3] Günter Graf, "Provisional Master Data in Integrated Business Planning for SAP Simple Finance."

plus a large set for more sophisticated functions (rounding, revaluation, statistical functions, etc.) are now available based on SAP HANA. These functions are the foundation for defining predictive scenarios.

All of these improvements are available after a seamless migration of existing plan data so that companies can continue to work with their existing numbers. SAP BPC for Finance provides end users with different means to enter planning data, such as Microsoft Excel or a web-based interface.

11.5.4 Business Planning Process

Figure 11.19 and Table 11.4 outline the process that many companies use as a best practice, in which all steps are supported by the new SAP BPC for Finance. Throughout the process, a central planning administrator orchestrates the steps using Business Process Framework (BPF; envisaged for a future release). The system supports this administrator, ensuring a proper sequence in the planning steps by sending corresponding mails and links to the affected users, and so on.

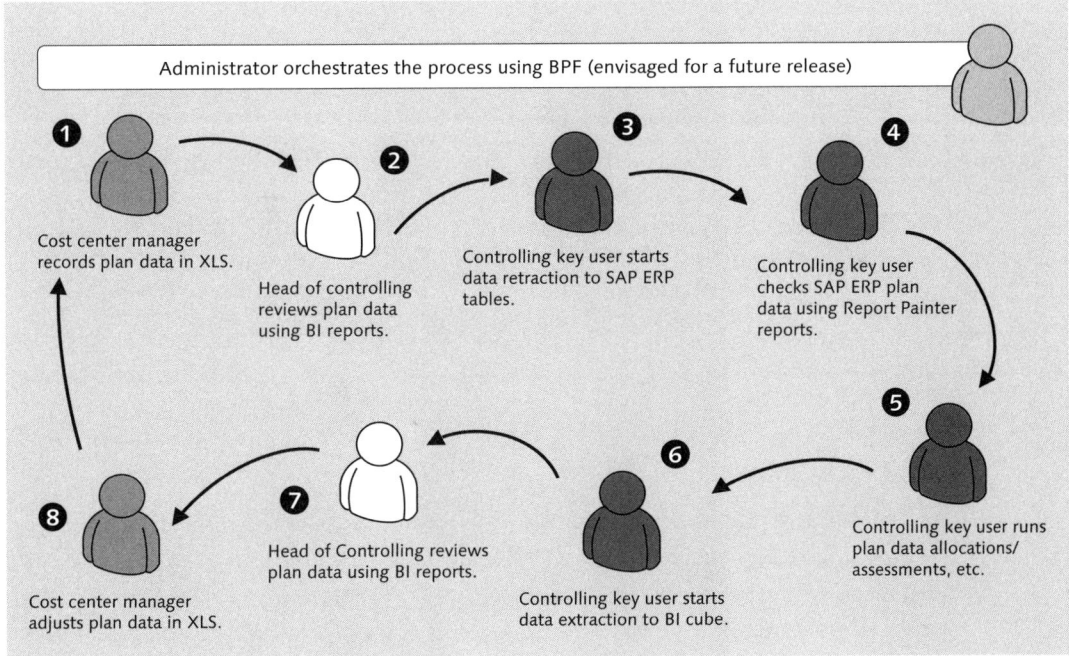

Figure 11.19 SAP BPC for Finance Workflow

Role	Process Step	Business Function Benefit
End user	❶: Cost center manager opens planning Microsoft Excel sheet and records plan data.	Personalized Microsoft Excel sheet. Plan data recording is limited to the end user's area of responsibility, resulting in a consistent set of data.
Manager	❷: Head of Controlling department verifies plan data completeness and correctness using SAP BW reports.	Increased plan data quality.
Key user	❸ and ❹: Controlling key user launches the retraction process and verifies plan data using existing reports.	No new investments are needed in this area.
Key user	❺: Process the plan data: allocations, distributions, order settlement, tariff calculation, and so on.	Consistent plan data processing ensures comparability with historic data.
Key user	❻: In case the plan data needs to be corrected, it can be extracted back to the SAP BW cube.	This process can be repeated as often as needed.
Manager	❼: The head of the controlling department can run a set of SAP BW reports to verify data completeness, and standard plan/actual reports can be executed.	Drilldown reports from a high-level income statement down to a detailed market segment report can be executed for actual data and plan data in parallel in a seamless way.
End user	❽: In case the plan data needs to be corrected, the key user can change existing data or create plan data by using a new category or version.	Plan data correction occurs in a very flexible and transparent way. Together with the comments functionality, the history of plan data can always be explained.

Table 11.4 SAP BPC for Finance Process

11.5.5 Outlook

As explained so far, the SAP BPC for Finance solution for SAP S/4HANA Finance creates significant business benefit for companies and addresses often-requested requirements. Among others, the benefits include the reconciled view on all financial data by bringing together FI and CO and the simplified system landscape that tears down planning silos. The simplified architecture lays the foundation for future improvements that will yield a few key additional benefits:

- The planned Business Planning and Consolidation Business Planning Framework (BPC-BPF) will allow companies to orchestrate their planning processes in order to ensure a smooth planning workflow with full governance over timelines, dependencies, and authorizations.
- SAP HANA has the potential to improve the allocation and assessment functionality with faster algorithms. Furthermore, the corresponding configuration and UI could be simplified drastically.
- Financial plan data for Management Accounting (with regard to the income statement) could be integrated with other planning applications in the areas of balance sheet planning or cash flow and liquidity planning. The planning engine could automatically consider dependencies among different senders and receivers, such as the ones shown in Figure 11.20. For example, an increased headcount (additional expenses) planned in one department will impact liquidity, and additional equipment for the new employees will have an effect on the balance sheet.

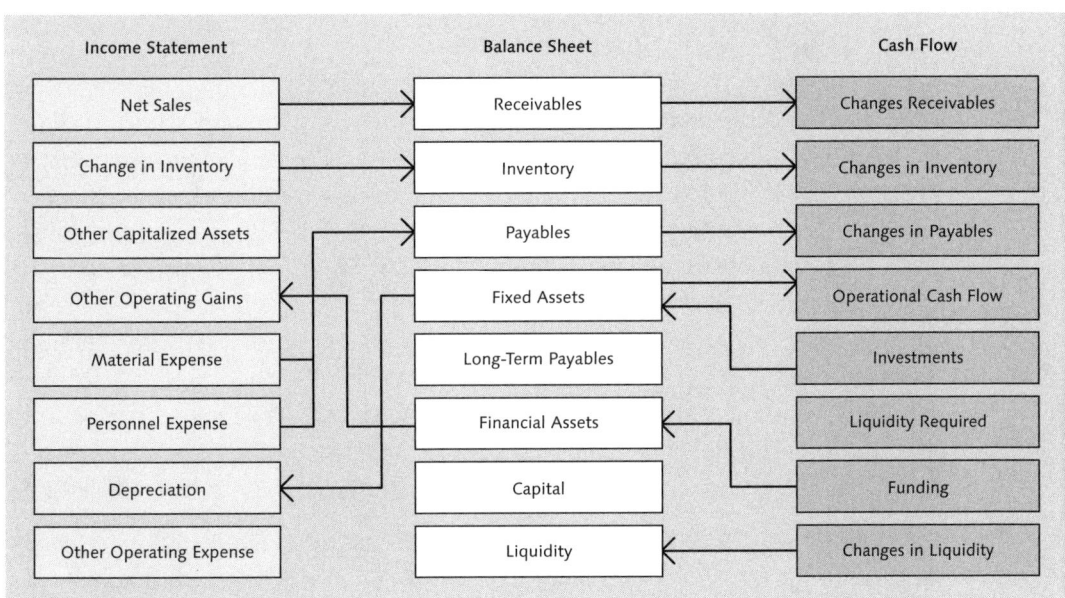

Figure 11.20 Potential Dependencies among Income Statement, Balance Sheet, and Cash Flow Planning

11.6 Profitability

We can determine the profitability of a company as a whole by viewing all income and expenses for the period in the income statement. However, to truly understand what drives their business, organizations need a more granular breakdown of their income statements. This helps companies understand which customers they are serving, which products they are selling, which channels they are serving, and where sales are taking place. Although the company as a whole may be profitable, some customers typically will be very profitable and some less profitable, and others may cause the company to lose money. It should be the company's goal to keep the profitable customers, grow the less profitable customers, and either retire or change the relationship with the customers who are not profitable at all. The same applies to the products and services that the company sells, the channels that serve the customers, and the geographies in which they operate. Although all companies are obliged to provide an income statement about their business activities as a whole, many struggle to create a more granular analysis of the profitability by customer, product, channel, region, or other dimensions for internal purposes and to make these figures available to their sales managers and marketing executives in a timely manner.

Understanding profitability is partly a data volume challenge: The number of customer invoices to aggregate typically is huge. In order to understand what has been spent to drive that business, companies often perform allocations to charge the sales and administration costs to the parts of the organization they served. We also find internal orders and projects used to capture event-based costs, such as those for a trade fair, and these costs also need to be assigned to the correct profitability dimensions via settlement. In addition, a manufacturing company will create cost estimates to determine the standard costs for each product and an engineer-to-order or professional service company will create a cost estimate for each project. This information also plays its part in setting standards for profitability analysis. Period close then brings a long chain of jobs to perform the allocations, settle internal orders and projects, settle variances with respect to original estimates, and generally assign all relevant costs to the revenues earned.

The story of SAP HANA in finance begins with costing-based Profitability Analysis. Selecting the relevant revenue items and cost items for each product, customer, region, sales office, and so on used to involve preselecting the information required for analysis and storing it in summarized form. Even with the summarization completed, care was needed in the definition of the reports in order not to mix products and customers in the same report.

With SAP HANA, the same profitability reports query huge datasets without the need for this preaggregation. This means that each time the manager opens the report, he triggers a new selection from the database and receives instant results. An accelerator for account-based Profitability Analysis quickly followed. Companies were able to benefit from the speed of SAP HANA not only in reporting but also in their allocations and top-down distributions. To allocate sales and administration costs, we typically use reference data (such as the revenue per customer) to determine how to split the costs. This selection step could represent around 30% of the entire run time of an allocation, so accelerating the selection of the reference data provides enormous performance benefits. Further improvements are achieved in top-down distribution by using SAP HANA's ability for parallel processing. The improved version of top-down distribution processes each sender (the dimension with costs to disaggregate) separately so that even better performance can be achieved.

SAP S/4HANA Finance goes further by addressing another big challenge in profitability: ensuring that the totals shown in the income statement match the more granular contribution margins in Profitability Analysis. Account-based Profitability Analysis was originally built with this kind of reconciliation in mind. Nevertheless, it was only as detailed as the accounts in the G/L. Hence, most manufacturing companies continued to rely on costing-based Profitability Analysis because they wanted to break out their cost of goods sold and production variances into more detail. Only the value fields in costing-based Profitability Analysis allowed them to leverage the information calculated in Product Cost Controlling to achieve this.

Let's look at how SAP S/4HANA Finance has been enhanced to update several accounts for the cost of goods sold and the production variances, where formerly only a single account was updated. This allows for a more detailed recording of the information.

Because of the complexity of the profitability reports, their usage was often limited to a handful of controllers. The actual target audience, such as sales managers, did not use the reports by themselves. With SAP S/4HANA Finance, however, there are new reports designed specifically for sales managers rather than controllers. To get an impression of the new Profitability Analysis, let's start by looking at the new SAP Fiori applications. We'll then look at the functional enhancements that enable organizations to see more details in their accounts.

11.6.1 SAP Fiori Applications

We discussed the reporting needs of a manager in Chapter 9. SAP S/4HANA Finance includes the Margin Analysis application for this user group, together with a number of key figures.

Figure 11.21 shows the margin analysis—and specifically the actual margin as a percentage of the actual revenue for a group of materials. Notice how easy it is to see the relative margins of each of the products and note the analysis paths on the left, which allow managers to display not only the margins but also the revenues, the direct costs, and the indirect costs for each product. The manager can set up further analysis steps (on the left) to display the same key figures by customer and by channel, also for various time slices. It is this detail that provides the transparency that was lacking in a classic income statement.

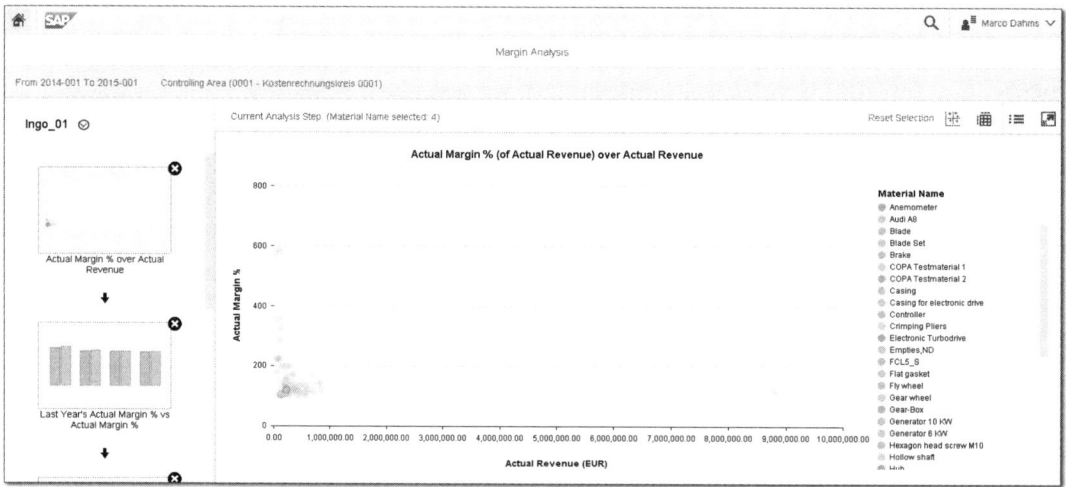

Figure 11.21 Margin Analysis

11.6.2 From Costing-Based to Account-Based Profitability Analysis

The figures displayed as margins in Figure 11.21 are calculated by looking at a group of accounts rather than value fields or key figures. In general, an account model (account-based Profitability Analysis) and a key figure model (costing-based Profitability Analysis) represent two different ways of looking at the same information.

In account-based Profitability Analysis, you look at the values by account (in other words, you use exactly the same format as the income statement). In costing-based Profitability Analysis, you assign the values to key figures or value fields. Depending on the definition, key figures (such as revenues or cost of goods sold) may actually be one and the same in the accounting view, but it is the transformation from accounts to key figures that makes reconciliation difficult. Sometimes, the values of ten accounts have been rolled up into one key figure: revenues. At other times, the value of one account—cost of goods sold—has been broken out into several key figures, such as raw material costs, internal activity costs, overhead costs, and so on. At still other times, key figures such as the quantity of goods sold are displayed, but they are not shown in accounting at all. This can make it difficult for the accountants working with the income statement and the controllers working with the profitability reports to be sure that they are dealing with one version of the truth.

The easiest way to imagine account-based Profitability Analysis is to imagine a journal entry for a cost center expense or an order expense, then replace the one-dimensional cost center, order, or project with a multidimensional set of characteristics. Typically, revenues and cost of goods sold are posted at a granular level: by customer, product, channel, region, and aggregates of these dimensions. When you allocate costs, you make a decision during configuration as to whether, for example, the trade fair served the Western Europe region (one of perhaps a dozen regions) or all customers in Western Europe (thousands of customers), because this affects the number of records created and the detail available for reporting. If you've worked with costing-based Profitability Analysis in the past, you'll know that such an allocation would typically credit the cost center/order, debit a reconciliation object (a placeholder for all the dimensions in Profitability Analysis), and create separate records to account for the marketing costs in costing-based Profitability Analysis. If you allocate to account-based Profitability Analysis, then you will be crediting the cost center/order and creating debits for each of the regions served and/or customers served. This simple sender–receiver relationship is much easier to visualize and check.

The next challenge is the timing of some of the postings. In the G/L, the creation of a delivery document triggers a goods issue and the associated cost of goods sold posting. In costing-based Profitability Analysis, the cost of goods sold is not realized until the invoice is posted. If a period close intervenes between delivery and invoice, then the two applications can be out of sync. In account-based Profitability Analysis, such a difference cannot happen.

Going forward, companies using SAP S/4HANA Finance will still be able to use costing-based Profitability Analysis, but for the benefits just outlined the main focus will be on account-based Profitability Analysis as part of the Universal Journal. In the following sections, we explain how existing processes have been extended to provide more detail in account-based Profitability Analysis.

Revenues

In general, revenue postings to account-based Profitability Analysis are easy, because the sales accounts already flow into the G/L. The only limitation is that statistical postings, such as freight calculations, do not generally flow into the G/L. If you want to include freight and other statistical calculations in your profitability reports, then you should continue to use costing-based Profitability Analysis alongside the account-based model for these items.

Cost of Goods Sold

Organizations that manufacture the goods they sell typically have used costing-based Profitability Analysis, because it allows them to take into account the standard costs for the goods sold to determine which part of these costs could be considered raw material costs, internal activity costs, overhead costs, and so on.

SAP S/4HANA Finance provides new options that allow organizations to break out their cost of goods sold to these separate accounts. To do so, they extend their chart of accounts to include new accounts for each cost component in their standard cost estimates and thus gain transparency regarding the relative weight of each cost type in their product costs. This allows these organizations to see where they are potentially exposed to risks due to changing commodity prices for their raw materials or changes in their wage structures.

Variances

Organizations manufacturing their products typically have also calculated production variances to determine the scrap, price variances, quantity variances, resource usage variances, and so on for each manufacturing order and assigned these to value fields in costing-based Profitability Analysis.

Again, SAP S/4HANA Finance provides the same options for account-based Profitability Analysis, allowing organizations to break out their price differences into separate accounts representing scrap, price variances, quantity variances, resource usage variances, and so on. Adding new variance and scrap accounts increases the transparency companies have regarding the efficiency of their production processes.

Allocation and Settlement

We already discussed the journal entries for allocation and settlement when we discussed the difference between account-based and costing-based Profitability Analysis. There are no changes to the allocation and settlement functions as such, but it makes sense to revisit your chart of accounts to check that the accounts you will use to record the allocation of marketing costs, sales costs, administration costs, and so on provide sufficient detail for your reports and to ensure that all these accounts are included in the financial statement version for reporting. You will need to create corresponding assignment cycles for account-based Profitability Analysis.

Quantities

Finally, in addition to reviewing the revenues and costs associated with their goods and services, many organizations also analyze the volume of goods sold. The quantities captured in logistics flow into accounting, but they are often in units (such as boxes and pallets) that make an aggregation across product lines impossible. For this reason, many organizations convert these quantities into comparable units, such as tons or kilograms. Again, account-based Profitability Analysis has been extended to support this type of analysis, allowing organizations to report not only the revenues earned but also the volumes shipped. This gives a good impression of how the operational business performed in a given period.

11.6.3 Outlook

Thus we see that with relatively small changes in the applications, a new approach to profitability reporting is possible with SAP S/4HANA Finance that provides increased transparency in several key areas and ensures that all stakeholders are working with one version of the truth. With the Universal Journal as the foundation, many more future improvements are possible.

The real-time provisioning of profitability attributes described in Chapter 8 already provides additional dimensions useful for Profitability Analysis. By expanding the set of dimensions that are automatically derived during posting, it will be possible to further enrich the data that forms the basis for Profitability Analysis to arrive at a more fine-grained level of reporting.

In addition, remember that in Chapter 8 we described our vision of how facts existing in the system can be used to arrive at more accurate predictions. The same train of thought also applies to Profitability Analysis in particular. Current events and transactions that will have an impact on profitability in the future (e.g., purchase orders with increased raw material prices) can be written forth as prediction documents and analyzed with standard profitability reports.

11.7 Financial Closing and Consolidation

No financial process of a company gets more external attention than financial closing and consolidation.

This process provides accurate and complete financial statements for local group companies, segments, and profit centers and consolidates them into a single corporate group statement. Timely, accurate, and transparent external reporting is a seal of quality and is representative of the overall process quality of the entire organization. Moreover, it is also the wish of managers to get an early (in-period) view of their external reporting. In the past, a lack of control, disparate data stores, and lower performance led to longer closing processes. SAP S/4HANA Finance improves the closing and consolidation cycles of companies in several ways:

- **Process control**
  Exercising control over processes ensures that your close processes are consistent across organizational units, whereas central monitoring reduces the execution risks across the entire cycle.

- **Avoiding reconciliation efforts**
  With the Central Finance deployment option (see Chapter 14), SAP S/4HANA Finance allows closing and consolidation processes to operate on a single data set. The Universal Journal ensures reconciled G/L, controlling, and subledger data.

- **Closing during the period with the speed of SAP HANA**
  Closing programs of SAP S/4HANA Finance have been optimized for SAP HANA by aggregating data directly on the database level. By running closing programs (such as project result analysis or work-in-progress calculations) frequently within the period, these programs serve as risk mitigation with earlier insight into the upcoming financial figures.

- **New closing applications**
  New or enhanced applications, such as SAP Intercompany Reconciliation, make closing tasks more efficient and transparent.

Let's take a closer look at each of these means to improve financial closing and consolidation.

11.7.1 Process Management

Fast and reliable financial closing and consolidation processes need efficient process management. The steps involved in a period-end close are highly interdependent and require alignment with clear scheduling and monitoring across the entire organization. Organizations that are able to monitor and react during the close cycle can reduce the impact of a breakdown in the process.

The SAP Smart Business cockpit for financial close of SAP S/4HANA Finance provides an easy-to-use, template-driven environment that enables business users to set up and schedule their companies' closing cycles. It enables financial professionals to create the closing schedule as a series of automated and manual time-based tasks. They can create tasks, assign them to task owners, or schedule them as automated jobs.

The SAP Smart Business cockpit for financial close monitors the status and progress of the financial close for all tasks and units. Figure 11.22 displays the overview the cockpit provides at a particular point in time during the closing process. As a manager, you can get an overview on your mobile device to quickly see which closing tasks are completed, in process, ready for execution, or nonexecutable. You can easily identify the overdue tasks and the potential overall delay in the closing cycle. Further analysis provides deeper insight into timelines and task owners. In order to resolve problems, you can trigger emails or initiate collaboration sessions with relevant stakeholders.

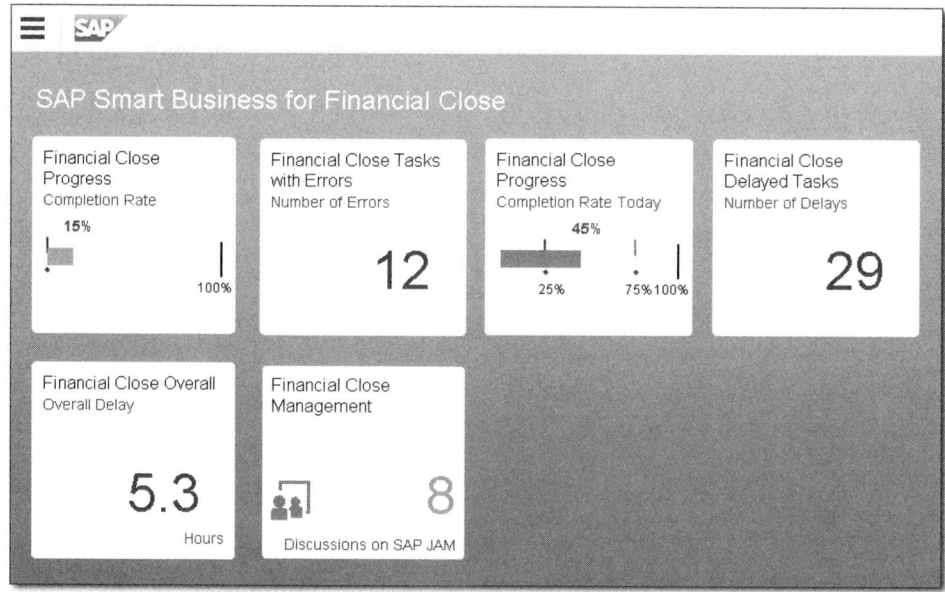

Figure 11.22 SAP Smart Business Cockpit for Financial Close

11.7.2 Avoiding Reconciliation Efforts

Operating the financial processes of an organization as a shared services center is a common business model. Centralizing administrative business processes goes along with harmonizing and centralizing the underlying IT system as well. SAP S/4HANA Finance supports this trend with its central deployment option, Central Finance (which we'll cover in more detail in Chapter 14). Instead of having data distributed over a diverse system landscape, the Central Finance system makes integrated closing and consolidation information centrally available at any time without spending effort on data transfer and transformation. The data transfer and transformation happens automatically in real time from local logistic and finance systems (possible also from older release versions or non-SAP systems). The postings are always processed in the Central Finance system, considering all authorization and compliance aspects. Data completeness is therefore always given without the usual reconciliation effort in case data is distributed across several IT systems.

Avoiding reconciliation effort on the system level is continued on the level of the data model within the system. As outlined in Chapter 8, SAP S/4HANA Finance has one single source of truth (the Universal Journal) for G/L, Management Accounting, and the subledgers AP/AR, Fixed Asset, and Current Asset Accounting. One Universal Journal entry is inherently reconciled so that time-consuming reconciliation tasks across components are no longer necessary.

11.7.3 Faster Period Close with SAP HANA

SAP HANA accelerates the month-end closing process. Many steps can even be run on a daily or weekly basis rather than only at period end. Thus, the accounting component of SAP S/4HANA Finance provides much earlier insight into the upcoming financials figures.

The general approach for reworking and speeding up period-close activities utilizes in-memory technology by performing tasks directly on the database layer, rather than in the application layer. For example, in the past, work-in-progress calculation selected orders for settlement and then looped over order by order, aggregating the relevant costs, performing the relevant calculations, and then writing the results to the database (see left side of Figure 11.23). As described in Chapter 2, set processing operations (e.g., aggregations) should be executed in the database to take full advantage of SAP HANA. In this manner, many period-end programs have been accelerated significantly. As shown on the right side of Figure 11.23, the selection of the relevant costs and their aggregation is moved to SAP HANA and performed for all orders in the initial selection with high speed before the process returns to the application server in order to calculate the works in progress, variances, and so on.

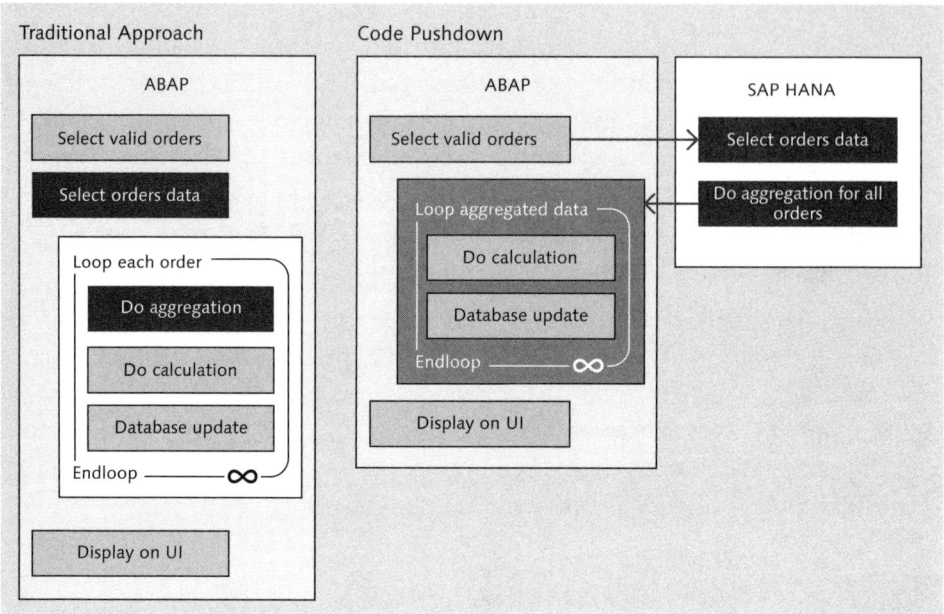

Figure 11.23 Code Pushdown to SAP HANA Database

11.7.4 New Closing Applications

In addition to SAP HANA speeding up existing processes, new applications improve other important close transactions. In the following sections, we look at two examples: intercompany reconciliation and monitoring accounts for goods received or invoices received.

SAP Intercompany Reconciliation

Corporate group consolidation eliminates intragroup deliveries among affiliated companies. Before this consolidation step can start, all mismatches, such as one-sided postings on sender or receiver sites or amount differences, need to be identified and corrected.

The SAP Intercompany Reconciliation app checks all intragroup deliveries and identifies mismatches. SAP Intercompany Reconciliation is optimized for the Central Finance scenario. In a multisystem landscape, intragroup delivery data is transferred to one SAP Intercompany Reconciliation system, in which the mismatches are calculated via batch processes. With Central Finance, SAP Intercompany Reconciliation gets direct, high-speed access to open items from the Universal Journal. Now, SAP Intercompany Reconciliation can be executed at any time with immediate results, thus avoiding bottlenecks at period end. An easy-to-navigate web UI (see Figure 11.24) provides transparent process insight via graphical reconciliation alerts and access to all relevant reports.

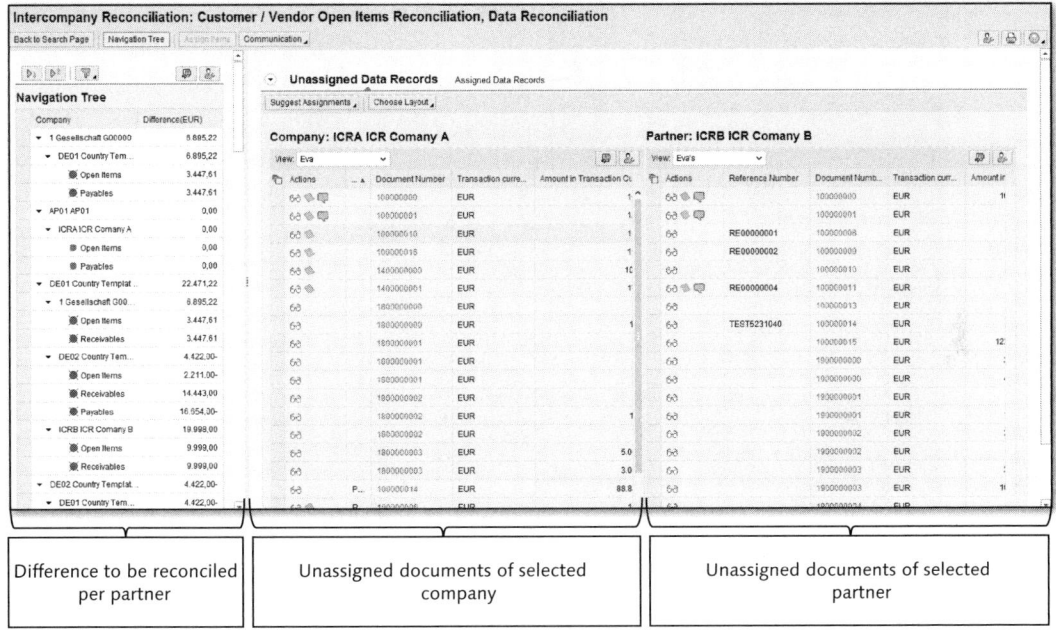

Figure 11.24 SAP Intercompany Reconciliation Dashboard

GR/IR Monitor

You use the goods receipt/invoice receipt (GR/IR) clearing account to post goods received that have not yet been invoiced and invoices for goods that have not yet been received. When you receive the missing goods (or invoice), the system makes an offsetting post to the GR/IR clearing account. Before creating financial statements, you need to analyze the GR/IR clearing account to check whether its balance is correct. An incorrect balance can happen, because in some cases an automatic offsetting post is not possible—for example, if quantities or amounts from goods receipt and invoice differ too much. SAP S/4HANA Finance makes this mandatory reconciliation step much faster and more transparent. A single app, SAP Invoice and Goods Receipt Reconciliation (see Figure 11.25), replaces multiple backend transactions with real-time insight into invoices, goods receipt, master data, and supporting information.

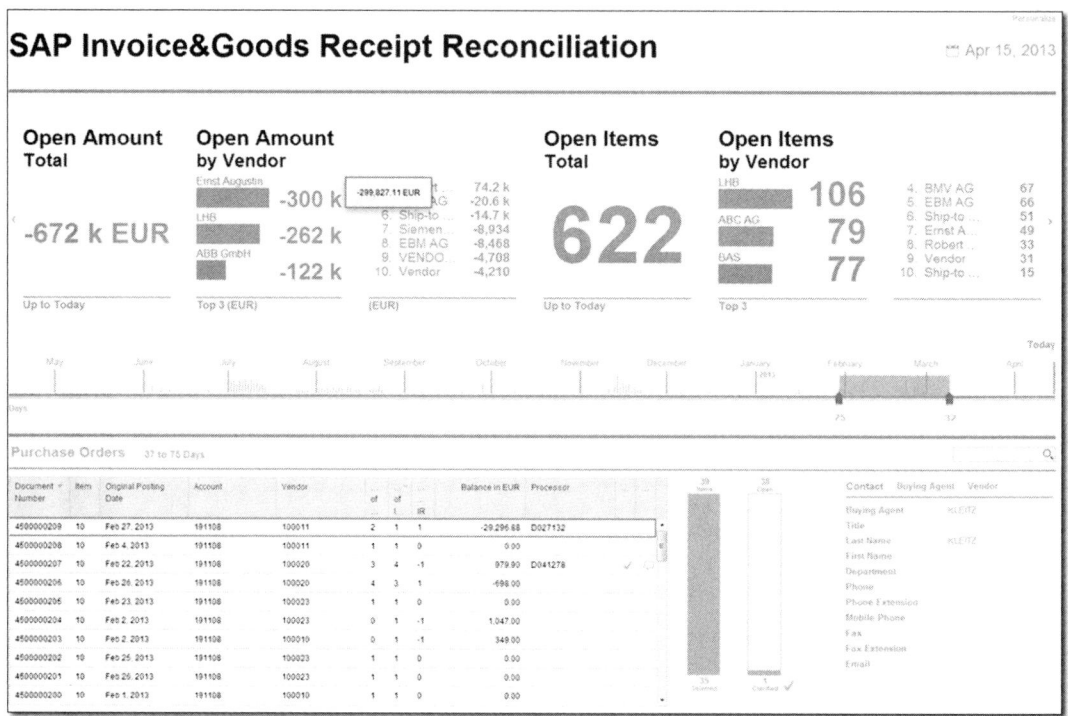

Figure 11.25 SAP Invoice & Goods Receipt Reconciliation

11.7.5 Outlook

SAP S/4HANA Finance accelerates the closing and consolidation cycle in several ways. As a closing manager, you can monitor the status and progress of the financial close for all tasks and units. As a business manager, you have earlier insight into financial key figures, because many closing steps can run on a daily or weekly basis.

The future development of closing in SAP S/4HANA Finance will continue in this direction and will continue to be an area of innovation. More local close processes will be processed during a period, such as allocation and settlement posting, which are triggered automatically for each individual journal posting. SAP plans for group consolidation methods to work directly on the Universal Journal entries without any of the extraction and transformation effort of a separate consolidation system.

11.8 Revenue Accounting

Revenue is one of the most important figures in a financial statement for assessing an entity's financial performance and position. Amount and timing for recognizing revenue have to be determined according to various accounting standards.

In order to clarify the requirements and principles for recognizing revenue, the International Accounting Standards Board (IASB) and the US Financial Accounting Standards Board (FASB) have recently defined a common standard for revenue from contracts with customers. It has been published as International Financial Reporting Standards (IFRS) 15 and as Topic 606 in FASB Update 2014-09 and will be effective for annual periods beginning on or after January 1, 2018. It clarifies some principles for determination of amount and timing for recognizing revenue, and it defines some new requirements, especially for disclosure.

With SAP S/4HANA Finance, SAP delivers SAP Revenue Accounting and Reporting as an add-on. With this solution, companies can determine the amount and timing of revenue postings in financial accounting for any sales process. The add-on can process events from any operational sales application, such as SAP ERP Sales and Distribution or third-party applications. In a system landscape with a centralized finance system and several systems for operational applications, you only need to implement SAP Revenue Accounting and Reporting once. Therefore, you can easily ensure that principles for revenue recognition are implemented and applied consistently for similar operational processes.

This new solution not only enables companies to comply with the new upcoming revenue standard but also makes recognized revenue available at the same time for management reporting. Because some of the general principles of the standard allow entities to define their specific company policies, the new solution offers configuration options accordingly. Companies can define their own rules in Business Rule Framework plus (BRFplus). With this flexible rules framework, the solution also can be applied for many requirements of existing revenue standards, such as IAS 18 and US GAAP standards.

Companies that have implemented parallel accounting principles can define different rules for revenue accounting separately for each accounting principle. If an accounting principle allows revenue recognition at invoice for certain processes, then companies do not need to implement SAP Revenue Accounting and Reporting for those processes.

The new revenue standard defines a model of five steps for revenue recognition:

1. Identify the contract(s) with a customer.
2. Identify the performance obligations in the contract.
3. Determine the transaction price.
4. Allocate the transaction price to the performance obligations in the contract.
5. Recognize revenue when the entity satisfies a performance obligation.

The following sections describe the detailed functionality of SAP Revenue Accounting and Reporting along this five-step model.

11.8.1 Contract Identification

Contracts with customers are usually entered into an operational application. However, according to the revenue standard IFRS 15.17, an entity has to combine contracts under certain conditions and account for them as a single contract. Therefore, different contracts from an operational application can be combined within SAP Revenue Accounting and Reporting into a single revenue accounting contract.

You can implement algorithms for automatic combination (e.g., based on the time between the inception dates of two contracts), but you can also manually combine contracts or even split a contract and assign only some items to another revenue accounting contract. It is also possible to combine contracts from different operational applications.

The system can manage contract modifications according to IFRS 15.21 and either allocate the remaining revenue to remaining performance obligations or calculate a cumulative catch-up.

11.8.2 Performance Obligation Identification

Usually, SAP Revenue Accounting and Reporting creates one performance obligation in a revenue accounting contract for one item of an operational contract. However, some special cases are handled differently.

If an operational contract contains items that are generally sold as a package with a special package price, then the single items can be distinct performance obligations, or the package as a whole may have to be accounted for as one performance obligation. In Figure 11.26, the Smartphone Pack as a whole is one performance obligation. In BRFplus, you can configure what kinds of items of an operational contract will be combined in one performance obligation. This combination becomes relevant for revenue recognition if the single items are not delivered to the customer at the same time.

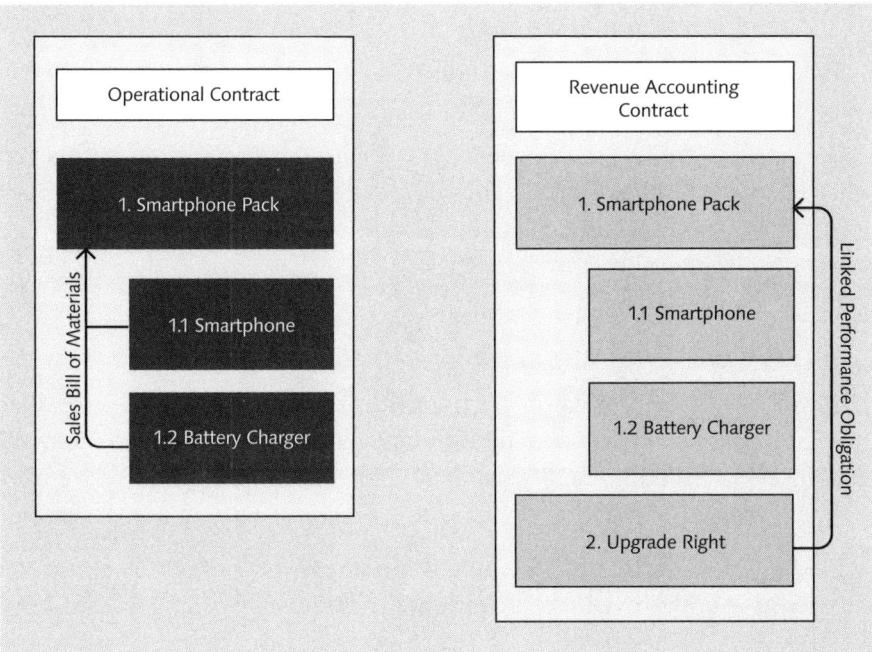

Figure 11.26 Operational Contract with a Package, and Revenue Accounting Contract with Linked Performance Obligation

Sometimes, a contract may include some implicit right that is not explicitly included as an item in the operational contract. For example, an entity sells hardware devices with software, for which customers have a right to receive updates over a defined timespan. The updates are not included as an item in the operational contract, because they will not be separately delivered or charged to the customers. Revenue can be recognized either over time or when upgrades are made available for download to all affected customers.

Within SAP Revenue Accounting and Reporting, you can configure (in BRFplus) what kinds of implicit rights exist for what kinds of items. For these implicit rights, the system will then create additional performance obligations that are linked to the "leading" performance obligation. In Figure 11.26, the Upgrade Right is an additional performance obligation that is linked to the Smartphone Pack leading performance obligation. The system will then allocate a part of the total transaction price to the linked performance obligation. Revenue for the linked performance obligation then usually will be recognized over time, starting with fulfillment of its leading performance obligation.

11.8.3 Transaction Price Determination

The pricing conditions of the items of the operational contract determine the transaction price of the corresponding performance obligations in a revenue accounting contract. SAP Revenue Accounting and Reporting takes into account changes in the pricing conditions in the operational application at any time before or after fulfillment or at invoicing.

11.8.4 Transaction Price Allocation

According to IFRS 15.74, the complete transaction price of a contract (in other words, the sum of the prices from all performance obligations of the contract) will generally be allocated to the distinct performance obligations in the contract relative to their standalone selling prices.

The standalone selling prices can be determined in flexible ways: They can be based on pricing conditions of the operational item, or they can be loaded from an external source. They can be defined as dependent on any attribute of the operational item (e.g., material and sales channel).

11.8.5 Revenue Recognition

SAP Revenue Accounting and Reporting supports several methods to satisfy a performance obligation and trigger revenue recognition:

- **Satisfaction at a point in time (event based)**
  A defined event in an operational application (e.g., goods issue) or manual entry delivers the satisfied quantity and triggers corresponding revenue recognition.

- **Satisfaction over time**
  Revenue can also be recognized over a period of time in increments. There are two alternatives:

  - **Time-based satisfaction**
    Spread revenue by a mathematical algorithm (e.g., a straight line) over a defined time

  - **Satisfaction based on percentage of completion**
    A percentage of completion can be entered manually or transferred via an interface from an operational application and trigger according recognition of revenue

SAP Revenue Accounting and Reporting allows for configuring which method will be used for what kind of performance obligation, giving companies full flexibility.

11.8.6 Flexible Adaptability

Although companies can configure flexible rules for automatic processing of contracts and performance obligations in SAP Revenue Accounting and Reporting, they can also enter manual adjustments for specific valuations. All manual activities will be tracked for a complete audit trail. Companies can also implement work lists for manual checking of automatic processing.

11.8.7 Outlook

In its current release, SAP Revenue Accounting and Reporting creates aggregated postings to the G/L (FI-GL) in a periodic batch run. This batch run also transfers revenue data to Profitability Analysis (CO-PA).

In a future release, SAP Revenue Accounting and Reporting will leverage the capabilities of SAP HANA and the new concept of the Universal Journal for integration into G/L and CO-PA. It will be possible for every relevant operational event (e.g., a goods issue or any cost event) to trigger immediate real-time posting of the corresponding revenue in the G/L and in Profitability Analysis. This will offer several advantages:

- Revenue figures always in real time and up to date in G/L and Profitability Analysis
- Less time-consuming batch jobs at period close
- Easy audit trail via direct link between a cost posting document and a corresponding revenue posting document
- No reconciliation required between posted amounts in G/L and single items in Revenue Accounting

SAP Revenue Accounting and Reporting already makes recognized revenue figures available at the same time for accounting and for management reporting. Figures can be determined in flexible ways that are consistent with regulatory standards and company policy.

11.9 Real-Time Governance and Compliance

As the level of process automation constantly increases in all lines of business, it becomes more difficult for organizations to stay compliant with legal regulations, such as administrative offence law (OWiG) §130, the Prevention of Money Laundering Act (PMLA), the Financial Action Task Force (FATF), or the External Trade and Payments Act (AWV).

At first glance, this might sound contradictory, because automated processes usually support the implementation of external and internal guidelines. However, the legal requirements and the entire business environment are permanently changing, which increases the risk of inefficient automated controls and thus incompliance. The big challenge is how to recognize that a process needs to be adjusted.

SAP solutions for Governance, Risk, and Compliance (GRC) comprises a wide range of products for these tasks. These products are available separately (with individual licenses) but integrate closely with SAP S/4HANA Finance. Together, this combination offers companies a comprehensive way to govern their processes and manage risks. Let's take a look at how SAP GRC simplifies the practice of automated controls in order to efficiently monitor and improve any kind of business transaction. This discussion is divided into three sections: Section 11.9.1 provides an overview of governance, risk, and compliance; Section 11.9.2 discusses current trends and the challenges of staying compliant; and Section 11.9.3 looks at one particular process and shows how you can secure outgoing payments by identifying high-risk payments in real time.

11.9.1 Introduction to Governance, Risk, and Compliance

Today, organizations are growing at an unprecedented rate. They are not only expanding into multiple markets but also venturing into new terrain. Although this expansion creates significant opportunity, it also entails tremendous risk. With highly regulated markets and complex legal requirements, stakeholders are demanding greater transparency and effective management practices.

Compliance management became more important due to globalization and its impact on the worldwide business. Corruption scandals of nameable international companies and the financial crisis underline the significance of compliance. In view of a broadening legislative basis and correspondingly intensified enforcement, the pressure increases on economic organizations to consider compliance from a horizontal and vertical prospective.[4]

Managing risk is no longer an afterthought but must be at the forefront of business in order to achieve organizational goals. Organizations need the proper resources, processes, and technology to monitor and manage different types of risk. This includes strategic, tactical, operational, and regulatory risk as well as behavior or reputational risk.

Driven by the need for greater predictability and efficiency, organizations require integrated solutions and a unified approach to manage risk and compliance. SAP GRC helps organizations leverage best practices with scalable enterprise solutions. The solutions enable repeatable, automated, and unified responses to risk.

Using both the computing power of SAP HANA and its ability to integrate and manage any kind of SAP and non-SAP data, SAP GRC solutions enable organizations to automate key processes in order to detect, remediate, and prevent violations. In this way, they reduce the cost of access management, audit, and ongoing compliance activities and minimize the risk of incompliance or fraud.

---

[4] R. Wagner and D. E. Steinhüser, "Agenda 2015: Compliance Management als stetig wachsende Herausforderung."

SAP Fraud Management, for example, drives down costs associated with continuous monitoring and issue management while minimizing the risk of fraud. Comprehensive automated controls can be applied that refer to the real business processes, not restricted by the underlying, often limited, technical data model. Using predictive capabilities and in-memory technology, business users can instantly simulate and calibrate controls based on big data in order to avoid inefficient false alarms. Users gain a 360-degree view of risk, control, and compliance management across all business systems.

To secure the entire value chain beyond internal business processes, SAP GRC also helps companies manage global trade operations, improve ongoing trade compliance, and streamline cross-border supply chain activity.

11.9.2 Changing Trends and Challenges of Staying Compliant

Today's compliance management requires more than economical and legal strategies. Moving from an era in which compliance was considered to be the pure application of legal regulations by implementing internal policies, current trends veer toward directly embedding compliance into the business processes, which is a cornerstone of SAP GRC. Furthermore, it is important to achieve a solid acceptance level from process owners and eventually all employees.[5] To this end, SAP GRC offers means to continuously fine-tune the efficiency of controls and reduce false alarms.

With an increasing level of automation, the need for automated controls is obvious in order to ensure the proper operation of your business. Controls can be differentiated into preventive controls and detective controls. Preventive controls are designed to avert problems rather than identify them. Detective controls are meant to identify errors or irregularities after an event has occurred.[6] Usually, common controls defined by legal regulations such as SOX regulations are directly built into the business application.

---

5 Jens C. Laue and Christoph B. Schenk, "Wirksames Compliance-Management — ein anhaltendes Topthema in deutschen Unternehmen."
6 R.W. Grünendahl, *Beyond Compliance.*

Covering the Gray Areas

Even having all these controls in place is sometimes still insufficient. There are obvious situations in which customers or employees actively conduct fraudulent activities for their own benefit, but often people do not even know that they are violating a regulation and creating a high risk for their company that might result in drastic penalties. Although companies address bribery in their codes of conduct, some employees think it is culturally appropriate to pay additional "fees" to get transactions processed or deals closed. Some people believe there is an area open for wide interpretation, which may lead to wrongful transactions, because the business opportunity is more important than the compliance risk.

Because there are no detailed instructions on how to implement most legal requirements in the business process, this gray area is a reality. The law or corresponding authorities are aware that the effort to implement the legal requirements may be too expensive or cause too much effort and thus exercise the practice of due diligence in order to find out if the balance between compliance and operative risks was met. Due diligence means that the effort to implement legal requirements has to be reasonable. This can lead to a situation in which preventive controls are not sufficient, because they have to allow the business enough room to maneuver.

Implementing Detective Controls

SAP GRC provides comprehensive and highly flexible detective controls that complement manual policies, guidelines, and thus static preventive controls. Detective controls allow organizations to monitor all activities within the gray area in order to identify irregularities that do not fall under the application of due diligence but can be classified as noncompliance or even fraud.

The major success factor of both preventive and detective controls is in whether they can reduce risk and thus prevent financial damage due to improper cash drains or fines. Ideally, controls are embedded directly into the business process and can react in real time on exceptions. Stopping a high-risk payment before the money leaves the organization is much smarter than claiming it back. Let's look at how SAP GRC enables organizations to implement risk-based controls, test and calibrate them on production data, automatically identify high-risk transactions in real time, trigger preventive measures, and continuously improve controls to ensure effective and efficient exception management.

11.9.3 Embedded Real-Time Monitoring of High-Risk Transactions

A typical detective control is the identification, checking, and governance of high-risk transactions in order to minimize risks in areas such as taxes, anti-money laundering, anticorruption, fraud, and export control. Figure 11.27 shows the individual steps of an embedded monitoring scenario within the payment process, which is just one example of how SAP GRC secures your business transactions.

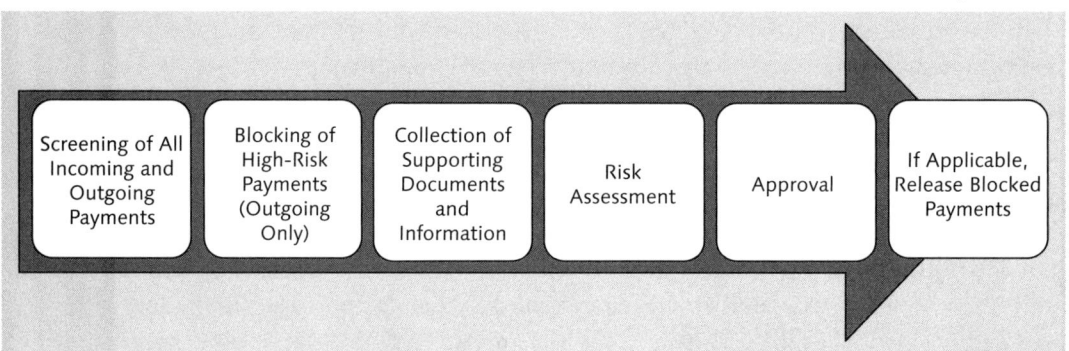

Figure 11.27 Real-Time Screening of Payments

SAP GRC screens all incoming and outgoing payments against a set of various rules that check, for example, for manual changes of the payee, payments on weekends or public holidays, bank accounts in high-risk countries, a different bank country from the country of registered office, or payment to an embargoed country. Each rule has an adjustable weighting and indicates a certain risk that contributes to an overall risk score per payment item. If the total risk score per payment item exceeds a defined threshold, SAP GRC automatically triggers an alert and blocks the outgoing payment item to avoid having the money leave the organization. In a review process, the payment items are investigated in order to decide whether the system was right to stop the payment or not.

In this phase, a workflow process is triggered to request additional documents and information from the accountant, assess a case-specific risk, and obtain approval from the business process owner—in this case, the accounting manager. If the accounting manager approves the payment item, then SAP GRC automatically releases the block and triggers the payment. All collected information, actions, and decisions are tracked within SAP GRC to guarantee auditing acceptability. A live dashboard provides an instant overview of all monitored business transactions, open alerts, total risk value, efficiency, and much more (see Figure 11.28).

Figure 11.28 Live Dashboard

Challenge of Staying Efficient

When you initially design a set of detection rules to identify high-risk transactions, they might work quite well. However, the entire business environment is constantly changing. The behavior of people changes both unconsciously and intentionally, official publications such as sanction lists are updated, average values and thresholds are adjusted, and even system parameters and process flows may change. These changes lead to the fact that your rules can easily fall out of date and produce more and more false positives or even false negatives. False alarms, also known as false positives, disturb regular business processes and create additional effort to resolve them. If the number of alerts exceeds a certain threshold, then users regard the system as waste and stop using it. Another related unwanted situation is one in which real cases are no longer detected (false negatives). Both false positives and false negatives decrease the efficiency of controls dramatically. To avoid this, you need the ability to constantly analyze, simulate, and adjust your controls.

As simple as this sounds, it is extremely difficult to change productive controls. First, you need an idea of what to change. Should you change the parameters of a rule, the weighting of each rule, the thresholds, or even the rules themselves? Classical systems required comprehensive and time-consuming analysis to identify efficiency drivers. Then, the business process or compliance owner had to hand over a corresponding change request to the IT department to provoke the necessary changes. Before these changes could be deployed to the production system, the IT department needed to conduct tests on sample data. Quite often, it took weeks or months before the changes were applied to the production environment.

Leveraging the power and flexibility of SAP HANA, SAP GRC reduces this lifecycle down to few minutes! A live dashboard permanently supervises the efficiency of each screening strategy. In case it changes for the worse, a business user can use a calibration tool to identify the root cause, apply and simulate changes, perform what-if analyses to predict the improvement, and create a new screening version. The easy-to-use calibration tool offers a feature to calculate an optimum for each screening strategy using statistical algorithms.

Figure 11.29 illustrates the contribution analysis within the calibration tool. For each rule within a detection strategy, a Sankey chart visualizes the corresponding contribution. For example, the user easily identifies weak rules that produce many false positives. Knowing the troublemaker, the user can directly change the rule's parameters or even deactivate it, immediately test the new setup, and directly apply the changes. All of this is possible within the production system on top of operative business data without any IT involvement.

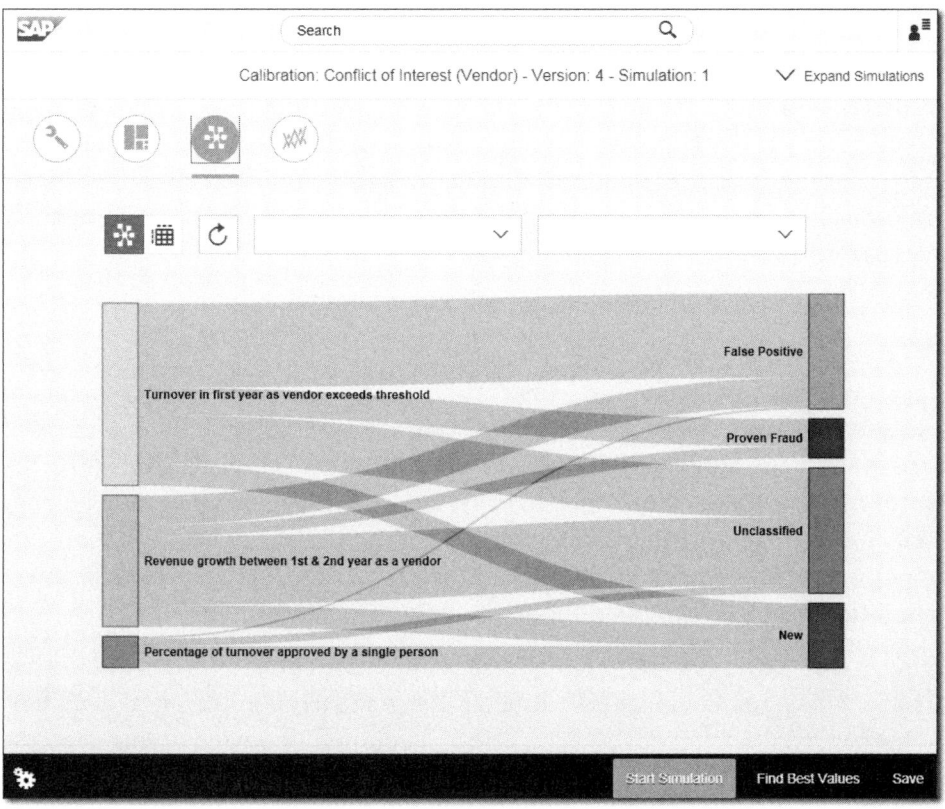

Figure 11.29 Real-Time Contribution Analysis

In addition to classical detection rules, SAP GRC allows business users to use statistical algorithms to train and integrate predictive models as part of a screening strategy. In contrast to rule-based approaches, a predictive approach does not require the knowledge of a concrete pattern. In fact, predictive models identify irregularities in the data and thus indicate new patterns. Combining both in one screening strategy offers new ways to optimize automated controls.

Using SAP HANA and the new in-memory paradigm allows for the simplification and acceleration of technical analyses to a degree that business users can directly utilize them. They can execute the aforementioned complex calculations at any time on production data in order to ensure efficient monitoring. Another huge enabler is SAP HANA's ability to collect data from various SAP and non-SAP systems to apply common rules or models. This enables you to implement detective controls across system borders, focusing on the business processes rather than on technical constraints.

As described in this chapter, SAP GRC not only provides you the flexibility to monitor all your business processes in real time; in comparison to classical rules-based continuous control monitoring systems, it also simplifies the entire process dramatically to give business users full control of the scope and impact of automated controls.

11.9.4 Outlook

As part of the finance value map, enterprise risk and compliance management are also key topics of SAP's future road map in finance. Corresponding solutions will benefit from the simpler and more streamlined architecture of SAP S/4HANA Finance and further performance improvements based on optimizations for in-memory processing. Throughout solutions in this area, the insight-to-action paradigm will become more prevalent and will allow risk managers to take direct action from any risk analysis.

With an ever-closer integration into financial processes in SAP S/4HANA Finance, managing risk and compliance will be an integral part of all financial activities, giving companies better governance. The dynamic definition and tuning of access and analysis rules based on the possibilities of SAP HANA will remain an important topic, as will a personalized and intuitive UI.

This chapter presents the new user experience of SAP Fiori delivered with SAP S/4HANA Finance. Intuitive and beautiful web apps replace the existing transactions. Task-based and role-centric apps allow users to follow their processes in an intuitive environment enriched with web capabilities.

12   Revamping the User Experience with SAP Fiori Apps

Research now confirms what we have known all along: People are drawn to things of beauty. SAP Fiori embraces this notion by creating a visually appealing and simplified consumer-grade user experience across SAP applications for frequently used business transactions. The flower in the logo of SAP Fiori (*fiori* means "flowers" in Italian) represents this sense for beauty (see Figure 12.1). However, we know that when it comes to closing the books, "simply beautiful" does not get the job done. Therefore, SAP Fiori goes beyond beauty alone, reimagining the end-to-end experience for enterprise users and reducing complexity throughout the process.

Figure 12.1 SAP Fiori Logo

In this chapter, we'll explain the SAP Fiori philosophy (Section 12.1), process (Section 12.2), and principles (Section 12.3) that bring "simplicity" to SAP S/4HANA

263

Finance. We then look at how these paradigms, combined with the application framework of SAP Fiori (Section 12.4), revitalize work in the enterprise (Section 12.5).

12.1   SAP Fiori Design Philosophy

SAP Fiori governs how applications look and feel, using design principles that ensure consistency across form factors and between applications.

We are inundated every day with information overload. Attention to aesthetic details, such as color, typography, and layout, bring structure to information so that it can be easily consumed, enabling us to work more productively and with a sense of satisfaction.

Yet design goes far beyond pretty pictures and graphics. It is a method of deliberately arranging information to appeal to our emotions and senses in the context of work. As shown in Figure 12.2, deliberate arrangement of information across form factors brings structure to information.

Figure 12.2 Arrangement of Information across Multiple Platforms

With a well-designed product, you are able to consume complex information and perform tasks without distraction or impediment. Tools and functions are available when you need them, and icons speak to your intuitive understanding of the functions they represent. A well-designed software product most prominently offers exactly those functions that the user most likely needs in the current context—for example, an option to call a customer when displaying that customer's overdue invoice.

We continually ask more of our products, and technology innovations such as SAP HANA and SAP S/4HANA Finance open up entirely new functional possibilities. At the same time, we demand that our products be easier to use. This tension presents designers with a great challenge, because simplicity is not simple to achieve. It requires rigorous and deep analysis of users' needs and pain points during their complex work. Based upon this analysis, SAP delivers an experience that is beautiful and intuitive.

The ultimate goal is to ensure that users achieve their tasks efficiently, without barriers. SAP Fiori supports this goal with processes, design principles, and concepts, as well as with technology.

12.2 Developing Intuitive Products

A structured design process is fundamental for creating beautiful, simple, and intuitive financial applications and for delivering the benefits outlined by this philosophy with SAP S/4HANA Finance. At the highest level, this process consists of "going broad" with research and contemplation, forming empathy with users, and then narrowing to tangible directions and ideas.

Design teams apply several methods to gain knowledge and understanding of the user, business, and market. To understand users, they observe them in the context of their work to gather insight into their core needs, pain points, work practices, and desires. Business-level needs are revealed through engagements and industry organizations (such as ASUG, DSAG, and the SAP Community Network) and through interviews with business leaders and key decision makers. SAP regularly researches the market to identify trends, understand the competition, and validate best practices.

This body of insight constitutes the basis of great design according to the needs and processes of financial users. Figure 12.3 illustrates the design process, with its characteristic flare and focus phases. In *flare phases*—for example, when getting an understanding of the problem at hand or prototyping solutions—a team should go broad and expand its mindset to look at more options and ideas. *Focus phases* are meant to converge on and arrive at a common artifact, such as the user's point of view or a refined product.

After design concepts solidify, the process moves into technical prototyping and development. Here, SAP Fiori utilizes the most modern and flexible UI technologies via SAPUI5. Based on industry-leading HTML5, SAPUI5 is a reusable code library and programming model optimized for consumption and display of SAP data. The benefits of SAPUI5 are enormous: It provides business agility, because it is available on any device and any platform, adapting seamlessly to different form factors. It increases user productivity and satisfaction through flexibility and openness. In addition, HTML5 is an open standard, so customers can easily adapt SAP S/4HANA Finance screens if required.

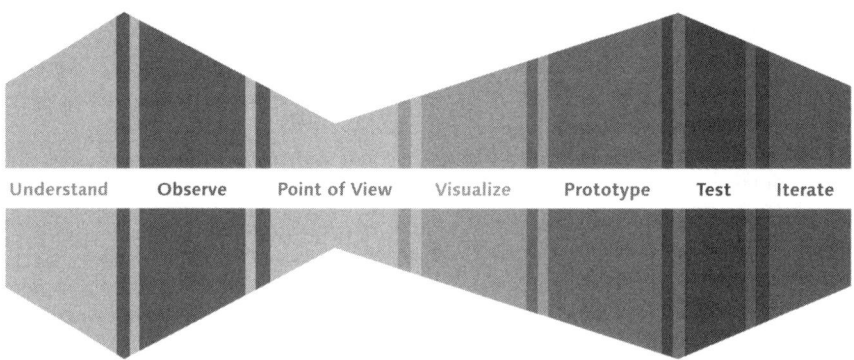

Figure 12.3 Design Process

12.3 SAP Fiori Design Principles in SAP S/4HANA Finance

Design principles guide the discussion when a product team evaluates multiple approaches during the design process shown in Figure 12.3. In addition to providing direction and rules, such principles act as tools that allow for sharpening and refining the system to meet the expectations of users. This section proposes and describes the five SAP Fiori design principles illustrated in Figure 12.4.

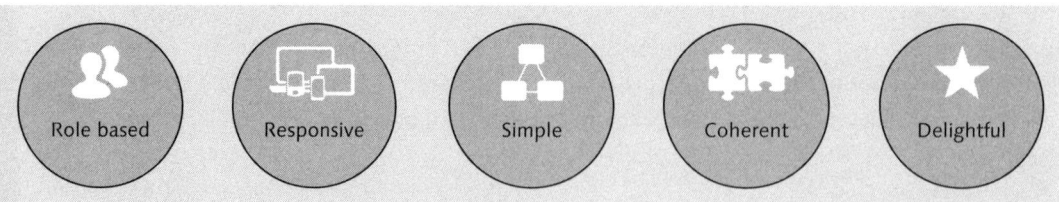

Figure 12.4 SAP Fiori Design Principles

The *role-based* principle ensures that SAP S/4HANA Finance speaks the language of your business. It requires designers to understand tasks and workflows across all roles so that solutions meet your needs based on an understanding of what you care about and how you work every day. The results (illustrated in the right part of Figure 12.5) are role-based applications that each match the specific requirements of a certain role instead of trying to incorporate various functions into a single screen (as shown on the left side of Figure 12.5). SAP S/4HANA Finance addresses each role within the finance ecosystem (accounts payable accountant, accounts receivable accountant, controller, auditor, etc.). Each user has a central (personalized) entry point into the system that gives access to all apps relevant to his role.

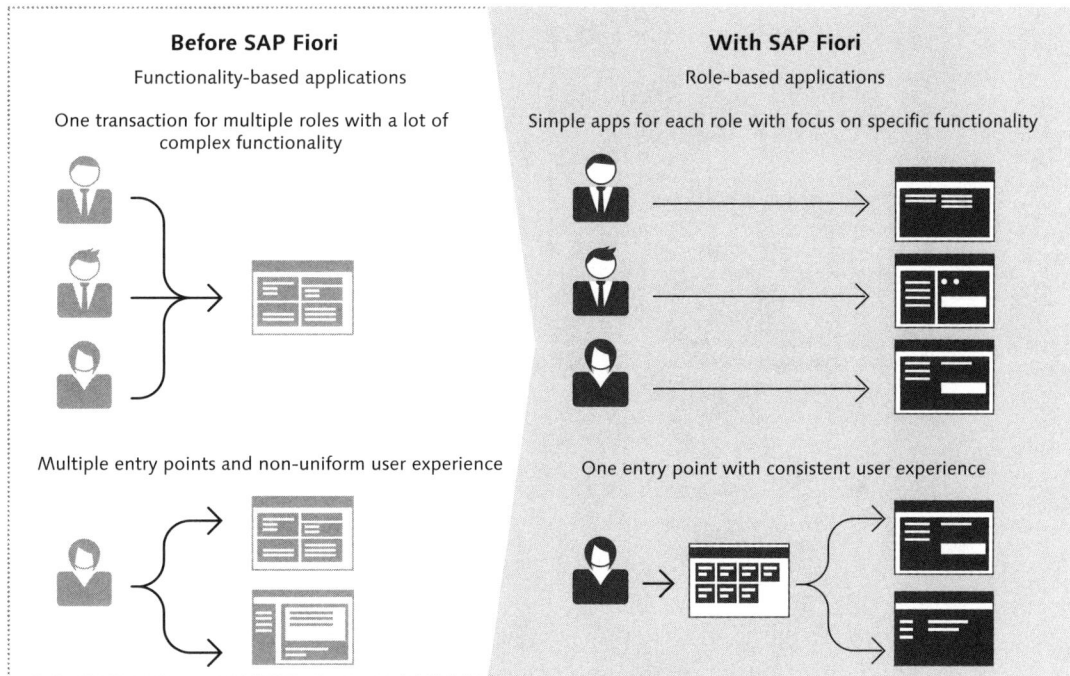

Figure 12.5 Translating Functionality-Based Applications into Role-Based Applications

SAP Fiori is designed around the idea that your work environment needs to be available to you wherever you are: on your desktop, tablet, or phone. The *responsive* design principle ensures that each app presents the best experience in the context of how and where you work so that actions are consistent across devices. Navigation collapses and expands with your screen real estate, and SAP S/4HANA Finance apps offer views of data and functions appropriate for context and form factor. On a desktop, for example, a user would have access to all details and actions associated with an account, whereas a smartphone-based experience would focus on essential KPIs and actions relevant to the mobile context of a phone (e.g., contact information).

Figure 12.6 illustrates how design can span across devices, enabling easy reading, minimal resizing, and logical navigation.

Figure 12.6 Responsive Design across Devices

The *simple* design principle is about freedom from complexity and direct access to essential functions. The goal is to put the most important tools and information in front of the user in order to reduce distraction and time spent searching. However, this principle goes beyond putting what you need at your fingertips; it also helps to automate the things you do most frequently. The simple principle of SAP Fiori applies the fundamental paradigm of simplification underlying SAP S/4HANA Finance to the UI.

Figure 12.7 shows an example of simple design, focusing a user on the key information and available actions (APPROVE and DECLINE, shown in the bottom right corner) required to complete a task.

To achieve a *coherent* multidevice experience, SAP Fiori establishes a familial resemblance across all applications and form factors. SAP Fiori includes a collection of standardized solutions for common design challenges that are extensible across all application types. The notion of coherence ensures that tasks, language, and controls have the same meaning and purpose within each application and from one application to the next. Consistent experiences based on reusable patterns (such as the ones displayed in Figure 12.8) enable you to quickly learn the system and reapply what you have learned when moving across applications. You will come across similar screen elements and patterns while navigating from one app to another, so you will have a sense of familiarity and improved learning.

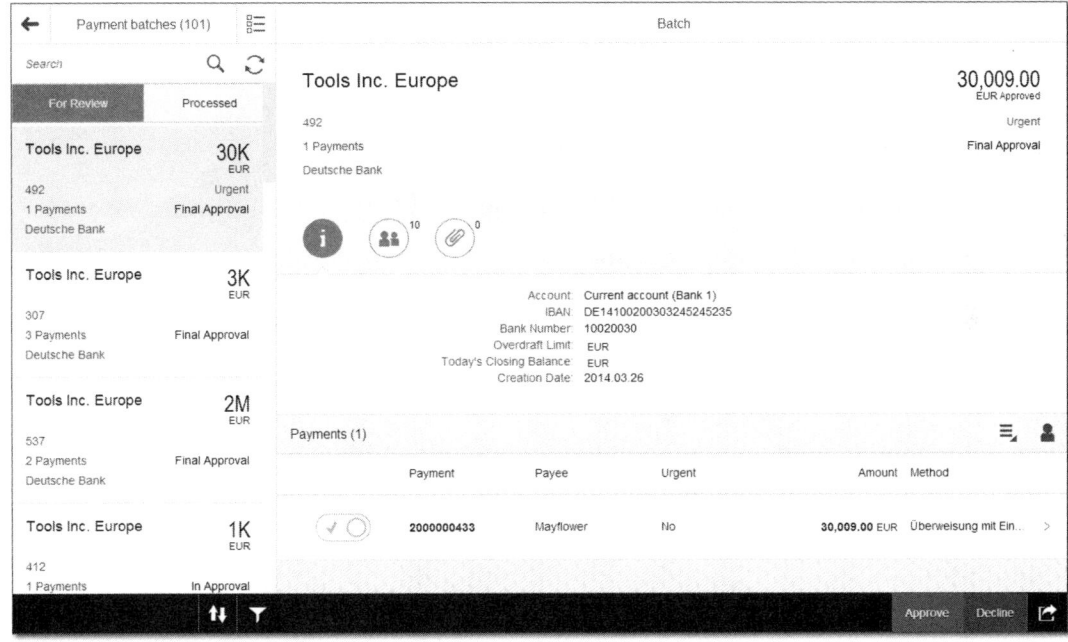

Figure 12.7 Simple Design

A *delightful* product goes beyond "accomplishing tasks" and extends into delivering an emotional connection to the work and letting you feel the impact of your contribution. In addition to supporting efficient task completion, SAP Fiori applications in SAP S/4HANA Finance go beyond what is expected by also being smart and proactive. The delightful product is not only a tool but also a fun assistant. SAP Fiori applications are designed to make users feel like experts when performing their work and to simultaneously provide a pathway to improve. Figure 12.9 showcases an application that delights users by means of visually appealing KPIs and makes them feel like part of a larger task through collaboration facilities, such as the right-side bar.

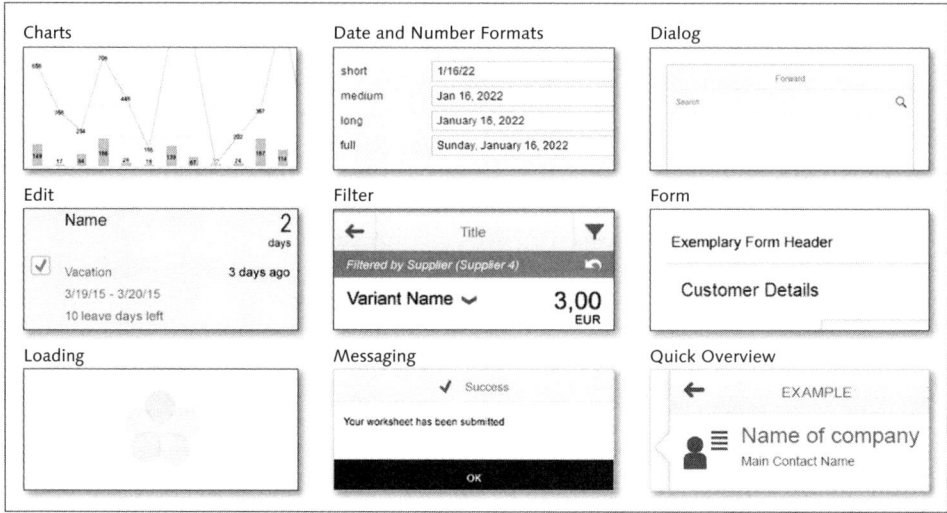

Figure 12.8 Example of SAP Fiori Design Patterns

Figure 12.9 Delightful Analysis of Operating Margin

12.4 SAP Fiori Application Framework and Finance

As we have just explained, process and principles are necessary inputs to great products, but not sufficient on their own. Between that foundation and the finished product, the application framework provides consistent high-level interaction patterns across categories of enterprise work. The SAP Fiori launchpad serves as a user's hub from which multiple application types are accessed. Therefore, let's first look at the launchpad before outlining different kinds of SAP Fiori applications. Finally, we will explore the patterns and UI controls that make up these applications.

12.4.1 Launchpad

The SAP Fiori launchpad houses the user's personal collection of SAP Fiori apps. It functions as a container that displays and groups tiles that are best suited for the user's needs. It serves as the home page, KPI dashboard, and role-specific entry point into the suite of financial applications.

For example, a manager's launchpad will mostly consist of his KPIs (see Chapter 11, Section 11.1) and self-service apps that let him control, for example, his department's budget or travel requests.

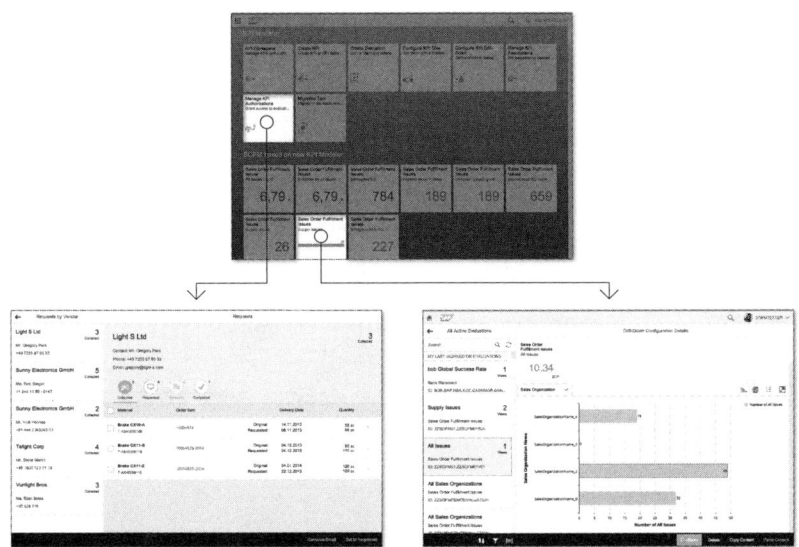

Figure 12.10 SAP Fiori Launchpad App Navigation

The launchpad of a collection specialist will instead highlight and give quick access to required tasks, such as processing open receivables, and to specific KPIs for the collection specialist's role, such as DSO. A launchpad also contains basic navigation tools, such as global search, to allow users to browse the application catalog or locate a specific business object, as shown in Figure 12.10.

12.4.2 Application Types

From the launchpad, a user accesses several application types, addressing the full range of financial tasks. Each application type shown in Figure 12.11 provides a basic interaction template and task-appropriate features, thereby improving learnability and reducing complexity—for example:

- Transactional apps allow for completion of business tasks, from simple tasks (such as workflow approvals) to more involved tasks (such as managing outstanding receivables).
- Analytical apps allow for monitoring of KPIs and other business data.
- Fact sheet apps provide a consistent 360-degree view of business entities by combining traditional transactional business data with related information, such as analytic views and related objects.

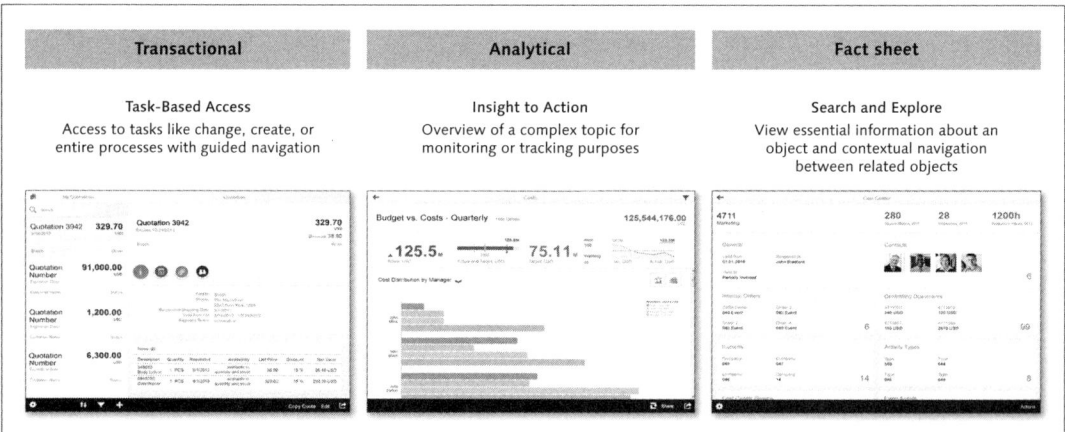

Figure 12.11 SAP Fiori Application Types

12.4.3 Application Patterns and Controls

Within each application, users achieve their goals through interaction with SAP Fiori patterns and controls. The framework includes dozens of these standardized solutions to common user needs, covering the range of enterprise tasks. Although each pattern and control is optimized to address a specific type of task in a simple, easy-to-use manner, they are flexible enough to be combined and work synergistically. The consistent use of patterns and controls ensures a coherent user experience and gives users a sense of familiarity across SAP Fiori apps.

The figures ahead show a few common SAP Fiori controls. The flow pattern shown in Figure 12.12 is useful for visualizing different states of a process or the sequence of steps. The filter bar in Figure 12.13 gives users quick access to a large range of selection criteria in reports. SAP Fiori also makes use of chart libraries (see Figure 12.14) to visualize information and includes means to improve collaboration by placing them directly next to the information under discussion (Figure 12.15). For users to take action, SAP Fiori consistently employs the toolbar pattern displayed in Figure 12.16, which gives access to context-specific actions in a central place.

Figure 12.12 Process Flow Pattern

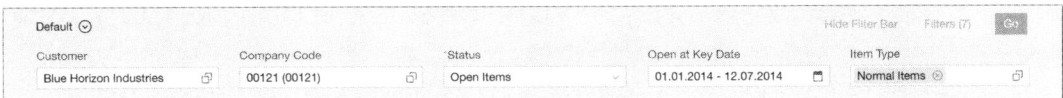

Figure 12.13 Filter Pattern

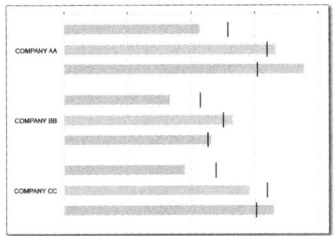

Figure 12.14 Chart Pattern

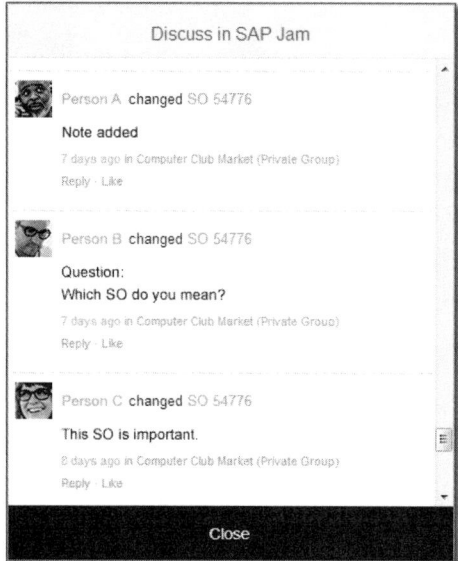

Figure 12.15 Collaboration Pattern

Figure 12.16 Toolbar Pattern

12.5 Extending SAP Fiori

Traditional enterprise software was structured around transactions that reflected complex underlying data stores. The resulting interfaces felt like containers for disparate features and functions rather than experiences crafted for a specific role and purpose. These types of transactions presented users with more options than needed, clouding the most important functions. Finance users ended up spending more time looking for the right tool than getting real work done.

Along with the sheer mass of features and functions included in traditional transactions, these transactions were often conceived with a single purpose in mind and did not look holistically across the business process. This resulted in a fragmented experience. Users were forced to toggle between transaction screens, gathering information from a variety of disparate sources and manually integrating it to accomplish their work.

The SAP Fiori design paradigm consciously breaks from the traditional model and is centered on creating experiences that cater to each user's needs and working style. SAP S/4HANA Finance apps incorporate lessons from many conversations with users to understand how real people work. These apps take what users know from apps and websites they use in their daily lives and bring it to the enterprise world. To this end, SAP Fiori makes use of the latest advances in web technology embodied in the SAPUI5 library.

In the end, SAP Fiori apps speak for themselves. Let's take a look at the My Spend application from SAP S/4HANA Finance, which beautifully demonstrates the SAP Fiori philosophy and principles. My Spend also shows different patterns and controls in action, such as charts and a toolbar with access to collaboration features. You can refer to Chapter 9, Section 9.4 for an explanation of the business context.

Figure 12.17 shows how My Spend is designed for a line manager to monitor his team's spending; the overview screen's heat map allows a manager to quickly identify hotspots through the visual means of color and size. In this case, the Singapore team in the top-left corner clearly demands attention.

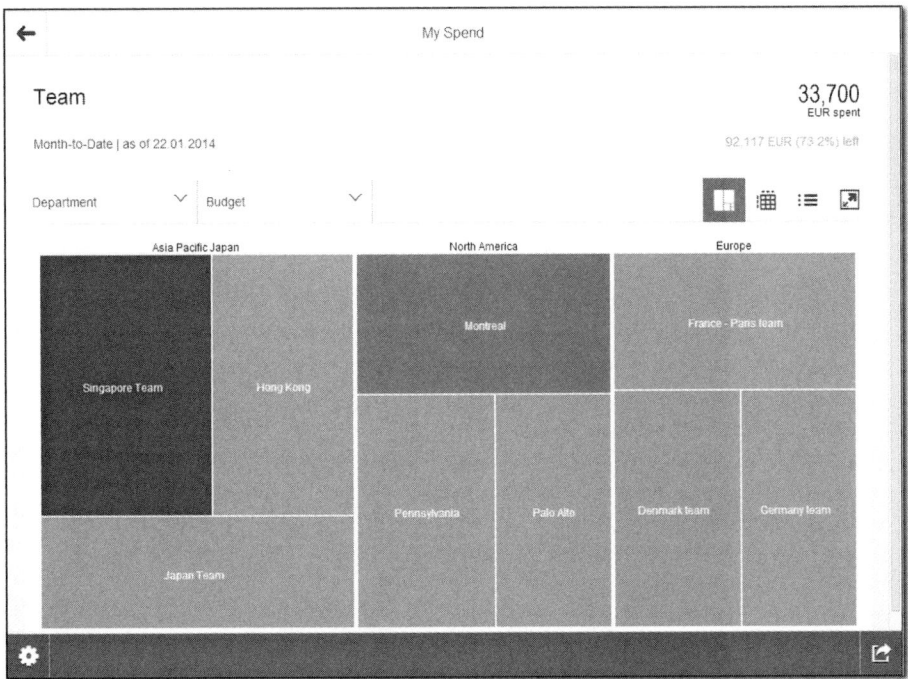

Figure 12.17 Overview of Budget Status by Location in My Spend

When the user drills down into the Singapore team (see Figure 12.18), the clear visuals of the My Spend app and the color representation reveal that THIRD-PARTY SPEND and especially TRAVEL EXPENSES seem to be the root causes of the high spending.

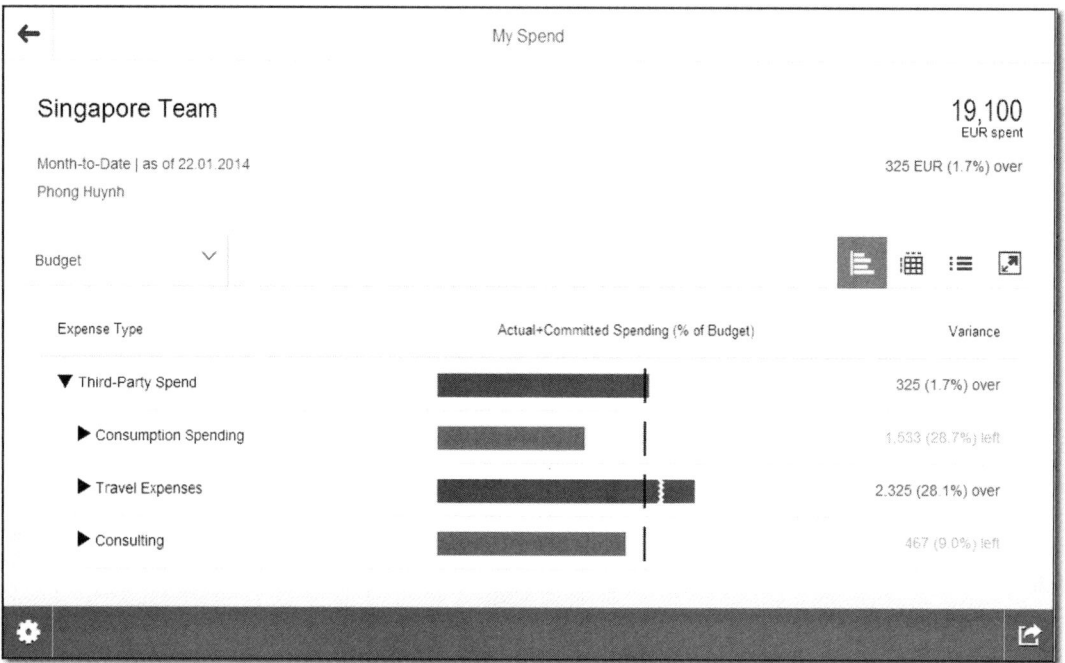

Figure 12.18 Use of Budget by Expense Type

Now that we've reached the level of the individual line items comprising the travel expenses spend (see Figure 12.19), the manager can identify the specific expenses that caused the budget overrun. From here, the manager can directly follow up with his team to address the overages, thanks to the consistent collaboration integration.

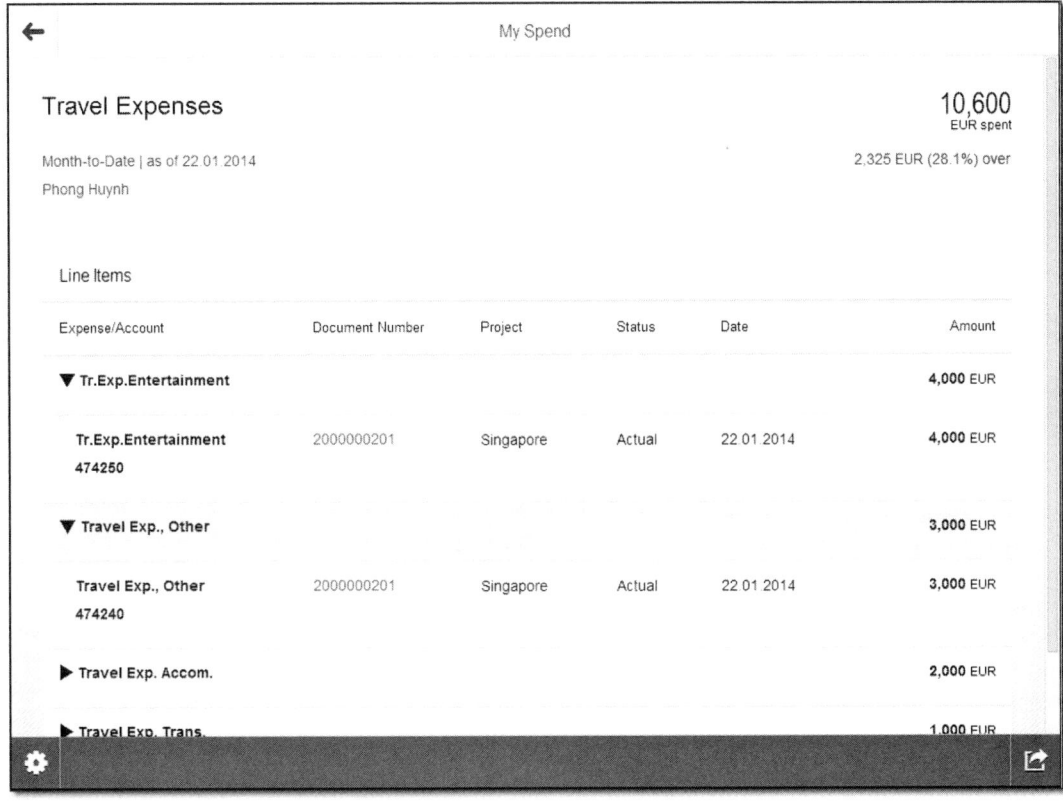

Figure 12.19 Access to Line Items in My Spend

In this chapter, we looked at how SAP Fiori simplifies the user experience of SAP S/4HANA Finance. Processes, design concepts, and technology come together to bring the end user into focus, revitalizing work in the enterprise.

PART III
Running SAP S/4HANA Finance

This chapter covers the wide range of delivery options for SAP S/4HANA Finance: on-premise installation, cloud delivery, or hybrid scenarios. How do you choose from among the available options, and how can you deploy SAP S/4HANA Finance in a seamless migration?

13   Deploying SAP S/4HANA Finance

SAP S/4HANA Finance is natively built on SAP HANA and offers a simple solution architecture with complete choice of deployment, consumable from the cloud, on-premise, or in a hybrid setup for lower IT costs and easy adoption.

In this chapter, we provide an overview on the deployment options to run SAP S/4HANA Finance. The deployment options we illustrate focus on the SAP S/4HANA Finance innovations, which can work seamlessly with other on-premise and cloud apps from SAP, such as SAP SuccessFactors, SAP Ariba, SAP Fieldglass, SAP Hybris, and Concur.

How can this book provide decision support for your project? The content of this chapter cannot replace the detailed guides, SAP Notes, or consulting and support services associated with the realization of an implementation project. However, it will give you clear indications of which of the following editions may best support your current and future business needs.

- **On-premise edition (Section 13.1)**
  In this section, we will discuss how to get a fresh on-premise installation, as well as how to migrate from an existing SAP ERP system. We will also look at the overall system landscape architecture and the handling of specific functionalities during migration situations.
- **Cloud editions (Section 13.2)**
  Here, we will look at SAP S/4HANA cloud editions, which include SAP S/4HANA Finance, and briefly discuss the scenarios they support.

► **Managed deployment based on SAP HANA Enterprise Cloud (Section 13.3)**
This section will focus on deployment options on SAP HANA Enterprise Cloud, including a specific case in point: the hybrid scenario.

In the last section of this chapter (Section 13.4), we will introduce you to the extensibility SAP S/4HANA offers through SAP HANA Cloud Platform.

Your individual business requirements inside the line of business as well as in the IT departments cannot be squeezed into a simple matrix—just as these offerings do not require you to make a black-or-white decision, be it cloud vs. on-premise or with regard to your timeline. You will learn that SAP S/4HANA Finance offers full choice and flexibility to adopt innovations at your own pace and in alignment with your business needs.

Nevertheless, there are some key criteria associated with some options, which we will make transparent, including the following:

► Level of modifications allowed
► Ease of adoption for new innovations
► License model

Overall, in this chapter we will outline key factors that will support your decision-making process, whether you already run a complex financials landscape or are starting a greenfield project.

This chapter also provides a bigger picture from a technology perspective: how the innovations from SAP—such as the SAP HANA platform (see Chapter 2), SAP Fiori user experience (Chapter 12), innovations inside the finance application layer, and opportunities of the cloud—enable new business processes focusing on simplicity (for example, enabling extended analytics capabilities with reduced landscape complexity).

13.1 On-Premise Edition

SAP S/4HANA Finance follows SAP's promise to support options for on-premise deployment of all the latest innovations.

If you want to leverage already existing data center investments or if your business processes need heavy individualization, including modifications to the system, then an on-premise installation or upgrade might be your best option. In addition, there might be specific policies in your company or industry that currently prevent the option to move forward into the cloud. On the down side, you have to take on the end-to-end responsibility for an on-premise system, including system governance and operations or the implementation of maintenance measures.

13.1.1 Architecture Overview

As shown in Figure 13.1, SAP S/4HANA Finance is based on the in-memory database technology of SAP HANA. The ABAP application core of SAP S/4HANA Finance deployments is an integral part of the SAP S/4HANA on-premise edition 1511 released at the end of 2015. In addition, it is available as an add-on product to EHP 7 and EHP 8 for SAP ERP 6.0 and replaces—in this case—the classic SAP ERP Financials applications. Of course, you are not limited to financials only; SAP S/4HANA Finance is part of a full-blown ERP system integrated with the other SAP ERP applications, like logistics processes (Materials Management, Sales and Distribution, and Production Planning), all in the same system: SAP S/4HANA.

As you learned in previous chapters of this book, the beautiful and intuitive user experience is enabled by the SAP Fiori apps. These HTML5-based web applications support a responsive screen design on mobile devices as well as on office desktop PCs based on the same application. To connect to the backend, the apps use SAP Gateway technology. Classic SAP GUI still works as well in on-premise scenarios. Users of the core financial roles may want to switch to SAP Fiori apps to benefit from the extended SAP Fiori coverage and the improved user experience.

By running the complete ABAP stack of SAP S/4HANA Finance on SAP HANA, you can run embedded analysis and integrated business planning by activating the relevant functionality on the SAP S/4HANA Finance instance itself. This option allows you to utilize the full power of an OLAP engine and flexibly slice and dice your data. Furthermore, you then have the advantage of working in real time by removing the latency of data replication. Remember that you still have the ability to extract data and utilize a separate data warehouse, such as SAP BW, if necessary for your scenario.

13   Deploying SAP S/4HANA Finance

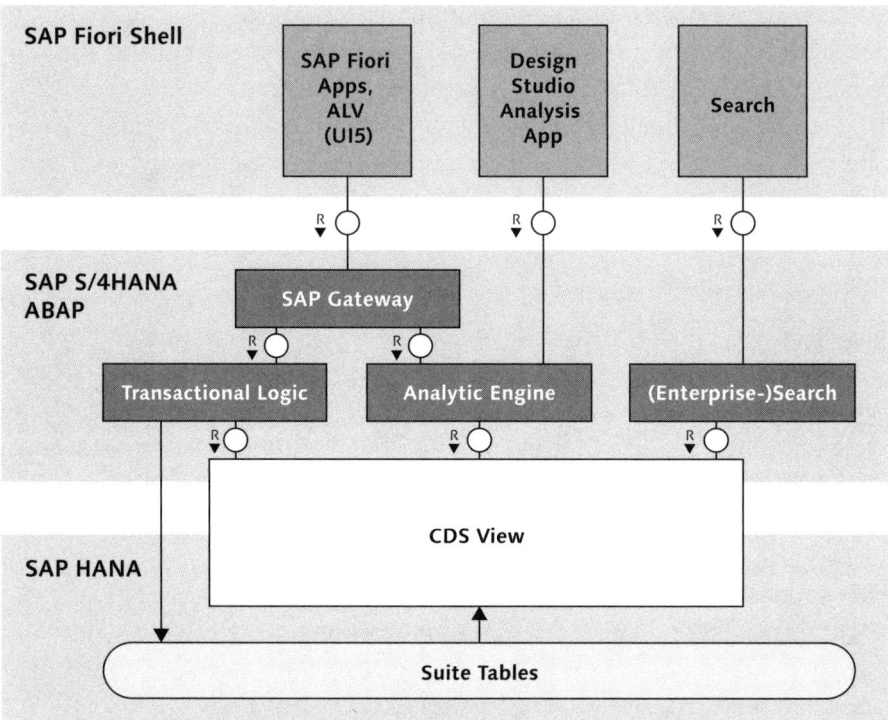

Figure 13.1 SAP S/4HANA Architecture Overview

13.1.2   New On-Premise Installations

In the context of this chapter, a *new* installation refers to the setup of an SAP S/4HANA Finance on-premise instance from scratch, without any customer data contained in the beginning—for example, a greenfield project.

This kind of installation is supported by a dedicated set of installation media. The so-called export packages contain the ABAP stack of either SAP S/4HANA or EHP 8 for SAP ERP 6.0 plus the current version of the SAP S/4HANA components and will be installed first on the server. Next, packages supporting SAP S/4HANA Finance, such as the relevant UI components, need to be deployed into the landscape before starting the business configuration.

SAP ERP 6.0-based implementation projects using SAP S/4HANA Finance via an add-on can quick-start by way of the various SAP Rapid Deployment solution packages and packaged service offerings.

SAP S/4HANA on-premise edition 1511 projects can benefit from the new SAP Activate services. This innovation adoption framework expedites SAP S/4HANA implementations throughout the customer lifecycle from the discovery of ready-to-run digitized business and integration processes to guided configuration, and with next-generation methodology. It accelerates the initial implementation of SAP S/4HANA and is designed for continuous innovation.

SAP Activate supports different starting points for customers to adopt SAP S/4HANA: new implementation, system conversion, and landscape transformation. SAP Activate is a unique combination of SAP best practices, methodology, and guided configuration that helps customers and partners deploy SAP S/4HANA.

SAP Best Practices for SAP S/4HANA are comprehensive, flexible, ready-to-run OLTP and OLAP processes optimized for SAP S/4HANA. They're easily integrated with other cloud solutions, such as SAP SuccessFactors and the Ariba Network. These business processes are cultivated from the collective implementation knowledge of thousands of SAP customers.

13.1.3 Landscape Migration for Existing SAP ERP Systems

Let's look at a high-level overview of the upgrade paths, including the required installation and migration steps, from a technical point of view. The required steps depend on the starting conditions of your existing system landscape.

The target stack of SAP S/4HANA Finance consists of either SAP S/4HANA on-premise edition 1511 or EHP 8 for SAP ERP 6.0, plus new software components that replace the classic SAP ERP Financials applications. In addition, new UI components need to be deployed to access the SAP Fiori user experience.

As outlined previously, the innovations provided in SAP S/4HANA Finance are closely connected to the in-memory database technology of SAP HANA. This implies a database migration as well if you have not yet been running your SAP ERP system on SAP HANA.

Figure 13.2 shows the upgrade paths to the required SAP S/4HANA Finance target stack from every SAP ERP 6.0 release state, including the migration from any database toward SAP HANA using the database migration option (DMO) feature, if required. There are service and support options available to assist at each step of the journey.

13 Deploying SAP S/4HANA Finance

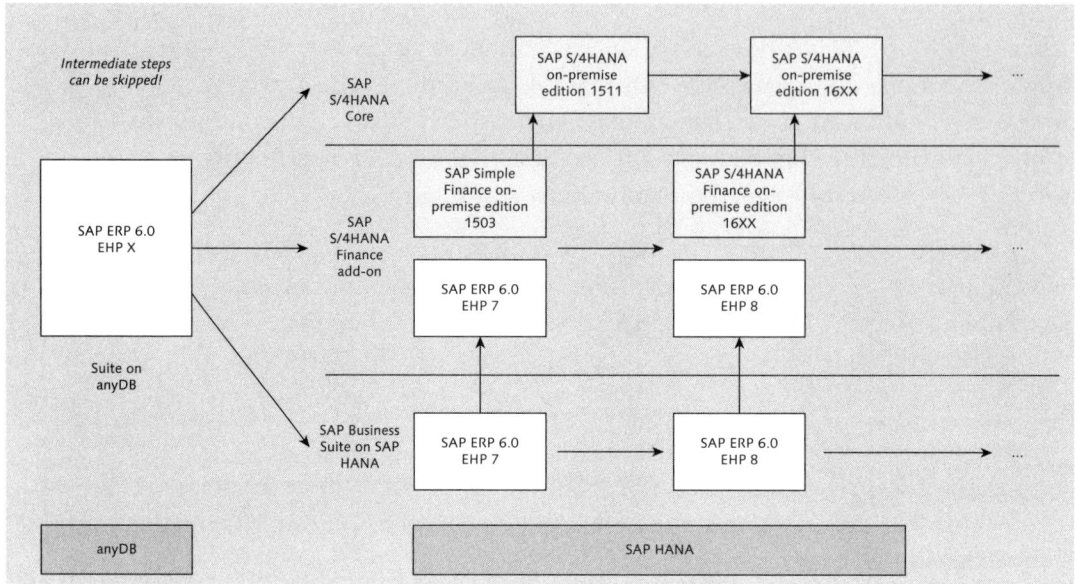

Figure 13.2 Upgrade Paths to SAP S/4HANA Finance

13.1.4 Handling General Ledger Functionality during Upgrade

SAP S/4HANA Finance leverages the capabilities of the latest feature state delivered via EHP 7 for SAP ERP 6.0. Depending on the system configuration of your start release, preparations for the new Asset Accounting, the General Ledger (G/L), and Controlling in SAP Accounting powered by SAP HANA are to be done as part of the upgrade to SAP S/4HANA Finance.

SAP S/4HANA Finance makes it easy to switch even if you have been using the classic G/L so far. The automated migration to the G/L in Accounting for SAP S/4HANA Finance does not imply an immediate full change to your financial business processes. As shown in Figure 13.3, the migration first converts the distributed data into the data model of the Universal Journal and allows you to run your accounting and reporting almost as before—but while leveraging benefits such as line item details and faster processes.

You can access the full capabilities of the "new" G/L, such as parallel ledgers and document splitting, by running the business migration at a later point in time.

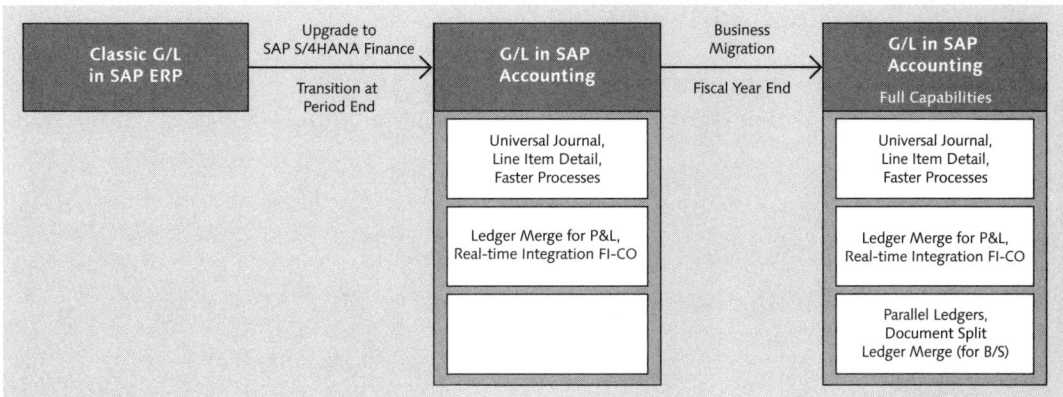

Figure 13.3 Migration Path to G/L in SAP Accounting

13.1.5 Simplification List

To allow its customers a better way to plan a path to SAP S/4HANA on-premise edition, SAP has created the Simplification List. This list describes on a detailed functional level what happens in SAP S/4HANA to individual transactions and solution capabilities of older releases you may have been running. If some transactions or capabilities seem to be missing, this does not mean that SAP is decommissioning that functionality, but rather that it has merged with other elements or is now reflected in a new solution or architecture.

The Simplification List consists of simplification items, each of which describes the impact on customers from business and technical points of view. For example, if a data structure has been simplified, related custom code must be adapted. In other cases, functionality may have been replaced with a new and simplified successor application, possibly even based on an unchanged data structure. Based on the simplification item, you can execute custom code check analysis. Related service offerings also are available (or will be available over time).

Currently, the Simplification List provides information for the SAP S/4HANA on-premise 1511 release and is provided as part of the SAP S/4HANA documentation.

13.2 Cloud Editions

The SAP S/4HANA cloud editions shown in Figure 13.4 are designed to help customers drive their digital business transformation with the simplicity of the cloud and currently include the following:

- SAP S/4HANA cloud marketing edition
- SAP S/4HANA cloud project services edition
- SAP S/4HANA cloud enterprise edition

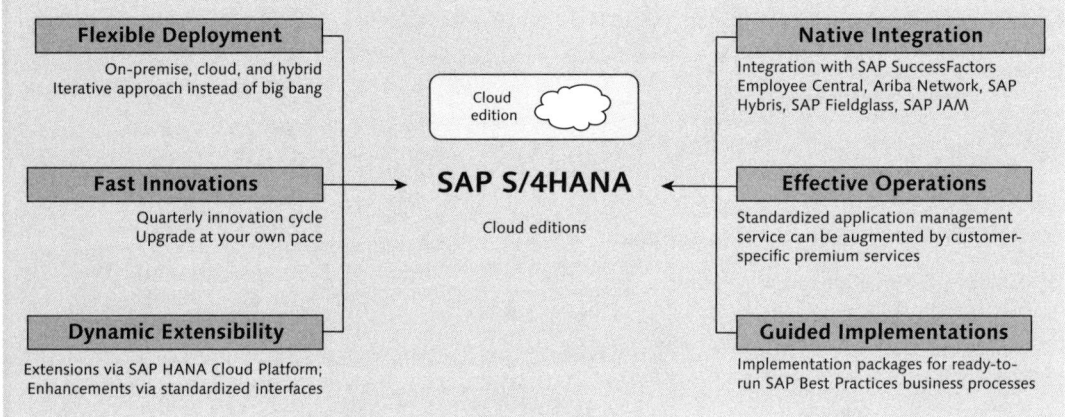

Figure 13.4 SAP S/4HANA Cloud Edition Characteristics

The last two editions include finance functionality. SAP S/4HANA cloud editions introduce the next wave of simplification and innovations across core business functions. In addition, they offer the opportunity for customers to deploy real hybrid scenarios (in other words, combining on-premise and cloud solutions) for unprecedented IT flexibility and accelerated business innovation.

The first two SAP S/4HANA cloud editions listed already cover specific business scenarios for the marketing line of business and for the professional services industry as well as the most essential scenarios to run an entire enterprise in the cloud with a digital core, including finance, accounting, controlling, procurement, sales, manufacturing, plant maintenance, project management system, and product lifecycle management. This comprehensive offering also provides native integration between SAP S/4HANA and other cloud solutions from SAP, including those from SAP SuccessFactors in human resources, SAP Ariba in procurement, and SAP Hybris in marketing. You can execute your IT strategy at your own pace, based on your needs, while keeping all the integration and business benefits of your existing SAP solutions. In addition, SAP S/4HANA Finance cloud editions are designed to connect easily with global business networks such as the Ariba Network and Concur.

13.3 Managed Cloud Options

Finance solutions have a long history and are at the heart of your business. Sometimes, moving into cloud-based offerings is not an easy decision for companies to make, as they often cite risks associated with a cloud deployment in the areas of data privacy and data security. The SAP HANA Enterprise Cloud provides answers to such questions as an offering certified by external auditors, such as TÜV and KPMG (for further details, please refer to *www.sapdatacenter.com*). This cloud offering takes the following into consideration:

- **Data security**
  Firewalls from different manufacturers protect data in the data center. Furthermore, an intrusion detection system monitors incoming data and identifies suspicious activities. Data and backup files are exchanged with customers in an encrypted format or transmitted via secure fiber-optic cables.

- **Data privacy**
  SAP ensures compliance with data protection provisions. Data from cloud customers falls under the jurisdiction selected by the customer and is not forwarded to third parties. SAP's support services ensure that data protection remains in place during required maintenance operations.

- **Data center locations**
  As shown in Figure 13.5, SAP HANA Enterprise Cloud data centers are located around the globe. Data centers are either owned and operated by SAP or co-located at partner sites. Moving forward, SAP will continue to build SAP-owned and -operated data centers and to pursue partner capacity.

  (Note that this map represents SAP's current plan at the time of publishing, but it is subject to change without any prior notification!)

13 Deploying SAP S/4HANA Finance

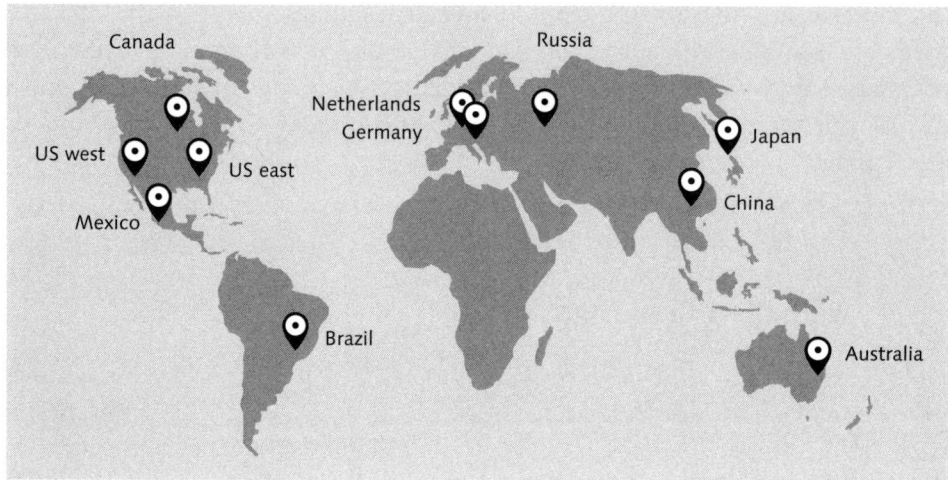

Figure 13.5 Data Center Locations

13.3.1 Service Offerings in the Cloud

Trends such as mobile, big data, social media, and the cloud change consumer behavior and, in turn, significantly change business models, which requires companies to react appropriately and adapt their highly optimized business processes.

Sometimes, companies hesitate to modify existing finance systems and maintain old releases with highly individualized system landscapes. Part of this relates to limited IT budgets that have to be managed to fund this transformation; there are also some costs, risks, and upfront investments associated with any disruptive changes.

Nevertheless, increasing globalization, rapidly changing conditions, and high pressure on margins force companies to seek potential cost reductions and simplifications. In addition, acquisitions and new subsidiaries may need a quick integration into existing landscapes, and companies are willing to streamline their processes.

SAP HANA Enterprise Cloud

In the spirit of the nondisruptive innovation paradigm underlying SAP S/4HANA Finance, SAP HANA Enterprise Cloud is the answer to these challenges. It offers a virtual private cloud infrastructure based on SAP HANA, with dedicated infrastructure for each customer in adherence with the highest standards for security and data privacy.

A closed-loop service offering complements the infrastructure as part of the Plan/Build/Run approach. Services of the Plan and Build phases, such as advisories on a roadmap or onboarding, are mostly relevant when transitioning to the SAP HANA Enterprise Cloud (see the next section of this subchapter). While running your system in the SAP HANA Enterprise Cloud, best-in-class managed services guarantee smooth operation of the system infrastructure, including the SAP HANA platform. The application-managed services (AMS) ensure the technical operation of SAP S/4HANA Finance applications. SAP Enterprise Support or SAP MaxAttention Support take care of the business process layer and corresponding business configuration.

The SAP HANA Enterprise Cloud operations model can be described by the following characteristics:

- Systems are dedicated to one customer. Each customer installation runs on a dedicated server that is not shared with other installations, ensuring full availability of resources.
- The customer has system governance. He decides on all operation-relevant matters, such as updates, and controls access to the system.
- With regard to licensing, both bring-your-own-license (BYOL) and subscription options are supported. This gives customers the option to use existing licenses and to subscribe to specific functionality.
- Applications offer the same functionality richness as on-premise modules. Functionality that is available in the on-premise deployment described in Section 13.1 is similarly offered via the same applications.
- Modifications on the software level are not recommended. Customers can tailor the solution to their needs by selecting additional services, and options for business configuration remain fully available.
- Customer involvement is part of the model. The customer has full transparency into system operations and is kept in the loop about upcoming innovations, which he can, but does not have to, adopt.

- Each customer can use individual software release levels. He has the option to update to newer releases, but is not forced to do so. Thus, he can schedule release changes as best suits his needs for stability and innovation.

Using the portfolio of services and products in the SAP HANA Enterprise Cloud is not an all-or-none decision. You can adapt the solution offerings to your individual business needs and add further managed services over time from the individual building blocks (see Figure 13.6). In addition to providing individually sized infrastructure, the SAP HANA Enterprise Cloud offers managed infrastructure services and application management services as additional options to add to existing software licenses. In addition, customers have full control over the building blocks highlighted on the left of Figure 13.6.

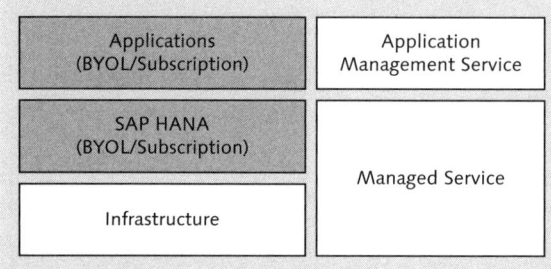

Figure 13.6 Building Blocks of SAP HANA Enterprise Cloud Solution Offerings

Transitioning to SAP HANA Enterprise Cloud

The process of transitioning to SAP HANA Enterprise Cloud must inherently be tailored to your company's situation. The process starts with an advisory service provided by consulting in order to compile an individual cloud innovation roadmap for your company.

Then, an assessment service details the transformation from on-premise into the SAP HANA Enterprise Cloud. You need to answer questions such as whether your system already runs EHP 7 or EHP 8 for SAP ERP 6.0 on SAP HANA or any database, which business processes need to be run in the cloud, and so on. Subsequently, SAP works with customers to define a solution that fits their individual needs (see Figure 13.7). The required activities are supported by packaged service offerings provided by SAP. Onboarding and migration services safeguard a quick and successful implementation.

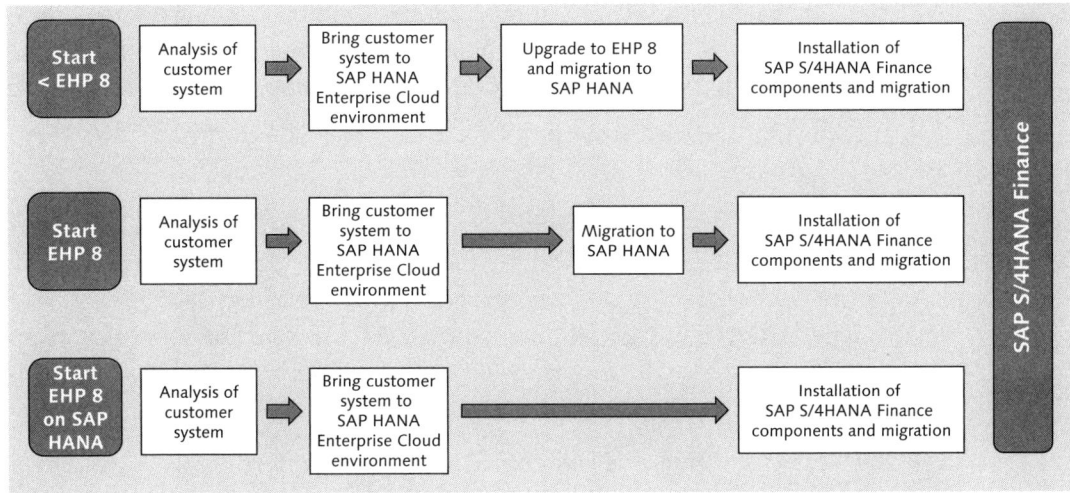

Figure 13.7 Getting Ready for SAP S/4HANA Finance in SAP HANA Enterprise Cloud

13.3.2 Hybrid Scenarios

Hybrid deployment scenarios bridge different deployment options. These scenarios can be combinations of on-premise and cloud systems or combinations of systems based on hosting or managed services and public cloud offerings.

With a hybrid approach, you can leave existing systems untouched in your on-premise environment, which might consist of SAP ERP instances of various levels or legacy systems. Adding an SAP S/4HANA Finance instance managed in SAP HANA Enterprise Cloud enables you to adopt finance innovations at your own pace.

A good example of this approach is the central reporting scenario described in Chapter 14, in which we discuss the fact that all sender systems stay untouched when using real-time replication logic. The SAP S/4HANA Finance instance in the SAP HANA Enterprise Cloud functions as a first step in a central reporting option that supports flexible reporting on data from all connected systems in SAP HANA—making use of features such as data harmonization and built-in data validation. All required landscape components—like the SAP Landscape Transformation Replication Server for real-time replication and optional SAP Master Data Governance—are available inside the managed SAP HANA Enterprise Cloud.

Over time, more processes (like central planning, cash management, and consolidation) can be moved to the Central Finance system inside SAP HANA Enterprise Cloud, and then obsolete on-premise components can be removed. The vision is that this move can help you to simplify your system landscape and reduce TCO.

13.3.3 Subscription Licensing and Options

SAP S/4HANA cloud enterprise edition, finance option is designed to provide the simplest experience for easy cloud adoption, from the discovery of the solution to its deployment and through actual use by finance users. The SAP Fiori user experience leverages modern design principles for personalized, responsive, and simple interactions across most common financial tasks.

SAP S/4HANA cloud enterprise edition, finance option offers packages that cover the requirements of end-to-end processes (see Figure 13.8). Starting with an attractive base package and building up, companies can choose optional value packages across all solution areas. For example, the corporate treasurer might ask for the Cash Management package so that his department can use the latest innovations of SAP S/4HANA Finance in that area (see Chapter 11, Section 11.4). The head of finance operations might require the shared services framework.

Common to all easy-to-consume value packages, nonfunctional capabilities (such as discovery, consumption, on-boarding, configuration, packaging, and extensibility) have been simplified. You can add more cloud capabilities progressively to the set of solutions in your subscription.

The subscription covers software license, support, infrastructure, and managed services for one price, as shown in Figure 13.9. Combination and standardization leads to an attractive and easy-to-understand price, allowing SAP to free you as a customer from worrying about the complexity of licensing. One business metric per package serves to characterize the customer's requirements with regard to sizing and similar operational measures, and also allows you to identify the best match for your business requirements. Onboarding and implementation costs are kept separate.

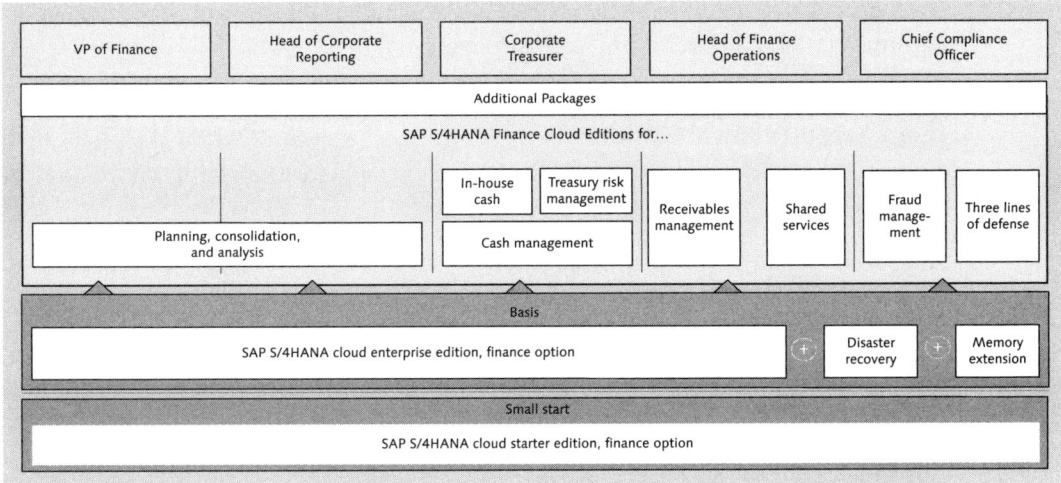

Figure 13.8 Packages in SAP S/4HANA Cloud Enterprise Edition, Finance Option

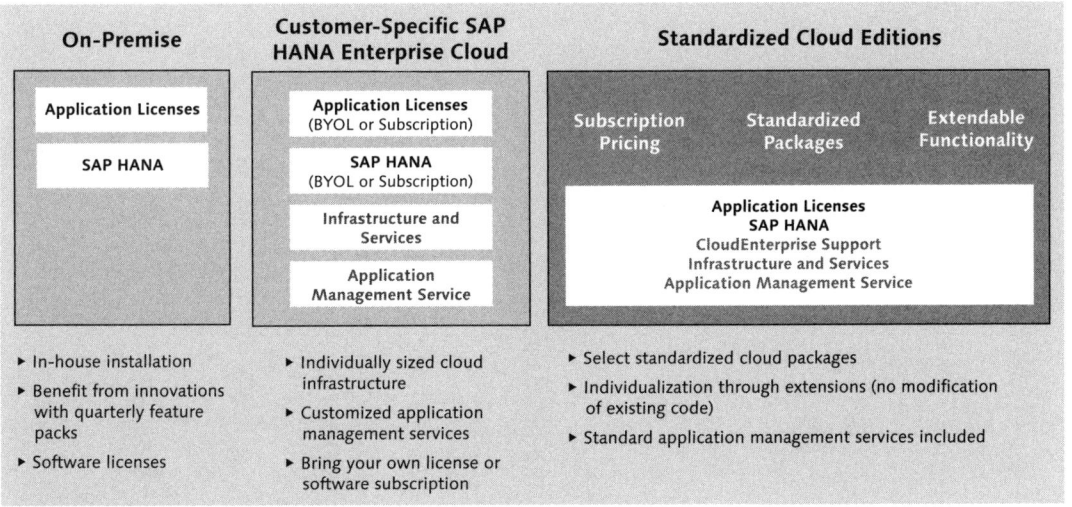

Figure 13.9 Delivery Options for SAP S/4HANA Finance

We expect that cloud deployment and consumption of enterprise software will increasingly become the new standard. Yet SAP is moving beyond simple cloud enablement with SAP S/4HANA cloud enterprise edition, finance option. With this new solution, it delivers on all the benefits of the cloud, such as ease of deployment and consumption, while not compromising on SAP's traditional

13 | Deploying SAP S/4HANA Finance

strengths: enterprise-caliber breadth and depth of functionality, high degree of automation, globalization, and industry support.

The SAP S/4HANA cloud enterprise edition, finance option may be your best choice whether you are a new or an existing SAP customer when starting a new project focused on finance. The solution can be added to existing landscapes in hybrid mode, as described in the previous section.

13.4 Extensibility

For many years, SAP has implemented successful processes for scalable and cost-efficient extensions in all product versions. This was a major driver of the large acceptance and adoption of SAP R/3 software, the SAP ERP application, and SAP Business Suite software (for example, by using the SAP NetWeaver technology platform for on-premise extensions of SAP Business Suite).

Today, this approach is taken to the next level with SAP S/4HANA: You can apply a tool-based and platform-based methodology, which is scalable for companies ranging from small startups to large enterprises.

As shown in Figure 13.10, we can distinguish between two kinds of extensibility.

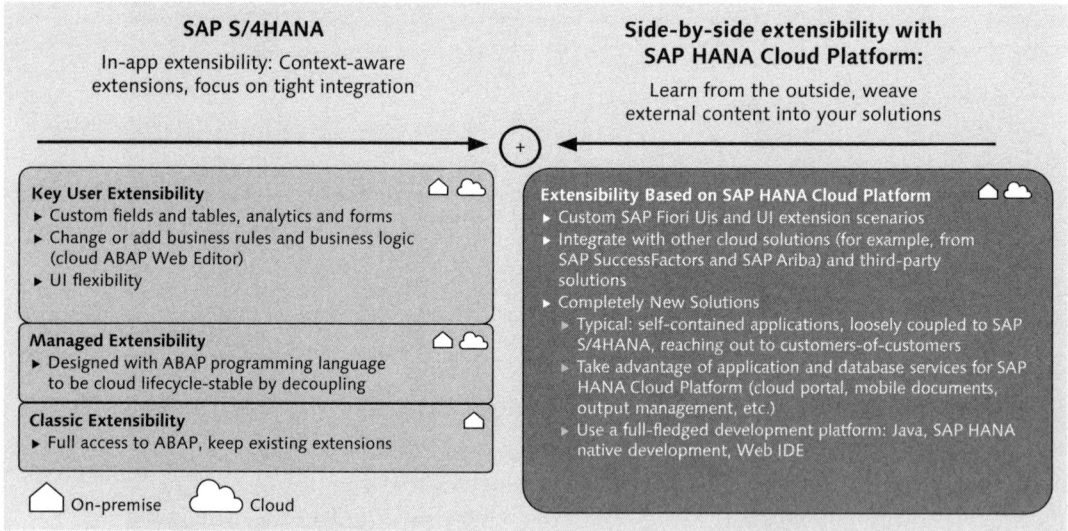

Figure 13.10 Extensibility Capabilities of SAP S/4HANA

In-app extensions, shown on the left, are implemented in the same system (or software stack) as the enhanced application.

- **Key user extensibility**
  Customers usually apply many small changes and extensions, because they want to increase user productivity or implement adaptations of the application logic without changing the major parameters of the respective business processes. Frequent examples include adding custom fields and tables.

- **Managed extensibility**
  In addition to using the key user and side-by-side extensibility capabilities (the latter will be explained ahead) available in all cloud edition deployment models, customers and partners may have a strong need for coded extensibility for SAP S/4HANA, cloud enterprise edition from within the context of the application. These types of managed extensions have a focus on tight integration with the ABAP-based SAP S/4HANA standard applications and thus are written in ABAP.

  To fulfill this requirement, SAP will offer customers and partners an additional service to use an SAP-hosted development landscape to develop ABAP add-ons that allow a high level of in-app extensibility, but with a restricted scope so that the operation of the add-ons does not break the cloud operations concept. For example, modifications of SAP objects are forbidden, and access to SAP objects will be allowed only through released "whitelisted" application program interfaces (APIs) so that the custom and partner code will be lifecycle stable.

- **Classic extensibility**
  With classic extensibility, customers and partners can extend and even modify SAP S/4HANA software with full access to development tools such as Eclipse or ABAP Workbench (Transaction SE80). This extensibility capability is only available in the on-premise edition of SAP S/4HANA.

On the right side of Figure 13.10, you will see a list of side-by-side extensions based on SAP HANA Cloud Platform. SAP HANA Cloud Platform is the PaaS offering from SAP that offers the broadest end-to-end capability in the market (from SAP HANA to SAP Fiori) and access to the broadest set of data sources (from SAP cloud applications to social data). For example, you can integrate business processes with applications from SAP SuccessFactors, SAP Ariba, or Concur, or from third parties. It is also possible to enable an SAP Fiori and mobile user experience for existing solutions. Since SAP HANA Cloud Platform is a full-fledged development platform, you can even build completely new solutions with a loose coupling to SAP backend systems.

SAP HANA Cloud Platform is designed to be 100% compliant with open standards (for example, using open-source software from Eclipse and Apache). When using SAP HANA Cloud Platform, you will benefit from a healthy ecosystem of partners that contribute value to existing solutions and services and can establish "best of breed" for small and large extensions. By definition, side-by-side extensions are loosely coupled with core SAP systems and therefore support a pace-layered IT strategy in which some areas of enterprise systems may innovate and receive updates faster than a stable core.

How should you handle extensions during transition from SAP Business Suite to SAP S/4HANA? As shown in Figure 13.11, in the cloud edition, existing extensions have to be reimplemented, either via the key user extensibility or managed extensibility in-app extensibility capabilities, or side-by-side using SAP HANA Cloud Platform. You can access SAP objects through public APIs only. In the on-premise edition, you can also use these capabilities, but you still have the freedom to create development objects using the classic development capabilities of the ABAP platform. The motivation for pushing extensions into key user extensibility, managed extensibility, or side-by-side on SAP HANA Cloud Platform is the reduced cost of operations for the customer, in particular the reduced cost of applying SAP software updates.

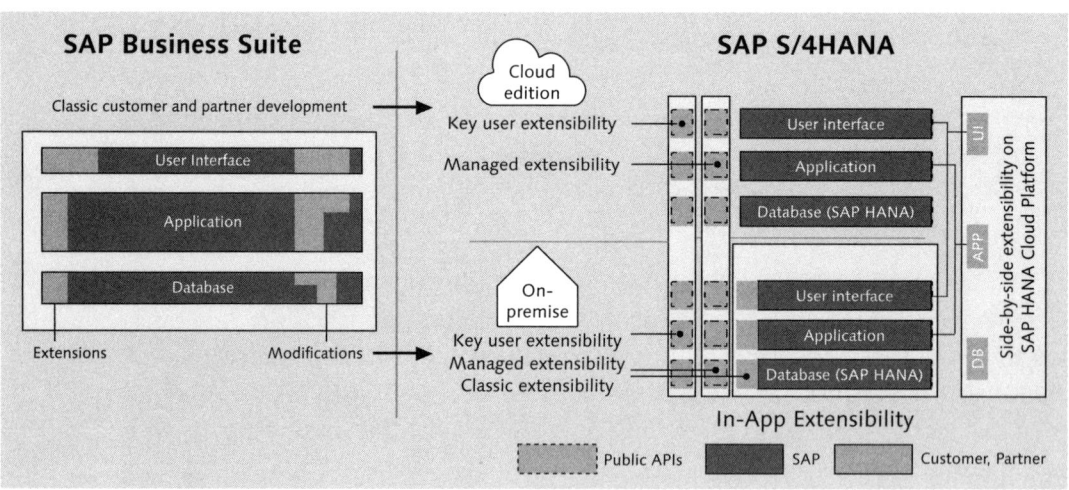

Figure 13.11 Extensibility Capabilities for Each Edition in Detail

This chapter presents Central Finance, the option to use SAP S/4HANA Finance as a centralized system that consolidates complex system landscapes consisting of a large mix of SAP and non-SAP systems.
Central Finance enables companies to harmonize their processes and integrate acquired companies more easily.

14 Landscape Consolidation with Central Finance

The idea behind Central Finance, an option and system architecture to use SAP S/4HANA Finance for centralizing finance, has been around for some time: A centralized finance approach has been implemented many times with finance systems on traditional databases. With SAP HANA, this idea becomes more compelling and feasible even for larger organizations thanks to performance improvements.

SAP S/4HANA Finance introduced many fundamentally new capabilities enabled by the sheer speed of processing and a new architecture. Together with the paradigm of a single source of truth in the areas of accounting, exposure, and planning, SAP S/4HANA Finance becomes a key enabler for centralized finance, while in return Central Finance can substantially simplify the adoption of SAP S/4HANA Finance—so it's a perfect match. Section 14.1 will shed light on the concepts of harmonization and standardization behind centralized finance. Section 14.2 shows how a central reporting scenario (formerly called the Central Journal) represents a first step toward these goals. Moving operational processes to the Central Finance system is the logical next step; Section 14.3 highlights ways in which this step can improve finance processes. Central Finance is also an ideal candidate for a first step into the cloud, as briefly outlined in Section 14.4.

14 Landscape Consolidation with Central Finance

14.1 Harmonization and Standardization

It is a widely established practice in large and medium organizations with international operations to decentralize leadership and responsibilities. Accountability for business success lies with the local or regional business owners, as does regulatory compliance. Subsidiaries use financial systems that run in their own locations and regions. With mergers and acquisitions, even more financial systems are added to the system landscape of the global organization, introducing more complexity.

In a world with grown and distributed system landscapes, CFOs and their finance departments are challenged by inconsistencies and late availability of financial data from the organization.

Group CFOs and global finance departments take a global view on financial operations and accounting. To this end, financial data is often replicated into a central data warehouse on a group level, which requires significant extraction efforts. Reliable data is only available with considerable delays due to the laborious processes of data collection, harmonization, transformations, and adjustment. Finance departments find it particularly difficult to get consistent insights that reflect the group's current financial situation, but it's not only internal reporting that suffers. In order to stay compliant, one consistent view for the global organization and one version of the truth is a must. Consolidated statutory reporting that fulfills legal requirements must build on a single set of finance data that has been harmonized at a global level. The same holds true for consolidated managerial reporting, which is necessary in order to run the enterprise at a group level.

Therefore, it has long been the desire of CFOs to have a single global system can centralize finance processes, providing the foundation for process efficiency and data quality for management decisions. There are different approaches available to resolve this conflict between decentral and central.

In a *one-system* strategy, one central transactional system (OLTP) is rolled out and used globally across all business areas, which means adjusting the centralized finance system subsidiary by subsidiary, taking into account all finance processes and local needs. This approach requires standardization and harmonization of all processes right from the beginning. Finance systems added by mergers and acquisitions are replaced by adding the new organizations to the single instance.

This strategy has the advantage of using the same semantics, consistent master data, best-practice finance processes, and comprehensive reporting across the board, plus providing access to data at any time—but there are limitations. Enterprises operating in multiple industries with fundamentally different requirements from accounting and IT find it difficult to agree on global definitions of data and standardized processes and operations. Although the flexibility for business is low due to the interdependencies of local and global settings, the total cost of operations for single global instances may be very high. Data volume can grow to a critical size and turn into a limiting factor for the one-system solution. Many large and medium organizations choose not to follow the one-system strategy.

One alternative to the one-system approach is to build on central business intelligence (BI) solutions, such as SAP BW. Data is replicated from decentral transactional systems into central data stores that are optimized for analytical processing (OLAP). The OLAP systems allow flexible analysis based on data from different sources and handling of high data volume. The challenges in this setup derive from different semantics and master data used in the source systems. Data is difficult to harmonize in the OLAP system, because finance business logic is missing; therefore, inconsistencies and disconnects arise. Deviating definitions create challenges when comparing planning data (OLAP) and actual data (OLTP). The loading of data to the data warehouse leads to delayed availability of information, and redundancies lead to multiple versions of the truth.

The preferred solution for the global finance organization comprises a combination of the functional capabilities of OLTP to run business processes with the analytical capabilities of OLAP in one system, without limiting the agility and flexibility of the decentral systems. This smart combination can give access to central and decentral finance information in real time and ensure accounting data consistency, fast reports, and availability of finance processes. In the past, it was hardly possible to combine online transactional processing and online analytical processing in one system, and doing so came with very high costs. This has changed with the introduction of SAP HANA and SAP S/4HANA Finance. The new finance architecture in SAP S/4HANA Finance delivers the ideal prerequisites for a central accounting data store, with all the capabilities the finance organization might want:

- A finance system based on accounting documents and accounting line items, providing the necessary level of detail

- Linking of Financial Accounting (FI) and Management Accounting (CO) data at a document line item level, ensuring a single source of truth
- One repository for cash-related data, offering a comprehensive view on cash exposure
- High processing speed through in-memory technology, enabling aggregation and analysis of large amounts of finance data online
- Ability to handle a sparsely populated matrix of heterogeneous accounting data—like asset procurement, material valuation, and distributions—in one table
- Analytical capabilities based on the virtual data model that allow flexible data modeling
- A single, consistent data model for financial planning that overcomes the traditional challenges posed by separate OLTP and OLAP deployments
- New UIs and dashboards that make it easy for even occasional users to consume data

The idea of Central Finance as an option to deploy and use SAP S/4HANA Finance was born from the dilemma of decentralized and centralized finance data, which has previously limited the agility and capabilities of centralized finance departments. Centralizing finance is a step-by-step approach that begins with collecting accounting data at a line item level in the central transactional system (OLTP), facilitated by SAP S/4HANA Finance. After this first step and based on this data, other processes can be centralized sequentially based on business priorities.

When accounting data is moved into the central system, data is translated to match global definitions using translation rules. This may include leveraging global master data management systems. This is a smooth way to achieve harmonization without impacting decentral system configurations, data, and business processes. Once the decision to centralize finance business processes in the central instance has been made, harmonization can continue and can be broken down into smaller, easily digestible steps. Over time, companies will achieve more and more harmonization of finance processes and operations across the organization while adding value to their business.

By building a centralized finance instance, there is no disruption to decentral systems and operations. This makes Central Finance an attractive adoption scenario for finance organizations that want to access the unique capabilities offered by

SAP S/4HANA Finance. Finally, Central Finance will add exceptional value and ease the move toward delivering finance services through shared service centers, which then operate in a more harmonized environment.

You've seen now that SAP S/4HANA Finance and Central Finance are the perfect match for companies that want to reap the benefits of SAP S/4HANA Finance without transitioning their whole landscape. The most logical starting point is to create a reporting scenario in which the central system collects accounting data from the different source systems. Central Finance establishes a single source of truth for group reporting, both for statutory and managerial purposes. We will look into that scenario in a moment in Section 14.2. For now, let's see what the next steps may look like.

The next phase of building the centralized finance system is to add business processes and capabilities to the central instance. This goes beyond the level of mere data and will require efforts on the business side to standardize and harmonize business processes.

Those business processes fall into different use cases. The following is a list of use cases of Central Finance supported today or planned for the future; each use case adds value to the global finance operations and makes Central Finance a good candidate for adoption:

- Central reporting (local and group reporting)
- Central working capital analysis
- Central financial planning
- Central open items management
- Central payments
- Central intercompany reconciliation
- Central bank account management
- Central cash operations, treasury, and risk management
- Central collections and dispute management
- Central credit management
- Central asset accounting
- Financial consolidation in central finance
- Central revenue accounting

Each use case comes with substantial added value for the global organization. The staged adoption of Central Finance divides the cumbersome and time-intensive standardization and harmonization endeavor into consumable chunks.

14.2 Principles and Capabilities

With Central Finance, postings from source systems are replicated into the central instance in real time. This is facilitated by a software tool called the SAP Landscape Transformation (SLT) Replication Server, which can be deployed centrally or decentrally.

Financial systems from most software vendors typically store data from financial postings in database tables. SLT operates at the database level. Once a data record is inserted or updated in the database table, the systems writes a database trigger. SLT responds to this database trigger and retrieves the data records that were inserted or updated.

This principle is in use at many companies for SAP HANA sidecar scenarios, which were introduced in 2011 as a deployment option for SAP HANA accelerators in order to speed up critical reports, processing steps, and transactions with SAP HANA's in-memory capabilities. The SAP ERP sidecar scenarios run an SAP HANA database in parallel with the classical database. The SAP HANA database is used to achieve better performance with high data volumes. In these scenarios, SLT performs a one-to-one replication at the database level; when a data record is inserted, updated, or deleted on the classical database, it is immediately inserted, updated, or deleted on the SAP HANA database as well.

SLT has a second mode of operation that makes it relevant for Central Finance. Instead of replicating a data record directly into the target database, it can move data records to a programming interface, such as an ABAP function module, as depicted in Figure 14.1.

Once a financial document is posted and stored in the database of the source system, the data record is retrieved by SLT and fed into the corresponding Central Finance interface. The interface posts a new financial document in the central instance running on SAP S/4HANA Finance. As part of this processing step, the standard accounting interface augments and completes the financial document based on the master data and customizing configured in the central system. It checks whether the financial document, the master data used, and the account assignments are consistent, and it persists the document in the data format required by the database tables of SAP S/4HANA Finance.

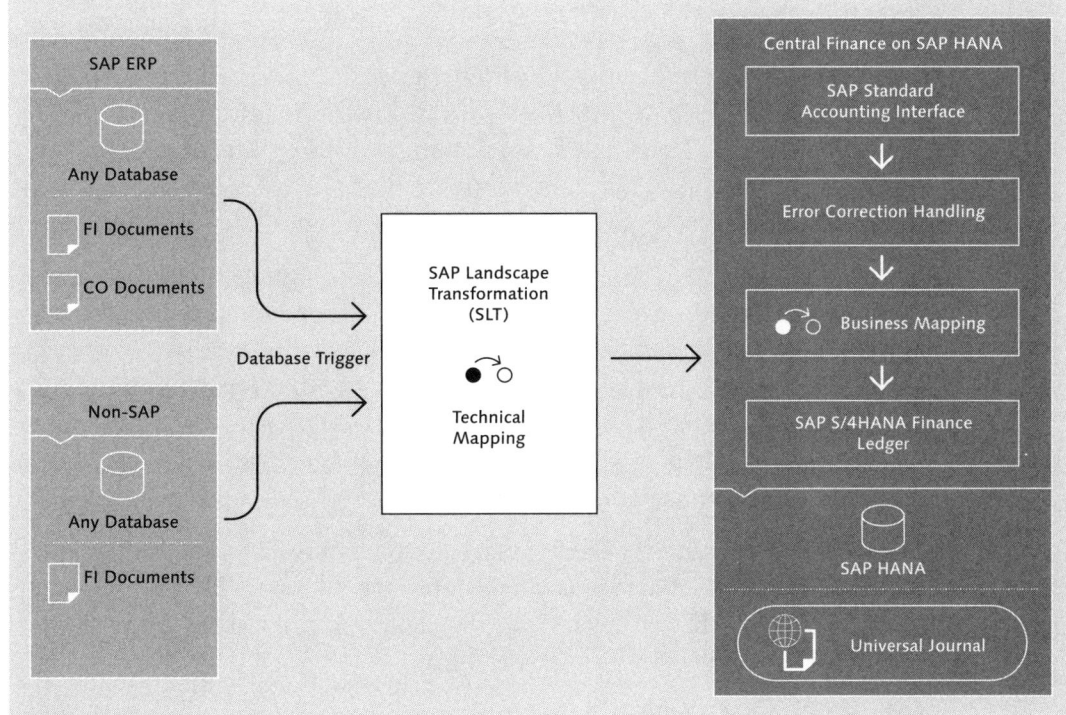

Figure 14.1 Data Replication Process with SLT

The newly posted financial document keeps the reference to the original document of the sender system and can be used like any document posted in the central system—even if it originates from a non-SAP source system.

Customizing settings in the sender and central systems do not need to be identical. Dependent master data is derived when posting the document in the central instance. For example, a cost center may derive a profit center that is different in the central system from the one derived in the source system. This is a smart way to reduce harmonization efforts in the organization. Mapping organizational structures and hierarchies in the target system can be achieved without master data harmonization in the existing system landscape.

In general, all kinds of master data used in the replicated financial document can be mapped before the new document is posted in the central system. Master data can be harmonized on the fly. For example, different charts of accounts can be harmonized in the central system, controlling areas and operating concerns can be merged, and cost centers and cost center hierarchies can be harmonized.

Some companies that operate in a distributed system landscape use master data management tools, such as SAP Master Data Governance, to distribute master data across the system landscape. A key feature of those tools is to store mapping information. For instance, after distributing a vendor master record, such tools store the corresponding vendor numbers used by the connected systems.

That type of information can be reused during the replication of a financial posting from the decentral system to the central system. For example, an accounting document with a payment may relate to one vendor with different numbers in the sending and in the receiving systems. In this case, the vendor numbers were mapped using the mapping information from the SAP Master Data Governance tool. This is independent of whether SLT and SAP Master Data Governance operate on the central instance or on separate servers.

Because the use of a master data management solution is optional for Central Finance, the mapping information can also be maintained in the central system. Alternatively, it may be retrieved from any data source of Central Finance using the available customer exits (business add-ins).

Although not strictly defined as master data, some accounting entities do have characteristics of and are used similarly to master data (e.g., cost objects such as internal orders, production orders, sales orders, etc.). In decentral instances, they are instruments to structure information and data, may be valid for restricted time periods, and so on. As a consequence, such entities are used in accounting documents and therefore must be replicated in a similar way as master data. Because they are not managed and distributed via the master data management tools, Central Finance can handle those entities as well. The replication from the source system to the central system is achieved with an interface that maps these entities automatically once documents are posted.

Posting FI documents in the central system may fail for various reasons. For example, a cost center in the central system may be blocked or mapping information may be incorrect, so the account cannot be determined. Those cases are handled by the Application Interface Framework (AIF) error-handling tool.

Incomplete or incorrect records are categorized so that different users can resolve issues depending on those error categories. AIF shows the unsuccessful postings along with the error message raised by the system. In this way, the problem can be resolved based on expert decisions and the document reposted.

Central Finance offers reporting capabilities for group-wide managerial accounting and reporting. Therefore, the replication of primary postings, secondary postings, and cost objects from source systems to the central system is available by default. Three interfaces are available:

- Central Finance interface for primary postings
- Central Finance interface for secondary postings
- Central Finance interface for cost objects

Primary postings are financial documents that are posted in the source system. Depending on the P&L accounts, they can lead to controlling documents that are posted simultaneously. For example, goods receipts into consumptions lead to an expense line item in the financial document with relevance for controlling.

Secondary postings are documents that are used for internal accounting, such as time confirmations and cost allocations from one cost center to another. Secondary postings do not lead to a financial document. Both primary and secondary postings can be replicated to Central Finance by using the respective interfaces.

The *cost objects interface* creates corresponding cost objects in the central system for cost objects in the source system. Based on the setup, the sender system triggers the creation of a corresponding cost object in the central system, and both objects are mapped. For instance, a user creates a production order in a sender system. This information is propagated and leads to a new production order created in the central system. When costs are posted to the production order in the sender system, the document is also replicated to the central system. In the central system, the sender production order number automatically maps to the number of the replicated production order in the central system and the document is assigned accordingly.

In order to improve transparency or to logically structure costs and revenues, it is common practice to use cost object structures. Costs and revenues may be collected on or transferred to cost objects that group multiple production orders on a higher level. The interface for cost objects can manage the assignment of several production orders to one aggregated production order or to the product cost collector. When a production order is created in such a setup in the sender system, the central system finds the higher-level cost object for this production order or, if it does not exist, creates one.

Configuring the financial document replication to Central Finance is easy for SAP systems and relatively straightforward for non-SAP systems. For source systems that are SAP ERP systems, the replication of primary postings, secondary postings, and cost objects via the interfaces is facilitated by delivered integration content. For source systems that are non-SAP systems, the same interfaces are used. Because SLT directly replicates from the database, you must state which database tables of the non-SAP system hold the financial document data. SLT performs a technical mapping of those database fields with the fields of the Central Finance interfaces, providing the corresponding financial document attributes to be replicated.

Based on this relevant finance data from across the company in Central Finance, users can benefit from the flexibility and speed of reporting in the central system. The harmonized and real-time data becomes the single source of truth for the group finance department. New qualities of insights are available for General Ledger Reporting, Profitability Reporting, and Overhead Cost Reporting. Analysts will take advantage of new reporting capabilities available with SAP S/4HANA Finance, such as SAP BusinessObjects Dashboards, SAP BusinessObjects Analysis for Office, SAP BusinessObjects Design Studio, and so on.

In addition to reporting, there is much more value to realize from the finance data in Central Finance. SAP HANA delivers comprehensive planning capabilities that use the speed of in-memory processing. SAP S/4HANA Finance leverages those capabilities in the new SAP Business Planning and Consolidation for Finance solution, allowing financial planning scenarios to be run in the central system. The new planning solution provides a new financial planning data model that is consistent and integrated (return to Chapter 11, Section 11.5 for more details).

The powerful planning engine removes the need to transfer actual and planning data to a separate business warehouse. Planning takes place in the same system that holds the actuals. This is of particular interest in combination with Central Finance, in which the results from planning can be used to interact with actual data—for example, to carry out adjustment postings and allocations.

With the central availability of harmonized finance data, Central Finance is a powerful asset that provides a global view of accounting for centralized finance departments.

14.3 Evolution to an Operational System

In general, financial operations are strongly integrated into business operations and managed under decentral responsibility. Although this approach has advantages from many perspectives, it comes with a price from the perspective of the global organization. Visibility is limited, as in the areas of exposure of cash and liquidity. Many effects for scale cannot be realized, as in procurement. Dependencies from the decentral finance organizations are high, as during period-end close. There are approaches to tackle those challenges and to move components of decentral finance processes to a more centralized process.

Centralization is not the right solution to all problems. In order to identify where the value of centralization lies, a more detailed view on business processes is needed. Examples can include purchase-to-pay or sell-from-stock scenarios. Key elements of the business process are the purchase order or the sales order. Those are essential entities that are used in the supply chain and to operate the business end to end, so they qualify to remain fully in the decentral system. Upon posting a goods receipt or a delivery with goods issue, a financial document posts. This financial document is replicated to the central system with relevance for internal and external accounting. With postings now on accounts and cost objects in the central system, business analysts have the choice to report on the business process both in the decentral system and in the central system. There will be use cases in which more in-depth analysis of a particular business process or transaction is needed, and this analysis will be performed in the decentral system. However, analysis on an aggregated level and across many business transactions will likely be performed in the central system, because it has the single source of truth from a corporate perspective, reflects the corporate view on business, and simplifies the communication across units.

In the next step of this business process in the decentral system, a customer invoice posts. This again leads to a financial document containing a receivables item. This document is again replicated into the central system. A collections manager can monitor the receivables item centrally, whereas the central cash manager may be interested in this receivables item for the liquidity forecast. Finally, dunning and payment take place in the central system. The corresponding situation is in procurement, in which supplier invoices are relevant for central payment processes as well as central liquidity analyses.

These examples have in common that the process starts in the decentral system and is owned by the business operations. Figure 14.2 shows that as soon as the processes have an impact on finance there is central representation of this process that allows the analysis of the impact on a local level and on a corporate level. Where decentral control of the business process is feasible from a business perspective, there are opportunities to centralize processing by leveraging the Central Finance system.

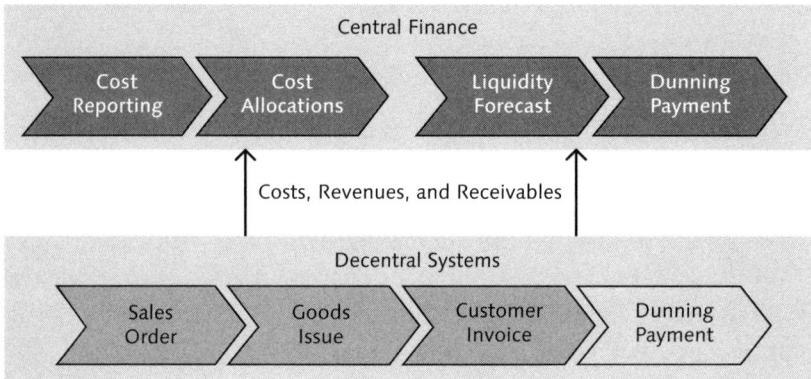

Figure 14.2 Processes in Decentral Systems and in Central Finance

There are other examples in the area of asset accounting. The building, procurement, and maintenance of fixed assets is reflected in financial documents and monitored in asset accounting. Selected parts of this process may even be moved to the central system, with central responsibilities and a central view. Depreciation runs, for instance, may be performed centrally.

These examples illustrate the value, savings, and optimization potential that centralizing the financial processes can achieve. Limitations for centralization arise when there are considerable dependencies between operational events and finance processes. There are many situations in which financial processing is linked to operational processes, such as confirmations or routing information, or to personal insights, such as customer account managers. When criteria for decisions are not available centrally or require high effort to replicate, centralizing finance operations becomes cumbersome. There are also situations in which finance operations are embedded into a network of dependencies that are managed by other applications, such as production systems. Centralization may technically be feasible through harmonization of master data and status information, but there is a point at which this option is not economically attractive due to the high effort required.

With limited insights or data required as a basis for decisions, centralization of financial operations will not provide optimization in all cases. Process analysis and conscious decisions will lead the way to use cases in which centralized finance processes add the most value.

Looking beyond the centralization of data and processes, we can imagine more attractive use cases for Central Finance for the future.

Material valuation is a candidate for a case in which a central store of finance data will help to rethink the possibilities. A central material ledger may give new options for material valuation. Product costs could be analyzed in different ways and without limits across the organization. If the underlying data from various sources was heterogeneous in the past, then the harmonization with Central Finance suddenly opens opportunities for new processes.

Financial consolidation is another example of a process that may be performed directly in the central system in the future. This option would speed up consolidation significantly. Considerable time is lost during close through adjustments of documents in decentral systems that lead to waiting times and delays. Today, the adjusted documents are again extracted and loaded into the consolidation system with subsequent loading cycles. With Central Finance, the adjustment will be replicated immediately. Alternatively, adjustments may even be made directly in the centralized finance system. Another use case in this context may be the handling of intercompany reconciliation, in which intercompany transactions already will be recognized at the time of posting. In this way, intercompany elimination may occur immediately.

A future consolidation solution in the central system may be instrumental to avoid replication and waiting times for extraction cycles, to rethink intercompany reconciliation, and to run significantly faster through the fast processing of large data volumes with SAP HANA. With the central store for accounting documents, possibilities arise to bring consolidation even closer to the operational ("logistics") processes.

We intend for the preceding ideas to outline the potential advantages of having all financial data in one central instance in real time, especially if the central system is an SAP S/4HANA Finance system. Most likely, once a company has actually established a Central Finance instance, a lot of ideas and desires will arise from the data in one system operating on a powerful database that can cope with all that data volume and analyze it flexibly with high performance.

14.4 Central Finance in the Cloud

In today's world, it is increasingly irrelevant where hardware is located. Software is consumed as a service, and companies want to invest their IT budgets where such investment will help them to stand out from the competition. Therefore, it is becoming more common for organizations to leverage the consumption and license models of the cloud for their finance operations. Depending on the level of influence and customization companies want to have for the system, they can choose from a variety of alternatives: a managed service, a hybrid consumption model with on-premise and cloud components, a public cloud model, or even a public cloud model that offers additional options that cater for individual needs.

Today, companies are testing cloud deployment models in combination with Central Finance. Central Finance makes moving into the cloud easier and presents an attractive scenario with many options that help to create additional value.

The initial stage of Central Finance delivers high value for companies and will easily justify the investments. The opportunities that arise out of the centralized finance system, however, are much greater. Reporting scenarios are only the starting point, and many more scenarios can be added to a roadmap that adds incremental value over time. The aspiration is to move beyond a centralized finance data store with reporting and planning capabilities, to drive centralization of finance processes, and to evolve from a reporting system to an operating system.

This chapter explains what typical implementation projects look like—in particular, how the nondisruptive paradigm allows SAP customers to quickly adopt SAP S/4HANA Finance. We also outline how organizations can embrace the additional possibilities created by SAP S/4HANA Finance.

15 Adoption Scenarios

Companies that have decided to adopt SAP S/4HANA Finance based on its benefits and features can choose between different deployment options, as shown in the first two chapters of Part III. Chapter 13 gave a general overview of on-premise installations and cloud offerings, whereas Chapter 14 explained Central Finance as a strategy and deployment scenario for a centralized finance system.

Independent of their choice of deployment, companies have a certain adoption scenario for SAP S/4HANA Finance in mind when switching. Such a scenario consists of their expectations with regard to business value, the project approach they are taking for switching to SAP S/4HANA Finance, and the specific measurable objectives of the project.

In this chapter, we introduce the various approaches that drive SAP's customers through selected customer cases. This should give you useful insights into what currently motivates companies to undertake the journey into the new world of finance, even as most companies just now begin to switch to the rather new product SAP S/4HANA Finance. Looking at the customer cases, you will probably be able to draw parallels to your own situation and learn valuable insights for your adoption from the approach others are taking. For reasons of brevity, this chapter is not a detailed implementation guide. SAP and its partners offer services that support you in your particular adoption scenario.

15   Adoption Scenarios

In this chapter, we first point out the two different approaches that need to be understood before starting an implementation project for your company, namely greenfield or brownfield (Section 15.1). Section 15.2 then highlights two particular customer cases of companies undertaking an on-premise installation of SAP S/4HANA Finance. Finally, Section 15.3 presents a case of a Central Finance adoption.

15.1   Greenfield vs. Brownfield Approach

With SAP S/4HANA Finance, you are given the option of a rapid, efficient, and integrated implementation of your financial and cost accounting processes. Before starting a project, it is essential to determine whether you want to reengineer the processes and when.

In this respect, we differentiate between a greenfield and a brownfield approach for established SAP customers. If you are a new SAP customer, you always use a greenfield approach in order to adapt your existing financial and cost accounting processes to the SAP solution. In contrast, brownfield approaches originate with a finance system in place and migrate to the SAP solution.

15.1.1   Greenfield Approach

In a greenfield approach, customers implement SAP S/4HANA Finance as a fresh start for their financial world. Greenfields usually start off with a blueprint phase, in which an implementing company takes the opportunity to review its existing processes (which may have developed over years or even decades) and to get more insight into the new architecture and processes by prototyping business use cases. Based on the results of the initial analysis, customers build processes that are slimmer, globally aligned, and make better use of resources.

Furthermore, the greenfield approach gives customers the advantage of setting up a company-wide template and delivering a standard business process map during the rollout to their companies. Table 15.1 walks through the pros and cons of this approach.

Advantages	Disadvantages
▶ Disposal of the outgrown and outdated process landscape. ▶ Kickoff with a new and efficient process landscape. ▶ Construction of a company-wide template for harmonization and standardization of processes. ▶ Excellent opportunity to implement the full range of innovations within SAP S/4HANA Finance.	▶ Depending on the size of the company, standardization and reengineering of processes may be very time consuming, in which case users can benefit from the advantages of SAP S/4HANA Finance only in the midterm.

Table 15.1 Greenfield Implementation Considerations

The Central Finance deployment option is always based on a greenfield approach, because you build up a centralized finance backbone next to the current system landscape. This scenario will be discussed in detail later.

15.1.2 Brownfield Approach

The brownfield approach presupposes an existing finance system landscape that a company migrates to SAP S/4HANA Finance. Such a migration can be carried out in a relatively short time, depending on the size of the company (see Chapter 13). Customers who have already migrated their SAP ERP system to SAP Business Suite on SAP HANA often switch to SAP S/4HANA Finance in a second step in order to benefit from the substantial enhancements in the financial applications. SAP SE, for example, switched its existing financial accounting to SAP S/4HANA Finance in only 2.5 months.

Customers who at present have not yet switched to SAP Business Suite on SAP HANA must upgrade their existing SAP ERP system to EHP 7 and migrate to the SAP HANA database. This means that all of their remaining SAP ERP applications also benefit from the existing improvements of SAP HANA.

Many companies who choose this approach intend to achieve results quickly, albeit without having to reengineer their processes. They can instantly benefit from the simplified architecture, the new transactions (e.g., intercompany reconciliation), and the included SAP Fiori apps (e.g., to display balance sheets or line items). However, as companies gain insights into the actual process acceleration after the completed migration they can subsequently analyze further potential for improvement by making individual changes—for example, in the closing processes.

Table 15.2 outlines the advantages and disadvantages that brownfield implementation projects bring.

Advantages	Disadvantages
▸ Short project runtime, because the migration to the SAP S/4HANA Finance add-on is a straightforward process. ▸ Users perceive the built-in benefits of the SAP S/4HANA Finance add-on right after migration. ▸ No need to change existing FI or CO interfaces.	▸ The migration does not eliminate naturally complex and obsolete processes. Customers may have to kick off an additional project and involve the business. ▸ In the case of earlier releases, an upgrade to EHP 7 is a project that may prove time consuming. Because EHP 7 is a prerequisite, this may delay the finance project.

Table 15.2 Brownfield Implementation Considerations

15.2 SAP S/4HANA Finance in SAP Business Suite on SAP HANA

Over the past months, we have discussed the capabilities of SAP S/4HANA Finance with numerous SAP customers. For many, SAP S/4HANA Finance provides a chance to review long-standing or obsolete processes and reports. Finance departments consider the implementation of SAP S/4HANA Finance as an opportunity to strengthen their position as innovative and trusted partners within the company.

The following examples illustrate possible project goals related to SAP S/4HANA Finance implementations for your reference. You will see that the motivation for adopting SAP S/4HANA Finance is quite similar but also that there are different approaches available.

15.2.1 Manufacturing Company

Our first example centers on a global manufacturing enterprise with five thousand employees and $1.8 billion of revenue. This organization has one of the largest

SAP Business Suite on SAP HANA installations, because all areas and modules of the enterprise run on a single SAP ERP installation. Through SAP S/4HANA Finance, the customer now has the opportunity to organize its processes, especially for reporting.

The following project goals were defined based on a customer pilot study:

1. To harmonize internal and external reporting:
    - Set up standardized and effective reporting. As with SAP S/4HANA Finance, the various individual documents in FI, CO, and CO-PA are made obsolete, because all reports access the same document in the Universal Journal (see Chapter 8). This means that no further reconciliation between the modules and reports is necessary, and the same reports can be used for differing requirements.
    - Introduce account-based CO-PA in order to retain real-time and fully aligned contribution analysis.
    - Achieve seamless reporting—for example, between FI and CO-PA, in order to branch directly from the balance sheet and the P&L statement to the profitability analysis segments using drill down.
    - Introduce SAP BusinessObjects Dashboards to SAP HANA views and analytical apps, such as SAP Smart Business apps, to enable intuitive reporting.
    - Introduce SAP Lumira for the plan-to-actual comparison.

2. To accelerate and simplify the closing processes:
    - Eliminate the reconciliation processes between FI, CO, and CO-PA and between totals and line items thanks to the Universal Journal.
    - Use online intercompany reconciliation to dispense with periodic reconciliation.
    - Replace the periodic settlements with online top-down distributions, resulting in short month-end cycles.
    - Implement integrated planning to enable both top-down and bottom-up planning for the P&L statement, separately for costs and revenues based on the last fiscal year, on any dimension (cost center, profit center, or segment), and rolled up to the superordinate hierarchies.

The customer works through two project phases and their respective steps. While in the first phase, the foundation for the G/L is laid; in the second phase, the functionalities of the G/L are implemented. Hence, the customer benefits quickly from technological enhancements coming from SAP S/4HANA Finance.

The first phase, in which SAP S/4HANA Finance is implemented, includes the following steps:

1. Reorganization of Profit Center Accounting
2. Migration to SAP S/4HANA Finance
3. Configuration of the G/L, but without document split
4. Implementation of account-based CO-PA
5. Go-live of the G/L and CO-PA
6. Reengineering of reporting based on PCA and CO-PA

The second phase of the implementation and extension of the G/L includes introducing document splitting and further ledgers.

The existing organizational structures in the logistics and finance areas do not change. The existing direct assignment of company codes to a controlling area is retained.

15.2.2 High-Tech Company

This case stems from a company with ninety thousand employees and $35 billion of revenue. With regards to objectives, this customer in the high-tech industry sees huge advantages primarily through the new data integrity (Universal Journal), the elimination of reconciliation efforts, and company-wide transparency. In addition, by using SAP Fiori apps, the customer can achieve an optimized and simplified process landscape for accounts payable and accounts receivable accounting.

The goals of the finance department are to further extend the business partner role and to support decision making even better in the future through optimized reporting.

The business seeks the following improvements via the implementation of SAP S/4HANA Finance:

- All divisions to access a common P&L statement structure
- Standardized P&L statement for both internal and external reporting
- Mapping of the P&L statement within cost-of-sales accounting
- Standardized segment reporting of the financial statements
- Elimination of missing cost and revenue assignment in month-end closing
- Improvement of individual processes by using SAP Fiori apps and replacement of the existing processes that this entails
- Support of decision-making for acquisitions or expansion into new markets by being able to simulate future options

In order to roll out new processes and reporting on a global level, this customer has opted for the greenfield approach. A first step in this project is the definition of a common group template that considers the requirements of all countries and business units. Rollout begins in one country, followed by a stepwise transfer of further countries to the group template.

15.3 Central Finance and Central Reporting

As explained in Chapter 14, Central Finance offers enterprises that have a particularly large and widely distributed system landscape new capabilities to implement financial processes and analysis across the enterprise and in real time. Let's look at the customer case of a trade company that demonstrates the motivation and goals behind adopting Central Finance.

15.3.1 Trade Company

This trade company has thirty thousand employees and $50 billion of revenue along with a huge, heterogeneous system landscape. This company faces the issue that its sources for both reporting and financial statements come from both SAP ERP systems and several non-SAP systems. In addition, the customer plans to grow the enterprise through acquisitions.

In the current system landscape, only a data warehouse made comprehensive reporting possible, some of which could only be performed on a monthly basis, depending on individual connectivity. In this case, the Central Finance system offers the customer the option to set up a global shared service center. Processes will be automated increasingly in the future in order to focus on value-adding measures.

Today, the customer faces several challenges:

- Different data sources with diverse data models.
- Only limited automation to the reporting systems for further processing due to numerous interfaces.
- Data can only be reconciled with a high input of time and resources due to incorrect master data and differing time zones.

For the company, the introduction of one financial system is an important step in eliminating these challenges within the implementation project. For this reason, the customer has defined the following project goals to realize the business case for Central Finance:

- Set up a global closing statements and reporting system.
- Generate financial statements anytime in the course of a month.
- Create KPI reporting across the group at any time by replicating data in real time to the financial backbone system.
- Massively reduce reconciliation efforts between the individual ledgers and areas.
- Enable additional and quicker reporting and processing capabilities by using SAP HANA.
- Enable group-wide controlling for tracking the entire company process (from planning and budgeting to reporting) and the plan-to-actual comparison in real-time divisions.
- Avoid adoption of related logistics systems for the planned finance transformation (all logistics processes remain unchanged and continue to run).

The following measures are planned for this project:

- **Error reduction**
  To recognize and correct errors quickly (e.g., in the master data area), a monitor is set up that reports the error directly during the data replication process. This enables accurate reporting even partway through the month. Errors can be corrected directly in the source system, and as a result further automatic processing is ensured.

- **Reduction in reconciliation tasks**
  Real-time replication of the data means that reconciliation can be carried out between the various source systems in the current month. The reconciliation tasks at month-end closing can be considerably reduced in this way.

- **Global KPI reporting**
  By centralizing financial data, the customer or product information is consolidated for the segments as well and can be evaluated across the various systems. The customer will now obtain its operating KPI reporting globally based on real-time data.

- **Performance improvements**
  The Central Finance system creates the necessary framework to implement performance-relevant measures that are controlled worldwide and subject to continual improvement.

- **Consolidation**
  Within the Central Finance system, company-wide consolidation is provided in addition to the financial statement for the individual company codes. The permanent replication of the data enables quick generation of consolidated financial statements anytime throughout a month. The enterprise thereby gains the greatest possible level of transparency for the key figures for the group.

The project is structured in two phases. The first phase includes the following tasks:

1. Definition of the global reporting template
2. Setup of a centralized finance system to enable global reporting
3. Integration of SAP and non-SAP systems to replicate documents into the Central Finance system

The second phase includes the following tasks:

1. Definition of the global template for overall finance processes
2. Enhancement of the Central Finance system according to the template
3. Enhancement of the SLT tool to enable replication of additionally required finance data

This chapter described adoption scenarios for SAP S/4HANA Finance. After explaining the greenfield and brownfield approaches, we looked at four concrete customer cases. They highlight the various objectives companies aim to realize with SAP S/4HANA Finance. We also explored the different approaches that customers of SAP take to switch to SAP S/4HANA Finance.

*SAP S/4HANA Finance is used already by several SAP customers—
but SAP SE itself has also replaced its core financials system with SAP
S/4HANA Finance and now materializes the benefits outlined in the
preceding parts of this book. In this chapter, we will explain how SAP SE
made this transition.*

16　Success Story: SAP SE Runs SAP S/4HANA Finance

SAP SE is the global corporation headquartered in Walldorf, Germany, that creates world-class enterprise software such as SAP S/4HANA Finance. As part of the SAP Runs SAP initiative, SAP SE adopted SAP S/4HANA Finance for its core financials system. Lessons learned from its experience with integrating SAP S/4HANA Finance into its system landscape can be valuable not only as yet another generic case study but also perhaps as a success story. In this chapter, we also refer to earlier releases with the product's previous name, "SAP Simple Finance," in order to describe the adoption process as SAP SE continuously adopted new releases.

In order to get the most out of SAP SE's example, let's begin by understanding its vision and the potential benefits it expected to reap by combining core finance functionality with the strengths of other innovative technologies and solutions offered by SAP (Section 16.1). After that, you will get some insights into SAP SE's overall roadmap, explaining in detail the starting point, the business requirements, the steps taken, and the experiences gained (Section 16.2). This overview is followed by a recap of what benefits have been achieved so far, giving concrete examples from SAP's internal processes, including facts and figures (Section 16.3). We continue our analysis with the steps planned toward the next editions of SAP S/4HANA Finance and the business value that we expect to be unlocked in the near future (Section 16.4). The chapter ends with a conclusion of this exciting journey toward a vision for the future.

16.1 Defining a Finance Vision

We all are used to certain conveniences in our private lives. We consume countless self-service apps from our mobile devices, purchase products and services in online shopping portals, read e-books, exchange information about experiences and opinions through ratings or blogs, connect with friends via social networks, and visit places via online maps—just to name a few cases. With the help of apps, we optimize our daily tasks—from monitoring energy consumption to opening or closing window blinds at home from a mobile device. We store personal data in the cloud in order to have it available whenever and wherever we need it.

We accept and use only those apps that are beneficial and easy to use. We don't want to worry about maintenance, upgrades, or bug fixes.

Most of us miss such an environment in the business context when performing our tasks at work. Given the technology revolution of the previous years, this situation should no longer be limited to the private space. Business users should be supported while working in a connected world to collaborate and exchange data with each other. They should enjoy the convenience and flexibility of accessing all data relevant to performing their tasks, and they should have fun doing it.

This intersection of expectations and functionality is where SAP SE sees the potential of SAP S/4HANA Finance, and its creator is not immune to its allure. The following nonexhaustive list names some of the core elements that influenced the decision to implement SAP S/4HANA Finance at SAP SE.

With SAP HANA and in-memory technology as the new basis of SAP's enterprise software solutions, the first benefit of SAP S/4HANA Finance that comes to mind is enhanced performance. Performance is considered an enabler for a reactive user experience, simulation of complex systems, and real-time jobs instead of batch jobs—just to name a few. However, this is certainly not the only relevant benefit. Given the potential of SAP HANA, being able to store and consume data on a line item level provides unlimited flexibility for analytics, seamless navigation, and independence from previously required but redundant aggregates. Standard Virtual data model (VDM) views provide the content to be used for native SAP HANA reporting and to be executed in real time on the respective source data. In addition, historical data becomes easier to access, because data aging reduces the in-memory footprint while at the same time keeping the original data available without limitations in case it is needed.

SAP SE sees immense potential in the integration of FI and CO in the Universal Journal for enabling data harmonization and consumption. This not only means that the reconciliation effort can be removed, but it also provides for an integrated legal and management view, which is a real single source of truth for reporting and analytics enabling—for example, by providing seamless navigation both from granularity and content points of view.

Furthermore, SAP SE expects to be able to automate existing business processes and to provide its finance users with new functionality and applications, such as cash management, planning, or predictive elements based on combined FI/CO data and the Exposure Hub, complementing actual and plan data.

The user experience plays a decisive role in the context of SAP S/4HANA Finance. Although the SAP Fiori launchpad helps to individually configure the user's personal entry point to his or her set of applications, the SAP Fiori apps support the user in efficiently fulfilling those tasks. Users can combine and navigate between transactional apps, analytical KPI visualizations, and fact sheets. They all follow the same user experience paradigms and can be used in a flexible, individual, role-based, and intuitive way, providing the opportunity to collaborate and share information with others and to switch instantly from insight to action.

In addition to the previously mentioned capabilities, the nonfunctional qualities in the context of adoption are important as well, because they enable SAP SE to move toward SAP S/4HANA Finance quickly. SAP SE relies on a nondisruptive transformation combined with the ability to proceed step by step in order to have the best possible change management process and finally to achieve overall user acceptance.

Combining these elements, SAP SE sees a chance to simplify business processes, its system landscape, and the user experience without disruption. Let's take this scenario and transfer it to the finance world: SAP SE envisions its finance staff working with beautiful SAP Fiori transactional apps optimized for respective tasks and roles. Employees may search and surf the systems with SAP HANA Enterprise Search, consuming SAP Fiori fact sheets connected to additional information and further functionality. They can share data or views and collaborate with colleagues via apps and SAP Jam, analyze business data via SAP Smart Business cockpits and other frontends, and create ad hoc evaluations, simulations, and predictions in real time.

The finance staff and managers explore and navigate through the business data and drill down when needed, not limited to prepared snapshots or aggregates. They can switch between legal, statutory, and management views all based on the same data in a consistent way without the need to start navigation from scratch. Prediction functionality provides simulation and prognosis for different scenarios or parameters considering the actuals and all data that might be relevant for respective calculations.

With SAP S/4HANA Finance, SAP SE envisions making its business processes more efficient and providing better transparency and decision support combined with significantly better usability and higher user satisfaction—all enabled by SAP HANA and the SAP HANA Cloud Platform.

How did SAP SE plan to reach its goals? What has the company already achieved?

16.2 Moving to SAP S/4HANA Finance

SAP SE aspires to be "the cloud company powered by SAP HANA" as it develops technology innovations for its customers to Run Simple and to improve people's lives everywhere. To support this and to deal with every business challenge of today and tomorrow, SAP provides solutions and services, from cloud and in-memory to mobile, analytics, and beyond. Currently, SAP helps 263,000 customers derive value from their SAP solutions in a cost-effective and predictable way, including professional services, support, and cloud delivery. SAP aims to simplify consumption of its products, business processes, and user experience.

To reach this target, SAP combines different innovative technologies covering five market categories: applications, analytics, mobile, database and technology, and cloud. The platform for all SAP solutions is SAP HANA, the in-memory database running complete enterprise applications in main memory, which is deployable as an on-premise appliance or in the cloud.

SAP also offers comprehensive services and support to maximize the business value of its customers' investments and to help them with faster innovation adoption and efficient solution implementation. SAP's services and support portfolio covers the entire end-to-end application lifecycle.

16.2.1 System Landscape and Organization

SAP SE's core systems consist of a central SAP ERP system with one client, linked to CRM, HR, BI, and several cloud instances: in total, more than thirty downstream systems. How does that break down?

- SAP SE handles more than 301 active company codes, 2.1 million customers, four hundred thousand vendors, one controlling area, and one operating concern.

- From a FI/CO perspective, the company has a volume of around 1,250,000 outgoing and around 650,000 incoming invoices, around 115,000 education and the same number of consulting billing documents per year, and more than one million trip entries, 4,500,00 posted FI documents, and fifteen million posted CO documents.

- Table entries in 2013 led to 6.3 million document headers, around twenty-five million FI line items, around ninety million CO line items, around thirty thousand active profit centers, and around twenty-one million profitability segments.

- More than seventy-four thousand business users work on different processes, such as quote-to-close, order management, invoicing, travel and expense management, record-to-close, purchasing, and controlling.

SAP SE's finance organization acts both as a steward with a focus on compliance, efficiency, and financial targets and as a conavigator advising the business on strategic and operational plans that improve SAP's business performance and effectiveness.

Therefore, the corporate CFO of SAP SE is leading the Global Finance and Administration (GFA) organization that covers the global finance functions. He is responsible for managing the financial risks of the corporation, financial planning, and financial reporting to upper management.

The GFA organization is structured along these five lines of business:

- Financial Planning and Analysis focuses on business-centric planning with embedded intelligence, integrated planning models, and simulation capabilities with real-time reference data and what-if scenarios.

- Accounting and Financial Close develops the closing process by automation, integration, processes acceleration, better collaboration, and intuitive self-service access to financial information.
- Treasury and Financial Risk Management optimizes payment, cash management, and treasury operations through improved automation, flexible deployments, and straight-through processing. Financial and commodity risks can be recognized proactively with an accurate global cash position.
- Collaborative Finance Operations standardizes and centralizes end-to-end finance processes for greater efficiency and lower costs by unlocking economies of scale and by automating service delivery along end-to-end processes in shared service centers. It focuses especially on simple, repetitive, regular, and predefined tasks, high-volume services, and tasks with a focus on standardization. Important aspects in this context are scalability, automation, and high quality.
- Enterprise Risk and Compliance Management has established an effective control environment and detects, investigates, analyzes, and prevents irregularities or fraud.

Facing sustained market volatility, increasing regulatory compliance, and growing pressure on margins, SAP's finance organization has to apply best practices to help the company meet its financial goals.

16.2.2 Finance Transformation

SAP SE started its finance transformation journey back in 2003. First, the company looked at globalization of the corporate functions, implementation of a shared services organization concept, and further standardization and automation.

In 2011, SAP SE decided to leverage its solutions and latest innovations with a focus on SAP HANA. In this context, SAP's internal IT department, Business Innovation & IT (BI&IT), is the partner for validation and implementation of new technologies and solutions. BI&IT is responsible for evolving SAP SE's IT strategy and executing on it. With expertise in both technology and business processes, BI&IT's goal is to drive the internal adoption of standard applications that support end users in the execution and reengineering of their processes in all lines of business, with a strong focus on end user centricity. Furthermore, BI&IT focuses on co-innovation with the product development units to extend the use of SAP standard products within SAP SE as the earliest adopter, to ensure zero distance between business and technology, and finally to act as the ultimate proof point in SAP SE's transition to being a cloud company.

SAP SE's roadmap to SAP S/4HANA Finance started with the adoption of SAP HANA as a side-by-side scenario in 2012, already leveraging some benefits in the area of analytics, such as real-time Profitability Analysis and Profit Center Accounting reporting. SAP SE integrated an initial set of SAP Fiori apps, such as SAP Receivables Manager. Next, SAP SE implemented SAP BW powered by SAP HANA with more than 4,500 users, which, for example, changed the currency evaluation for constant currency calculation to document currency and also made use of optimized planning functionality, such as SAP BPC and the Planning Application Kit. Since then, SAP SE continuously optimized analytics not only from a backend perspective but also from a frontend perspective, leveraging different tools, including SAP BusinessObjects Analysis for Office, SAP BusinessObjects Design Studio, SAP Lumira, and more. Afterwards, SAP SE migrated its CRM system to SAP CRM powered by SAP HANA, which is used by more than fifteen thousand users for marketing, sales, and services processes. A big step towards SAP HANA adoption was taken in 2013 by migrating to SAP ERP powered by SAP HANA, with its sixty-seven thousand users covering all core financial processes. In parallel, the company continued with new functionality, such as SAP Fraud Management and the financial fact sheet integrated with SAP Receivables Manager.

Finally, in April 2014, SAP SE went live with SAP Simple Finance 1.0 after completing a fifty-five-day implementation project between initial kick-off and go-live, followed in May 2015 by the migration to SAP Simple Finance, on-premise edition 1503, establishing the new Universal Journal.

16.2.3 Scope and Structure of the Project

At a very early stage of SAP SE's adoption journey, several Design Thinking workshops were executed to identify potential for improvement and to define future scenarios. SAP SE intensified its co-innovation activities, bringing together development, IT, and business expertise and offering a dedicated innovation landscape as a scrambled and anonymized copy of the production system for early validation activities. Hence, a first system running SAP Simple Finance was available already in January 2014.

Given the target date for go-live in April, a phased approach with an initial migration followed by stepwise adopting of enhancements was chosen.

For Wave 0, due April 2014, the following elements were in focus:

- Implementation of G/L as a basis for SAP Simple Finance (technical migration)
- Removal of aggregates and indices in FI and CO
- Harmonization of FI and CO data

From Wave 1, due in November 2014, SAP SE planned to leverage the new potentials step by step:

- Reporting scenarios to leverage one logical document
- SAP Fiori analytical and transactional apps addressing the Accounts Receivable, Accounts Payable, and G/L Accountant
- Enabling SAP HANA Enterprise Search/CBON/fact sheets
- Data aging for application logs, IDocs, and FI documents

In parallel, SAP SE continued with co-innovation activities to prepare the adoption of the Universal Journal as well as further modules (e.g., Cash Management). Apart from the functional implementation, SAP SE explored opportunities through possible process enhancements or combinations of new features in the context of prediction, automation, and more.

These aspects were targeted for Wave 2, due in May 2015:

- Migration to the new Universal Journal
- SAP Cash Management powered by SAP HANA
- Ongoing go-live of SAP Fiori analytical and transactional apps
- Further reporting and dashboard scenarios for leveraging the new Universal Journal
- Planning and simulation
- Process automation scenarios (e.g., P&L on the fly)

SAP SE's major requirement was to adopt SAP S/4HANA Finance in a smooth and nondisruptive way with the shortest possible system downtime and full data integrity, especially before and after the migration in Wave 0. Therefore, the business engaged with Active Global Support (AGS) for safeguarding services and with an external auditor to certify data consistency. SAP SE also executed three test migrations with near-production data in integrated systems to optimize the procedure and duration. This included technical preparation, consistency checks, and system clean-up activities to have a consistent source as well as clear and documented step-by-step processes for the go-live of SAP S/4HANA Finance.

SAP SE also took the chance to combine and support the migration activities with basic housekeeping tasks in the areas of archiving, custom code retirement, and code remediation. From a change management perspective, it was essential to involve the respective business stakeholders continuously and closely for concept validation and acceptance testing. The solution support teams ensured a smooth handover after go-live. End users have only been impacted marginally by the rather technical changes performed within Wave 0.

After fifty-five days, the execution of 1,100 test cases by 444 business testers, and one cutover weekend with an onsite task force setup, SAP Simple Finance went live in an amazingly smooth and fast way.

Technical Setup for Wave 0 Go-Live in April 2014

- System: IS* (SAP ERP)
  - ECC 6.0 EHP 7
  - SAP NetWeaver 7.40 SPS 06, kernel 7.41 PL26
  - SAP_FIN 700 SP 0
  - SAP HANA SPS 07 Rev. 74
- System: PG* (Gateway)
  - SAP NetWeaver 7.40 SP 05
  - SAP_UI: 740 SP 06

For Wave 1, the focus was on native reporting scenarios to leverage the existing SAP HANA Live views and the enhanced data model in general. Furthermore, SAP SE integrated more analytical and transactional SAP Fiori apps with a focus on Accounts Receivable (e.g., Display Customer Balances, Overdue Receivables, and

Manage Customer Line Items), Accounts Payable (e.g., Display Vendor Balances, Future Payables, Manage Vendor Line Items, and Manual Clearing), and G/L Accountant (e.g., Display G/L Account Line Items, Display Financial Statement, and Post G/L Document). Because SAP Fiori delivery is structured in waves with different system requirements, SAP SE split Wave 1 into two go-lives, one for October 2014 (1a) and one for November 2014 (1b). SAP Fiori Search apps, the so-called fact sheets (e.g., Accounting Document, Sales Order, General Ledger Account, and Cost Center), complemented the offering due to being accessible by SAP HANA Enterprise Search and also linked to other SAP Fiori apps as well as dedicated backend transactions.

Because the new functionality was offered on top of existing transactions or reports, SAP SE did not have to worry about retirement of existing processes or transactions. The project could focus on business feedback on one hand and performance measurements on the other to optimize the offering for end users, so it wasn't forced to reach full coverage of existing functionality immediately from the beginning.

While SAP SE covered the performance aspect with measurements during user tests and dedicated volume tests, business validation workshops for each covered role were initiated for development, IT, and business. These workshops aimed at identifying the functionality with the highest expected benefit and at receiving feedback for product enhancements. This was important especially because SAP SE decided to implement plain standards for SAP Fiori. In the area of SAP HANA Live, the company made use of delivered standard views simply embedded in its views (e.g., to add authorization checks based on real-time SAP ERP authorizations). With regards to the UI of analytics, SAP SE took a broad approach and chose tools that fit best respective use cases, such as SAP BusinessObjects or SAP Smart Business. For reports and dashboards, SAP SE took a native SAP HANA approach to the overall architecture in line with its requirements.

The go-live of Wave 1 was not critical; it simply helped to make the new possibilities more tangible and provided time to prepare the next step.

Technical Setup for Wave 1a Go-Live in October 2014
- System: IS* (SAP ERP)
    - SAP ERP 6.0 EHP 7 SP 05
    - SAP NetWeaver 7.40 SP 07

- SAP_FIN 700 SP 02
- SAP HANA Live 1.0 SP 07 for SAP ERP
- SAP HANA Live 1.0 SP 02 for SAP Simple Finance add-on
- SAP Fiori wave 4 to 5
- SAP Smart Business Analytics Foundation 1.0 SPS 01
- SAP HANA SPS 08 Rev. 83
- System: PG* (SAP Gateway)
  - SAP NetWeaver 7.40 SP 07
  - SAP_UI SP 09

Technical Setup for Wave 1b Go-Live in November 2014

- System: IS* (SAP ERP)
  - SAP ERP 6.0 EHP 7 SP 06
  - SAP NetWeaver 7.40 SP 09
  - SAP_FIN 700 SP 03
  - SAP HANA Live 1.0 SP 08 for SAP ERP
  - SAP HANA Live 1.0 SP 03 for SAP Simple Finance add-on
  - SAP Fiori wave 6
  - SAP Smart Business Analytics Foundation 1.0 SPS 01
  - SAP HANA SPS 08 Rev. 84
- System: PG* (SAP Gateway)
  - SAP NetWeaver 7.40 SP 09
  - SAP_UI SP 10

For Wave 2, the migration to SAP Simple Finance, on-premise edition 1503 was targeted to adopt SAP's next major innovation, the Universal Journal. In the course of this wave, 715 million items were migrated into the new Universal Journal entry table (table ACDOCA). Further SAP Fiori apps and new analytic solutions were added, leveraging the new data structures, and new modules (such as Cash Management) were introduced. In addition to implementation and migration, SAP SE sought process enhancements. As with the previous waves, it continued the close collaboration between business, IT, and development.

The Universal Journal is also an important source for SAP's digital boardroom, which leverages enhanced data structures and enables new business steering by bringing all relevant insights to the decision makers in real time. First used in a board meeting in July 2015, the functionality of SAP Digital Boardroom and the underlying SAP Cloud for Analytics solution is continuously enhanced to cover transparency aspects as well as instant simulation along a driver tree and system-based tracking of follow-ups. Its intuitive analysis, navigation down to the line item level, and ability to slice and dice data across all elements during analysis perfectly fits the new data foundation provided by SAP S/4HANA Finance.

Technical Setup for Wave 2 Go-Live in May 2015

- System: IS* (SAP ERP)
    - SAP ERP 6.0 EHP 7 SP 07
    - SAP NetWeaver 7.40 SP 10
    - SAP_FIN 720 SP 0
    - SAP HANA Live 1.0 SP 09 for SAP ERP
    - SAP HANA Live for SAP Simple Finance add-on 2.0 SP0
    - SAP Fiori wave 7
    - SAP Smart Business Analytics Foundation 2.0 SPS 0
    - SAP HANA SPS 08 Rev. 84
- System: PG* (SAP Gateway)
    - SAP NetWeaver 7.40 SP 10
    - SAP_UI SP 11

Before we look at the next steps, targeting the completion and implementation of existing product capabilities as well as enablement of dedicated business value scenarios, let's pause and examine what has been achieved so far.

16.3 Reaping the Benefits

On April 28, 2014, SAP SE went live with the SAP Simple Finance add-on to its central SAP ERP instance. The whole migration project took place in 2.5 months, including the switch to G/L. The go-live of SAP Simple Finance, on-premise edition 1503 on May 4, 2015, was the next major milestone, establishing the new Universal Journal as the single source of truth for finance and controlling. Since then, new capabilities have been leveraged, covering reporting scenarios, transactional and analytical SAP Fiori apps, and system optimizations that use data aging for FI documents. Also, FI-specific SAP Fiori fact sheets have been introduced in the context of SAP HANA Enterprise Search. Apart from the immediate benefits, the foundation is laid for further enhancements to be provided and for process improvements to be implemented in the course of 2016 and the following years.

Looking at the benefits so far, we have to differentiate between technical and business values. However, it is almost impossible to allocate each benefit to either SAP HANA or SAP S/4HANA Finance individually, because they are closely interconnected. From a technical perspective, SAP SE has continued its path of reducing its data footprint. Starting from 7.1 TB of data, the footprint could be reduced to 3.7 TB through rigid data management and then to 1.8 TB on SAP HANA through database compression. By utilizing data aging not only for FI documents but also for IDocs and application logs, SAP SE targets a data footprint of less than 1 TB. In finance, materialized aggregates have been replaced by SAP HANA on-the-fly views, indices can be dropped, and the respective code has been simplified. All in all, the footprint reduction factor in FI/CO is about 2.2.

SAP SE has started to move reporting processes (e.g., purchase order content, Profitability Analysis, etc.) to its corporate SAP ERP system. This helps to simplify the system landscape and to reduce the overall data footprint, data redundancies, and data transfers. This move goes hand in hand with reincorporation of components such as SAP SRM, which also took place in 2014. This means that the relevant data is consumed directly without delay and without the risk of inconsistencies caused by replication.

From a business process point of view, fast close enablement is one example of enhancement: 28% of processing time has been removed. Real-time analysis and continuous intercompany reconciliation are especially important here, not to mention process acceleration due to significantly faster response times and a higher data quality. The financial closing cockpit helps to automate processes, to start steps as soon as necessary predecessors are finished, and to provide process transparency.

Looking into a bit more detail, one important aspect of SAP HANA is the revenue split along master codes (industries) in CO-PA that changed from a month-end process into a real-time process. In the past, this process took two days during quarter-end closes with efforts on the business and IT sides to complete the settlement. Currently, the master code split job takes place every day for the open periods. Business analysis is therefore possible on a daily basis, and no business corrections are required during the closing.

When adjustment postings are necessary, the process was accelerated as well due to real-time reporting capabilities. In the past, data was extracted only three times per day, and the verification of the posting sometimes could happen only after eight hours of waiting time. Now, the controller can immediately check and make corrections, thus reaching a better data quality even faster. Even complex iterations can thus happen in a very short time frame. This of course is also valid in the case of allocations; for example, the IT allocations can now be checked in real time on a global, company code, or line item level to identify reasons for potential deviations.

Apart from this, the complexity of report definitions has also decreased significantly. In the past, lots of expertise and effort was needed to analyze reporting requirements and to decide on needed dimensions and necessary aggregates (e.g., in the area of CO-PA), but the business can now include all objects. Instead of several reports for different purposes, now one or two are sufficient in some areas. For CO-PA, SAP SE currently needs only two reports, one real time and one with staged data in SAP BW, providing additional dimensions available only in SAP BW.

Other examples of accelerations in the context of the closing process include the significantly faster maintenance spreading report and the real-time intercompany reconciliation, which in the past took place every thirty minutes only and thus could cause a waiting time of up to one hour. All 173 entities at SAP SE are now able to check their intercompany differences at any time and to take the appropriate actions.

In the area of receivables management, SAP SE was able to remove offline backend processes and media breaks. Taking into consideration that finance and sales are now working on a unified record level, a DSO reduction of 10% is expected.

Batch processing is no longer necessary for many jobs (e.g., chargeback), because these now run within seconds instead of over several hours. Given this improvement, the month-end batch processing can be removed, and processes can be run at any time during the current period.

Meanwhile, SAP SE is top among its peers for fast close, according to the German magazine FINANCE.[1] SAP SE claimed the top spot with twenty-one days; for context, the average in DAX (the German stock index) is fifty-nine days, the average in MDAX (Mid-Cap-DAX) is seventy-seven days, and the average in the United States is twenty-nine days.

Knowing that fraud is an important factor for today's companies that can have a significant impact on their margins, the new SAP HANA–based fraud detection monitoring functionality provides an enormous benefit, not only allowing for real-time screening for anomalies but also temporarily blocking critical payments to give Accounts Payable accountants the opportunity to check such payments upfront.

In analytics, SAP SE sees much more business agility to adapt to new business realities, because the line item level makes the reflection of organizational changes independent from precalculated aggregates.

The new digital boardroom at SAP leverages the Universal Journal to provide transparency in real time based on live data. It offers a 360-degree view of the business and an up-to-date view of any detail of the new single source of truth. Complemented with simulation capabilities (e.g., along value-driver trees), SAP Digital Boardroom supports the decision-making process by offering alternative scenarios on the fly. The paradigms underlying SAP S/4HANA Finance are the fundamental building blocks of this boardroom of the future.

SAP SE believes that the Universal Journal will bring the line item–based integration of legal and internal management views forward. SAP SE further sees a massive reduction of high transaction volume at month end through continuous process execution throughout the month, which allows it to avoid peak loads and to gain efficiency. Not yet taken into consideration are cost savings gained by leveraging the cloud due to reduced hardware and operational costs.

SAP SE already uses new tools and frontends that follow the new user experience paradigms introduced with SAP Fiori and SAPUI5. Its end users can bundle transactional FI-related apps, analytical KPIs, time recording, approval workflows, HR processes, and more in an individual way. With the cloud launchpad, this feature is platform independent and also available securely over the Internet, so employees are no longer even limited by a mandatory connection to the

---

[1] Michael Hedtstück, "Deutsche CFOs bummeln beim Reporting. SAP am schnellsten."

company network. Examples of apps providing business benefits include the Financial Statement app, with the possibility to drill down to FI line items or single documents, enabling fast insight to action. Drilldown, filtering, visualization via graphics and geo maps, commenting, and mailing functionality are the new normal.

These are some examples of concrete benefits that SAP SE enjoys today as a result of its journey toward SAP S/4HANA Finance. How will it proceed from here?

16.4 Anticipating the Next Steps

For its next steps, SAP SE is targeting the completion and implementation of existing product capabilities as well as enablement of dedicated business value scenarios. Furthermore, SAP SE currently evaluates different strategies to migrate the internal business processes in areas besides finance to SAP S/4HANA as the next-generation business suite.

A huge potential is expected in the areas of simulation, prediction, and automation. Based on first experiences with the digital boardroom and considering SAP HANA's powerful on-the-fly capabilities, the business can think of completely new ways of getting forward-looking business insights and decision support, including scenarios such as P&L statements on the fly or a kind of soft financial close where and when needed. These are just ideas now, but they may become reality in the near future.

As part of its transformation journey, SAP SE also sees a chance to establish new steering dimensions and KPIs consistently for analytics and planning, leveraging the attributing and reporting capabilities within SAP S/4HANA Finance as well as the new SAP Cloud for Analytics.

Coming back to SAP SE's vision and summarizing its achievements, will SAP SE achieve its finance transformation goals?

16.5 The Takeaway

SAP S/4HANA Finance applies elements of main innovation areas: SAP HANA, SAP Fiori, and SAP HANA Enterprise Cloud. This is the basis for a fast, intuitive, and simple solution offering. By combining such elements, SAP S/4HANA Finance shows that the sum is greater than its parts.

SAP SE has made its financials in SAP ERP more agile in a nondisruptive way. The accounting architecture has changed completely by fully leveraging the native capabilities of the SAP HANA platform. Finance data is available on a line item level, which enables the business to react to reporting requests on an ad hoc basis. The Universal Journal is the single source of truth for both regulatory and managerial accounting and for both transactional and analytical processes. Aggregation and transaction processing can now be performed on the fly. The end user has more flexibility to drill down to the line item level, to slice and dice all financial data across all dimensions, and to search functionality throughout the system.

In SAP S/4HANA Finance, SAP SE sees an opportunity to simplify business processes, system landscapes, and user experiences. This fits perfectly with SAP SE's promise to its customers to do the most sophisticated things in simple ways and with its strategy to be the cloud company powered by SAP HANA. Hence, SAP S/4HANA Finance helps SAP SE to Run Simple. SAP SE is convinced that its vision will become a reality sometime in the near future.

PART IV
Moving Forward with SAP S/4HANA Finance

Design Thinking can be a means for companies to think about their business processes. We introduce the Design Thinking approach briefly and show how it can be used to design business processes from scratch based on the needs of all stakeholders.

17　Design Thinking

Part I and Part II of this book explored the important paradigms and new features of SAP S/4HANA Finance. Part III then outlined how easy it is to switch to SAP S/4HANA Finance. Throughout the book, we have highlighted the immediate benefits that companies get when using SAP S/4HANA Finance. Before we conclude the book in this last part with an outlook into the future of Finance, let's take a look at how companies can embrace the further new opportunities to improve the efficiency of their business processes.

Because SAP S/4HANA Finance goes beyond adding a few new options here and there, companies may want to (but are by no means required to) rethink their processes in order to fully leverage the radical new capabilities offered by SAP S/4HANA Finance. To this end, this chapter describes how Design Thinking can be used in the context of business process analysis and design and in the area of process opportunity identification. As an empathetic approach for problem solving and design, Design Thinking is often used and widely known in product development; however, there are many more areas in which it is of value:

- Use case identification
- Service portfolio collaboration
- Business model innovation
- Development and implementation
- Operational excellence
- IT strategy definition
- Shaping the profile of a new organizational unit
- Business strategy transformation

17   Design Thinking

In this chapter, we closely look into the areas of operational excellence and use case identification. Before we dig in, though, let's get an understanding of where Design Thinking comes from and what it can enable (Section 17.1). After this introduction, we'll study the impact that software changes may have on business processes (Section 17.2) and how to identify and address those to achieve operational efficiency (Section 17.3). We then give detailed hints for how to take action and set up a Design Thinking workshop for the purposes of process design (Section 17.4). We conclude by applying Design Thinking to identify use cases and business opportunities (Section 17.5).

17.1   Foundation of Design Thinking

Based first in academic design research and architecture, Design Thinking was adapted for business purposes primarily by the design consulting firm IDEO. David Kelley, one of the founders of IDEO, describes Design Thinking as "a human-centered approach to innovation that draws from the designer's toolkit to integrate the needs of people, the possibilities of technology, and the requirements for business success." In 1999, IDEO demonstrated this approach by applying it to the creation of a new shopping cart for a TV episode of "Nightline."[1]

Today, IDEO still delivers prominent examples of the strengths of Design Thinking. The field of application ranges from digital experiences to social services to medical products and to financial services. The commonality in all of these projects is the user-centered approach and the aim to focus on the "problem space" first.

This is innovative. When creating new products or services, most companies tend to think directly about solutions. They brainstorm new concepts and features that quickly lead to management pitches or technical prototypes. However, new ideas can be more pioneering and disruptive if they are based on profound knowledge about challenges in specific domain areas for different stakeholders. It's important to understand the problems and wishes of the people you're designing for. In this case, *understanding* does not mean *market analysis with a large sample*; rather, it's about understanding the emotional and implicit behaviors of people.

These days, Design Thinking has been adapted in a lot of companies (including SAP SE, where the development of SAP S/4HANA Finance also followed this

---

[1] IDEO, "Shopping Cart Concept for IDEO: Redesign of the Shopping Cart for ABC's Nightline."

approach) and is taught at several universities and institutions—including at the Hasso Plattner Institute of Design at Stanford in California and the HPI School of Design Thinking in Germany. Students from a variety of different subjects get to know to Design Thinking in a "learning-by-doing" style while working together on projects from different domains. The diversity of a team is an important factor, because it's helpful to include different points of view. During most people's academic and work lives, they have learned to be experts in specific domains and have adapted to a certain way of thinking that is relevant for their work lives. When talking to a person from another background, it can sometimes be hard to understand the other person's way of thinking, and communication is more difficult. However, often we also notice that another perspective helps to see a problem from another angle and reveals aspects that we might have missed on our own. For this reason, the Design Thinking approach pushes for a diverse team setup with stakeholders from different areas. Looking at industry-related work, this means that a mix of business- and IT-related roles is preferable.

There are a lot of different Design Thinking process descriptions and names for the different phases and methods. Although there is not one official process and different methods can be applied in different sequences and iteratively run through several times, there is a common denominator visible in all instantiations of the Design Thinking process. This denominator involves three tasks: to understand the problem space, to imagine the ideal, and to move on to the solution space.

Design Thinking also follows an iterative approach, in contrast to a traditional waterfall model. However, it takes some experience to know how to apply different methods in an optimal way for each respective project. Educational programs and introductory courses for Design Thinking therefore usually teach a sequence of phases and methods that has been proven to be useful for several projects. At SAP and at the HPI School of Design Thinking, the following phases or steps are commonly included (as shown in Figure 17.1):

- **Understand**
  Define and analyze the design challenge, and compare different understandings regarding the challenge within your team. Perform a quick first research to find out more about the scope of the challenge. If necessary, redefine the scope, and make sure that everybody shares the same understanding. Make a research plan for the Observe phase.

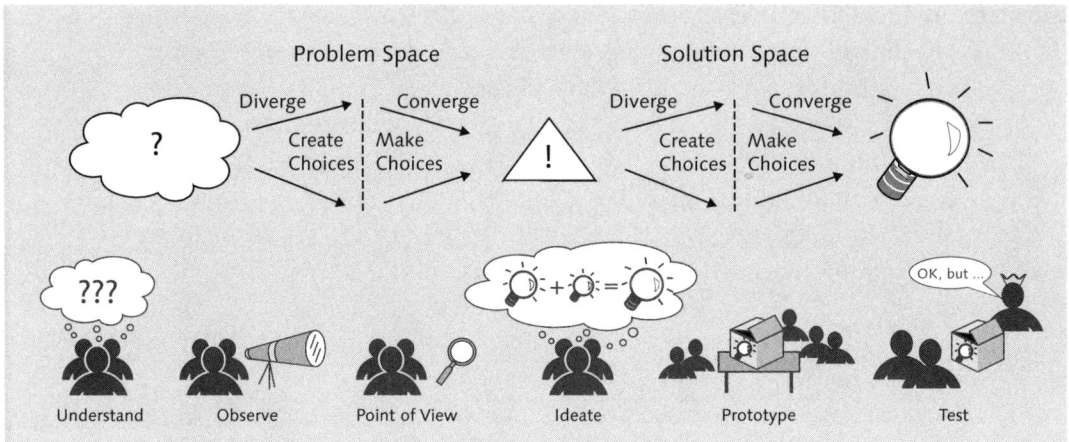

Figure 17.1 Design Thinking Phases in Problem and Solution Spaces

- **Observe**
  Engage in qualitative user research with end users. The most commonly used methods are interviews, observations, and tryouts. The goal is to understand *why* users behave in a certain way and what their goals and aspirations are. Quantitative market research usually only reveals how many users act or would act in a certain way. Ethnographic methods help to clarify the reasons that people act in certain ways. The reasons might be implicit and irrational and often require careful reading between the lines. Observing users during their actions can also reveal contradictions between behaviors and verbal statements.

- **Point of view**
  Create a common point of view of research results within your team. As shown in Figure 17.1, observation is a diverging working mode that offers broad perspectives on a topic. In the Point of View phase, the different perspectives have to be consolidated, and the team needs to come to one point of view. Surprising insights from research should be shared and contradictory findings discussed. One common method is to create a "persona," because doing so helps a team decide for whom they want to design a solution and helps to create empathy for the persona's needs, motivations, and expectations. For example, a persona description of a CFO includes typical responsibilities he has in his job as well as his main goals and most urgent pain points. Assigning a fictional name (e.g., Charles Fisher) and background (e.g., age 51 and, for the last three

years, the CFO of fictional company Good Consumer Products) to the persona helps a team develop a common understanding and language.

- **Ideate**
Create a large amount and broad range of ideas as a basis for prototyping and testing based on the Point of View phase. The team is encouraged to also propose "wild" ideas that are not realistic. Building on the ideas of others is a central concept. Therefore, even unrealistic ideas often carry certain aspects that can be merged with conventional ideas and in this way lead to new, innovative ideas. Ideation is again a diverging phase, in which it is important to create a large pool of ideas without judgment. In the end, as a transition to the next converging phase, the team should decide on the most promising ideas they want to prototype.

- **Prototype**
Prototype to find out whether an idea has potential or not. In engineering or other technical fields, prototyping is a detailed, functional, preliminary version of the future solution. However, prototypes can have different granularities and purposes. In the beginning, a prototype should help to communicate an idea and make it more tangible. It should be done quickly, though; if the idea turns out to have no potential, then it must be thrown away. If the idea *does* seem to have potential, then the prototype should be designed in such a way that it can be tested with users to collect their feedback. Depending on granularity and purpose, prototypes can be made of paper, be interactive click-through programs, involve roleplaying, or be made of LEGO blocks.

- **Test**
Collect feedback on your prototypes. The actual potential of a prototype can only be evaluated with the help of feedback from future users. An idea might seem very promising and useful within your company, but users might not see its usefulness or might encounter difficulties in using it. Although the prototype might have "failed," testing can help creators learn which details of the prototype have problems and how to circumvent them. "Fail early, fail often, and fail cheaply" is a main guiding principle of Design Thinking. By using low-fidelity prototypes, people do not get emotionally connected to their ideas and as a result are more open to criticism. An initial prototype does not need to be made out of polished metal. First, it's important to see how the prototype works and feels from a user's point of view. Once the idea becomes a great story, the prototype can be refined.

Depending on the results of the testing, it might be necessary to go back to the Prototype phase and change the prototype (if the idea seems to have potential), to the Ideate phase (if new ideas based on the feedback are needed), or even to the Observe phase (if new insights are necessary).

17.2 Impacts on a Business Process Landscape

Every introduction of software such as SAP S/4HANA Finance requires a strategy that defines how an organization and the inherent process landscape adopt the new solution. Basically, there are two main directions. Either the software needs to be adapted to function within existing company processes or the company processes need to be adapted to the functionality and processes defined by the software solution. Both ways are valid approaches, and very often the final approach lies somewhere in between them. Extreme, standard software solutions, especially in public cloud scenarios, require companies to adhere to the processes given by the software solution. On the other hand, custom-built software mirrors existing processes within a company. Of course, there is a lot to discover between these two directions, and sometimes this decision needs to happen process by process.

Today, more and more companies follow a *core and context* principle when it comes to deployment and software selection. *Context processes* are supported by standard software and proven industry best practices, whereas *core processes* that differentiate against competitors in the market need highly customized software solutions.

Let's apply this to the finance business function. For a lot of companies, finance might be a context process, because it supports the core business and provides financial services. SAP S/4HANA Finance also gives those companies a competitive advantage thanks to more advanced insights and lower TCO. However, for other companies finance is considered a core process (e.g., in leasing or core banking companies, etc.). Therefore, companies need an approach that enables them to understand the impact of a new solution not only in terms of functionality and IT architecture–related impact but also in the context of organizational change management, process management, and process design. This is the first case in which Design Thinking as an approach for problem solving and design can make a difference, which relates to the area of operational excellence.

There's another key area in which Design Thinking can be used. Regardless of which direction or core dependency a company is facing in the context of the introduction of a new software solution, there could be a side effect that implies an innovative and sometimes also disruptive impact on the existing process landscape: What if new financial software could deliver financial data without overnight batch-mode calculations and reporting? This would not only have an immense impact on existing financial processes but could also have an unforeseen positive aspect on other processes. SAP S/4HANA Finance enables companies to enter the realm of real-time finance. To identify, understand, validate, design, and deliver ensuing opportunities requires a creative and collaborative approach. This is the second area in which Design Thinking can be applied, which refers to the area of use case identification (e.g., for SAP HANA real time, mobility, cloud, etc.).

17.3 Identify and Define Changes

Design Thinking can be used in the context of operational excellence, including process analysis and design and software requirement definitions. Let's look at how to apply Design Thinking in this context.

Figure 17.2 shows the relationship between software introduction and process landscape implications. Upon introduction of new software, such as SAP S/4HANA Finance, business and IT departments should decide on the implications the new software has for its current process landscape. On one hand, these implications may require or enable changes to the processes, but on the other hand certain company-specific cases may also require changes to the software or its configuration—something that SAP S/4HANA Finance makes possible as well via the well-known customer modification and customizing options. The introduction of new software should also be used to identify unknown opportunities. We will look at this last step in Section 17.5 and will focus on the process and software changes in the current section.

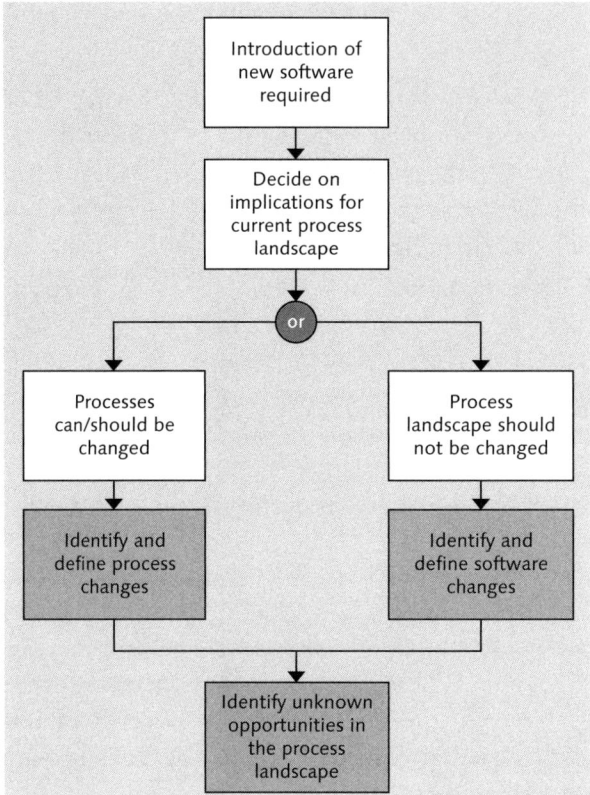

Figure 17.2 Software Introduction and Implications for Current Process Landscape

17.3.1 Team Setup

Design Thinking strives for multidisciplinary teams, which means ensuring a mix of perspectives, backgrounds, cultures, and expertise in a team. This approach ensures controversial discussions, but also leads to better and more valuable ideas. Some often-involved roles include process owner, line of business manager, business architect, software developer, IT architect, and, last but not least, the end users who "live" the process and shape it through their behavior. Especially important may be people who act as a hub between different departments and who know about bottlenecks and challenges that arise. We suggest including participants with different ages, genders, and cultural backgrounds, because these factors often influence a person's habits and perspectives. It might be hard at the beginning, because the terms and language might not be so compatible, but by exchanging and capturing different perspectives the team will build better empathy for the people that are affected by the new solution and/or processes. If a team is not used to working in a Design Thinking mode, we suggest having a dedicated Design Thinking moderator. It is possible to run through all Design Thinking phases in a workshop setup within one or two days, depending on the complexity of the process and the knowledge and empowerment of the people involved.

17.3.2 Problem Space

The problem space represents the challenges and wishes of stakeholders in the domain at hand. As in other Design Thinking projects, the problem space phases should help people to better understand the current situation and to come to a shared point of view. The problem space phases are as follows:

- **Understand**
  First, you need to discuss the design challenge and its scope. This means articulating something more concrete than just "redesign the process"; articulating the challenge should include the actual demand or change of prerequisites, as in, "redesign the process to leverage the possibilities of SAP S/4HANA Finance with regard to real-time editing without batch jobs by minimizing software customizing." The design challenge needs to take both software capabilities and relevant processes into account. The relevant processes also help to determine needed stakeholders.

- **Observe**
  The objective of this phase is to gather data points that enable the team to understand the as-is process as well as areas for improvement.

  Depending on your team setup and the stakeholders you have identified, you may need to do additional user research outside of your team. That is, you either do interviews with other stakeholders and then retell what you have heard within your team or you invite these stakeholders to your workshop and let them talk about their experiences. If stakeholders are not already pointing such issues out by themselves, then ask them about bottlenecks and difficulties with the current process.

  As a research technique, the customer journey map can be used to capture the as-is flow of a process and also the emotional journey of the people or stakeholders involved. The customer journey map is a template that uses swim lanes to represent (process) steps and activities, touch points with other people or systems, relevant information, and the emotional situation of people. New swim lanes can be added or old swim lanes removed if needed. Because Design Thinking is a methodology in which empathy for people plays a major role, the emotional situation of people in the context of a process is reflected. A bad emotional situation within a process could be turned into an opportunity to turn the process into an exciting experience for users.

In this phase, you can also study best practices from other companies or general industry trends.

- **Point of view**
 Create personas for the different stakeholder roles. "Stakeholder" does not only refer to users that interact during process steps; it also refers to process owners, predecessors, and successors and to roles that require reporting of relevant data from this process for another process. Don't pick employees of your company, because this may limit participants to design only for the people they know or think that they know. Instead, think about a fictional character and reflect on that character's roles. However, give this persona a name and define his or her needs, motivations, and expectations. This helps to put you into the shoes of a person with this role and to create a process that fits his or her needs. You should also point out in which part of the current as-is process you see room for enhancements and optimization.

Of course, you can change this sequence iteratively. For example, it may be necessary to reframe your design challenge after conducting interviews with the different stakeholders, or the stakeholders may have already talked about their experiences during the visualization of the as-is process. An experienced moderator helps to find the most appropriate methods for your setup and situation.

17.3.3 Solution Space

In other Design Thinking projects, often even the type of solution (product, service, or so on) is deliberately left open, but it is already established in our case that the solution should be an improved business process. However, the specific points of where and how the process can be improved thanks to SAP S/4HANA Finance need to be defined, and we have the following different options to prototype the new process:

- **Ideate**
  Based on the identified areas for optimization, the team should ideate on different ways the improvement could look. For example, one ideation topic could be, "How might we decrease the number of coordination loops between stakeholders?" Unlike in greenfield approaches, at some point in time this phase should also take the capabilities of SAP S/4HANA Finance as the new software into account. Otherwise, the team might pursue ideas that are not part of the standard functionality or that require extensive custom development.

- **Prototype**
  There are different options to prototype a new process model. On a conceptual level, the process should be visualized with all of the involved steps and interactions with the stakeholders (e.g., via a customer journey map). To foster the possibilities for feedback collection and testing with end users, the team should think of more concrete ways to prototype the new process. One example could be to simulate the process in a role-play activity in which workshop participants mimic the different stakeholders within the process and interact with a test person. To ensure feasibility, it is necessary to constantly validate the prototype and ideas against the selected software solution. This reveals process and organizational requirements as well as customizing and modification requirements for the software solution.

- **Test**
  As a first step, the new process concepts should be shown to different employees (from different stakeholder roles) of the company. These employees can give early feedback on the process improvements and detect possible obstacles and gaps. Afterwards, the process should be presented in a more "tangible" way. The test persons should be able to experience what the new process would be like and how it would influence their work.

Again, the described steps should be repeated in the desired sequence until the team comes up with a new process model that receives positive feedback from all stakeholders.

17.3.4 Packaging and Handover

After the team has decided on a new process model, it should prepare a realization roadmap and define what is necessary to implement the process. This concept then should be handed over to the realization team. Ideally, one person on this team should have been part of the Design Thinking activities, which lowers handover efforts and knowledge loss.

17.4 Set Up a Design Thinking Workshop

A Design Thinking workshop is often best suited to achieve an open-minded and creative working mode focused on the intention of the workshop. The workshop should take place in a room that supports creativity, team activities, and tangible prototyping. Ideal setups include sufficient whiteboard space or other writable areas. Sticky notes or index cards (plus magnets or fixing pins) with different shapes as well as other office supplies, such as pens in different colors, scissors, glue, and so on, should be available.

It is difficult to define a general time frame, because the scope of intended changes varies a lot. The minimum will be a one-day workshop, but it probably will extend to follow-up workshops or meetings. To make sure that the participants' valuable time is used most efficiently, time boxing should take place during the whole workshop, which means that each step should be concluded in a preset time in order to ensure that there is an outcome at the end of the day. Of course, this involves careful planning of the different steps. An experienced moderator can define which time frames are realistic and how much time is usually needed for a satisfying result.

Setting up such a workshop also requires preparation in terms of goal setting and expectation management. In which direction the process should be improved must be clarified. This can also be influenced by the IT infrastructure you are planning to use. For example, if you want to introduce SAP S/4HANA Finance, then you analyze the opportunities it offers for your company and define the focal points for improvement.

Remember that people from different stakeholder groups should be participants in your workshop. Therefore, you need to define the stakeholder groups and begin early on to ask people whether they have the time and interest to participate in a process-modeling workshop.

You should also clarify the surrounding conditions: How much time would you have to implement a new process? Should it be finished quickly, and would that therefore limit the scope of possible changes? What would be the budget for this, and who would be the sponsor? Is it supported on a board level or rather by one department?

Often, there are general challenges or concerns that could influence the workshop or its participants. For example, new processes could lead to downsizing of certain job roles. Even though this is not planned, if employees feel they could be affected, then they may express great concerns regarding a process-modeling workshop. Whether these concerns are relevant or not, it makes sense to think about possible obstacles and concerns beforehand to ensure that they do not influence the workshop procedure.

An experienced moderator helps to achieve the predefined workshop goals in the given time frame. In addition, he or she will help to find appropriate methods and the overall structure for the workshop.

In summary, these are next steps you should take:

- Clarify the main goal of a business-modeling process workshop.
- Define who should be invited to the workshop.
- Clarify the surrounding conditions.
- Identify possible obstacles or concerns.
- Find an experienced moderator in the area of Design Thinking for business process design.

17.5 Opportunities in the Business Process Landscape

Design Thinking can be used to identify use cases for many different enablers (e.g., mobility, cloud, and, in this context, SAP HANA). How can we apply Design Thinking to identify new and valuable use cases for a business?

New software solutions like SAP S/4HANA Finance can imply unknown and positive impacts on other parts of the business process landscape—that is, beyond finance processes. In the case of SAP S/4HANA Finance, this is possible because the solution is based on the SAP HANA in-memory platform. SAP HANA in this context not only enables accelerated and simplified finance processes but also can create totally new business process opportunities. Using Design Thinking to identify these opportunities sounds a little strange. It feels almost upside down, because you try to find a problem (use case) for an existing solution or, better put, an "enabling environment," like accelerated execution due to SAP HANA. Even though identifying new use cases based on existing enablers is not the initial intention and application of Design Thinking, in our experience it is the most powerful approach to identify use cases in a lot of different areas (e.g., mobility, cloud, SAP HANA, social, and so on).

It's important to understand that Design Thinking is not a straightforward set of activities and techniques. The phases remain stable, whereas the techniques that need to be used within these phases differ depending on the initial challenge. Therefore, you can still use Design Thinking to explore and unveil those promising use cases that might help you to run totally new processes or existing processes in an exciting new way. These use cases can be identified by looking at a situation from three different angles (as illustrated in Figure 17.3):

- **Process perspective**
  During the research phase of Design Thinking, you can use interview questions such as the following to capture relevant data points:
  - Where did we define processes and/or process steps due to performance restrictions?
  - Where did we define workarounds?
  - Where do we have exceptions in processes due to missing information?
  - Where do we have challenges to define the right reporting structures?
  - Where are most of the change requests in the context of reporting?
  - What processes run in batch mode (e.g., overnight)?
  - What processes run more than once per day?
  - What information is most relevant to support decisions?

  Questions like these reveal data points and insights that can be used to create points of view for a later ideation. You can use simple ideation techniques such as multiplication to understand, for example, the impact of an SAP HANA–based SAP S/4HANA Finance solution. Multiplication uses a simple question format—for example: "What if we multiply this situation/point of view/process step/or so on with an SAP HANA in-memory enabler? What would change or be possible?"

- **Business model perspective**
  Not only companies need a business model; every line of business, every organizational function, and every team needs a business model. Moreover, every

individual needs a business model. Everybody offers some skills, needs some resources to deliver these skills, and hopefully finds some addressee that appreciates the work.

In fact, this idea is not really about "needing" a business model, either. Business models are everywhere. A business model simply describes what the value proposition is (e.g., products or services), who the customer (segment) is, how the customer is being served, and how the value proposition is being fulfilled (activities, resources, partners, etc.). Of course, there is also an element of costs and revenue involved.

An excellent template to capture a business model has been developed by Alexander Osterwalder.[2] Some might think that if they do not earn "real" money, then there is no revenue stream and therefore no business model. However, the currency for the revenue stream doesn't have to be in real dollars. For example, for a marketing unit the revenue stream could be "market share" or the "success of the latest promotion." For a development unit, it could be "customer satisfaction" or "ease of maintenance."

Using the business model perspective to identify new process opportunities is a powerful concept. You can use research techniques to capture the relevant data points in order to understand the business model of a certain company, line of business, organizational unit, or so on, synthesize this data into points of view, and use different ideation techniques (e.g., the Eliminate, Reduce, Raise, and Create technique by Blue Ocean Strategy).[3] All of this can identify positive or even disruptive impact for an existing business model with a given enabler (e.g., SAP HANA).

▶ **People perspective**
The people perspective builds on the concept that individuals have a business model, but it adds an empathic angle to it. Every person in a company has a job to do, and those jobs have exciting elements and not-so-exciting ones. If you design a value proposition that helps to boost the exciting moments and erase some of the not-so-exciting ones for a certain person and role, then this person will most likely buy your proposal.

---

[2] Alexander Osterwalder and Yves Pigneur, *Business Model Generation: A Handbook for Visionaries, Game Changers, and Challengers*.
[3] Blue Ocean Strategy, "ERRC Grid."

By understanding the job to be done and the positive and negative events, you can gain a lot of insights and data points that help you to ideate around possible new value propositions for a certain role in your company. Again, the multiplication technique can be used to reveal ideas, including questions such as, "Where could we boost the exciting moments by using SAP S/4HANA Finance?" or, "What if this person receives reports not the next morning, but instead at anytime? Would this change the positive and negative moments or even the job to be done?"

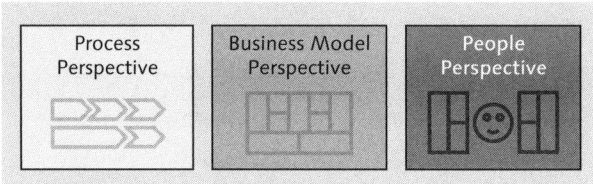

Figure 17.3 Different Perspectives for Identifying Use Cases

In general, these ideas, no matter from what perspective they're coming, require a low-fidelity prototype to test desirability, viability, and feasibility.

Design Thinking is a powerful yet flexible methodology. In this chapter, you've read about the basic concepts of Design Thinking, how it can be used to gain operational excellence, and how to apply it for use case identification to reveal unknown opportunities. In the end, it's always *people* that design, use, enhance, and ultimately buy any kind of solution. Therefore, the empathic nature of Design Thinking ensures that ideas and designs are always put into the user's context. This is also the reason that we believe that it can be applied to an endless variety of questions and problem statements. In the end, the concept is all about people.

This chapter looks at trends and technologies that will drive the digital transformation of the finance function. It also takes a look at the potential future of SAP S/4HANA Finance, the long-term vision, and specific features that are in discussion.

18 Digital Enterprise and the Future of Finance

So far in this book, we've taken a look at the features and power of SAP S/4HANA Finance as it stands today. Now, we turn our eyes towards the direction the world is heading and the opportunities that lie ahead for SAP S/4HANA Finance.

The ideas presented in this chapter are not yet part of the current product offering of SAP S/4HANA Finance, but rather a sneak peek into what we might expect in the future and a discussion of SAP S/4HANA Finance's benefits for the digital transformation of business.

The vision for finance systems of the future is a solution that achieves four primary goals:

- Shifts the focus from the mechanics of accounting to the ownership of enterprise analytics by leveraging a progression from mechanics to robotic software through machine observation to machine learning.
- Connects all internal and external data through the enterprise, rooted in actual financial results via the Universal Journal on the SAP HANA in-memory platform, and builds patterns to identify anomalies to predict performance.
- Liquefies information so it flows like water throughout the organization, seeking the path of least resistance to decision makers.
- Improves quality of decisions by providing comprehensive simulation and prediction capabilities, thus allowing business users to proactively understand the decisions they need to make and have the system recommend a course of action.

18 Digital Enterprise and the Future of Finance

We begin in the context of a digital enterprise, and discuss it not as a buzz word, but in terms of what it really entails for the finance function (Section 18.1). Then, we venture into solution space and see how technology-driven paradigms such as shifting the role of finance and machine learning (Section 18.2) and the related concept of simulation and predictive analysis (Section 18.3) can go a long way toward solving problems faced by finance managers. This builds up to the idea of a proactive finance solution, discussed in Section 18.4, before we wrap up our discussion in Section 18.5.

18.1 Behind the Term "Digital Enterprise"

Today's digital enterprises can attribute their existence largely to disruptions caused by modern technology trends: hyperconnected smart devices, in-memory supercomputing, cloud computing, and cyber security, to name a few. These trends enable enterprises to reimagine their traditional business models with new capabilities.

The digital enterprise is no longer a distant vision. It is a reality, and today's financial executives are focusing on digital business transformation while seeking to respond to challenges of the digital economy and managing the most volatile economic and regulatory environment in decades presented to them every day. Digital transformation is an all-encompassing phenomenon that affects every link in the industrial value chain, from lead generation to sales to logistics through production to delivery. These transformations challenge status quo and demand adoption and deployment of new business models and digital technologies to improve performance. While many see the current environment as a challenge, others see it as an opportunity and are moving to turn the digital economy to their advantage.

As we briefly discussed in Chapter 1 and Chapter 5, finance executives have been the trusted advisors that management and shareholders have turned to in times of uncertainty for centuries. Their role is now more important than ever because of demands placed on them to direct the business in stormy, unpredictable global markets and changing business landscapes. Study after study shows finance's boardroom influence increasing, job scope expanding, and salaries rising. But to stay relevant, finance has to undergo its most fundamental transformation since

ERP was invented. It is at the center of the digital transformation, and as the keeper of business data it will have to manage the rapid growth of massive datasets, distributed computing, and advancement in statistical methods for common learning problems.

Furthermore, finance must continue to support flexibility, scalability, and responsiveness to address global opportunities and challenges. It must empower companies through insightful information and analysis to deliver products and services that create value and delight customers.

What impact does this change bring? Let's find out in the following sections.

18.1.1 Change Has Never Been So Rapid

The changes we discussed in the last section are bringing together people, process, data, and things in ways that have never been seen in the past. The boundaries between customers and vendors are disappearing across all industries, creating unparalleled opportunities for countries, businesses, and people. Not limited to just "tech-oriented" companies, the changes—though uneven—are observed in all areas of the economy. This is an opportunity in which early adopters are rewarded.

Technology has made everything real-time, and connectivity is more vital than ever before. Partners, suppliers, and customers want to deal in real-time without the "frictions" of missed phone calls and delayed paperwork. Market rumors are easily validated and hit the stock markets in real time. Concepts which were unimaginable are a reality. For example, today's business travelers use real-time updates from a ride-share company to know when they are going to be picked up. They use real-time systems to pay, and update their expense report at the same time. They use real-time navigation with Google Maps.

The digital economy is driving industry transformation into a "digital center" in which operating models, solutions, and value chains are digitized to the maximum extent possible. This process creates a radical structural transition in global economies. Consumers are migrating to technology and apps that change how we perform our day-to-day activities, such as listening to music, shopping for groceries, or reading our favorite books. Distribution channels operate instantaneously. The communication protocol is changing as well; scheduled broadcasting is replaced by frequent interactions and messaging.

Digital dynamics are weakening barriers to entry and competition is no longer confined to players within an industry sector. Cross-industry moves are more common than before and firms are set against a competitive landscape that is swiftly changing.

Latency and nonresponsiveness are things of the past, and this is only the beginning of the change.

18.1.2 Automation and Big Data Handling Are Becoming Imperative

In the past decade, the amount of data generated has increased rapidly. This data is diverse and spans a variety of domains, from social data created on Facebook or Twitter to log data generated by customer and partner interactions. In today's business environment, this data drives critical decisions and business strategy. Analytics goes beyond simple graphs and reports and has evolved into an environment in which companies combine business and social data to create new financial transactions that go directly to the bottom line. Data-driven enterprises can react to market changes and apply methods and techniques that can produce effective results and firm profitability consistently.

As a result, the success of an enterprise is likely to heavily depend on its ability to automate key components of business, IT, and business networks (the latter driving automation, collaboration, efficiency, and insight to allow highly effective interaction with partners, suppliers, and customers in core business processes), from source to pay, to sell to cash, and everything in between. Combined with business networks, the automation of businesses facilitates faster and more efficient provisioning of new policies and services. This helps digitization across user and partner channels and leads to efficient processes and simplified systems.

18.1.3 Finance Is the Score Keeper of Business Performance

The digital economy presents unique opportunities for the finance function to help businesses create and sustain value. Traditionally, finance departments have always played a role of supporting the business and being a keeper of financial data, policies, and internal controls, but things have changed. Finance's role has moved from being a back-office function to being a trusted partner and decision-maker. As the leaders of today's finance functions work hard to boost their relevance and the value added to the business, they shift their focus outward to those management activities that contribute the most to better business decisions that improve the bottom line.

In business, the ultimate goal is maximizing wealth. Everything in business comes back to financials. Members of the organization, from senior executives to front-line employees, need timely insights and visibility into financial results to drive efficiency. "Now-casting" is becoming the need of current times, especially for finance, to empower every member of the organization with flexible, personalized, and on-time information in order to accurately forecast business performance.

As data boundaries diffuse and data from operations blends into finance, the need to rethink existing systems becomes more profound. The onus will be on finance departments to look for opportunities to move away from long, tedious business processes toward more agile ones. For example, driving a shorter soft financial close outside of period-end closing provides more timely information to operations. This allows business leaders more time for analyzing key business metrics and taking necessary actions as needed in real time. In another approach, finance organizations can aim to enhance efficiencies with shared services and collaboration, thus removing information silos and simplifying collaboration across departments. This will provide complete information in one place and build assured, strategic decision-making processes with key stakeholders, further enhancing efficiency.

In a digital enterprise, alternate costing methods will run parallel to the standard cost and retail method of accounting to identify the true opportunity cost to a manufacturer with a more precise understanding of total cost to serve. Planning will evolve from a periodic process to an ongoing embedded process into daily operations, and spot analysis projects that took days or weeks will be reduced to hours by leveraging in-memory technologies.

Let's look into how this change can be achieved.

18.2 From Mechanics to Analytics

Transitioning into a digital enterprise is an evolutionary process.

When we hear about the digital enterprise and how it will revolutionize business, we often just want to say, "How can we get to insightful analysis when we're bogged down in the mechanics of running the business?"

There are four themes along this evolutionary road for finance departments to reach digital enterprise that will help transform from the mechanics of accounting to revolutionizing business management through analytics:

- Eliminating the drudgery of accounting mechanics
- Creating a connected enterprise
- Integrating planning and analytics as standard operating procedure
- Enhancing everyone's use of information within the organization

Let's examine each theme a little more closely.

18.2.1 Eliminating the Drudgery of Accounting

Technology and the evolution to the digital enterprise will bring significant change in the way work happens. The current processes and working methods in finance have developed over decades and were designed to support the analog business. These processes now represent "friction points" that prevent or slow the transformation to the digital enterprise.

There is an estimated 95% probability of accounting processes being replaced by software "robots" for tracking and paying for orders (source-to-pay), invoicing customers and applying payments to invoices (sell-to-cash), and performing credit checks on new vendors and new customers.

It would be naïve to think that the first step to automate these types of robotic operations would be a magic *machine learning* algorithm—that is, an algorithm that can learn from data and build a model from example inputs in order to make data-driven decisions about processing.

Instead, the evolution of the robotic accounting department started with static program instructions or rules. Many accounting applications have implemented rules to different degrees; some are hidden from users, others are fully exposed and configurable, some handle relatively basic functions, and some are quite sophisticated. In the current state, the implementation of these rules is uneven.

Some areas have brilliantly automated processes, whereas other processes are barbarically manual.

The evolution of these rules will accelerate in the next three years as they create successes in the enterprise and free up headcount to reallocate to analyzing the business. The rules will start by helping with the procedural problems in an *if this, then that* format. These simplistic rules will help the user understand outliers that don't fit the rule and help accelerate the discipline of machine observation.

Machine observations are facilitated through a set of tools and techniques to help the user recognize relationships in information they normally don't think about or look for. An example of machine observation is fraud detection, which we explored in Chapter 11, Section 11.9. Fraud detection is about identifying transactions that don't look normal. In many companies, the basis of fraud detection is a series of rules that point to questionable transactions, like material changes to asset values via journal entries, nonroutine journal entries altering cash balances, or using outlier rates on currency conversion. With in-memory technologies, we can provide machine observations; in other words, we can allow programs to help the user navigate through transactions in real time that these programs identify as out of the ordinary. These transactions may involve system users who reverse significantly more transactions than other users, for example, or transactions performed when or where transactions shouldn't typically be performed.

These observations will facilitate the understanding and development of increasingly fuzzy algorithms that plug in to and replace static rule logic to make them more flexible and to identify the calculation of fraud statistics.

An additional area for creating efficiency will be through business partner engagement and business networks (see Chapter 11, Section 11.3). This is an area where forward-thinking organizations are eliminating paper and electronic bottlenecks and, with the help of business networks, streamlining the exchange of documents with customers and vendors. Business networks inherently create a stronger trusted relationship between supplier and customer that results in tighter security and stronger partnerships. Breakthroughs in in-memory technologies allow for dramatic leaps forward in process automation. In addition to providing more time for analytics vs. mechanics, these techniques also provide for a nimbler organization and provide access to information on a more consistent and timely basis.

18.2.2 Creating an In-Context Enterprise

An in-context enterprise understands that all transactions, from physical goods movement to virtual funds transfers, are related. It provides visibility and access to information across all systems, understands how they relate to other transactions, and provides the necessary information to make sound business decisions.

Users will no longer be satisfied with drilling down and its limitations; they will want to "roll around" the information, submerge themselves in it, experience it, understand every aspect of it, look at it from every perspective, and do it at the speed of thought. Information needs to flow like water, seeking the path of least resistance, filling every nook and cranny of detailed attributes. Reporting will provide live navigation to every level of detail in every direction, and machine observation technologies will be key to create the in-context enterprise.

As an example, a material purchase is not just an invoice for the vendor: It is also the purchase order that identifies the agreement between the buyer and the seller. It is the receiver in the warehouse identifying when the product was received. It is the movement of the material from inventory to the plant floor and work in process inventory. It is the movement of product out of work in process to finished goods and ultimately to the customer.

An in-context enterprise requires data structures be simplified so business users understand how to access the information and connect the dots between financial data with other major operational data. The Universal Journal in SAP S/4HANA Finance and the Material Document Table in SAP S/4HANA Manufacturing are examples of data simplification supported by in-memory technology and will be the cornerstone of the in-context enterprise.

A third key component of the in-context enterprise is technologies that merge and analyze huge volumes of data from multiple sources, such as data from ERP systems, gathered from sensors throughout the ecosystem of the enterprise and from external providers of data. Linking these sources is key to obtaining meaningful insight with the help of machine observations.

The final component of the in-context enterprise is access to information, anywhere, anytime, and on any delivery platform, including delivery platforms that haven't been developed yet.

18.2.3 Integrating Planning and Analysis with Daily Operations

Planning and analytics will be integrated into daily operations of finance and the rest of the organization. It will no longer be a separate siloed function characterized by separate systems and data architecture, with periodic updates at month end. Different planning areas will not be separate, either. Strategic plans will no longer be documents rewritten once each year, capital plans a series of disconnected spreadsheets, or operational plans only managed by operations and solely used to run day-to-day operations in the short term. Planning will be an ongoing daily process.

Much of this planning won't be new. Organizations do a lot of planning now. However, in most cases today's planning isn't connected. It's characterized by departments or groups performing isolated planning, with little integration with the other plans. Chapter 11, Section 11.5 discusses how to address this situation.

As an example, manufacturing operational planning is carefully coordinated with purchasing and shipping. However, these plans are typically disconnected from the financial plan.

Planning in the digital enterprise will be rooted in actual results at a detailed level. Drivers will be identified by merging actual financial results with operational inputs and outputs and external information about products, customers, the industry, and the economy. These drivers then will be selectively modeled as levers to steer the business, cost centers, and profit centers. As the business changes, models will be updated with different drivers and levers, and because the system reads from actual results in real time, updated information will be readily available.

In addition to planning for stakeholders and stockholders, planning will help provide guidelines for making decisions. Planning will help organizations understand the key decisions they need to make along with their implications, risks, and rewards before they need to make them.

Planning models will also evolve—from hard-coded logic leveraging robotic-type models to models leveraging machine observations to associate different characteristics together and then to machine learning techniques for predictive and prescriptive modeling.

The result of integrating planning and analysis into daily operations will be the ability to sit in a planning meeting and understand the financial and operational implications as projects, programs, and strategies are discussed.

18.2.4 Enhancing the Use of Information

Companies are realizing the valuable skills the finance department brings to the organization beyond being a scorekeeper of results. Finance will be the catalyst to bring everyone in the organization forward in the use of information.

Finance departments will be challenged. They will be challenged to extend existing financial measurement models to include operational metrics. They will also need to extend existing methods of connecting ratios and KPIs to include detail-level information from every perspective and to link information to new analytic methods such as the following:

- Enhanced analytics and insights leveraging operational drivers to provide a new perspective
- Predictive analytics to predict the future
- Prescriptive analytics to suggest different courses of action
- Machine observations that allow tools to point out relationships that are difficult to see
- Machine learning pattern recognition and computational algorithms that can learn from and make predictions about data

These methods will need to be implemented without requiring much effort and time to collect, analyze, and present them. In summary, they will need a platform. SAP HANA provides the basis for combining data, structured and unstructured, from different sources and for making it available in real time for read access and analytical processing. On the inbound side, transactional data streams and sensor measurement data streams allow users to understand what is happening in the physical world like never before.

In the following two sections, we will see how digitalization can bring SAP S/4HANA Finance to new frontiers.

18.3   Simulation and Predictive Analysis

Decision makers in innovative businesses need to keep up with the pace at which the economy runs. They need instant insight into the impact of shifts in customer demand or changes to cost drivers on KPIs. They need transparency on the financial impact of decisions, such as the introduction of new products or changes to the supply chain. To assess impact, forecasts of KPIs in a business-as-usual scenario will be compared to KPIs simulated under the assumption that a specific decision alternative is chosen. Results of such comparisons are required without delay and with a high level of precision.

Because SAP S/4HANA Finance allows online access to all transactional line items from the current and past periods, completely new ways of analyzing and learning from the data are enabled. This means that not only can aggregated business trends be extrapolated, but also forecasting models can understand and predict when certain line items occur and under which circumstances. Consequently, this enables far more accurate models and increases prediction quality.

Thanks to the flexibility of the in-memory platform SAP HANA, external influences (such as growth rates, currency exchange rates, tax regulations, legal obligations, and nonfinancial data, such as weather forecasts or upcoming sport events) can be incorporated into the prediction process. The combination of predicted data from previous periods, external data, and additional reporting-specific data (e.g., sales pipeline, HR-related data, purchase orders, and so on) will lead to precise and role-specific recommendations for users.

The forecasted data can be used by several financial users, such as managerial accounting, treasury, or liquidity management, who are in charge of providing timely and accurate forecasts for important business decisions (e.g., budget, investment, or cash management).

Real-time simulation that can track trends related to and transparency into the impact of multiple dimensions is of key strategic value. Thanks to the removal of aggregates, it is possible to create what-if scenarios by designing new potential structures (e.g., hierarchies) and models (e.g., KPI systems) and then applying the current or predicted line item data within those new models in real time. In this way, users can observe the impact of the simulated changes on the organization. In addition, this allows for the creation of multiple different scenarios that the company does have control over in order to see how to best optimize their operations.

Any business-critical decision (such as an organizational restructuring) should be supported through an impact analysis. This applies in particular when appropriate data is missing or certain models cannot be extracted from the available data. Far too often, these key decisions are made based on gut feelings rather than on real information. Therefore, SAP S/4HANA Finance also has to deal with simulation aspects in the future. Simulation can be realized on three levels.

First, potential courses of action can be specified in an abstract way and on an aggregated level. The system can then support translating this specification into effects on financial key figures and help determine how these aggregated changes are distributed on more granular levels.

Second, using line item–level simulations, the impact of individual hypothetical transactions on performance metrics and budgets can be analyzed. This means that a controller or accountant can apply hypothetical changes to certain attributes of financial transactions. For example, a line manager wants to simulate whether certain pending expense requests still fit into his budget. By relabeling certain transactions, he or she can play with the data until an appropriate expense scenario has been identified. Furthermore, line item data can be augmented by user-specific attributes—that is, by providing new characteristics on the fly that are not provided by the financial system by default. For example, a manager could add certain priorities to projects (e.g., WBS elements or internal orders), which can be used in rollups and other aggregations.

Third, performance metrics other than those currently used may be appropriate for the decision at hand, which requires defining new sets of KPIs on the fly. For example, a user in a treasury department may use existing methods to calculate cash flows and balances per company, using different parameter sets corresponding to alternative financing options. However, the user may want to use a performance metric that takes into account the funding needs of different parts of the organization in order to understand the performance effects of the different financing options. As another example, a manager can use the structural simulation capabilities to observe what effect restructuring the internal profit centers would have on the margins of the subdivisions of the organization.

Figure 18.1 shows a comprehensive overview of how simulation and prediction is incorporated logically into SAP S/4HANA Finance. First, the current system contains the actual line items ❶ in the financial system as well as standard economic models and procedures to derive KPIs ❷. Second, financial dashboards ❸ allow the user to visualize and interact with these models and to drill down to the line item level. Third, besides the system of records, simulated ❹ or predicted ❺ line items enhance the actual data layer. On top of this data, users can freely define their own models (e.g., KPIs) to run what-if analysis or to derive their individual insights ❻. Finally, important models can be exposed to the financial dashboards in order to be consumed by other parties.

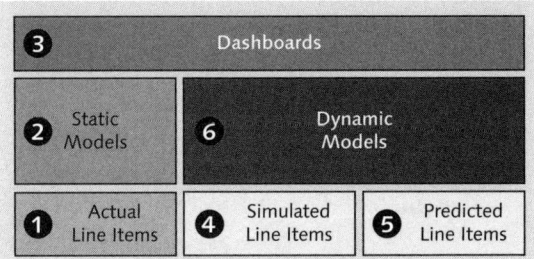

Figure 18.1 Enhanced Simulation and Prediction in SAP S/4HANA Finance

18.4 Proactive Finance Solution

The longer-term vision is a finance solution that proactively supports the finance users of an organization. By proactively, we mean that the system actively reacts to business events instead of merely reacting to user queries. The first steps toward a proactive finance system are alerts that call the attention of users to changes in the system—that is, alerts that are triggered by a KPI that increases beyond a defined threshold or in case a trend manifests. As a next step, the system proactively proposes mitigation strategies for defined scenarios. Finally, we envision a system that will autonomously take actions in a predefined scope.

The underlying motivation for this vision is to reduce the time to decision. By merely providing more information upon user request, users have more facts to base their decision on. This enables users to make better-informed decisions. However, consuming all available information and filtering the relevant information becomes the dominating time factor, potentially increasing the time to decision.[1]

---

1 Chris Taylor, "A Better Way to Tackle All That Data."

Figure 18.2 illustrates this principle. Row A demonstrates the decision processes in a traditional finance system: The user issues a request to the system. After the system has produced the requested results (computation time), the user has to interpret the results (human think time). This can be an iterative process until the user has come to a decision. Note that, as we discussed in Chapter 6, some requests that a user might want to make of the system could take so long that this iterative process actually is not possible, because the user would not be willing to wait for the results; hence, requests may be limited to a predefined set.

With SAP S/4HANA Finance in Row B, the computation time is drastically reduced. This either shortens the time to decision or allows the user to make more requests in the same time, potentially increasing the quality of the decision.

Now, the time to decision is dominated by the human think time. The vision for SAP S/4HANA Finance in the future (Row C) is to further reduce the time to decision by proactively proposing actions that then only need to be approved and executed by users. The foundations for realizing this vision are solid simulation and prediction capabilities in SAP's finance solution. Based on these features, SAP plans to implement capabilities in SAP S/4HANA Finance that autonomously evaluate scenarios and propose strategies to help finance users make informed decisions more quickly.

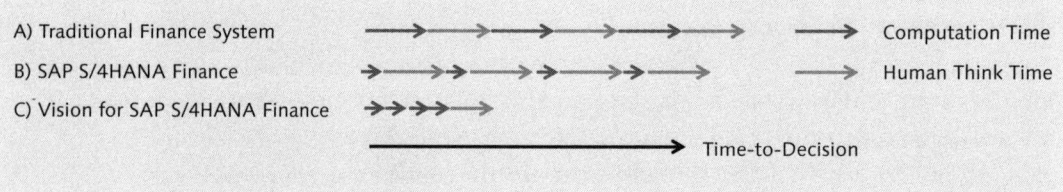

Figure 18.2 Reduction of Time to Decision with SAP S/4HANA Finance

The fast progress of computational capabilities affects every function of the business world. In an interview by McKinsey, Andrew McAfee, coauthor of *The Second Machine Age*, explains what managers need to ask themselves.[2] The key question, he said, is, "Where do I actually add value, and where should I get out of the way and go where data takes me?"[3] He mentions several fields in which

---

[2] Rik Kirkland, "Artificial Intelligence Meets the C-Suite."
[3] Erik Brynjolfsson and Andrew McAfee, *The Second Machine Age: Work, Progress, and Prosperity in a Time of Brilliant Technologies*.

human abilities are indispensable, such as effective negotiations or leading and motivating a team. However, there are other areas in which trained machine learning algorithms operating on large data sets provide better results and operate more efficiently.

The number-driven finance function of a company is an area in which we see a lot of potential for the application of algorithms from machine learning and artificial intelligence. The finance function in todays' companies is increasing in complexity. This is caused by increasing organizational complexity of companies, as well as increasing regulatory requirements. Furthermore, the finance function is expected to create business value in addition to fulfilling the minimal requirements of financial reporting—for example, by "providing foresight and protecting the business from internal and external shocks, through predictive analytics and risk reporting."[4] With this increasing complexity, staying on top of all finance reports and drawing the right conclusions becomes an organizational challenge and, if the time to decision takes too long, a risk for an organization.

Consequently, the vision for the finance solution centers on two main objectives:

- Proactively identifying situations that require action
- Proposing actions and, where reasonable, autonomously performing them

From an algorithmic perspective, these two objectives are distinctive. The first problem can be categorized as a *classification problem*, because the finance system needs to classify incoming transactions or statuses of one or several KPIs as those for which an action needs to be taken or those for which no action needs to be taken. The second problem falls in the class of *optimization problems*. Once the system itself or a user has identified that some action needs to be taken to mitigate a certain situation or reach a defined target, the system can assist in finding an optimal solution while considering a defined set of parameters.

In the following paragraphs, we discuss these two objectives and starting points for solutions. Note that these objectives are not reflected in the current SAP S/4HANA Finance product offering and that the solutions that will be implemented are subject to further evaluation.

We've already said we envision a finance system that identifies situations that require actions. We understand this problem as a classification problem, because

---

4 PwC, "Finance Function of the Future."

we need to classify a set of parameters into the "requires action" or "does not need actions" classes (more fine-grained alert levels are also conceivable). This can be achieved by different means that require different degrees of system intelligence.

In Section 18.2.1, we introduced the concept of robotic software to reduce the drudgery of accounting mechanics. This translates to a rule-based alerting and processing system with predefined rules as a straightforward way to let the system proactively raise alerts once a certain situation occurs that requires action and in well-defined situations to take a prescribed action. This feature is implemented already by many of SAP's applications. As an example, the SAP Receivables Manager mobile app provides personalized alerts and notifications to focus the attention of users in case receivables of a defined amount become overdue. A more complex example is SAP Fraud Management powered by SAP HANA. However, rule-based systems with predefined rules have two main drawbacks: They can only identify situations that are predefined in the rules, and maintaining a large number of rules becomes very complex.

A different approach is to apply machine learning algorithms to discover patterns (e.g., rules) in the data in order to predict that an action needs to be taken.[5] In contrast to rule-based algorithms with predefined rules, these algorithms are designed to classify parameter sets that have not been encountered before based on the patterns discovered in previously encountered situations. An algorithm is mainly distinguished by its main learning style. For classification algorithms, the main classes are supervised and unsupervised learning. In *supervised learning*, the algorithm is trained with a set of parameter combinations for which the result is known. In *unsupervised learning*, the system deduces structures from parameter sets it has seen. It can detect if a given parameter set deviates from all sets seen so far and raise an alert in that case. These algorithms can potentially detect anomalies and alert a financial user to check the situation. Because SAP S/4HANA Finance is based on SAP HANA, finance applications can leverage many algorithms for anomaly detection or clustering (e.g., k-means) implemented in SAP HANA's Predictive Analysis Library. Deciding which approach is best suited for which application of SAP S/4HANA Finance is subject to further evaluation. Examples of potential application areas are matching payments to invoices, detecting fraud, and forecasting liquidity.

---

5 Mehryar Mohri, Afshin Rostamizadeh, and Ameet Talwalkar, *Foundations of Machine Learning*.

The second objective, beyond identifying situations that require action, is proposing action and potentially performing these actions autonomously within a predefined scope. Conceivable optimizations that can be proposed or built in a system include optimizing the cash position and optimizing the investment or product portfolio based on a set of constraints, such as financing or scarce resources. For the finance system of the future, we envision that specific applications, such as Cash Management or Liquidity Management, will provide built-in optimization algorithms that proactively provide optimizations to finance users. Scope, some of these optimizations could also be carried out by the system autonomously, without any user interaction required.

18.5 Summary

What we have described here is based on the current projected trajectory of the digital enterprise, but the digital enterprise is a moving target driven by technological innovation. Wearables, the Internet of Things, and technology on driveables and flyables, including vehicles, all serve to change the landscape of available information about the physical world. Technology also enhances our understanding of how changes in the real world impact financial results and plans. Last but not least, technology changes how information is consumed, not just on a phone or watch, but also in ways we cannot even imagine today.

Transforming to the digital enterprise is not a technology problem, but a leadership challenge that requires a vision of how different streams of information are interconnected when constraints are lifted through in-memory technology and how access to this information can help us reimagine growth, efficiency, stewardship, and business performance.

In this transformation to a digital enterprise, the role of the finance function will transform from a reporter of historical results to a driver of results using real-time information. The ultimate goal is to create an environment in which software provides information and decision support where, when, and to the extent that it helps humans to take appropriate decisions and actions.

Appendices

A Changes to the Data Model 379

B Additional Information 381

C The Authors 391

A Changes to the Data Model

As we outlined throughout the book, the data model of SAP S/4HANA Finance underwent a thorough simplification. Because SAP S/4HANA Finance removes redundancy (see Chapter 3), the materialized views and materialized aggregates listed in Table A.1 and Table A.2 were eliminated and replaced by compatibility views to ensure nondisruptive innovation (see Chapter 4). Table A.3 lists tables that have been eliminated or reduced in size and purpose due to the introduction of the Universal Journal (see Chapter 8).

Table	Description
BSIS	Index for G/L Accounts
BSAS	Index for G/L Accounts (Cleared Items)
BSID	Index for Customers
BSAD	Index for Customers (Cleared Items)
BSIK	Index for Vendors
BSAK	Index for Vendors (Cleared Items)
FAGLBSIS	Index for G/L Accounts—New G/L
FAGLBSAS	Index for G/L Accounts—New G/L (Cleared Items)

Table A.1 Eliminated Materialized Views

Table	Description
GLT0	General Ledger: Totals
GLT3	Summary Data Preparations for Consolidation
FAGLFLEXT	New General Ledger: Totals
KNC1	Customer Master (Transaction Figures)
LFC1	Vendor Master (Transaction Figures)
KNC3	Customer Master (Special G/L Transaction Figures)
LFC3	Vendor Master (Special G/L Transaction Figures)
COSS	Cost Totals for Internal Postings
COSP	Cost Totals for External Postings

Table A.2 Eliminated Materialized Aggregates

Table	Description
COEP	CO Object: Line Items (by Period)
COBK	CO Object: Document Header
ANEP	Asset Line Items
ANEA	Asset Line Items for Proportional Values
ANLP	Asset Periodic Values
CKMI1	Index for Accounting Documents for Material
BSIM	Secondary Index, Documents for Material
MLHD	Material Ledger Document: Header
MLIT	Material Ledger Document: Items
MLCR	Material Ledger Document: Currencies and Values
MLCRF	Material Ledger Document: Field Groups (Currencies)
MLCD	Material Ledger: Summarization Record (from Documents)

Table A.3 Tables Eliminated or Reduced by Universal Journal Refactoring

B   Additional Information

Throughout this book, we have referenced a number of helpful publications and sites. We recommend the following references for further reading on topics mentioned throughout the book and new information to take the conversation further.

B.1   Bibliography

- Ailamaki, Anastassia, David J. DeWitt, Mark D. Hill, and David A. Wood. "DBMSs on a Modern Processor: Where Does Time Go?" *Proceedings of the 25th International Conference on Very Large Databases (VLDB)*. Edinburgh, Scotland, 1999: 266-277.

- Barringer & Associates. "Risk-Based Decisions." 2004. *http://www.barringer1.com/nov04prb_files/nov04prb.pdf.*

- Bloomberg Businessweek Research Services. "Finance as Analytical Partner to the Business." 2013. *http://www.sap.com/bin/sapcom/en_ae/downloadasset. 2013-02-feb-11-14.finance-as-analytical-partner-to-the-business-pdf.html.*

- Blue Ocean Strategy. "ERRC Grid." *http://www.blueoceanstrategy.com/concepts/bos-tools/errc-grid/*.

- Brynjolfsson, Erik, and Andrew McAfee. *The Second Machine Age: Work, Progress, and Prosperity in a Time of Brilliant Technologies*. New York: W. W. Norton & Company, 2014.

- Castelluccio, Michael. "Accounting Most Likely to be Subsumed by Automation." *Strategic Finance*, November 24, 2015. *http://sfmagazine.com/technotes/november-2015-accounting-most-likely-to-be-subsumed-by-automation/*.

- CFO Research Services. "Shaping the Finance Function of Tomorrow: Finance's Strategic Mandate—and the Innovations That Will Help Them Meet It." January 6, 2014. *http://www.cfo.com/research/index.cfm/displayresearch/14703644*.

- CFO Research Services. "The Next Stage in Creating the Value-Added Finance Function: Turning Data into Insight and Business Actions." October 31, 2014. *http://www.cfo.com/research/index.cfm/displayresearch/14716829*.

- CFO Research Services. "Thriving in the Digital Economy: The Innovative Finance Function." December 3, 2015.
  http://ww2.cfo.com/innovativecfo/2015/12/thriving-digital-economy-innovative-finance-function/.

- Cisco Systems Inc. "Cisco Global Cloud Index: Forecast and Methodology, 2014–2019 White Paper." October 28, 2015. *http://www.cisco.com/c/en/us/solutions/collateral/service-provider/global-cloud-index-gci/Cloud_Index_White_Paper.html.*

- Codd, Edgar. "A Relational Model of Data for Large Shared Data Banks." *Communications of the Association for Computing Machinery* 13, no. 6 (1970): 377–387.
- Codd, Edgar. "Further Normalization of the Data Base Relational Model." IBM Research Report RJ909, 1971.
- Edelman. "2013 Edelman Trust Barometer." 2013.
  http://www.edelman.com/insights/intellectual-property/trust-2013/.

- Graf, Günter. "Enhancing an Input-Ready Query with a Comments Column in Integrated Business Planning for SAP Simple Finance." SAP Community Network. Last modified November 13, 2014. *https://scn.sap.com/docs/DOC-59001*.

- Graf, Günter. "Provisional Master Data in Integrated Business Planning for SAP Simple Finance." SAP Community Network. Last modified January 19, 2015. *https://scn.sap.com/docs/DOC-59000*.

- Grünendahl, R. W. *Beyond Compliance*. Wiesbaden: Springer, 2006.
- Hedtstück, Michael. "Deutsche CFOs bummeln beim Reporting. SAP am schnellsten." *FINANCE*, May 14, 2014. *http://www.finance-magazin.de/bilanzierung-controlling/bilanzierung/deutsche-cfos-bummeln-beim-reporting/*.

- Hindle, Tom. *Guide to Management Ideas and Gurus (The Economist)*. London: Profile Books, 2008.
- IBM. "The New Value Integrator: Insights from the Global Chief Financial Officer Study." 2010. *http://public.dhe.ibm.com/common/ssi/ecm/en/gbe03277usen/GBE03277USEN.PDF*.

- IDEO. "Shopping Cart Concept for IDEO: Redesign of the Shopping Cart for ABC's Nightline." http://www.ideo.com/work/shopping-cart-concept.

- Jesse, Andrew. "Safeguarding Yourself against Invoice Fraud." *Proformative*, August 28, 2014. http://www.proformative.com/blogs/andrew-jesse/2014/08/28/safeguarding-yourself-against-invoice-fraud.

- Kirkland, Rik. "Artificial Intelligence Meets the C-Suite." *McKinsey Quarterly*, September 2014. http://www.mckinsey.com/insights/strategy/artificial_intelligence_meets_the_c-suite.

- Krüger, Jens, et al. "Fast Updates on Read-optimized Databases Using Multi-core CPUs." *Proceedings of the VLDB Endowment (PVLDB)* 5, no. 1 (2011): 61-72.
- Laue, Jens C., and Christoph B. Schenk. "Wirksames Compliance-Management—ein anhaltendes Topthema in deutschen Unternehmen." *Compliance Berater*, 2013: 140-142.

- Lesser, Adam. "Projecting the Technology Path to the Smart Home." *Gigaom Research*, October 6, 2014. *http://research.gigaom.com/report/projecting-the-technology-path-to-the-smart-home/*.

- Mehryar, Mohri, Afshin Rostamizadeh, and Ameet Talwalkar. *Foundations of Machine Learning*. Boston: MIT Press, 2012.
- OECD Publishing. "Interconnected Economies: Benefiting from Global Value Chains." 2013. *http://dx.doi.org/10.1787/9789264189560-en*.

- Osterwalder, Alexander, and Yves Pigneur. *Business Model Generation: A Handbook for Visionaries, Game Changers, and Challengers*. New York: John Wiley and Sons, 2010.
- Plattner, Hasso. "A Common Database Approach for OLTP and OLAP using an In-Memory Column Database." *Proceedings of the 35th SIGMOD International Conference on Management of Data (SIGMOD09)*. Providence, Rhode Island, 2009: 1-2.
- Plattner, Hasso. *A Course in In-Memory Data Management: The Inner Mechanics of In-Memory Databases*. Heidelberg: Springer, 2013.
- Plattner, Hasso, and Bernd Leukert. *The In-Memory Revolution: How SAP HANA Enables Business of the Future*. Cham: Springer, 2015.

- PwC. "Finance Function of the Future." 2014. http://www.pwc.co.uk/finance/finance-matters/insights/finance-function-of-the-future.jhtml.

- Solis, Brian. *What's the Future of Business? Changing the Way Businesses Create Experiences*. New York: Wiley, 2013.

- Taylor, Chris. "A Better Way to Tackle All That Data." *Harvard Business Review*, August 13, 2013. https://hbr.org/2013/08/a-better-way-to-tackle-all-tha/.

- Tyagi, Ankita. "From the Shadows to the Forefront: AP Automation and the Strategic Vision." *Aberdeen Group*, October 1, 2013. http://www.aberdeen.com/research/8671/ra-accounts-payable-automation/content.aspx.

- Wagner, R., and D. E. Steinhüser. "Agenda 2015: Compliance Management als stetig wachsende Herausforderung." *BearingPoint*, 2010. http://bearingpoint.com/de-de/adaptive-thinking/insights/agenda-2015-compliance-als-stetig-wachsende-herausforderung/

B.2 Resources

- SAP S/4HANA Finance: *http://go.sap.com/solution/lob/finance/s4hana-finance-erp.html*

- SAP Solutions for Financial Management and Accounting: *http://go.sap.com/solution/lob/finance.html*

- SAP Fraud Management: *http://www.sap.com/pc/analytics/governance-risk-compliance/software/fraud-management/index.html*

- SAP HANA Predictive Analysis Library Documentation: *http://help.sap.com/saphelp_hanaplatform/helpdata/en/32/731a7719f14e488b1f4ab0afae995b/frameset.htm*

- SAP Receivables Management: *http://go.sap.com/solution/lob/finance/receivables-management.html*

- The SAP Data Center: *http://www.sapdatacenter.com*

C   The Authors

Dr. Jens Krüger heads the Finance LoB in the board area of Products & Innovation, where he reports to Bernd Leukert, a member of the SAP Executive Board. Jens oversees a global development organization that is dedicated to developing innovative applications in SAP's core business. Jens and his team were key in developing the first module of SAP S/4HANA—SAP S/4HANA, Finance edition, formerly known as SAP Simple Finance.

In his responsibility as co-head of the SAP Innovation Center Potsdam and managing director of the SAP Labs Berlin, Jens plays a key role in shaping SAP's future Finance portfolio and in further building thought leadership across the SAP ecosystem.

Before joining SAP in September 2013, Jens was co-representative of Prof. Hasso Plattner's research chair at the Hasso Plattner Institute for Software Systems Engineering. He was one of the founding members of the prominent joint research project with SAP that built the first prototype of SAP's award-winning in-memory platform, SAP HANA.

Jens has a master's degree in business administration from the Free University of Berlin, Germany, and received a doctorate degree for his dissertation "Enterprise-Specific In-Memory Data Management" from the Hasso Plattner Institute at the University of Potsdam.

Akhil Agarwal works as a development architect at SAP Innovation Center, Potsdam, currently focusing on development of cloud applications for SAP S/4HANA Finance and other strategic projects. He also acts as hub scrum master for Potsdam.

In his career of over fourteen years at SAP, he has worked on several global projects in development and managerial roles, spanning across financials, logistics, HCM, and industry solutions.

With an electronics engineering background, he holds a postgraduate in IT from IIIT–Bangalore and an executive MBA in Finance and Strategy Management from IIM Kozhikode, India.

Alfred Schaller works as a product expert in the development of SAP Revenue Accounting and Reporting.

After earning a university degree in business administration, he joined SAP in 1982. He has worked as a developer, architect, development manager, and product owner in the development of several software solutions in the financial areas of fixed asset accounting, investment management, leasing, financial consolidation, and master data governance.

In 2011, he joined the development project that then started to evaluate new IFRS requirements for revenue recognition.

Dr. Arndt Köster has over seventeen years of experience in SAP development, including four years as the chief product owner for the area of Financial Operations.

Prior to his current activity, he had several roles in development for receivables management, payments, cash management, and treasury management solutions.

Bastian Distler is the chief product owner for Central Finance. He started at SAP in 2003 and joined the development department for SAP ERP Financials in 2005, where he has spent most of his time involved in integration topics between Financials and different modules of SAP ERP and across different systems in a distributed system landscape.

Ben Tomsky is the principal user experience designer and has been designing business software for over fifteen years, ranging from Sarbanes-Oxley compliance systems to sustainability applications to analytics tools. With degrees in symbolic systems and art history from Stanford University, he enjoys solving design challenges with both sides of his brain engaged.

Birgit Starmanns is a senior director for product marketing at SAP, with a focus on SAP S/4HANA Finance. She has over twenty-four years of experience across product and solution marketing, solution management, strategic customer communities, and consulting. Prior to joining SAP, she had been a consultant at Price Waterhouse and several boutique firms, redesigning business processes and implementing SAP at Fortune 500 and SME companies, with a focus on management accounting. Birgit holds a bachelor's degree and a master's degree in business administration from the College of William and Mary. She is a coauthor of the SAP PRESS book *Accelerated Financial Closing with SAP* and the SAP Labs guidebook *Product Costing Scenarios Made Easy*.

Christian Klensch acts as the chief development architect for financials development in the context of SAP Business Suite.

He has a twenty-three-year record in financials development and architecture in various areas, including SAP ERP on-premise, financials performance management, and financials in the cloud.

He is accountable for SAP HANA adoption architecture for financials in the SAP Business Suite context and was among the inventors of the SAP S/4HANA Finance approach.

Christian joined SAP in 1991 and is located in Walldorf, Germany.

Christin Schmidt is a development architect in the LoB Finance. Prior to joining SAP in 2014, Christin held various project leadership positions in the Global Technology Division of Deutsche Bank Group in Frankfurt and Berlin. Christin holds a master's degree in IT systems engineering from Hasso Plattner Institute at Potsdam University.

Christin is based at the SAP Innovation Center in Potsdam.

Daniel Lou is a development architect at SAP and a member of the SAP Technology Strategy and Services group. He has over sixteen years of experience working with database technology. He has led many implementations of large-scale enterprise database and data integration applications for customers worldwide and has taught extensively on these subjects.

David Mahlmann is responsible for driving design thinking to customer experiences across offerings, improving design processes, and fostering innovation at SAP Labs, Palo Alto, California.

In the past, he has held several leadership positions with organizations such as Intuit (where he envisioned and designed a new Design Language System), Waggener Edstrom, frog design inc., Ramp, Corbis, and Starwave. He also spent nine years at Microsoft in various creative leadership roles.

Ekkehart Seip works as a development architect in the SAP Innovation Center in Potsdam. In that role, he is responsible for the delivery process of SAP's financials solutions powered by SAP HANA.

Ekkehart joined SAP in 2004 as a technology consultant, and prior to his current position he managed validation programs for multiple SAP Business Suite releases inside SAP's Quality Governance & Production Unit.

He holds a master's degree in industrial engineering with an emphasis on information technology from the University of Offenburg, Germany.

Dr. Franz Weber joined SAP S/4HANA Finance product management beginning in 2013, with a focus on integrated business planning and financial cockpits for managers. Before that, he had been the architect for the SAP BusinessObjects Enterprise Performance Management solution since 2010. He first joined SAP ten years ago as the development architect for the SAP NetWeaver Business Process Management products.

Dr. Georg Dopf is the development senior manager at SAP SE and currently leads the Universal Journal program in LoB Finance.

His career at SAP started in 1991 as a developer in the Special Ledger team. Since then, his passion has been to work on business architectures. He shaped the renewal of the General Ledger module in SAP Business Suite (New G/L).

During his long career in development, he gained expertise in on-premise and public cloud deployment models and held a variety of different management positions.

Dr. Henning Heitkötter works at the SAP Innovation Center in Potsdam as part of the LoB Finance development team. He is responsible for strategic projects, including the project management for the book at hand. Before joining SAP in 2013, he completed his doctorate degree in business information systems at the University of Münster, with a focus on cross-platform development of mobile apps.

Holger Faber is driving coinnovation in the context of Planning, SAP S/4HANA Finance, SAP Fiori, Search/CBON, data aging, and general UI-related topics as the chief consultant for business innovation and early adoption. As a project manager, he was responsible for the internal implementation of CO-PA on SAP HANA, SAP BPC 10 on SAP HANA, SAP S/4HANA Finance, and more. Before that, he was the manager of the global IT department Application Services Controlling and a known expert on internal planning processes and SAP's planning solutions.

Janet Salmon is currently the chief product owner for Management Accounting. She joined SAP in 1992 and has worked as both a solution manager and product manager for Controlling. Over the last two years, she has been working primarily on SAP S/4HANA Finance. She is the author of *Controlling with SAP—Practical Guide* (SAP PRESS), *SAP HANA for ERP Financials* (Espresso Tutorials), and numerous articles for SAP Financials Expert.

The Authors

Johannes Wust heads the strategy and program office in the finance development organization at SAP. Prior to joining SAP, Johannes worked in Dr. Hasso Plattner's research group at the Hasso Plattner Institute in Potsdam, mainly driving research and industry projects in the area of in-memory databases for enterprise applications. Before that time, he worked as a consultant at McKinsey & Company, mainly helping large international companies with transformational IT projects and lean process implementations.

Kai Bi worked as chief product owner of Cash Management in SAP, responsible for roadmap definition and product delivery in the Cash Management solution. Kai joined SAP Labs China in Shanghai in 2001 and since then has worked mostly in the financials area: SAP Strategic Enterprise Management, SAP Business Consolidation System, SAP Business Planning and Consolidation, and cash and treasury management products. Kai currently works as the director of product development at Utegration Inc, an SAP partner in the utility industry in United States.

Marc Dietrich is an innovation consultant in the global SAP Services Innovation team. With the first customer showcases, he applied Design Thinking to the SAP Services business and is now responsible for its global rollout to SAP's field services organization.

Marc has been with SAP Consulting since 2006 in different roles, including business and technology consultant, enterprise architect, and team and project lead, and he has experience in multiple industries. Earlier, he worked as a developer for four years and was self-employed for six years.

He holds master's degrees in both computer science and in economics and engineering.

Michael Emerson is a chief project expert in LoB Finance, providing guidance to the development organization. He studied mathematics and computer science at the University of Edinburgh, after which he moved to Paris, where he worked at Société Générale CIB as a developer and manager. In 2011, he started his MBA at the University of British Columbia, specializing in finance and IT management, which led him to work with SAP in the Sales Intelligence team before taking up his current role.

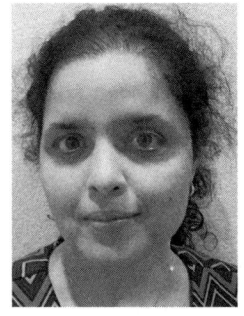

Monica Bhat works as the Financials domain expert in LoB Finance. She has more than twenty-five years of experience in enterprise software development and has worked in financial applications areas including core Financials, SAP Enterprise Performance Management, and SAP Governance, Risk, and Compliance. Prior to joining SAP, Monica worked in product management and development functions at Workday, Oracle, and PeopleSoft. Monica has a Bachelor's degree in electronics engineering from the University of Mumbai, India, and an MBA from Haas School of Business, University of California, Berkeley.

Dr. Oliver J. Kroneisen is the vice president for the Financials Operations development in LoB Finance. After studying physics, mathematics, computer science, and economy, he joined SAP in 2000 and held different positions in project management and development, centering on accounts receivable, accounts payable, contract accounting, and collections management, as well as integration with other parts of enterprise resource management. His primary area of interest is in leveraging financials operations improvements to achieve better business results along the value chain of large companies.

Peter Cholewinski is the chief of staff of LoB Finance at SAP and works at its Innovation Center in Potsdam. Prior to his current role, he worked for McKinsey, for Google, and as an executive assistant to the SAP Executive Board. He holds one master's degree in computer science and another in business administration.

Dr. Raja Gumienny is a user experience designer at the SAP Innovation Center in Potsdam. In that role, she is responsible for introducing and applying user-centered design methods in development and moderating workshops with customers.

Raja joined the Innovation Center in May 2014 after finishing her thesis within the HPI-Stanford Design Thinking Research Program on digital support for remote design thinking teams. She holds a master's degree in communication and computer science and a PhD in computer science.

Ralf Ille is currently the chief product owner for Financial Accounting at SAP SE. In this role, he has worked since the beginning of SAP S/4HANA Finance with a focus on harmonizing external and internal accounting. He joined SAP in 1989 and has accompanied many developments in Financial Accounting and Controlling components, such as General Ledger, Profit Center Accounting, Profitability and Overhead Controlling, Planning, and Financial Shared Services. He holds a bachelor's degree in business computer science and a master's degree in mathematics methods and models.

Dr. Ralf Sabiwalsky works for the SAP Innovation Center in Potsdam as a finance domain expert. He joined SAP in 2012 as a developer of high-performance, in-memory, financial risk management applications. He previously worked as a PhD student and postdoc in the fields of credit and market risk, IFRS, and international tax law.

Reiner Wallmeier is the chief product expert in financials at SAP SE. He has been at SAP since 1987 as a developer, development manager, product manager, and solution manager, and was one of the founders of R/3 development. He now has worldwide responsibility across all industries. Over the years, he has focused on scope and business architecture of financials, especially SAP S/4HANA Finance. He is a coauthor of the book *The CFO as Business Integrator* (Wiley 2003). Prior to joining SAP, he was head of accounting and controlling at a Japanese trading company and customer of SAP.

Ric Ratkowski is a domain expert in Finance and Analytics as part of the Customer Coinnovation team in LoB Finance. He spent the first twenty-plus years of his career in accounting, internal audit, financial planning, and information technology. The remaining fifteen-plus years of his career were spent with leading software companies in product management and as a subject matter expert. Ric has a bachelor's degree in accounting and a master's degree in finance, and is a CPA.

Sabine Otholt leads the Finance Customer Coinnovation office, focusing on alignment with solution management for go-to-market, coinnovation for product and solution strategy with customers, and driving customer-facing activities, such as supporting early adopters.

Throughout her career, she has held several positions in SAP, including global account director of BMW, consulting manager in South Germany for financials, project/program manager, architect, and finance consultant.

Stefan M. Fischer leads Finance Cross-Applications development at SAP SE, aiming to simplify the adoption of SAP S/4HANA Finance and to ease the consumption of SAP innovations on SAP HANA. His responsibilities include Central Finance, CFO dashboards, and knowledge management. Previously, Stefan managed the industry solution portfolio for midsized service industry companies and the go-to-market activities. He led SAP implementation projects at international customers in construction, facility management, and real estate. His career at SAP started in 1997 in product and solution management.

Steffen Vollmert is the product owner for financial planning in the SAP S/4HANA Finance development department located in the German headquarters in Walldorf. After joining SAP in 1994, he gained extensive hands-on planning experience through numerous SAP implementation projects in Latin America, Europe, and Asia. His focus was always to find the appropriate tradeoff between business benefit and implementation/maintenance effort.

Susanne Kollender is a knowledge manager in the LoB Finance development department and leads a team of technical authors and translators, responsible for creating and translating the product documentation for SAP S/4HANA Finance.

She joined SAP in 2002 and worked as a translator and technical author in the Customer Relationship Management development department before she became the team lead. She has been in her current role since 2009.

Tilman Ulshöfer works as a principal business support specialist, supporting customers worldwide and across industries in business process management, Design Thinking, and business model development and innovation.

He joined SAP in 2006 and previously worked for a global SAP customer and an international SAP consulting partner. He has supported companies as an application and business process management consultant and as a project manager on international business transformation and implementation projects.

He holds a degree in business administration from the Baden-Württemberg Cooperative State University in Mosbach, Germany.

Torsten Zube is chief products strategist in the area of Products & Innovation. In his former role as area product owner, he was responsible for the development of software solutions in the areas of fraud detection, anticorruption, antibribery, money laundering, and partner screening. He has a sixteen-year record in governance, risk, and compliance and foreign trade software development in various positions. Torsten holds a bachelor's degree in information systems and a master's degree in business administration.

**Dr. Winfried Schmitt** has been responsible for the development program management of SAP S/4HANA Finance core products at SAP, which includes Accounting and Financials Close, Financial Risk Management, Financial Performance Management, Invoice to Pay, Receivables Management, and Shared Services. After finishing his physics studies, he joined SAP in 1994 to develop products for financial consolidation and strategic enterprise management. Since 2006, he has been responsible for continuous innovation of financials-based industry solutions and core solutions. During his career, he has held different positions at SAP, including software architect and development manager.

Index

A

ABAP, 99, 155, 283, 297
Accounting document, 90, 91, 301
Accounts payable, 46, 140, 205, 209, 211, 214, 228
Accounts receivable, 46, 139, 140, 205, 208, 211, 228
Actual data, 301
Actual line item, 371
Adjustment, 300
Adoption, 302, 313
Aggregated data, 107, 171
Aggregation, 74, 76
Allocation, 154, 172, 177, 234, 239, 241
Analytical apps, 272
Analytics, 136, 185, 189, 337
Analyze Liquidity Plan app, 225
Annotations, 192
Application Interface Framework (AIF), 306
Application management services (AMS), 291
Application patterns, 273
Application program interface (API), 297
Architecture, 301
Ariba Invoice, 214
Ariba Network, 212, 215, 285
Assessment service, 292
Asset Accounting, 46, 140, 151, 153, 157, 245, 310
Assignment cycle, 241
ASUG, 265
Automation, 362

B

Bad debt, 206
Balance sheet, 43, 119, 138, 151, 153, 161, 164, 179, 235
Bank Account Management, 50, 143, 219, 225, 303
Bank statement import status, 220
Batch job, 106, 118, 210, 230, 336
Big data, 290, 362

Bring-your-own-license (BYOL), 291
Brownfield, 314, 315
Budgeting, 118
Business add-in, 306
Business cockpit, 54, 144, 197, 198, 201
Business intelligence (BI), 55
Business model, 130, 290
Business network, 144, 212
Business Planning Framework (BPF), 233, 235
Business process, 348
Business Rule Framework plus (BRFplus), 249, 251
Business transformation, 106

C

Calculation principle, 118
Calibration, 260
Carbon Copy Invoices app, 214
Cash discount, 209, 215
Cash Discount Utilization app, 209
Cash flow, 49, 119, 205, 220, 223, 224, 228, 235, 370
Cash Management, 49, 92, 143, 144, 211, 216, 303
Cash position, 220
Cash Position app, 222
Central Finance, 103, 123, 244, 246, 294, 299, 302, 303, 310, 311, 312, 315, 319
Central Finance interfaces, 307
Central Journal, 303, 312
Centralization, 217, 311
Centralized finance, 48
CFO, 27, 121, 300, 327
Change management, 348
Chart of accounts, 170, 306
CIO, 37
Classic extensibility, 297
Classic G/L, 101
Classification problem, 373
Closing, 31, 45, 106, 144, 145, 148, 158, 170, 177, 242, 243, 245, 248, 335
Cloud, 23, 33, 282, 289, 293, 295, 312

405

Index

Cloud deployment, 295
Code pushdown, 60
Coherent principle, 268
Collection worklists, 207
Collections Management, 142
Column scan, 74, 88
Column store, 69, 70, 71, 73, 75, 77, 78, 93
Company code, 176
Compatibility view, 91, 92, 98, 99, 101, 152, 155, 170
Compatible refactoring, 98
Complexity, 17
Compliance, 31, 255, 256, 257, 260
Concur, 281
Connected enterprise, 364
Consistency, 40, 82, 84
Consolidation, 47, 242, 243, 246, 248, 311
Consumption views, 193
Core data model, 89
Core Data Services (CDS), 186, 187, 198
   ABAP, 190, 191
   SAP HANA, 190
   VDM, 187, 190, 193, 194
Correlation, 112, 114
Cost center, 117, 153, 157, 159, 160, 170, 171, 172, 173, 174, 176, 179, 229
Cost Center Accounting, 170
Cost element, 151, 153, 154, 170, 178, 179
   secondary, 156
Cost Element Accounting, 141
Cost object, 306
Cost object structures, 307
Cost of goods sold, 240
Costing method, 363
CPU cache, 65, 69, 74
Credit Risk Analyzer, 142
Customer journey map, 351, 353
Customizing, 305

D

Dashboard, 201, 213, 259, 271, 371
Data aging, 334
Data availability, 185
Data bucket, 117
Data centers, 289
Data collection, 300
Data compression, 72, 73, 88
Data definition language (DDL), 191
Data dictionary, 99
Data distribution, 111
Data governance, 185
Data harmonization, 126
Data latency, 185, 232
Data privacy, 289
Data replication, 232
Data security, 289
Database footprint, 85, 94, 101, 157, 335
Database migration option (DMO), 285
Days sales outstanding (DSO), 57, 110, 206, 229, 272
Decentral system, 301, 306
Decentralization, 217
Delightful principle, 269
Delta merge, 79
Delta store, 77, 78
Delta version, 151
Deployment, 23, 33, 281
Depreciation, 158
Design process, 265
Design Thinking, 329, 343, 344, 349, 355
   in business, 355
   process, 345
   workshop, 354
Detective control, 257, 258, 262
Device agnosticism, 266
Dictionary, 73
Dictionary encoding, 72, 73, 74
Digital economy, 361
Digital enterprise, 359, 363
Dispute Management, 142
Document splitting, 150, 153, 286, 318
Double-buffer concept, 80
Drill down, 122, 173, 176, 198, 200, 205, 220, 366
DSAG, 265
Due diligence, 109, 257
Dynamic models, 371

E

Early adopters, 361
EHP 7, 283, 284, 286, 292, 315
EHP 8, 283, 284, 285, 292
Error handling, 306
Exposure Hub, 226, 325
Extensibility, 151, 162, 296

F

Fact sheet apps, 272, 325
False negatives, 260
False positives, 260
Financial Accounting, 22, 90, 91, 136, 138, 147
Financial close, 34
Financial closing cockpit, 335
Financial operations, 142, 144, 205
Financial planning, 34
Financial statement, 148, 156, 167, 170, 173, 179, 241, 242, 249
Flexibility, 18, 94, 108, 136, 187
Forecast, 33, 118
Fragmented landscape, 105
Fraud, 337
Functional area, 171, 176
Functional Area Ledger, 149

G

General Ledger (G/L), 46, 90, 101, 139, 151, 153, 157, 162, 171, 176, 178, 229, 240, 243, 245, 253, 286, 318, 330, 334
   account, 93, 151, 153, 154, 156, 159, 173, 178
Goodwill, 109
GR/IR, 189, 247
Greenfield, 282, 314, 319, 353

H

Hard disks, 68
Harmonization, 300, 302, 311, 325
Hierarchy, 108, 115, 369
High-performance application, 102
HTML5, 266, 283
Hybrid deployment, 281, 293

I

Ideate, 347, 353
IDEO, 344
In-context enterprise, 366
Individualization, 282
Industry requirements, 130
Information loss, 108, 110
Information silo, 105
In-memory computing, 32, 67, 85, 89, 93, 135, 261, 302, 324
In-memory database, 66, 70, 285
Input/output (I/O) access, 65
Insert, 78
Intercompany reconciliation, 61, 303, 317
Interface views, 193
Internal order, 153
International Accounting Standards Board (IASB), 249
International Financial Reporting Standards (IFRS), 139, 148, 153, 249, 250, 252
Invoice clearing, 190
Invoice collaboration, 214

J

Joint Venture Accounting, 148, 149
Journal entry, 365

K

Key figure, 239
Key performance indicator (KPI), 27, 50, 110, 122, 124, 198, 201, 205, 206, 218, 268, 369, 371
Key user extensibility, 297

Index

L

Latency, 362
Ledger, 153, 154, 162
Licensing, 294
Line item, 43, 87, 90, 91, 136, 301
Liquidity, 123

M

Machine learning, 360, 364
Machine observation, 365
Main memory, 65, 68, 70
Managed extensibility, 297
Management Accounting, 22, 46, 136, 140, 147, 151, 153, 229, 243, 245
Margin, 122, 201
Margin Analysis app, 238
Market Risk Analyzer, 142
Market segment, 153, 159, 161, 164, 229
Material Document Table, 366
Material Ledger (ML), 153, 157
Materialization, 91, 93
Materialized aggregate, 82, 85, 86, 87, 88, 89, 90, 92, 94, 98, 99, 152, 335
Materialized result set, 83
Materialized view, 82, 84, 89, 90, 91, 92, 98, 152
Mergers, 109, 300
Migration, 285, 315, 316, 330, 334
Migration services, 292
Mobile, 268
Modifications, 291
Multidevice experience, 268
Multidisciplinary team, 350
My Spend app, 180, 200, 275

N

Navigation, 267, 272
Net margin, 200
New G/L (see also General Ledger), 139, 140, 150

Nondisruptive, 17, 89, 92, 97, 98, 103, 136, 152, 290, 331
Normalization, 82

O

OData, 193
OLAP, 40, 83, 94, 107, 157, 186, 226, 283, 301
OLTP, 40, 83, 107, 157, 186, 300, 301, 302
Onboarding services, 292
One price, 294
One-system strategy, 300
On-premise deployment, 23, 38, 281, 282, 291, 293, 312
On-the-fly calculation, 47, 83, 88, 92
Operational contract, 251
Operational efficiency, 206
Optimization problem, 373
Order management, 213
Overhead Cost Controlling, 141

P

P&L statement, 43, 113, 119, 123, 138, 149, 151, 161, 163, 166, 167, 169, 173, 176, 177, 319
Parallel accounting, 150, 151, 250
Parallel ledger, 153, 286
Parallel processing, 67, 75, 87
PayMeNow, 215
Payment Details app, 220
Payment proposal, 215
Percentage of completion, 253
Performance obligation, 251, 252
Persona, 346
Planning, 45, 51, 52, 114, 118, 124, 144, 145, 224, 226, 227, 228, 229, 231, 232, 235, 308
Planning and analysis, 364, 367
Planning Application Kit (PAK), 329
Planning data, 301
Planning models, 367
PO-Flip technology, 214
Point of view, 346
Portfolio Analyzer, 143

Preaggregation, 237
Precalculated data, 107
Predefined aggregates, 108
Predicted line item, 371
Prediction, 34, 118, 256, 261, 372
Prediction journal entries, 165
Predictive payment, 211
Problem space, 351
Process Collections Worklist app, 207
Process control, 243
Process Receivables app, 208
Product Cost Controlling, 141, 237
Profit center, 117, 171, 176, 179, 242
Profit Center Accounting, 101, 148, 149, 179, 318, 329
Profitability, 119, 236
Profitability Analysis, 38, 46, 141, 145, 149, 151, 153, 158, 170, 236, 253, 329
  account based, 153, 156, 176, 237, 239, 240, 241, 317
  costing based, 149, 153, 176, 236, 237, 239, 241
Project, 153, 159
Prototype, 347, 353
Public Sector, 149

Q

Query language (QL), 191

R

Real time, 31, 34, 106, 109, 119, 126, 131, 232
Real-time data, 185
Real-time simulation, 369
Reconciliation, 27, 31, 84, 106, 107, 108, 136, 147, 148, 156, 159, 239, 243, 245, 317, 320, 325
Redundancy, 81, 82, 83, 84, 85, 86, 89, 91, 92, 94, 157
  removal of, 17, 81, 89, 94, 136, 152, 226
Regression, 112
Relational database, 69
Relational model, 82

Replacement, 97, 98
Replication, 293
Replication server, 304
Reporting, 41, 136, 137, 169, 170, 173, 177, 317
Responsive principle, 267
Retroactive analysis, 118
Revenue, 164, 166
Revenue accounting, 250
Revenue recognition, 164, 249, 251, 252
  rules, 166
Risk, 28, 35, 121, 124, 131, 303
Robotics, 359, 364
Role-based principle, 267
Row store, 70, 71
Run Simple, 17, 18

S

SAP Ariba, 144, 212, 281
SAP Best Practices for SAP S/4HANA, 285
SAP BPC for Finance, 53, 224, 228, 229, 231, 233, 234
SAP Business Planning and Consolidation (BPC), 329
SAP Business Suite, 39
SAP Business Suite for SAP HANA, 17, 315
SAP Business Warehouse (BW), 283, 301, 336
SAP BusinessObjects, 37
  SAP BusinessObjects Analysis for Office, 329
  SAP BusinessObjects Dashboards, 317
  SAP BusinessObjects Design Studio, 329
SAP Cash Management, 219, 220, 224, 225, 226, 330
SAP Community Network, 265
SAP Customer Engagement Intelligence app, 102
SAP Customer Relationship Management (CRM), 329
SAP Enterprise Performance Management, 37
SAP ERP, 52, 232, 283, 285, 292, 308
SAP ERP Financials, 17, 37, 85, 89, 90, 97, 136, 138, 143, 148, 149, 283
SAP Fieldglass, 281
SAP Financial Supply Chain Management, 142, 143

Index

SAP Fiori, 23, 38, 137, 138, 180, 181, 198, 226, 238, 263, 264, 268, 273, 275, 283, 294, 318, 330, 332
  design principles, 266
  launchpad, 218, 271, 325
SAP Fiori apps, 191, 271, 315
SAP Fraud Management app, 102, 256, 374
SAP Gateway, 283
SAP GUI, 98, 283
SAP HANA, 17, 38, 40, 42, 48, 60, 65, 71, 81, 83, 94, 97, 99, 107, 127, 135, 138, 149, 151, 152, 154, 157, 173, 185, 198, 218, 227, 231, 233, 236, 245, 253, 255, 260, 265, 281, 299, 301, 304, 324, 369, 374
SAP HANA accelerator, 103
SAP HANA Cloud Platform, 326
SAP HANA Enterprise Cloud, 281, 289, 290, 292, 293
SAP HANA Live, 331
SAP Hybris, 281
SAP Intercompany Reconciliation app, 246
SAP Invoice and Goods Received Reconciliation app, 190, 248
SAP Jam, 210
SAP Landscape Transformation (SLT), 293, 304, 306, 308, 321
SAP Lumira, 55, 317, 329
SAP Master Data Governance, 306
SAP Predictive Analysis Library (PAL), 374
SAP Rapid Deployment solution, 284
SAP Receivables Manager app, 57, 374
SAP Revenue Accounting and Reporting add-on, 145, 249, 250, 252, 253
SAP S/4HANA, 37, 275
  flexible analytics, 102
  manufacturing, 366
SAP SE, 323
SAP Smart Business, 56, 198, 202, 317
SAP Smart Business cockpit for financial close, 243
SAP solutions for Governance, Risk, and Compliance (GRC), 37, 145, 254
SAP SuccessFactors, 281, 285
SAP Treasury and Risk Management, 142
SAP Working Capital Analytics app, 58
SAPUI5, 266, 275, 337
Sarbanes-Oxley (SOX) Act, 256

Segment, 171, 176, 242
Semantics, 301
Settlement, 241
Shared service center, 113
Side-by-side adoption scenario, 329
Side-by-side extension, 297
Sidecar, 304
Simple principle, 268
Simplicity, 84
Simplification, 17, 18, 81, 91, 117, 135, 137, 163, 225, 232
Simplification List, 287
Simulated line item, 371
Simulation, 359, 370, 372
Single source of truth, 40, 81, 107, 123, 136, 144, 185, 189, 229, 299, 303
Smart device, 360
Smart Invoicing, 214
Soft close, 34, 46
Solution space, 352
Special Ledger, 101, 149
SQL, 65, 107, 192
Stakeholders, 113
Static model, 371
Statutory reporting, 300
Structural change, 130
Subledger, 139
Subscription, 291, 294
System governance, 291

T

Table
  BKPF, 90, 101
  BSEG, 90, 101
  BSID, 101
  COEP, 101, 155, 156
Template, 314, 319
Throughput, 59, 85, 93, 94, 157
Time boxing, 354
Total cost of ownership (TCO), 85, 94, 108, 157, 231, 232, 294
Transaction KB11N, 163
Transactional apps, 272, 325
Transactional line items, 369

Transformation, 300, 359
Treasury, 126, 303

U

Universal Journal, 22, 46, 83, 89, 92, 101, 119, 135, 136, 137, 147, 151, 152, 153, 158, 159, 162, 166, 167, 169, 173, 176, 179, 229, 243, 245, 317, 330, 337, 359, 366
US Financial Accounting Standards Board (FASB), 249
US Generally Accepted Accounting Principles (GAAP), 139, 153
User experience (UX), 23, 34, 137, 325
User interface (UI), 185, 284
User research, 346, 351

V

Value integrator, 128
Value map, 17, 36, 137
Variance, 241
Verifications, 190
View, 82
Virtual data model (VDM), 41, 102, 188, 193, 198
Visualization patterns, 203

W

What-if scenarios, 115
Work breakdown structure (WBS), 171
Working capital, 110, 124
Work-in-progress calculation, 245
Write operations, 78

- ▶ Get step-by-step instructions for moving from SAP ERP to SAP S/4HANA Finance
- ▶ Configure important SAP S/4HANA Finance functionality
- ▶ Employ data migration best practices for SAP S/4HANA Finance

Anup Maheshwari

Implementing SAP S/4HANA Finance

Get into the nitty-gritty with this guide to your on-premise SAP S/4HANA Finance implementation project. Migrate your data from SAP ERP Financials to SAP S/4HANA Finance, and then customize its key functionality: General Ledger, Asset Accounting, Controlling, and Cash Management. Consult expert tips, learn transaction codes, and join the brave new world of SAP S/4HANA Finance.

approx. 550 pages, pub. 6/2016
E-Book: $69.99 | **Print:** $79.95 | **Bundle:** $89.99

www.sap-press.com/4045

► Explore the entire financial close process from financial accounting to entity and corporate closing

► Maximize the potential of SAP Financial Solutions like FI, CO, and Disclosure Management

► Meet the latest regulatory and reporting requirements with ease

► Based on ERP 6.0 and EPM 10.0

Elizabeth Milne, James Fisher, Birgit Starmanns

Accelerated Financial Closing with SAP

Navigate the complex last mile of finance with speed, efficiency, and ease with this end-to-end process guide for closing your books books. Address regulatory requirements, manage disclosure management and report results to key stake holders. Develop a single financial close workflow and maximize the potential of SAP's financial solutions. Close your books faster with this one-stop resource for all your financial closing needs!

296 pages, pub. 10/2013
E-Book: $59.99 | Print: $69.95 | Bundle: $79.99

www.sap-press.com/3227

www.sap-press.com

▶ Understand how SAP Enterprise Performance Management enables financial planning processes

▶ Learn best practices for streamlining strategy, planning, and profitability analysis

▶ Preview SAP's vision for EPM, including SAP Business Planning and Consolidation, SAP HANA support, and more

William D. Newman, Malcolm J. Faulkner

Financial Planning and Analysis with SAP

SAP Solutions for EPM

Hit your financial target by carefully mapping your course with the applications in SAP Enterprise Performance Management. From financial planning through integration, this book will help you understand the business steps and requirements needed to work with the core EPM applications. With this book, understand how EPM can help you create detailed financial plans, monitor actual costs against budget, and analyze profitability based on products and customer behavior.

440 pages, pub. 5/2014
E-Book: $69.99 | **Print:** $79.95 | **Bundle:** $89.99

www.sap-press.com/3507

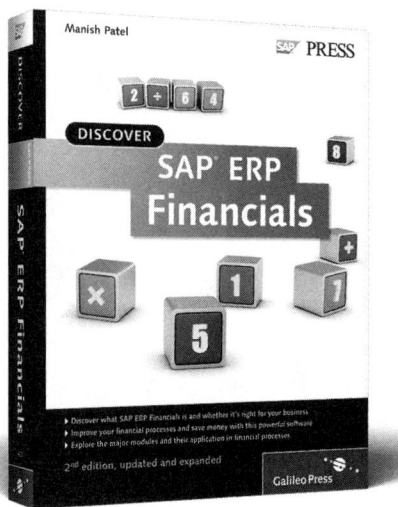

▶ Discover what SAP ERP Financials is and whether it's right for your business

▶ Improve your financial processes and save money with this powerful software

▶ Explore the major modules and their application in financial processes

Manish Patel

Discover SAP ERP Financials

Business financials is an essential part of every business, large or small. This title offers a very detailed, reader-friendly reference that will give you an in-depth overview of the key components of SAP ERP Financials. Perfect for new users, decision-makers, and power users, you will learn how to improve your efficiency in key financial areas, including profitability analysis, financial supply chain management, cost-accounting, and more. Updated for SAP ERP 6.0, EhP 5 and 6 with a focus on expanded real world scenarios and practical case-studies.

604 pages, 2nd edition, pub. 9/2012
E-Book: $34.99 | **Print:** $39.95 | **Bundle:** $49.99

www.sap-press.com/3133

www.sap-press.com

Interested in reading more?

Please visit our website for all new
book and e-book releases from SAP PRESS.

www.sap-press.com